D0083402

A Living of Words

A LIVING OF WORDS

American Women in Print Culture

Edited by
Susan Albertine

Released from
Samford University Library

The University of Tennessee Press • Knoxville

Samford University Library

Copyright © 1995 by The University of Tennessee Press / Knoxville.
All Rights Reserved. Manufactured in the United States of America.
First Edition.

The paper in this book meets the minimum requirements of the
American National Standard for Permanence of Paper for Printed
Library Materials. ⊖ The binding materials have been chosen
for strength and durability.

Library of Congress Cataloging in Publication Data

A living of words: American women in print culture / edited by Susan Albertine.
      p.   cm.
    Includes bibliographical references (p.) and index.
    ISBN 0-87049-867-3 (cloth: alk. paper)
    1. Women in the book industries and trade—United States—History.
I. Albertine, Susan L., 1950-   .
Z473.L79 1995
381' .45002'092273—dc20   94-19670
                                                   CIP

Z
473
·L79
1995

For Al, Benjamin, and Hannah

Contents

Illustrations

Acknowledgments

Having become a mother twice while preparing *A Living of Words*, I must thank Benjamin Albertine Filreis and Hannah Filreis Albertine for their good nature and unencumbered happiness, which I have found entirely infectious and energizing.

Among the many persons who helped make this book possible, Crystal VanHorn, of Susquehanna University, made it her business to turn out excellent professional copy and manage the extensive correspondence that the project entailed. In addition to nearly one hundred persons who have suggested names of contributors, many friends and colleagues have offered advice and criticism along the way: Martha Banta, James L. W. West III, Daniel Traister, Cathy N. Davidson, Ellen Cronan Rose, Katharine Rodier, and Nina Auerbach deserve special thanks. I am greatly indebted to the authors of these essays, two of whom, Noel Riley Fitch and Elizabeth Horan, collaborated with me from the outset—a panel discussion entitled "The Word and the Market: American Women in Literary Enterprise since 1850," given at the 1988 convention of the Modern Language Association.

Archivists and scholars who have been indispensable to my work on the career of Harriet Moody are Cathy Henderson and Cynthia Farar, of the Harry Ransom Humanities Research Center, University of Texas at Austin; Jonathan Walters, Richard L. Popp, and Stephen Duffy of Special Collections, University of Chicago Library; Virginia Renner and Carolyn Powell of the Huntington Library; John Hoffmann, of the Illinois Historical Survey, University of Illinois at Urbana-Champaign Library; Professor Mary Lago, of the University of Missouri, Columbia; and Peter A. Gilbert, of Dartmouth College, Executor and Trustee of the Robert Lee Frost Estate. Peggy Roche and Sharon Smith, of the Morris Library, Southern Illinois University, provided essential help in preparing the essay on Caresse Crosby.

This collection came into being at the suggestion of Carol Wallace Orr, former director of the University of Tennessee Press, who was instrumental in guiding my early work to compile the essays. Meredith Morris-Babb, acquisitions editor, and Kimberly Scarbrough, acquisitions assistant, worked faithfully with me to bring the project to completion. I wish also to thank Stan Ivester, managing editor, and Alexa Selph, copyeditor, for their expert handling of the text.

For child care extraordinaire, I wish to thank Sarah Thomforde, whose summertime escapades with Benjamin gave me and Alan Filreis the confidence to devote ourselves to our writing. For sustenance that helped me to complete this project and the many others of our shared lives, I have relied on Alan Filreis and the balance of love and work that makes our partnership.

Introduction

With the arrival of the printing press, women in the English colonies that became the United States began to participate actively in print culture—the network of production and reception that creates the communications circuit.[1] Thanks to recent work in women's history, we can say with confidence that American women of the middle class and above, irrespective of race and ethnicity, have always been writers. But ever since Elizabeth Glover set up the Cambridge (later Harvard University) Press, the first in the English colonies, women have also been printers, compositors, publishers, booksellers, patrons, editors, promoters—entrepreneurs of the word.[2] While this fact hasn't gone unnoticed by bibliographers and social historians, in the work, for example, of Elisabeth Anthony Dexter, Madeleine B. Stern, Richard L. Demeter, and Leona Hudak, women's literary studies since the second wave of feminism have tended to focus on women as writers. Examples include Mary Kelley's influential *Private Woman, Public Stage* and Susan Coultrap-McQuin's *Doing Literary Business,* two studies of women's literary professionalism in the nineteenth century; studies of women writers and modern literature include Bonnie Kime Scott's critical anthology *The Gender of Modernism,* Gillian Hanscombe and Virginia L. Smyers's *Writing for Their Lives: The Modernist Women, 1910–1940,* and Suzanne Clark's *Sentimental Modernism: Women Writers and the Revolution of the Word.*[3]

This attention to authorship is, I think, entirely understandable. In the rush to rediscover and position women writers in a newly conceived canon, literary historians have devoted relatively little energy to women's *other* work in print.[4] Elevated above women's business in the production, marketing, and delivery of the printed word, women's writing—especially published, literary writing—stands at the top of a hierarchy. The purpose of this collection is to conceive of print culture not only as a hierarchy, which it unquestionably is, but also as a network in which writing is but one of many interlinked activities.[5] We want, in short, to supply some of what is missing, to suggest what women's full contribution to print culture has been, and to emphasize the business practices of some individuals who made their careers between the English colonial period and the early twentieth century.

By print culture, we mean *literate* as well as *literary* culture. The history of the book, of the printed word, requires this broader definition. Despite the inequities of power and privilege, print culture embraces popular culture just as commodiously as it does literary. The term *literary* itself, when freed from the narrow, exclusive confines of high art, applies as accurately to Ann Franklin's lively, narrative "filler" for her almanacs as to her printing of the almanacs themselves; as correctly to Elizabeth Palmer Peabody's publishing of the *Dial* as to her writing of the *Kindergarten Guide*. The advocacy journalism of such editor-publishers as Josephine St. Pierre Ruffin and Ida B. Wells-Barnett is no less literary for having been conducted during a period when women of African descent were largely excluded from print culture. We choose not to accept the duality of high and mass culture, or that of literary and nonliterary production, for if we did, we would be foreclosing on much of women's work.[6]

The careers under study here are made in and out of high culture, and have been chosen with this dynamic in mind. Caresse Crosby's transformation of the Black Sun Press from elite, limited-edition publishing to commercial publishing is a case in point, an economic move directly challenging the academic construction of high modernism. Crosby's venture suggests a pattern evident in many female enterprises. It is often the case that these businesswomen succeed because they are, problematically, at once accommodating and resistant to the values of the dominant culture. Women's careers in the communications circuit are made across the spectrum of work, crossing and recrossing the arbitrary line between popular and high culture—tying it, as it were, in knots.

The careers we discuss are situated at different points along the communications circuit. Compiling this anthology, we have sought to document the wide range of occupations in print culture open to American women in positions of privilege. Some of the women wrote books—Elizabeth Peabody, Sarah Josepha Hale, Martha Dickinson Bianchi, Harriet Monroe, Margaret Anderson, Sylvia Beach, Caresse Crosby—but their professional identity was not defined so much by authorship as by editing and publishing. One of them, Mary Austin, made her career in imaginative writing, but the focus here has been shifted from writing to business and the writer's entrepreneurial behavior. Austin's case in particular explodes a number of stereotypes of womanly behavior, both positive and negative, and suggests that easy conclusions will not apply to women's conduct in the marketplace. Ann Franklin dedicated her professional energies to printing; Josephine St. Pierre Ruffin and Ida B. Wells-Barnett owned, edited, and published newspapers; Mabel Loomis Todd devoted herself to editing and literary promotion; Harriet Moody undertook work only partially encompassed by the word *patronage*. This selection is intended to suggest the broad reach of women's professional roles and to cross the boundaries of literary periods, especially Victorian and modern.

We propose, through social and literary history and biography, to lay the groundwork for more comprehensive study. Our first goal is to move toward a capacious definition of female professionalism in print culture, one that will allow for the great range of activity and attitude evinced by these relatively few but indicative careers. How, specifically, has professionalism been shaped by gender? How has female professional behavior changed in the two centuries spanned by the lives of women under study here? Does it enact the slow but steady progress in the expansion of women's sphere that Mary Beth Norton traces to the Revolutionary period (xiv)? How do patterns of socialization—anxious or assured responses to the ideology of True Womanhood, for example—mark these careers?

Professionalism requires a secure competence in a given field, a confident self-awareness of one's capacity and one's calling, a serious commitment to a line of work. Professionalism is a pattern of conduct specific to a given social context—here, emergent industrial capitalism—and like other such patterns in a society dominated by men, it cannot be gender-free or neutral.[7] This is a broader definition of professionalism than some would accept. Concerning female novelists in Victorian Great Britain, Gaye Tuchman has argued that a strict definition must exclude writers of either gender, since authors have never had the rights and autonomy of professionals (19, 194, 205); authors do not "define the nature of their work," "control entrance to and departure from their occupation," or "define how they will get paid" (217). Yet it would be difficult to apply Tuchman's strict definition to the careers presented in this book. Presumably, a printer like Ann Franklin would have professional status, but she lacked the autonomy Tuchman describes, as did critics and editors like Sarah Josepha Hale or Harriet Monroe, or any of the women in publishing, including Sylvia Beach, Margaret Anderson, Jane Heap, or Caresse Crosby. Ida B. Wells-Barnett's freedom to practice her chosen profession meant facing the threat of racist violence; her offices were once burned by a white mob. Professional autonomy of the kind guaranteed by organizational affiliation and high social status, as for example in the medical and legal professions, was actively denied to entrepreneurial women in print culture through the early twentieth century.

Tuchman argues that in the late nineteenth century female authors were gradually edged out of the production of the high culture novel. Although it remains to be seen whether conditions for writers in the United States were similar—to date, no quantitative study like Tuchman's has been done for American writers—it is also interesting to speculate about Tuchman's conclusions in an American context. If *all* female work in print culture could be measured, in other words, would the gradual exclusion of women in the late nineteenth century emerge as a dominant pattern? How, then, might we explain the role of such women as Harriet Monroe, Harriet Moody, Margaret Anderson, Jane Heap, and Caresse Crosby in high-cultural, international modernism? Might it be, as Suzanne Clark argues, that women's "unwarranting"— the rejection of the sentimental by modernism—"reversed the influence of women's writing," confined female modernists to the margins and forced them to deny their gender or devise other strategies for dealing with emo-

tion (1, 13–14)? Women's writing and the sentimental have long been pejo-
ratively associated, as have all female emotions and sentimentality. How stul-
tifying it would be to evade emotion for fear of being trivialized as a senti-
mentalist, as if emotion were merely a feature of a lesser literary tradition,
rather than a human necessity.[8] Did the reaction against the sentimental edge
women out of authorship and into different, less prestigious roles along the
communications circuit? According to Joan Brumberg and Nancy Tomes,
women in the United States have engaged in the "dirtiest" kinds of professional work—"those involving the most human contact with all its attendant
complexities." For the most part, professional opportunities for women arise
in fields "unwanted or abandoned" by men (287). Is this true of print culture? Or is it possible that the edging out, the push to the dirty margins, is
itself a creation of historiography? The careers discussed here point toward
the latter conclusion.

Discussing professionalism among women writers in the nineteenth
century, Coultrap-McQuin draws several conclusions useful to our project.
Although their conduct was by no means uniform, the writers she discusses
"were literary professionals in the most positive sense of those terms" (xiii).
This interpretation differs from those reached by Mary Kelley, Mary Poovey,
and Sandra Gilbert and Susan Gubar, for example, who argue that women
felt ambivalence or anxiety about themselves as professional authors, having
been socialized for the private, domestic sphere and consequently limited in
their authorial ambitions (Coultrap-McQuin 20, 205n). Coultrap-McQuin's
reading complements those of Judith Fetterley and Nina Baym, who note
professional self-confidence among women writers, and of Lawrence Buell,
who finds that women gained professional identity as writers proportionally
more often than men did in the period through the Civil War.[9] Coultrap-
McQuin argues that each of her writers acquired the professional skills to handle
her business while preserving for herself a female identity neither incom-
patible with True Womanhood nor rigidly determined by that ideology.[10]
Her biographical examples show that the range of self-conception, attitude,
and conduct within these parameters was surprisingly broad. The women
she studies justify their public, professional standing by citing the moral or
cultural uses of their work. Their professional behavior frequently depends
on a willingness to receive advice from mentors, often female mentors, although Coultrap-McQuin stresses the tendency of women to take a traditionally
female position in relations with their male publishers. The women she describes learn to intertwine private and professional matters, behavior encouraged by "familial" or "spousal" affiliations with the men who publish their
work. What they gain, finally, is an expertise in business—flexibility, judgment, bargaining skills—tailored to female needs and desires acceptable in
the realm of middle-class conduct. They learn, consciously or not, to adapt
their gendered position as a strategy. Their professional identity is not fixed

but dynamic, evolving over the course of a career. This is an important point. Because of female socialization, American middle-class women have rarely been encouraged to develop an "autonomous outlook" (Norton 151). Yet the experience of spinsterhood, by choice or chance, or of widowhood may foster both independence and strong affiliation with other women, as well as a growing and by no means uniform professional self-conception over time.[11]

To illustrate the degree to which these professional markers can be found in women's careers and to challenge the all-too-common stereotyping of female behavior are primary goals of our study. What professional characteristics are evident in the deportment of a colonial woman of affairs like Ann Franklin? What form of professionalism obtains for Elizabeth Peabody, Sarah Josepha Hale, Mabel Loomis Todd, Martha Dickinson Bianchi? Peabody's female self-awareness suggests ambivalence, as she regrets the restrictions imposed on her speech, while devoting herself with True Womanly zeal to social housekeeping. Hale's attitude toward traditional feminine rectitude and duty evolves in a complex way with her career; her editorial decisions do not align themselves neatly with True Womanhood.[12] The feud over literary property between the Dickinson family and Mabel Todd shows how intricately intertwined personal and professional identity can be, even as it illustrates the particular constraints gender can impose on professional self-definition. In the cases of Josephine St. Pierre Ruffin and Ida B. Wells-Barnett, professional identity and the very existence of one's business had to be negotiated on the dangerous terrain of late nineteenth-century segregation; the political and class differences between these two women, as evidenced in their professional behavior, cautions against reflexive assumptions of similarity based on race and gender.

And in the transition to modernism, what changed, particularly for politically aware lesbians like Sylvia Beach, Margaret Anderson, and Jane Heap? If a kind of edging out occurred, what effects does it appear to have had on professional identity and self-esteem? Certainly Harriet Monroe's ambivalence about her calling was rooted in nineteenth-century feminine ideology. At the same time, she presented herself as a public persona engaged in the making of culture. Harriet Moody's abundant, delectable patronage is of like ideological origin. She, however, did not assume a public persona even as she positioned herself surely as a creator of culture. The pattern is different in the case of Sylvia Beach. Her pastoral fervor for her work is not clearly an artifact of nineteenth-century attitudes toward women. Mary Austin's assertive self-promotion utterly rejects the tradition of womanly deference to male authority. She locates otherness in herself in a reified Native America and thus promotes racist stereotypes of indigenous culture as a defiant gesture of self-definition. Would such aggressive self-assertion in a man be as reprehensible? Does her defiance of patriarchy mitigate her racism? An intrepid bookwoman, Caresse Crosby used critical and economic power to reshape modernism while acting out a parody of Victorian domesticity and female economic behavior.

In compiling this collection, we have not sought a fixed reading of women's participation in print culture, nor do the essays imply such a pattern. We want to suggest what it means to be a woman *and* a professional in print culture—even as we argue that there is no one female response to the print business, any more than there is a set patriarchal reaction to women who venture into traditionally male preserves. Rather, we find accommodation on both sides of the gender divide, accommodation that seems often to serve class interests. For as self-interest and class interest converge, gender recedes into the background. Middle-class women have traditionally been given professional latitude when their work fosters middle-class hegemony.[13] One observes this in the careers of widows like Ann Franklin, especially when they have dependent children, or of single women like Harriet Monroe. Even so, there are lines women "cannot" cross, as the story of Margaret Anderson and Jane Heap's obscenity trial tells us. Yet, while men unquestionably hold the vast majority of positions of power and authority in the communications circuit through the early twentieth century, women have been more widely present and active than commonly thought, their positions more various and fluid. Indeed, fluidity is the most salient characteristic of women's careers. The women whose work we discuss evince female self-awareness, regardless of ideological differences, but the degree to which they accept or resist their socialization is not uniform.

Because a collection of this kind is necessarily limited in scope, we think it imperative to recognize significant absences. It seems a truism to say that women of color of whatever class and all women of the lower class have been closed out of the communications circuit. In fact, however, as the essays in this book on Ida B. Wells-Barnett and Josephine St. Pierre Ruffin attest, much work remains to be done before such a conclusion is drawn.[14] We need to know as well about the collaborative publishing ventures of black and white women in the antebellum period, about the business of Harriet Jacobs's career and her relations with Lydia Maria Child and Amy Post, for example, and the work of Susanna Strickland, who transcribed Mary Prince's narrative.[15] Virtually no study has been done of Native-American women in publishing. Daryl Morrison has published a biographical essay on Ora Eddleman Reed, a part-Cherokee woman who at age eighteen edited *Twin Territories: The Indian Magazine* (1898–1904); similar studies of such Native women as Muriel Wright (1889–1975; Choctaw) and Gertrude Bonnin, or Zitkala-Sa (1875–1938; Sioux), have yet to be undertaken.[16] The extent to which Latinas have been active in publishing is open to question. Hudak notes that in 1594, forty-five years before the first New England imprint, one Maria de Sansoric took over her late husband's press in Mexico to become the first woman printer known in North America.[17] There were no known printing presses or independent publishers in the Spanish colonies that were made part of the United States; I have been unable to identify a single Latina in publishing in the United States before the turn of the twentieth century. However, at the time of the Mexican Revolution of 1910, a group of women including Sara Estela Ramírez, Jovita Idar, Andrea and Teresa Villarreal, Isidra T. de Cárdenas, Blanca de Moncaleano, and Leonor Villegas de Magnón worked in political publishing on the Texas-Mexico border. Beatriz Blanco became editor of the society page of *La Prensa,* published in San Antonio in the 1920s. Clearly, these careers merit attention.[18] As for Asian-American women, I have identified none active in print culture before the 1940s except Edith Maud Eaton (Sui Sin Far, 1865–1914)—an absence that is in large part the legacy of such laws as the Chinese Exclusion Act of 1882.[19]

Judging from the experience of writing the essays for this collection, we find that the effort to recover women's careers in print culture ought to be broadly rather than narrowly political, and it should be interdisciplinary as well. We think it constructive for literary historians to collaborate with social historians, bibliographers, and historians of journalism and speech communications, allowing for comparative work across the professions, as Brumberg and Tomes suggest (287). Only in this way is it possible to discover the deep and broad context of women's employment and to understand the effects of gender on the structuring of occupations. It seems especially important to bring the history of women's journalism together with literary studies, for the publication of newspapers, magazines, little magazines, and scholarly journals is linked at many points to the business of both small presses and major publishers. Sherilyn Cox Bennion's *Equal to the Occasion: Women Editors of the Nineteenth-Century West* documents the labor of almost three hundred female editors of more than 250 publications in eleven western states between 1854 and 1899 (2). These are careers that merit discussion alongside those of Sarah Josepha Hale, Harriet Monroe, Josephine St. Pierre Ruffin, and Ida B. Wells-Barnett. Ann Russo and Cheris Kramarae's anthology of radical women's journalism from the 1850s provides a rich sampling, including excerpts from newspapers proudly "owned, edited, published and printed by women" (31). As Russo and Kramarae contend, women's necessarily public enterprise in periodicals indicates that the barrier between the public and private spheres was lower and weaker in the nineteenth century than many contemporary historians have seen: "the connections among women through newspapers, letters, conversations, work, speeches, teas, reform societies and discussion groups (some 'dress reform pic-nics' were attended by hundreds) move these women outside the home into public life" (9). Elizabeth Peabody's, Josephine St. Pierre Ruffin's, and Harriet Moody's careers may be similarly described.

The labor of bringing ancillary or peripheral careers into the realm of creativity has necessitated a certain kind of scholarship—painstaking, deliberate, archive-combing, and source-searching. We believe that interpretation will best proceed from scrupulous, informed, self-aware research. Much as women's history has rediscovered and rewritten, we are only beginning to understand the degrees of freedom and constraint that characterize women's participation in literate culture in the United States. If the particulars of these careers contradict received interpretations of women's work, so much the better. Insofar as we are looking for ourselves when studying history, we stand to learn more when scholarship reveals a difference.

Susan Albertine
Susquehanna University

Notes

1. See Darnton (esp. the diagram on 31). The communications circuit, an interpretive schema of the history of the book, links authors, publishers, printers, suppliers, booksellers, binders, and readers; it describes the full social context of literacy—the production, marketing, and reception of the printed word.
2. On Elizabeth Glover's career, see Walker (117); and Hudak (9–24). In 1853, British journalist Eliza Cook noted that in the United States "female compositors are becoming a large class of workwomen" (qtd. in Nestor 105n).
3. Hanscombe and Smyers do, however, note as a theme the importance of women's patronage, both financial and literary, of the writers under study (xv); Bonnie Kime Scott's anthology "features women writers, without strictly limiting itself to them—a decision in line with the current profile of gender studies" (7).
4. For biographical sketches of women in print culture, not primarily authors, see Dexter, Stern, Hudak, and Demeter. Studies of individual women include Fitch's *Sylvia Beach,* Williams's *Harriet Monroe,* Chisholm's *Nancy Cunard,* Harris's essay on Carro Morrell Clark, and Gollin's essay on Annie Adams Fields. Hahn briefly discusses the careers of Natalie Barney, Mabel Dodge Luhan, and Janet Flanner; Ford provides an overview of women's publishing activities in Paris in the 1920s. See also Wickes's biography of Natalie Barney and Rudnick's biography of Mabel Dodge Luhan. Dennison includes a chapter on Anaïs Nin in *(Alternative) Literary Publishing.*
5. See Benstock, *Women of the Left Bank,* for a model study of the literary community in Paris, 1900–1940, that considers the full extent of women's professional work. See also Brumberg and Tomes: "Only by charting the development of women's fields in relation to one another, as well as to the male-dominated fields, can we begin to comprehend the interconnections between sex roles and the occupational structure. Women's professional opportunities did not develop within a vacuum, but as part of a larger occupational hierarchy shaped by interprofessional competition and accommodation" (287).
6. See Baym, "Melodramas," for a discussion of women's invisibility in traditional literary history; see Anne Firor Scott on women's history.
7. See Brumberg and Tomes for a historiographical survey of female professionalism.

8. On the sentimental and women's writing, see Radway; and Tompkins, esp. chap. 5, "Sentimental Power: *Uncle Tom's Cabin* and the Politics of Literary History" (122–46), and chap. 6, "The Other American Renaissance" (147–85).

9. See Fetterley's introduction and headnotes to selections in *Provisions;* Baym, *Woman's Fiction;* and Buell (378).

10. On True Womanhood, see Welter.

11. Norton finds a "noticeable" minority of women who "either sought independence or had it thrust upon them," who "had to forge roles for themselves that extended beyond the boundaries of the standard feminine sphere" (125, 133). See also Brumberg and Tomes: "While the need to support one's self or one's family first sent the middle class woman outside the home, the economic imperative did not long remain the sole rationale for women's work. . . . [O]nce outside the home environment, some girls and women kept working for their own reasons" (279).

12. See Marchalonis, ed., for a collection of essays that freshly interpret mentorial relations between male and female writers.

13. Brumberg and Tomes cite studies that document familial support for female professionalism (281, 293n); see Antler; and Palmieri.

14. For a discussion of relations between African-American women and the publishing world, see Berry.

15. I am grateful to Harryette Mullen for information about Harriet Jacobs, and to Sandra Pouchet Paquet for introducing me to the work of Susanna Strickland and Mary Prince.

16. I wish to thank A. LaVonne Brown Ruoff and Daniel Littlefield for their suggestions for further scholarship on Native American women in publishing. For a biography of Zitkala-Sa, see Welch.

17. Maria de Sansoric's name itself seems questionable. Hudak gives Sansoric's husband's name as Pedro Ocharte, and adds that she printed *De Institutione Grammatica,* by Father Alvarez (4).

18. According to Asunción Lavrin, no printing presses or independent publishers have been identified in New Mexico, Texas, California, or Florida during the colonial period (letter to author, Nov. 21, 1990). I am grateful to Clara Lomas for material on Latinas in publishing on the borderlands and to Juanita Luna Lawhn for information on *La Prensa.*

19. For information on Edith Eaton (Sui Sin Far), see Ling.

Works Cited

Antler, Joyce. "After College What? New Graduates and the Family Claim." *American Quarterly* 32 (1980): 409–33.

Baym, Nina. "Melodramas of Beset Manhood: How Theories of American Fiction Exclude Women Authors." *The New Feminist Criticism: Essays on Women, Literature, and Theory.* Ed. Elaine Showalter. New York: Pantheon, 1985. 63–80.

———. *Woman's Fiction: A Guide to Novels by and about Women in America, 1820–1870.* Ithaca, NY: Cornell UP, 1978.

Bennion, Sherilyn Cox. *Equal to the Occasion: Women Editors of the Nineteenth-Century West*. Reno and Las Vegas: U of Nevada P, 1990.

Benstock, Shari. *Women of the Left Bank: Paris, 1900–1940*. Austin: U of Texas P, 1986.

Berry, Faith. "A Question of Publishers and a Question of Audience." *Black Scholar* 17 (1986): 41–49.

Brumberg, Joan Jacobs, and Nancy Tomes. "Women in the Professions: A Research Agenda for American Historians." *Reviews in American History* 10 (1982): 275–96.

Buell, Lawrence. *New England Literary Culture from Revolution through Renaissance*. New York: Cambridge UP, 1986.

Chisholm, Anne. *Nancy Cunard: A Biography*. New York: Knopf, 1979.

Clark, Suzanne. *Sentimental Modernism: Women Writers and the Revolution of the Word*. Bloomington: Indiana UP, 1991.

Coultrap-McQuin, Susan. *Doing Literary Business: American Women Writers in the Nineteenth Century*. Chapel Hill: U of North Carolina P, 1990.

Darnton, Robert. "What Is the History of Books?" *Reading in America: Literature and Social History*. Ed. Cathy N. Davidson. Baltimore, MD: Johns Hopkins UP, 1989. 27–52.

Demeter, Richard L. *Primer, Presses, and Composing Sticks: Women Printers of the Colonial Period*. Hicksville, NY: Exposition P, 1979.

Dennison, Sally. *(Alternative) Literary Publishing: 5 Modern Histories*. Iowa City: U of Iowa P, 1984.

Dexter, Elisabeth Anthony. *Career Women of America, 1776–1840*. Francestown, NH: Marshall Jones, 1950.

———. *Colonial Women of Affairs: A Study of Women in Business and the Professions in America before 1776*. Boston: Houghton Mifflin, 1924.

Fetterley, Judith. *Provisions: A Reader from 19th-Century American Women*. Bloomington: Indiana UP, 1985.

Fitch, Noel Riley. *Sylvia Beach and the Lost Generation: A History of Literary Paris in the Twenties and Thirties*. New York: Norton, 1983.

Ford, Hugh Douglas. "Publishing in Paris." *Women, the Arts, and the 1920s in Paris and New York*. Ed. Kenneth W. Wheeler and Virginia Lee Lussier. New Brunswick, NJ: Transaction Books, 1982. 65–73.

Gollin, Rita K. "Subordinated Power: Mrs. and Mr. James T. Fields." *Patrons and Protégées: Gender, Friendship, and Writing in Nineteenth-Century America*. Ed. Shirley Marchalonis. New Brunswick, NJ: Rutgers UP, 1988. 141–60.

Hahn, Emily. "Salonists and Chroniclers." *Women, the Arts, and the 1920s in Paris and New York*. Ed. Kenneth W. Wheeler and Virginia Lee Lussier. New Brunswick, NJ,: Transaction Books, 1982. 56–64.

Hanscombe, Gillian, and Virginia L. Smyers. *Writing for Their Lives: The Modernist Women, 1910–1940*. Boston: Northeastern UP, 1987.

Harris, William E. "Women in Publishing: The Story of How Carro Morrell Clark Made a Dramatic Success of Publishing Nearly Thirty Years Ago." *Publishers Weekly* 113 (March 24, 1928): 1353–55.

Hudak, Leona M. *Early American Women Printers and Publishers, 1639–1820*. Metuchen, NJ: Scarecrow P, 1978.

Kelley, Mary. *Private Woman, Public Stage: Literary Domesticity in Nineteenth-Century America*. New York: Oxford UP, 1984.

Ling, Amy. "Edith Eaton: Pioneer Chinamerican Writer and Feminist." *American Literary Realism* 16.2 (1983): 287–98.

Marchalonis, Shirley, ed. *Patrons and Protégées: Gender, Friendship, and Writing in Nineteenth-Century America*. New Brunswick, NJ: Rutgers UP, 1988.

Morrison, Daryl. "Twin Territories: The Indian Magazine and Its Editor, Ora Eddleman Reed." *Chronicles of Oklahoma* 60 (1982): 136–66.

Nestor, Pauline A. "A New Departure in Women's Publishing: *The English Woman's Journal* and *The Victoria Magazine*." *Victorian Periodicals Review* 15.3 (1982): 93–106.

Norton, Mary Beth. *Liberty's Daughters: The Revolutionary Experience of American Women, 1750–1800*. Boston: Little, Brown, and Co., 1980.

Palmieri, Patricia A. "Patterns of Achievement of Single Academic Women at Wellesley College, 1880–1920." *Frontiers* 5 (1980): 63–67.

Radway, Janice A. *Reading the Romance: Women, Patriarchy, and Popular Literature*. Chapel Hill: U of North Carolina P, 1984.

Rudnick, Lois Palken. *Mabel Dodge Luhan: New Woman, New Worlds*. Albuquerque: U of New Mexico P, 1984.

Russo, Ann, and Cheris Kramarae, eds. *The Radical Women's Press of the 1850s*. New York: Routledge, 1991.

Scott, Anne Firor. *Making the Invisible Woman Visible*. Urbana: U of Illinois P, 1984.

Scott, Bonnie Kime, ed. *The Gender of Modernism: A Critical Anthology*. Bloomington: Indiana UP, 1990.

Stern, Madeleine B. *We the Women: Career Firsts of Nineteenth-Century America*. New York: Schulte, 1962.

Tompkins, Jane. *Sensational Designs: The Cultural Work of American Fiction, 1790–1860*. New York: Oxford UP, 1985.

Tuchman, Gaye, with Nina E. Fortin. *Edging Women Out: Victorian Novelists, Publishers, and Social Change*. New Haven, CT: Yale UP, 1989.

Walker, Gay. "Women Printers in Early American Printing History." *Yale University Library Gazette* 61 (April 1987): 116–24.

Welch, Deborah Sue. "Zitkala-Sa: An American Indian Leader, 1876–1938." Diss. U of Wyoming, 1985.

Welter, Barbara. "The Cult of True Womanhood, 1820–1860." *American Quarterly* 18 (1966): 151–74.

Wickes, George. *The Amazon of Letters: The Life and Loves of Natalie Barney*. New York: Putnam, 1976.

Williams, Ellen. *Harriet Monroe and the* Poetry *Renaissance: The First Ten Years of* Poetry, *1912–22*. Urbana: U of Illinois P, 1977.

1.

Types and Gender:
Ann Franklin, Colonial Printer

Margaret Lane Ford

Ann Franklin is not an unusual historical figure. She was the first woman to print in New England, only the second in North America, but in the context of her time, the first half of the eighteenth century, this claim was worthy of little note. Ann Franklin is rather a prime example of a "deputy husband," a role observed and elucidated by Laurel Ulrich: "should fate or circumstance prevent the husband from fulfilling his role, the wife could appropriately stand in his place" (36). The welfare of the family was the overriding responsibility of a colonial wife, and this required that she act as helpmate to her husband, sharing his duties and assisting in his trade to better provide for the family. Thus colonial women were unofficially trained in trades and professions ranging from mercantile business to cobbling to silversmithy to printing. In the event of widowhood these skills became vital for the continued well-being of the surviving family. In addition to Ann Franklin, seven out of the nine other women colonial printers came to the trade through widowhood: Dinah Nuthead, Elizabeth Timothy, Cornelia Bradford, Anna Catharine Zenger, Anne Catherine Green, Clementina Rind, and Margaret Draper.

James Franklin, Ann's husband and a printer, died in 1735, leaving her with young children and only the tools with which to earn an income: a printing press and types. She took over the printing business and ran it herself until her son, James Franklin, Jr., returned from an apprenticeship in 1748 and assumed active management. She resumed primary responsibility once again at his death in 1762, until her own demise in 1763. While the pattern of her professional life was typical of colonial widows in first depending on a husband and then acting as caretaker to the family business until a son came of age (Keyssar 83–119), there are signs of Ann Franklin's own growing self-awareness and self-reliance, as can be seen in contrasting the two documents that mark the beginning and end of her printing career. In the first, her petition to Rhode Island colony, quoted in full below, she defines herself solely through her husband, "Ann Franklyn widow of James Franklyn." In contrast, her obituary of 1763 does not even mention her husband explicitly but rather cites her own many virtues of integrity, faith, friendship, and generosity in addition to her "Oeconomy and Industry in carrying on the Printing Business."[1] By the time of her death Ann Franklin had managed the printing shop alone for fourteen years and was active in it for almost thirty, a long business career for anyone of either gender at that time. In addition, she was printer to the colony of Rhode Island and Providence Plantations, a writer of almanacs, a cutter of woodblocks, and a mother of five children. This last role should not be overlooked, for it was the impetus behind her professional achievements.

All these roles, however, arose from her marriage to James Franklin. Having served an apprenticeship in his father's hometown of Ecton, Northamptonshire, England, James returned with a press and types to Boston in 1716–17 (Kane 17). He soon founded his own paper, the *New-England Courant,* and made it a forum for criticizing the clergy and the Massachusetts Bay government. His outspoken criticism of the authorities led to imprisonment and a government censure on the *Courant,* which he circumvented by publishing the paper in the name of his apprentice and younger brother, Benjamin. Benjamin Franklin supposedly "published" the *Courant* from February 1723 until 1726, although the young apprentice had run away from his brother's printing business in September 1723. It is amidst this controversy, after James's imprisonment and immediately before his censure, that James Franklin and Ann Smith, then twenty-six years old, married on February 4, 1723 (Chapin, "Franklin, Printer" 461). Franklin continued to court controversy, and the family's move to Newport in 1726–27 must have been to the relief of all concerned. In common with other colonial women who learned the family business as helpmates to their husbands, Ann had learned to print by the time of James's early death in 1735, when she emerged as a printer in her own right.

She entered the printing business with no illusions. When James died, he left behind the tools of his trade: various unsold books, ballads and pamphlets, leather skins and leaf silver (presumably for binding), lampblack for ink, "about 4 reams of waste paper," and "Sundry Lotts of Types for Printing."[2] He also left behind four young children, a fifth, Ann, having died in 1730 (Chapin, "Franklin of Newport" 338). Although the appraisers of Franklin's estate were stumped by the types, admitting "the vallue thereof at Present we cannot find out," Ann knew full well their value: they were the key to her and her children's survival. She issued her first book that same year, *A brief essay on the Number Seven,* with the imprint simply "Printed for the author" (Alden 35).[3] It was not until later that year that she used her full imprint: "Printed and sold by the Widow Franklin At the Town School House." The next year she petitioned the General Assembly of Rhode Island colony to become the colony printer. In the petition she expresses clearly the situation of her assuming management of the printing press:

> The Petition of Ann Franklyn widow of James Franklyn late of Newport aforesaid Printer Deceased Humbly Sheweth That Whereas your Petitioner being left with Several Small Children which is a great Charge to her, & haveing not Sufficient Business at the Printing Trade Humbly Prays your Honours will grant her the favour to Print the Acts of the Colony & what other things that shall be Lawfull and necessary to be printed, in order for your Petitioners Support & Maintainance of her family she having no other way to Support her Self.[4]

Ann Franklin had no heroic aspirations other than to provide for herself and her family using the only means left and known to her. These circumstances were shared by other colonial women printers. For instance, Elizabeth Timothy requested of her husband's benefactors that they "continue their Favours and good Offices to his poor afflicted Widow and six small Children and another hourly is expected." Clementina Rind forthrightly lamented that she was "now unhappily forced to enter upon Business on my own Account" (Hudak 133, 301). Rhode Island colony complied with Ann Franklin's petition and regularly granted her contracts to print its resolves and arranged for her to print a digest of the Charter, Acts, and Laws, published in 1744–45.

One significant difference between Ann and James in their respective tenures as colony printers concerned their maintenance salaries. Rhode Island colony had offered a fixed sum of fifty pounds per annum to Andrew Bradford in its first efforts to encourage a printer to set up shop in Newport in 1709 (Bartlett 4: 65). Bradford declined the offer. When James Franklin settled in Newport twenty years later, however, while the colony gave him official business, it paid him no retainer. In 1730 James petitioned the colony for a salary, and the General Assembly complied by voting him twenty pounds per annum in exchange for twenty copies of each act passed by the assembly within each term, thus guaranteeing a minimum annual income.[5] Although James's petition makes it clear that he considered it an affront not to have been granted a salary from the beginning, Ann neither requested nor received one and was paid for her work as colony business arose. This reveals much about the colony's attitude toward Ann and Ann's expectations for herself. While the colony was willing to have Ann continue printing in Newport, which was clearly to the colony's benefit since she would thus be self-supporting and not become a charge to the state, it did not encourage her beyond its own convenience: she was allowed to survive but not necessarily to thrive. Ann accepted this position and saw herself, at least at the beginning of her career, primarily as a provider for her family and not as an aspiring businesswoman.

Perhaps this lack of a regular income inspired or necessitated Ann's attempt to increase her profit from printing official business, for she offered remaining copies of the Charter, Acts, and Laws (1744–45) for sale in her shop. She was sternly reprimanded for this marketing attempt and threatened with a fine of five pounds per book (Bartlett 5: 120). Ann was, however, given leave by the General Assembly to sell copies for herself in an act passed during the October session of 1747: "The Printer shall have the Liberty to make as many more Copies as he or she shall think fit, and dispose of the same for his or her private Profit or Advantage" (*Acts and Laws* 44). In the first case, the colony had provided the paper, so that it was objecting to Ann's private use of a public commodity, if indeed she used leftover colony paper for her extra copies. In the latter case, in which she was granted permission to print more than required, Ann provided the paper herself, as is clear from the bill submitted to the assembly for printing and the actual amount of paper used.[6] Most of the bills submitted by Ann to the General Assembly from then on are for "paper and printing," and no restrictions on the number of copies are specified. Further evidence that paper was the basis for the General Assembly's first objection is a resolve pertaining to printing the 1752 digest of Rhode Island laws. For this edition the colony provided paper, and it ruled "that five hundred such books, and no more on any pretence whatsoever, be printed . . . [and] that the said committee take security of the printer [i.e., James Franklin, Jr.], that he will not print, or suffer to be printed in his press, any greater than the above mentioned number" (Bartlett 5: 334). The Franklin bill submitted was for printing, folding, stitching, and cutting, but not for paper (Alden 128n).

After her slight infraction in 1745, Ann had no further problems with the colony, and she proved competent and reliable. James Jr. took over the press when he returned to Newport from an apprenticeship with his uncle Benjamin in 1748. Ann, however, remained active in the business, and although James's name appeared alone in the imprints, the bills for colony printing were submitted jointly by James and Ann until 1758. From that time until his death four years later James alone submitted bills.

Ann Franklin's absence from active management was apparently acutely felt and resulted in James's delayed printing of the colony's issues, which, as might be expected, angered the General Assembly. More directly, the delay in printing the session laws was caused by his printing a new Rhode Island newspaper, the *Newport Mercury,* which he had recently founded. James recognized the delay and apologized, promising to take on an assistant. His troubles did not end, however, and the General Assembly noted his lack of promptness. Thomas Ward, the colony secretary, noted the length of delay on at least two copies of 1759 session laws: "Exactly, Six months, three weeks & five days, since the Copy was delivered the Printer."[7] The situation worsened. Ward brought the unsatisfactory delays to Franklin's attention, but "the careless Mortal mislaid" the May session laws until October. Incensed at Franklin's "intollerable Laziness," Ward sent the remaining Acts and Orders to Boston to be printed (Alden 216n). As a result of Franklin's irresponsibility, the General Assembly repealed its 1747 act that had granted the printer residing in Newport the exclusive contract for printing official business. The assembly sent one session's laws to Boston but thereafter resumed using James as printer with no dissatisfaction, and its printing was accomplished by James until his death, and then again by Ann until her death.

Aside from printing official Rhode Island colony business, Ann Franklin also printed for private citizens, many of whom wished to address publicly wrongs they had suffered. The personal grievances or vindications that brought Ann business arose from both ordinary citizens and important townspeople. A Mrs. Maylem publicized in a broadside printed in 1742 the injustice done to her by her late husband's former associate and fellow distiller, Mr. Gardiner, who swindled the still and stock from the unsuspecting widow. Richard Ward, formerly secretary to the colony, had printed a remonstrance to clear his name concerning a mortgage in 1737. John Alpin, a Providence lawyer, openly criticized the religion of John Walton, claiming it was not "the Religion of Jesus." The quantity of work arising from personal confrontations was not large, typically consisting of only a few leaves or a broadside, but the subject was immediate, and a local printer could benefit from local controversy merely by virtue of proximity. Indeed, printing in Rhode Island began with a private controversy: James printed each side of an argument between John Hammett and John Wright, producing the colony's first two known pieces of printing.

Religious institutions also contributed to the business of Ann Franklin, although it is the lack of business supplied by the Society of Friends that merits closer examination. It is striking that the Society, which constituted a large and active body in Rhode Island and published works during the time of her management of the press, bypassed Ann Franklin in every instance. The Society had contracted with James to print works such as John Hammett's *Vindication* already mentioned, and Robert Barclay's *Apology*. It is this latter book, Barclay's *Apology,* that provides an explanation for what proved to be a strained relationship between Ann and the Society. The book appeared in 1729 in time for the Yearly Meeting held at Newport that year, and, upon publication, a drawn-out settling of accounts began. In 1734, 745 of 1,000 copies printed had been finished and delivered, and James had been paid £486. Only a few more copies were finished the next year, 1735, the year of James's death, and Wanton and Richardson, in charge of production, were instructed "to settle that Affare with the Printer's Widow." Precisely what stalled completion of the book is uncertain, but probably it was finishing the binding, for again in 1736 the two Friends were urged "to settle with her and get the Books bound and finished." Either Ann Franklin was not a binder, or she was a very slow one. She did finish the job in 1739, at which time the Meeting was saddled with 141 unsubscribed books and a debt of

£183 to the treasurers, who had paid the outstanding costs. Only two years later was the ordeal ended by dividing the books and debt among the Quarterly Meetings.[8] A publication and printing ordeal that lasted over ten years did not make for good business on either side, and the Friends went elsewhere, to Boston and Philadelphia, with their publishing until James Franklin, Jr., uneventfully published Barclay's *Catechism* for them in 1752.

Inadvertently Ann became publisher of the sole Rhode Island newspaper. Her husband James had founded the first newspaper in that colony, the *Rhode-Island Gazette,* but it had languished after only eight months. Ann made no attempt to revive newspaper publishing during her tenure at the press, but in 1758, after Ann had retired from the printing shop, her son James Jr. founded the *Newport Mercury.* After his death, Ann, then sixty-six years old, continued to publish the newspaper, issuing it in her name alone until she took on the young Samuel Hall as a partner later that year.

Ann Franklin, like her husband and son, was a printer and only rarely a publisher. She was hired by congregations to print sermons, by individuals to print grievances and advertisements, and, of course, by the colony to print its resolves and laws. Of the books which Ann may have published herself there remain three titles: *The Christians Daily Exercise,* by Mordecai Matthews; *The Chronicle of the Kings of England,* by Nathan Ben Saddi (Lord Chesterfield?); and *Fair Rosamond,* by Thomas Deloney. All are British works and were highly popular, high-volume, low-risk books. The Deloney ballad, for instance, had had several editions printed in England over the previous century and attracted a large reading—and buying—public. Such works represent what was probably a significant portion of business in verses, ballads, and moralizing exhortations. James Franklin had printed a similar title, *The Virgin's Advice: or the Oxfordshire Tragedy,* and advertised in its imprint: "Printed and sold by James Franklin at his Printing House on Tillinghast's Wharf: Where may be had many other Sorts of Verses." Without a doubt such verses and ballads constituted a remunerative aspect of the publishing, as well as printing, business of the Franklins.

Almanacs were a staple in the business of many colonial printers, and Ann Franklin too realized their annual income was advantageous—up to a point. She published five *Rhode Island Almanacs* in the years just after her husband's death. The first two were written by Joseph Stafford and the last three by Ann herself, using the pseudonym Poor Robin. Almanac "writing" was actually composed of several parts, typically an address to the reader, astronomical calculations, verses, prognostications, and "filler," which comprised maxims and pithy sayings interspersed among the tables. An examination of the text of the almanacs themselves reveals, on the one hand, that Ann Franklin had a greater role in writing those by Joseph Stafford than previously thought and, on the other, how closely she followed the precedent set by James in producing the *Rhode Island Almanac.*

Little, if any, of the literary material in almanacs was original, except perhaps for the introductory addresses to the reader. Benjamin Franklin drew heavily on such anthologies as James Howell's *Lexicon Tetraglotton* for the early editions of his Poor Richard's almanacs and on Lord Halifax's *A Character of King Charles the Second* for the later ones (Franklin xii). Although such an anthology used by James and Ann in preparing the *Rhode Island Almanacs* has yet to be identified, it is most likely that one from which the poems, proverbs, and adages derived did exist in their household. Some text was undoubtedly original, such as James's "as good a knack at advertizing as the two printers of the Weekly Journal," referring to his Boston colleagues Samuel Kneeland and Timothy Green, Jr., who published and printed the *New England Journal* (Brigham 540), and Ann's simple "astronomers do their almanacks." It is this filler which distinguished the *Rhode Island Almanac* from its contemporaries and which reveals Ann's greater role in preparing the almanacs for 1737 and 1738 than is implied by the title page declaring "by Joseph Stafford" in large type.

A quick comparison of the Stafford almanacs printed by Ann with those printed thereafter by Thomas Fleet in Boston reveals a marked difference in tone. Although the prose sections are equally dry in all the Stafford almanacs and deal with fact, such as the tides and eclipses, the Stafford almanacs printed by Ann are enlivened with filler, silly at times but amusing. In the almanac for 1737 the filler tells rather consistently the story of Moll in excerpts such as "She says He stole the butter. Moll runs after him. A matchmaking between Tom and Old Moll—They live a poor life." Interspersed are lively observations such as "she kicks up her heels and shows her fine legs" or "grin, but don't bite." Compare that with the filler, of which there is little, of the first Stafford almanac printed by Fleet: "Do unto all Men as you would have them do unto you. Honest dealing is the best."

This difference is typical of comparisons between Rhode Island and Boston almanacs of earlier years as well. Clarence Brigham points out that whereas James Franklin in the *Rhode Island Almanac* for 1728 had two poems, advice on health or weather, and a plethora of proverbs and sayings inserted into the calendar pages, the three Boston almanacs of the same year printed by Ames, Whittemore, and Bowen had dull poetry and almost no proverbs. Ames inserted three in his almanac, Bowen only one, and although Whittemore used nearly twenty, they consisted of rather less than titillating advice such as "use the Golden Rule" (Brigham 540). James's humorous filler, which preceded Ben Franklin's use of it by seven years (Brigham 541), was characteristic of the *Rhode Island Almanac* as a series, independent of "authors" such as Stafford hired in by the printer.

No only did Ann Franklin follow her husband's example by injecting personality into the filler for the *Rhode Island Almanacs* "written" by Stafford and those published later, she also followed the format used by James in his

Rhode Island Almanac so that the astronomical tables vary slightly from the
Stafford almanacs printed in Rhode Island and those printed in Boston. The
Rhode Island Almanac had seven columns indicating the date, the day of
the week, the weather forecast, the part of the body governed by the stars
that day, the time of the sun's rising and setting, the time of the moon's
rising and setting, and the tides. The Boston Stafford almanacs omitted the
part of the body and substituted the moon's place in relation to the signs.
Therefore, Stafford apparently supplied the astronomical calculations to fit
the already existing format of the *Rhode Island Almanac,* rather than molding the almanac to his own format.

Ann must have hired Stafford principally to provide the astronomical
calculations, for when he was late in giving her his copy the next year, Ann
was angered at the inconvenience, but not deterred from producing the rest
of the almanac while waiting on him. By the time he did deliver copy, Ann
had completed much of the almanac so that there was no room to accom-
modate his prose sections. Ann chastised Stafford publicly in this same almanac in an address to the reader which makes clear Stafford's responsibility, or rather irresponsibility, in supplying her with copy. She writes: "Friendly
reader, this copy of Mr. Stafford's came but lately to hand, and for want of a
Vacant Place in the Almanack I am obliged to omit several Things of considerable Consequence which I think will be very proper to insert (the general
Heads of) in the following Manner." She then lists the things by Stafford she
has had to omit: the seven mathematical questions, observations on the influences of the planets, and an explanation of the almanac. Stafford's delin-
quency led Ann to stop printing his almanacs. Ann then began writing her
own under the pseudonym Poor Robin, and Stafford had his almanacs printed
by Thomas Fleet. It is interesting to note that Stafford economized on his almanac writing for Fleet by using the text excluded by Ann from his 1738 almanac, so that the explanation of the almanac and observations on the influences
of the planets appear in Fleet's edition of the Stafford almanac for the following year, and the seven mathematical questions in the year after that.

After severing her ties with Stafford, Ann took on the persona of Poor
Robin, as James had done. He, incidentally had been drawing on the well-
established comic Poor Robin almanacs produced in England since the
middle of the seventeenth century, and she established a continuity between
the Rhode Island almanacs issued under that guise by explaining:

In one of my Almanacks publish'd some Years past, I gave a short Hint
that Almanack-making was a Labour I did not over-much delight in, and
therefore should never have troubled the World with any of my Composi-
tions, had not some malignant Planet or other compell'd me to expose myself in Print, which I did (sorely against my Will) for several Years succes-
sively, 'till about four years ago, when happily I receiv'd a Quietus from the

> Stars, which I promis'd myself would be of a much longer Continuance than
> I find it, for, to my great Grief, they have revok'd it, and like an angry Town-
> Council, call upon me to account for the small Stock I have received.

Still in the same role as wit and living up to the "poor" in the name "Poor
Robin," she explains the true motive behind reviving almanac writing:
money.

> If what the stars have impos'd on me be of any Benefit or real Service to
> you, you shall be most heartily welcome, if you pay honestly for it: Quid
> pro quo, herein being the principle Aim of thy faithful Friend, Poor Robin.

It was a motive that no doubt had a far more serious side than the jesting
tone admits. In succeeding almanacs Ann dropped an address to the reader
by Poor Robin, replacing it first with a verse dialogue between a Red-hot
Jeroboam Tory and a Jerusalem Whig and later with a poem of prognostications. Even with all the complaining posturing in her letters to the "friendly
reader," almanac writing did indeed seem to be "sorely against [her] will,"
and she neglected to calculate the rising and setting of the sun for the almanac of 1741, so that this column is blank. That is a rather large oversight for
an almanac. Her lack of enthusiasm for almanac writing is further reflected
in the fact that almost half of the proverbs and sayings of this last almanac
are taken from earlier *Rhode Island Almanacs,* primarily from those of 1730
and 1734 (Henry 133). Whether she had exhausted the household anthology
for such filler or was simply exhausted herself by this annual task is not
clear. After the almanac for 1741 Ann gave up the writing and printing of
almanacs altogether and relied instead on selling other people's, largely Poor
Richard's, written and supplied by her brother-in-law.[9]

To the list of achievements which can be credited to Ann Franklin, such as
colony printer, bookseller, and almanac writer, another may be added: wood-
cutter. Due to the lack of any certain identification of Ann Franklin as a wood-
cutter we must rely on circumstantial evidence, all of which supports such an
assumption. First of all, the man who taught her the art of printing, her husband James, was himself an engraver and cutter of metal- and woodblocks.
Lawrence Wroth and Marion Adams convincingly argue that James was employed in such a capacity after his return from England and before setting
up his own shop in Boston in 1718, and they have identified wood or metal
cuts from his hand (Wroth and Adams 41–44). Many of the ornaments appearing in Newport books were first used in 1718 by James, Bartholomew
Green, and Samuel Kneeland, frequently for books published for one of the
so-called Boston booksellers: Benjamin Eliot, Daniel Henchman, Samuel
Gerrish, and Joseph Edwards. One ornament which can safely be assigned
to James in Newport is a crown device and Rhode Island colony seal[10] ap-

pearing in the edition of Rhode Island Laws in 1730 and thereafter only in Franklin imprints. This was, obviously, a cut specific to Rhode Island.

James himself attested to his abilities as a metal cutter in a 1728 petition to the General Assembly concerning paper money: "the Cutting the Idents and Escutcheons, casting the Flowers and Letters, as well as Printing the Publick Bills of Credit in the Method above Proposed, may be Performed by your Petitioner, without Assistance of any other Person."[11] He outlines the method of cutting blocks and its advantages over engraved plates in foiling counterfeiters. With James a self-professed metal cutter, it is entirely feasible that Ann observed and learned the same technique and was able to apply it to cutting woodblocks. Cutting on wood requires little special skill, and given a design, there is no reason to believe that Ann could not have produced blocks for illustration.

While it would have been impractical to borrow or buy a special wood-cut in Boston or Philadelphia for one edition of a ballad or story, it is more likely that a preexisting design was copied and cut on the spot. Two books which exist in unique copies at the American Antiquarian Society point both to the practice of copying designs for recutting and to creating and cutting simple, new illustrations. One book is *Old Ireland's Misery at an End,* printed by James Franklin, Jr., around 1752. On the six (of probably eight) surviving pages are four illustrations: a macabre headpiece (Reilly no. 22), the figure of a man (Reilly no. 1527), the figure of a woman (Reilly no. 1529), and a figure of death carrying an axe and hourglass (Reilly no. 1018; fig. 1.1). Of these illustrations, two closely resemble woodcuts used much earlier by Thomas Fleet. The macabre headpiece is the exact design of a headpiece (Reilly no. 21) used by Fleet in 1729 to illustrate "An elegy upon his excellency William Burnet," a text more appropriate than the Franklins' verse to the skull and crossbones (fig. 1.2). The recutting of the headpiece resulted in slight variations in eye shape and spacing, but otherwise one is clearly modeled after the other. The allegorical cut of death is a mirror image of a block used by Fleet in 1738 (Reilly no. 1016) and is also a recutting, noticeable not only in its reverse image but also in the slightly finer lines. It too was first used in a piece more suited to the depiction of death, intriguingly entitled the *Dying Lamentation and Advice of Philip Kennison,* who apparently was a burglar with literary aspirations reaching beyond his execution for his crimes in 1738 (fig. 1.3). Both cuts are taken from patterns in Fleet's books, with which the Franklins would have been familiar. Ann or James Jr. needed only to place the Fleet woodcut on a block and cut accordingly to reproduce it for their own book.

Of the remaining illustrations in *Old Ireland's Misery,* the figure of a man is unique to this book. The figure of a woman, however, takes us back to Ann Franklin and to a book printed by her in 1746 with the delightful title *Fair Rosamond.* It tells the story of the piety of Rosamond and is suitably

1.1. *Old Ireland's Misery at an End.* Newport: James Franklin, Jr., about 1752. Courtesy, American Antiquarian Society.

1.2. *An Elegy upon His Excellency William Burnet.* Boston: Thomas Fleet, 1729. Rare Books and Manuscripts Division, The New York Public Library, Astor, Lenox, and Tilden Foundations.

illustrated by a woodcut of a woman in a room kneeling in prayer (fig. 1.4). To the right is the figure of a woman, the same figure that later appears alone in *Old Ireland's Misery*. Here the figure is much less worn, and details such as the face and clothing decoration are distinguishable. Both woodcuts in *Fair Rosamond* (Reilly no. 1528), one of which James Jr. reused six years later, then, originate in this book printed by Ann Franklin.

Whereas the Franklins freely used stylized ornaments such as head and tail pieces in much of their work, pictorial representation was reserved for their more fanciful books, as is evident in these titles. By their nature, these thin, popular pamphlets have not survived, as the American Antiquarian Society copies so tellingly attest: six of probably eight pages of *Old Ireland's Misery* exist, and only two and a fragmentary third page of *Fair Rosamond* exist. Although it may seem peculiar that so little illustrated material exists for a family who had the skill and desire to cut woodblocks—particularly in the case of James Sr., the most expert of the three, from whose hand in Newport no woodcut illustrations are known—the two books that do survive must be considered a very tiny part representing a much larger and popular side of the Franklin printing business.

As much as it may seem from the discussion of Ann Franklin so far, she was not working in a vacuum, and it may be appropriate to relate her at least briefly to two colleagues with whom she had business dealings: Thomas Fleet and Benjamin Franklin. Thomas Fleet is a name that crops up frequently in relation to the Franklins. A printer in Boston and contemporary of Ann and James Franklin, Fleet was intimate with them from their years there. He was involved with James's trouble with the authorities and even helped release James from prison by being one of his sureties. Once the Franklins moved to Newport, Fleet ran advertisements for the *Rhode-Island Gazette* as well as advertising and selling their almanacs. Beginning with the second *Rhode Island Almanac,* for 1728, its imprint read "Printed and sold by J. Franklin, sold also by T. Fleet, at the Heart and Crown in Cornhill, Boston." All of James's *Rhode Island Almanacs* were also advertised in Fleet's

1.3. *Dying Lamentation and Advice of Philip Kennison*. Boston: Thomas Fleet, 1738. Rare Books and Manuscripts Division, The New York Public Library, Astor, Lenox, and Tilden Foundations.

newspaper, the *Weekly Rehearsal*. When James died in 1735, the almanac for that year was still selling in Newport and Boston, fortunately for Ann, and the advertisement in Fleet's paper was simply changed to read "sold by T. Fleet . . . and the Widow Franklin in Newport."[12]

As suggested above, Thomas Fleet also lent, or the Franklins pirated, designs from his woodblocks. It is undoubtedly no mere coincidence that the two woodcuts in *Old Ireland's Misery* match those in earlier Fleet books, although it may be significant that they date from books in 1738 and earlier and that there was a decline in the friendship after the elder James died. Part of this decline may have been precipitated by the Joseph Stafford almanacs. As already outlined, Ann printed the first two Stafford almanacs and was very unhappy with Stafford's performance for the second; thereafter Fleet printed Stafford's almanacs. No matter where the blame lay in the Franklin-Stafford dispute, it may have rankled Ann that Fleet immediately took up Stafford as an almanac writer.

Her brother-in-law, Benjamin Franklin, appears to have been the major supplier of paper, ink, and type for his Newport relatives, or at least the best documented of them. Aside from almanacs and books, Benjamin also provided lampblack to James, paper to Ann, and paper and type to James Jr. Although it is not recorded in his account books, I believe Benjamin was the source for Ann's new type, introduced in 1745 (Ford 85). It was a Caslon type, and Benjamin's connections with Caslon are well known.

Within the printing shop, there is no evidence of outside help employed by Ann Franklin. Aside from her Negro slave, who presumably worked in the printing house as slaves of other printers did, two of her daughters are said by Isaiah Thomas to have worked there as compositors (315). Ann Franklin had three daughters, in addition to her son James, who could have worked and undoubtedly did work in the printing shop, at least until they

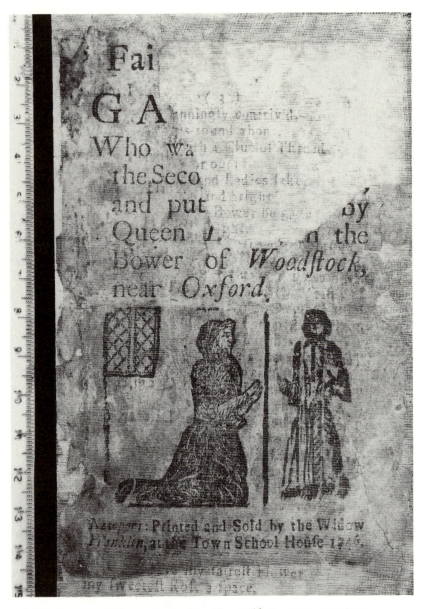

1.4. *Fair Rosamond*. Newport: Ann Franklin, 1746. Courtesy, American Antiquarian Society.

married. Thomas could be referring to any combination of Abiah, the eldest, who married in 1743; Mary, who married in 1752; or Elizabeth, who married in 1761.[13] It is likely that Abiah and Mary were most active during the time of their mother's running the press alone. James Jr., as we have seen, took on a helper in 1758 shortly after he founded the *Newport Mercury*.

The press on which Ann and both Jameses printed still exists, its fame resting on its having been the press on which Benjamin Franklin learned to print while an apprentice to James, and not, sadly, on its connection with Ben's sister-in-law Ann. It is an old-fashioned English press, one of six surviving from the colonial era, all of the same sort.[14] It is appropriate perhaps that this press is also known as a common press, for Ann Franklin, assuming her husband's role and occupation, was following a common course. She did not need to hide or highlight her identity, and the resulting absence of information proves, to an extent, that she was neither anachronism nor anomaly. In this she takes her place beside many other colonial widows such as her Newport contemporary Mrs. Sueton Grant. Mrs. Grant, widowed in 1725 with several small children, successfully managed the family importing business with its international dealings, later assisted by her son, up to the days of the Revolution (Dexter 33). She too broke free of the economic dependence on men which typified colonial women's lives, and she asserted her competence and self-reliance in business, even in representing herself in court. While noting in this and other cases the fact that Ann was not alone among colonial women in practicing a trade or profession, it is not to say that her femaleness did not affect business relations. I have described a changed, less encouraging attitude of the colony toward its printer and a decline in the Fleet-Franklin relationship once Ann took over the shop, and I am sure there are other unrecorded indications of affected transactions. Such evidence points to the contemporary perception of Ann Franklin as a "deputy" printer, always filling in for her husband or son, but her career shows that she was in practice a competent and successful printer. One should therefore look again at the pattern of colonial widowhood and see it as just that, a pattern which each individual woman tailored to herself. By the end of her career, having survived husband and son and indeed all her children, Ann had outlived any of her roles as "deputy." She acknowledged this by changing, after almost thirty years, from being Widow Franklin to Ann Franklin, and her imprint in the *Newport Mercury* in 1762 resolutely read for the first time: "Printed by Ann Franklin."

Notes

This is a revised version of a paper read before the American Printing History Association on October 7, 1989, and published in *Printing History* 24 (1990). I remain grateful to the Bibliographical Society of America and the American Antiquarian Society for fellowships granted to pursue work on Ann Franklin and to the libraries which kindly made their collections available to me and have permitted archival material to be used here: American Antiquarian Society, Rhode Island Historical Society Library, Newport Historical Society, John Carter Brown Library, Massachusetts Historical Society, New York Public Library, and the New England Yearly Meeting of Friends at the Rhode Island Historical Society Library.

1. *Newport Mercury,* Apr. 25, 1763. It is also quoted in full in Hudak 47.
2. James Franklin estate inventory. Town Council Book 7, p. 237, Newport Historical Society Archives.
3. I will refer to Franklin imprints by their number in Alden.
4. Petitions, vol. 4, 32, Rhode Island State Archives.
5. Petitions, vol. 2, 26, Rhode Island State Archives; and Bartlett 4: 472–73.
6. For a transcript of bills presented to the colony, see notes accompanying specific entries in Alden, in this instance Alden 79.
7. This is recorded on copies at the John Carter Brown Library and the Rhode Island Historical Society Library. Alden 215n.
8. The transaction may be followed in the minutes for Meetings held 17 of 4th month, 1734; 12 of 4th month, 1735; 10 of 4th month, 1736; 7 of 4th month, 1739. Society of Friends, New England Yearly Meeting Minutes in the Archives of the New England Yearly Meeting of Friends at the Rhode Island Historical Society Library.
9. Benjamin Franklin had begun sending almanacs to the Franklins in 1731 while James Sr. was still alive, usually in quantities of three hundred per year. This continued once Ann took over the printing shop, and the numbers increased significantly for the years 1742–48, when she was not producing an almanac herself. See *Account Books Kept by Benjamin Franklin,* ed. George S. Eddy (New York: Columbia UP, 1928–9), entries for Aug. 17, 1733; Dec. 8, 1735; Nov. 1737; Nov. 28, 1740; Dec. 1, 1742; Nov. 8–9, 1743; Jan. 5, 1744–45; Nov. 28, 1745; and Nov. 17, 1747.
10. Reilly no. 303. I will refer to all following illustrations by their numbers as listed in Reilly.
11. Petitions, vol. 1, 25, Rhode Island State Archives.
12. *Weekly Rehearsal,* Mar. 31–Apr. 7, 1735.
13. Arnold, First Series, 8: 401, 418, 439, 459; 4: 412.
14. The press is owned by the Massachusetts Charitable Mechanics Association and is now on permanent loan to the Franklin Institute, Philadelphia. I am indebted to Mrs. Gladys E. Bolhouse of the Newport Historical Society for updating me on the whereabouts of this press.

Works Cited

Acts and Laws of His Majesty's Colony of Rhode-Island, and Providence Plantations, 1745–1752. Newport, RI: 1752.

Alden, John. *Rhode Island Imprints, 1727–1800.* New York: Bowker, 1949.

Arnold, James A., ed. *Vital Records of Rhode Island, 1636–1850.* Providence, RI: Narragansett Historical Pub. Co., 1896.

Bartlett, John Russell. *Records of the Colony of Rhode Island and Providence Plantations in New England.* 10 vols. Providence, RI: A.C. Greene, 1856–65.

Brigham, Clarence S. "James Franklin and the Beginnings of Printing in Rhode Island." *Massachusetts Historical Society Proceedings* 65 (1936): 536–44.

Chapin, Howard M. "Ann Franklin of Newport, Printer, 1736–1763." *Bibliographical Essays: A Tribute to Wilberforce Eames.* Cambridge, MA: Harvard UP, 1924. 337–46.

———. "Ann Franklin, Printer." *Americana Collector* 2 (1926): 461–65.

Dexter, Elisabeth Anthony. *Colonial Women of Affairs: A Study of Women in Business and the Professions in America before 1776.* Boston: Houghton Mifflin, 1924.

Ford, Margaret Lane. "The Types of the Franklin Press of Rhode Island, 1727–1763, with Addenda to Alden's *Rhode Island Imprints.*" *Papers of the Bibliographical Society of America* 82 (1988): 83–95.

Franklin, Benjamin. *The Complete Poor Richard Almanacks Published by Benjamin Franklin.* Facsimile. Introd. Whitfield J. Bell, Jr. Barre, MA: Imprint Society, 1970.

Henry, Susan. "Ann Franklin of Newport, Rhode Island's Woman Printer." *Newsletters to Newspapers: Eighteenth-Century Journalism.* Ed. Donovan H. Bond and W. Reynolds McLeod. Morgantown: West Virginia U, 1977. 129–43.

Hudak, Leona M. *Early American Women Printers and Publishers, 1639–1820.* Metuchen, NJ: Scarecrow P, 1978.

Kane, Hope Frances. "James Franklin, Senior, Printer of Boston and Newport." *Americana Collector* 3 (1926–27): 17–26.

Keyssar, Alexander. "Widowhood in Eighteenth-Century Massachusetts: A Problem in the History of the Family." *Perspectives in American History* 8 (1974): 83–119.

Reilly, Elizabeth Carroll. *A Dictionary of Colonial American Printers' Ornaments and Illustrations.* Worcester, MA: American Antiquarian Society, 1975.

Thomas, Isaiah. *The History of Printing in America.* New York: Weathervane Books, 1970.

Ulrich, Laurel. *Good Wives: Image and Reality in the Lives of Women in Northern New England, 1650–1750.* New York: Oxford UP, 1983.

Wroth, Lawrence C. *The Colonial Printer.* 2d ed. Charlottesville, VA: Dominion Books, 1964.

———, and Marion W. Adams. *American Woodcuts and Engravings, 1670–1800.* Providence, RI: John Carter Brown Library, 1946.

2.

Sarah J. Hale,

Selective Promoter of Her Sex

Barbara A. Bardes and Suzanne Gossett

Sarah Josepha Hale (1788–1879), author, biographer, and editress (her preferred term), was arguably the most prominent woman engaged in literary
enterprise in the middle of the nineteenth century. Enterprising she was.
Widowed in 1822 at the age of thirty-four with five children to support, she
tried but failed to earn a living as a milliner and promptly embarked on a
literary career as a poet. After a few successes competing for prize money,
she was emboldened to publish an anthology of her own verse as well as a
two-volume novel, *Northwood.* The success of *Northwood* in 1827 led within
the month to a letter from "a publishing firm in Boston, proposing to establish a periodical for Ladies and offering me the editorship" (qtd. in Finley
39). The new *Ladies' Magazine,* which appeared first in 1828, was published
by John L. Blake, D.D., and was the first journal in America dedicated to
"women coping with life on serious terms, earnest about philanthropies and
progress . . . women interested in extra-mural activities but for intra-mural
ends" (Martin 48). Unlike her competitors, Mrs. Hale did not "clip" from other
magazines, largely British. Instead, the contents of the *Ladies' Magazine* were
original; the magazine was largely by women; and the contributors were
almost all American. When at a loss for material, Mrs. Hale guaranteed meeting all three criteria by writing the filler herself.

By 1836, publisher Louis Godey was looking for a way to expand the
success of his own magazine and began wooing Sarah Hale to join his establishment by printing frequent favorable comments on her periodical in
the pages of his own (Finley 62–63). The *Ladies' Magazine* merged with
Godey's in January 1837, beginning a forty-year career for Mrs. Hale and a
dizzying cycle of prosperity for the journal. Between 1839 and 1860 the circulation of *Godey's Lady's Book* went from 25,000 to 150,000, though it lost
ground after the Civil War (Mott 581n). Every month Mrs. Hale spoke to her
readers, first in a column called "The Ladies' Mentor," and then in her regular columns, the "Editor's Table" and the "Editor's Book Table" of reviews.
In these spaces Mrs. Hale articulated her personal philosophy, her social
concerns, and her literary criticism; these were also implicit throughout the

Book in her editorial choices. Throughout she kept herself conspicuously before her public, reminding them that she was the sole support of her family, sharing milestones in her life, and not hesitating to give firm and unqualified opinions about issues from literary quality to compensation for women's work.

Interpretations of Hale's life and career have varied widely, depending largely upon the period and upon the interpreter's attitude toward powerful women. Yet as we survey Hale's works, the most consistent element, the invariable factor whether one considers Hale radical or conventional in her activities, is her dedication to the promotion of her own sex. Within her own ideologically inflected definition of what was appropriate, she unwaveringly favored women's activities and, specifically, their literary achievements. These ideals are continuously expressed from her earliest editorials in the *Ladies' Magazine* to her final revision of *Woman's Record,* her encyclopedia of women's achievements.

It is not surprising that those who compare Hale to other major nineteenth-century figures in publishing are most struck by what she was able to accomplish despite her gender. Mott, the historian of magazines, describes Hale simply as "a great woman" (583), praiseworthy especially for her commitment to female education (349). For Eugene Exman, writing about the house of Harper, Hale was "demonstrating how much a woman could do in a man's world" (237); and for James Playsted Wood her editorial achievements justify referring to her as "the stalwart feminist from Boston . . . the militant Sarah Josepha Hale" (54).

Since the beginning of the second feminist wave, however, interpretations of Hale have been more divided. The negative view is clearest in the writing of Ann Douglas, who while conceding that Hale was "the most important arbiter of feminine opinion of her day" (51), condemns her as the "chief exponent of the doctrine of the feminine sphere" (54), one who even when seeking "partially feminist goals" does so by "largely anti-feminist means" (52). A more moderate analysis comes from Angela Zophy, who presumes that Hale's goal was to promote a traditional kind of "true womanhood" but nevertheless notes that in her monthly editorials Hale worked "to promote advances in women's education and employment opportunities" (1), and "used the concepts of true womanhood, woman's sphere, and woman's influence to broaden the scope of women's activities and interests to suit the times" (48).

Zophy, though more favorable than Douglas, denigrates Hale's accomplishments by asserting that Louis Godey was the controlling force at the journal and that, especially after Hale moved to Philadelphia in 1841, her "proximity to her publisher seemingly increased his influence over her and therefore over her formulation of editorial policy" (72). Consequently, Zophy concludes, by "following her publisher's policy of offending no one . . . Mrs.

2.1. Sarah J. Hale, from *Woman's Record; or, Sketches of All Distinguished Women from the Creation to A.D. 1868,* 3d ed. (New York: Harper and Brothers, 1872).

Hale tacitly accepted a diminished role as a lady-like reformer" (77). Cheryl Walker generalizes this picture, claiming that "women like Sara [*sic*] Josepha Hale . . . nominal editors of the ladies' magazines. . . . were in fact controlled by their publishers, who were male" (Walker 34). Such a structure would place Hale in a situation comparable to that which Susan Coultrap-McQuin argues obtained for most of the nineteenth century in the book publishing industry, a situation in which male publishers took a paternalistic attitude toward the female or feminized writers who worked for them and set the terms for their involvement in the literary marketplace (Coultrap-McQuin passim).

The view of Hale as Godey's puppet diminishes unjustifiably Hale's significance in the world of nineteenth-century publishing. Though Hale was no doubt grateful to Reverend Blake, the publisher of the *Ladies' Magazine,* for giving her the opportunity to enter the literary world as a professional (Martin 46), there is no proof that she adapted her opinions to suit him. It is true that the pages of *Godey's* have more fiction and more fashion plates than the *Ladies' Magazine,* but such marketing decisions did not force Sarah

Hale to change her intellectual and political positions once she moved to the larger journal. Instead, Baym has argued, "editorial policy and content were Hale's domain, while Godey attended to sales, format, and publicity" ("Christian Women" 249n). Significantly, before Hale joined his operation, Godey's magazine had been largely made up of reprints from English publishers: it was Hale who once again insisted on an American magazine "made up of articles written by American authors on subjects of special interest to an American public."[1] And she chose those articles.

Furthermore, the extent to which Hale can be dismissed as an uncomplicated advocate of "true womanhood" has been challenged by Laura McCall's content analysis of *Godey's Lady's Book* from 1830 to 1860. Analyzing a random sample of 120 short stories chosen from among all those published over that thirty-year period, McCall tested the women characters in the stories for the four presumably cardinal feminine virtues: piety, purity, submissiveness, and domesticity.[2] She was surprised to find that the majority of women characters reflected no interest in piety, that many were openly erotic (in the Victorian mode), and that quite a few were admired for their intellect. McCall concludes that "the categories historians have formulated to describe the ideal woman were not prevalent in either the fiction or the editorials of *Godey's*" (235).

McCall's analysis of the fiction in *Godey's* complements several other revisionist interpretations of Hale's ideology. From a political point of view, we have argued elsewhere, Hale must be seen in a context more nuanced than feminist or antifeminist. *Northwood,* her 1827 novel, reveals her advocacy of a particular subset of activities for female citizens, undertaken in subordination to male authority and within the family, yet clearly understood as fundamental to the political order. This novel, typical of the "nationalist historical fiction" written by women in the 1820s (Baym, "Women Writing History" 24), makes manifest the bases of Hale's political attitudes throughout her life. As a proto-Victorian, Hale accepted the premise that the differences between men and women were both physical and moral, such that each sex had a different but essential role to play in the preservation of the republic. Deeply patriotic, in keeping with her view of woman's role in the republic, throughout her life Hale expressed her dedication to the national cause through such activities as her successful campaigns for a national Thanksgiving Day and for the completion of the Bunker Hill monument.[3] Others have extended the political analysis of Hale's early work: Nicole Tonkovich Hoffman, for example, sees Hale as "continually politically involved" (50).

In two recent articles, "Onward Christian Women: Sarah J. Hale's History of the World" and "Between Enlightenment and Victorian: Toward a Narrative of American Women Writers Writing History," Nina Baym points the way to analyzing Hale's compendium *Woman's Record* as an indication of her most profound beliefs. Here Hale attempts "nothing less than to reconstitute world history . . . as the history of women" ("Christian Women" 252). And rather than showing the contribution of true womanhood or the conventional female virtues to the advance of a civilization led by men, Hale demonstrates that progress in world history depends explicitly on the progress of women. As Baym summarizes the argument implicit throughout the encyclopedia, "the Christian message is precisely the superiority of women, the destined mission of women is to Christianize the world, and the story of history is of inevitable progress toward a world dominated by Christian and Christianizing women" (253). *Woman's Record* is thus typical of Victorian women's history because, unlike the Enlightenment historians of the late eighteenth and early nineteenth centuries, who believed that "mind has no sex and that language, by which mind makes itself known and effective, also has no sex" ("Women Writing History" 29), Hale rooted her understanding of women's mind in the weaker female body and argued that women, though inferior in physical strength to men, developed compensatory superior moral and spiritual senses (38).

Baym's analysis of *Woman's Record* focuses on its place in nineteenth-century women's historiography and on its vision of women's moral and religious power. She says little about the *form* of the work, a series of biographies, though she does comment that "from Hale's own perspective her very decision to include particular women marked her admiration and high regard, her sense of their historical importance" ("Christian Women" 267). While Baym notes with some astonishment a few of the women that Hale did include—Agrippina, mother of Nero; Lucretia Borgia; and the African Princess Zinga, "licentious, blood-thirsty, and cruel"—she does not pause over the women who are absent, with the exception of Mary Wollstonecraft ("Christian Women" 254).[4] Baym also says nothing about the work's persistent emphasis on woman as writer. The last section of the book, for example, is headed "Fourth Era. Of Living Female Writers." Yet we can learn much about the way that Sarah Hale promoted her sex, and about her commitment to seeing women into print, by following these two lines of analysis, biographical and literary. Believing that only women could provide the necessary moral and spiritual leadership for the young nation and for Western civilization in general, Hale used her position as an author, editor, and historian to advance the careers of women authors, to promote a few other occupations and activities for women, and to provide models for her readers to follow in their own lives. She did this by exclusion as well as inclusion, by selection among the biographical facts as well as by selection among the subjects of the biographies. The ideology of *Woman's Record* is profoundly tied to Hale's lasting commitment to the selective promotion of her sex and even more specifically to the selective promotion of women writers.

Throughout her life Sarah Hale used biography as a way to establish female role models and judged publication the most concrete measure of approbation. That there could be conflict between success in publishing and Hale's standards for women was something that she only gradually acknowledged. In 1834, in the seventh volume of the *Ladies' Magazine,* she announced a series of "female biography," which she promised would include those who "have been eminent for domestic virtues and benevolence, as well as those who have exhibited brilliant talents and literary excellence. We are by no means in favor of exalting intellectual attainments above moral virtues" (41). This announcement, nineteen years before the appearance of *Woman's Record,* shows how early Hale began to accumulate her card files, with plenty of opportunity to add and delete.

She had, perhaps, borrowed the idea. As early as 1829, in volume 2 of the *Ladies' Magazine,* she reviewed Anna Maria Lee's *Memoirs of Eminent Female Writers,* which she calls a "manual of biography." She explains the interest of the book thus:

> The private histories of eminent persons are always sought after with eagerness; and were this passion for biographical literature, rightly fostered and directed, it would have a most powerful influence in promoting the intellectual and moral improvement of women. But to do this, greatness, in its worldly sense, either as applied to talents or station, must not be the object of eulogy; or rather, the domestic virtues must possess a prominence in the pictures which are held up for the admiration and consequent imitation of women." (393)

With this comment, Hale begins to outline her own ideal of womanhood. "We do not, in our country . . . want exhibitions of those talents and acquirements, which have fitted women to rule empires and manage state intrigues,—we want patterns of virtue, of intelligence, of piety and usefulness in private life." Still, Lee's book does include biographies of some whose fame "rests solely on the merit of their knowledge and writings." Hale's ambivalence about the respective importance of "virtue" and "intelligence," especially when that intelligence leads to publication, surfaces almost immediately, as she explains that she will reprint sketches of "two, eminent for profound and brilliant acquirements," and then add "specimens of that kind of eminence, which seems to have been the result of goodness of heart, rather than pride of understanding." Her purpose is to allow "our young ladies" to "decide in which class of these distinguished females, they should prefer to see their names enrolled." The first two are Madame de Chastelet, who studied philosophy with Voltaire and wrote about Newton, and Sappho; the others are Elizabeth Carter and Elizabeth Smith, both of whom wrote poetry, and Madame de Sevigné (2 [1829]: 395–400). That both exemplars of the first category, who are less notable for their character than for their accomplishments, are foreign and not Anglo-Saxon, is one of several patterns that would coalesce in *Woman's Record.*

Hale began her own sketches soon, and from the beginning they were not purely domestic. In 1832 the *Ladies' Magazine* carried one of Mrs. Fry, as an example of "just what our charitable ladies require, to invite them to act, as well as talk" (5 [1832]: 444). Fry, whose life was "devoted to acts of virtue," was a comfortable model for Hale because she combined religious devotion with a mission to women. The sketch pointedly describes Fry reading the Bible in prison and helping female prisoners' children. In the years that Hale edited the *Ladies' Magazine,* she identified herself with many of the causes that she would advocate throughout her life—female education, temperance, female missionaries, the control of their own property by married women—and praised women like Elizabeth Fry who worked for these causes. In the *Ladies' Magazine* Hale also delineated the methods she preferred: "I am not advocating what is termed *blue-stockingism.* No one can dislike a thorough dogmatical, dictatorial, demonstrating, metaphysically learned female more sincerely than I. But it is necessary, if men would improve, that women should be intelligent" (2 [1829]: 377).

Among these intelligent women, preeminently, were women writers. Writing had been Hale's own road to independence, and she always justified publication as the way by which intelligent, moral women could contribute to society while carrying out their domestic responsibilities. She promoted women authors at every step of her career and missed few opportunities to remind her readers of her special attention to female writers. For example, in volume seven of the *Ladies' Magazine* (1834) she lists her contributors for the past six years, including "Sigourney, Sedgwick, Gilman, Embury, Smith . . . Child, Gould, Wells, Willard, Phelps, Locke" (48). In 1837 she published *The Ladies' Wreath,* a collection of poetry by women from England and America, once again proposing two grounds for her choices and ignoring any possible conflict between them: "Two principles have guided my selections; one, to admit no poetry unless its aim was 'upward and onward;' the other, to allow place to those writers only whose style had some peculiar stamp of individuality, which marked their genius as original" (4). Some of those included had appeared in the list in the *Ladies' Magazine*—for example, Lydia Sigourney, Caroline Howard Gilman, Emma Catherine Embury, Elizabeth Smith—and all but one of those in *The Ladies' Wreath* would appear again in *Woman's Record.*

During her years as editor of *Godey's Lady's Book,* Hale published at least three special issues that included only female writers. The January 1840 issue of *Godey's* contained articles and stories by Hale, Elizabeth Ellet, Harriet Beecher Stowe, Lydia Sigourney, and Mary Russell Mitford, all of whom would appear in Hale's *Woman's Record.* In the Editor's Table of the January 1843 issue of *Godey's,* which again contained only women writers, Hale described her magazine as "the only Periodical in the world which embodies the piety, genius, intelligence, and refinement of perfect womanhood" (58). Once again Hale's stated ideal of womanhood went beyond the domestic virtues to include intelligence; McCall's quantitative analysis of the fiction in *Godey's* demonstrates that Hale's selection of stories reinforced this attitude for her readers. Finally, in the July 1845 all-female issue Hale provides yet another statement of her goals for the periodical and for American women. She is defending her temporary exclusion of men: "We make this arrangement, not as disparaging our gentlemen contributors, but to show the great progress of female literature, and the vast moral influence the genius of woman is obtaining in our country" (284).

Thus *Woman's Record,* which appeared first in 1853, with a second edition in 1855 and a third in 1872, was the apex of Sarah Hale's lifelong career as the discriminating promoter and patroness of members of her own sex and especially of the writers among them. In publications and reviews in the *Ladies' Magazine* and in *Godey's,* in the special issues of *Godey's,* in the *Ladies' Wreath,* Sarah Hale had regularly had opportunities to choose which women to feature and which to ignore. Viewed from the perspective of its exclusions as well as its inclusions, *Woman's Record* culminates a lifework of ideological choices. The volume argues, as Baym has said, for the superiority of women and of Christianity, but it has other, specific targets. In it Hale has the last word in her disputes with advocates of women's rights and of abolition, reveals the lower standard of morality she required of women not fortunate enough to be Americans, and again demonstrates her profound belief that there was nothing more important for a woman to do than to write. Especially in the 1872 edition, completed in 1869 when Hale was over eighty years old, *Woman's Record* closes the canon of Hale's writing by creating a print canon of the women she wished to have remembered—or forgotten.

Woman's Record; or, Sketches of All Distinguished Women from the Creation to A.D. 1868 was far more than a reference work or dictionary of biography. The *Record* provides at least a short biographical sketch for more than 1,800 women in world history, and names, in toto, more than 2,500 outstanding women, including a list of female missionaries in the appendix. In the general preface to the first edition, in the introduction to the second edition, and in the prefaces to each era, Hale states her goals for the *Woman's Record* quite clearly. She begins with the statement, "The want of the world is moral power" (xxxv), and then proceeds to outline her theory that educated, intelligent women will provide that moral power to the world. Her compendium will both prove her theory and serve as an example to women for their own lives: "The wide field of my plan, gathering records of women from every age, country, condition and character, presents an opportunity, never before accessible, of ascertaining the scope of feminine talent, and the effect the cultivated intellect of the sex, when brought to bear on Christian civilization, would exercise" (xlvii).

The third and last edition of *Woman's Record* is the best place to study the progress of Hale's ideas over the years from the 1840s until 1869, when the third edition went to the publisher. In complications, second thoughts, divided opinions, Hale reveals much about herself, as the construction of the book demonstrates much about her purposes. *Woman's Record* is divided into four eras: from the Creation to the birth of Jesus Christ, from the birth of Christ to 1500, from 1500 to 1850 (that is, to appear in this section a woman must have died by 1850), and the contemporary era "of living female writers." At the end of the contemporary period, Hale added a section on young writers and others, arranged by nation, a section on benefactresses that includes both philanthropists and Dorothea Dix, yet another section of supplementary names, and lists of female American missionaries. In the 1872 edition, she added another seventeen women in a second supplement and some brief notes updating the activities of women previously profiled, as well as notes on female progress since the first edition.

When it comes to the world of the living, Hale is more interested in women who have distinguished themselves by writing than in those in any other field. Of the 119 women profiled in the fourth era, the period of Hale's younger contemporaries, more than 90 are writers—poets, playwrights, historians, and novelists. For these women writers the *Record* goes beyond biography: it is also an anthology and a handbook of criticism, printing selections of their work as well as Hale's often hard-headed reviews and analyses. For example, after noting that Emma D. E. Nevitte Southworth, known to readers as E.D.E.N. Southworth, was left destitute with two infants to support, Hale praises the author for her "great powers of the imagination, and strength and depth of feeling," but along with selections from Southworth's gothic novel, *The Deserted Wife,* comes criticism of Southworth's "wild and extravagant manner" and "fervid imagination," which carries her "beyond the limits prescribed by correct taste or good judgment" (794). In another case, like many Victorians Hale saw serious flaws in Charlotte Brontë's *Jane Eyre:* "Vigour, animation, originality, an interest that never flags, must be conceded to it. . . . But the hero of this book, Mr. Rochester, is a personage utterly distasteful and disagreeable." She even proposes that "the chapters which immediately follow Mr. Rochester's most singularly managed declaration of love . . . have the air of being a contribution from some male friend." On the other hand, though she recognizes it as a literary "digression," Hale praises the section of the novel where Jane runs a parish school for girls, because it exemplifies "what may be effected by an intelligent woman, in awakening the torpidity of those classes of her sex to whom knowledge has but few opportunities of 'unrolling her ample page'" (597–98).

It is when we examine closely the women who are not writers that the extent of Hale's quiet exclusion becomes most apparent. Included are famous actresses and singers (Jenny Lind among others), scientists such as Maria Mitchell, teachers, at least one preacher, several European revolutionaries, and women rulers (Victoria and the queens of Spain and Portugal). Most of these women could be best described as intellectuals who were also examples of domestic virtue.

Women carrying forward the Christianization of the world of course merit approbation: with the exception of Phillis Wheatley, who appears as a poet, those women of color who are included figure because of their active Christianity. These include Kamamalu, daughter of the king of the Sandwich Islands; Kapiolani, another Hawaiian who overthrew the "idolatrous worship of Pele"; Pocahontas, "the first heathen who became converted to Christianity by the English settlers"; and Catherine Brown, a half-blooded Cherokee who also "brought many to Christianity." Even the odious Zinga was "the first of her tribe who made any attempt to adopt Christianity."[5] Yet Hale does not entirely support the religious thesis of her preface in the majority of the biographies. Not only are several Jewish women included, among them an actress and a singer, but Hale rarely mentions the religious denomination of the women or their dedication to the work of church or parish. Most surprising, given the anti-Catholic sentiment of nineteenth-century American society, she never identifies the European women by baptismal affiliation.

Hale's deeper purposes emerge if we compare the list of women discussed by Susan Conrad in *Perish the Thought: Intellectual Women in Romantic America, 1830–1860* to the selections in Hale's fourth era. Only seven of the thirteen described by Conrad appear in *Woman's Record*. Hale writes biographies of Margaret Fuller, Lydia Maria Child (with a rebuke we will discuss below), Elizabeth Fries Ellet, Louisa McCord, Sarah Whitman Power, Elizabeth Peabody, and Elizabeth Oakes Smith. All were authors, and many were contributors to Hale's periodicals. A look at the women whom Conrad proposes as intellectual leaders but whom Hale excludes provides a strong indication of Hale's goals and standards: Sarah Grimké, Elizabeth Cady Stanton, Antoinette Brown Blackwell, Paulina Wright Davis, Caroline Dall, and Mary Booth do not appear. Except for Mary Booth, all of the excluded women were politically active, either for women's rights or abolition, or both.

Woman's Record is, among other things, a continuation of Hale's literary dialogue on the proper response to slavery in America. Early in her career she gave some indication of uncertainty, though later her opposition to the abolition movement hardened. In the first edition of *Northwood* (1827) slavery was acknowledged as a problem that the northern hero would face by moving south, but was not a major topic. Two years later, while editing the *Ladies' Magazine,* Hale even reprinted a "southern lady's" appeal on behalf of the slaves (2: 515–17). Her comment, however, was not about the ethics of slavery but about the appropriateness of women's taking political action:

> We presume the writer had no idea of advocating female interference or usurpation of authority, in directing the affairs of state. . . . The establishment of "female emancipation societies," as has been suggested by the writer, would not, we think, be perfectly in accordance with woman's character. . . . The influence of woman, to be beneficial, must depend mainly on the respect inspired by her *moral* excellence, not on the political address or energy she may display. (515–16)

Nevertheless, she did reprint most of the appeal.

By the 1850s, Hale, like many Americans, had become more concerned about the issue, and her position had hardened. Typically, she engaged in the debate about slavery and abolition through fiction. As a response to *Uncle Tom's Cabin,* which had begun running in the *National Era* in 1851, Hale prepared a revision of *Northwood: A Tale of New England* with the new subtitle *Life North and South: Showing the True Character of Both* (1852). In the preface she insists that "the great error of those who would sever the Union rather than see a slave within its borders, is, that they forget the *master* is their brother, as well as the *servant"* (iv). In this version Hale concludes the novel with an additional chapter of twenty pages, in which the hero and his bride read his late father's journal instructing them on how to manage the plantation they inherit. The journal has a section on "slavery and its reformers," which expresses opposition to abolition by condemning the use of *"fraud, falsehood, or force,* rather than wait God's time for the liberation of the slave," and another on "What the Bible says of Slavery," which argues that slavery is not sinful, though undesirable (395). The wife's chief duty will be to Christianize the slaves, after which they may return to Liberia and spread the gospel they have learned.[6]

In 1852 *Uncle Tom's Cabin* appeared in a hardcover edition. Thomas Gossett comments that Hale's next response, *Liberia, or, Mr. Peyton's Experiments* (1853) is one of those "difficult to classify as pro- or anti-slavery" (235). The novel begins with a Negro uprising and, despite the sentimental portrait of some slaves devoted to one idealized master, is quite negative about the possibility that freed slaves will be able to handle independent life on this continent. Hale's eventual solution, repatriation to Liberia, connects her work with Stowe's, where George and Eliza, and eventually Topsy, choose to return to Africa as missionaries. However, by including a section on the unhappiness of freed slaves in Canada—where George and Eliza do well—and another on their inability to manage their own farms, Hale deprecates all other possibilities that Stowe includes. Her conviction is that only in Africa can Africans take charge of their own destinies. The final section of *Liberia* is an "Appendix" in which she subjoins "documents for the most part written by colored persons from and about Liberia, showing the estimation in which that country is held by those who have the best opportunity of judging" (247). To these are added the Declaration of Independence of Liberia, its constitution, and a number of papers on colonization, as well as a statement of the failure of emancipation in the West Indies. This collection seems to be Hale's attempt to meet Stowe on the ground of documentation she had claimed as her own in *The Key to Uncle Tom's Cabin* (1853).

Given her attitude toward female public speakers and toward abolition, it is not surprising that in *Woman's Record* Hale exercises her editorial power to express disapprobation of female abolitionists. She excludes almost all the women active in the abolition movement from the compendium as she had excluded them from her magazine. Of the fifty-one women whom Blanche Glassman Hersh identifies as working for abolition during the period coinciding with Hale's fourth era, only six appear in *Woman's Record:* Elizabeth Blackwell, Lydia Maria Child, Julia Ward Howe (a brief mention under "Young Writers"), Lucretia Coffin Mott, Elizabeth Oakes Smith, and Jane Grey Swisshelm (mentioned in passing in a summary paragraph). Blackwell is excused because she is the model for female physicians, a career choice Hale strongly supported; Smith is praised for her intellectual achievements.

The portraits and editorial comments on Child and Mott, however, embody Hale's peculiar blend of praise and criticism and demonstrate her difficulty in setting boundaries for the action of the intelligent and committed women she admired. Hale devotes considerable space to Child and prints a number of passages from her writings. What Hale finds appealing is Child's "warm sympathy with the young," as shown in her editorship of *The Juvenile Miscellany*. She anthologizes a selection from a book for children, *Fact and Fiction,* claiming that it "discloses the impulse of [Child's] own nature, always seeking to do good." But Child's abolitionist sympathies do not escape Hale's sharp tongue. She concedes that "the design of the abolitionists, let us believe, is the improvement and happiness of the coloured race; for this end Mrs. Child devoted her noblest talents, her holiest aspirations. . . . The result has been, that her fine genius, her soul's wealth has been wasted in the struggle which party politicians have used for their own selfish purposes" (619–20). If, instead, Child had spent her energies on sending "free emigrants" to Liberia and working for schools there, Hale imagines "what blessed memorials" would have come to her. Thus Hale praises a woman's character, rebukes her for her life choices, and promotes her own solution to the national problem within one profile. This mixed analysis characterizes many of the portraits of active women whose beliefs Hale did not share.

A particularly delicate problem for Hale was how to deal with Harriet Beecher Stowe. In this case the successive editions provided an opportunity for second thoughts. Hale includes a highly laudatory portrait of Catharine Beecher, Stowe's elder sister, in the first edition of the *Record*. Her profile of Stowe there is short, noting her first collection of stories, *The Mayflower,* and her promise as a young author; she had published Stowe herself, in

Godey's. There is no mention of *Uncle Tom's Cabin,* though Forrest Wilson asserts that by November 1851 "the fame of the *National Era's* serial had penetrated into an elegant sanctum in Philadelphia. Harriet received a letter from Sarah J. Hale, asking for her daguerreotype and biographical facts about herself which Mrs. Hale could use in writing a compendious book about distinguished women writers of the earth" (274). Stowe may bear part of the responsibility for this omission—Wilson reprints her reply to Hale, in which she calls her life uneventful, uninteresting, and domestic, and adds in a postscript, "In answer to one of your enquiries, I would say that I have never published but one book, 'The Mayflower,' by the Harpers."

Yet Hale deliberately used her editorial expertise to evade consideration of *Uncle Tom.* In the 1872 edition she includes a brief update under the heading of "List of the Living not Found in the 4th Era." Here she notes the novels Stowe had written "since *Uncle Tom's Cabin"* (902). However, in her summary at the end of the second supplement to the edition of 1855 she had commented, "But the book of the three years is, as all the world knows, 'Uncle Tom's Log Cabin.' . . . We have no room here for an analysis of the story or the history of its triumphs: these matters will be more suitably discussed ten years hence" (898). In this passage she also complained of "another work," presumably *The Key to Uncle Tom's Cabin,* which she claimed would "do more to lower the standard of [Stowe's] genius and destroy the prestige which her assumed philanthophy [*sic*] had given to 'Uncle Tom's Cabin.'" Thus by emphasizing the storm of criticism which greeted the *Key* in the second edition, and then in the third edition ignoring her own proposal to consider the major work after a·suitable time lapse, Hale, the advocate of women writers, managed never to review or discuss the most important novel by an American woman in the nineteenth century.

If Hale disapproved of and therefore excluded female abolitionists, who presumably were working for the benefit of an oppressed race, her views on women who were active in the women's rights movement were even more hostile. In an editorial in the *Ladies' Magazine* of 1833, Hale issues her judgment: "the term *rights of woman* is one to which I have an almost constitutional aversion. It is a kind of talisman, which conjures up . . . the image of a positive, conceited, domineering wife, than whom scarce any object in nature can be more disgusting" (6 [1833]: 496). It is no surprise to find that of all the women involved in the planning of Seneca Falls or the first few national women's rights conventions, only Lucretia Mott is included in the *Record.* Yet given Hale's position in Philadelphia, her comments on Mott, and her penchant for updating her work, she cannot have been unaware of the women's rights movement or unable to include profiles of its leaders. Such omissions were certainly deliberate.

In her rather lengthy profile of Lucretia Mott, Hale praises her for attending well to the duties of motherhood and for her support of her husband. She shows her familiarity with abolitionist activities by crediting Mott with being the most able representative sent to the World Anti-Slavery Convention, notable particularly for her power of speech. However, rather than attack Mott on the issue of abolition, she criticizes the Quaker preacher for her stand on the rights of women, for her position on marriage, and for her erroneous views of woman's place in society. Hale comments, "It is evident that Mrs. Mott places the 'true dignity of woman' in her ability to do 'man's work,' and to become more and more like him. What a degrading idea; as though the worth of porcelain should be estimated by its resemblance to iron" (753). She summarizes her estimate of Mott as follows: "In short, the theories of Mrs. Mott would disorganize society. . . . Woman's 'best gifts' are employed to promote goodness and happiness among those whose minds take their tone from her private character. Measured by this standard, Mrs. Mott deserves an estimation higher than her public displays of talent or philanthropy have ever won" (753).

Mott was, at least, an American; *Woman's Record* culminates the nationalist vision Hale had first expressed almost fifty years earlier in *Northwood*. Baym believes that the *Record* is meant to show not only Christian but also American progress; in America, both women and Christianity are closest to Hale's ideal ("Christian Women" 261). Yet of the 119 profiles in the fourth era, 79 are of European and British women. Among those who are not American, Hale was willing to include a fair number whose morals she condemned—for instance, George Sand, Bettina von Arnim, and Maria Christina, dowager queen of Spain—as well as several women who fought for their countries in man's dress and a number of female monarchs. We can justify these choices and Hale's glossing over the political, social, and sexual behavior of such women only by assuming that she set a higher standard for Americans. No toleration of moral laxness or unseemly political activism could be afforded American women because they were to be the model for all women; nevertheless, Hale's fascination with the foreigners she describes complicates any attempt to imprison her or her text within the limits of "woman's sphere."

Sarah Hale was not only the promoter of other writers, she was herself a boon to the literary markets of her era. *Godey's*, of course, was a continuing success. For her books Hale used and benefited publishers in different cities: for example, in Boston, Bowles and Dearborn for the first edition of *Northwood*, and Marsh, Capen and Lyon for *The Ladies' Wreath* and *Poems for our Children*; in New York, H. Long for the second edition of *Northwood*; in Philadelphia, first Grigg and Elliot, and then Claxton, Remsen and Haffelfinger for her *Complete Dictionary of Poetical Quotations*. She wrote and edited so many books that Paul Boyer concludes that "'Sarah Josepha Hale' eventually became a kind of trademark" (*Notable American Women* 2: 113).

Woman's Record was published by the largest publisher in America at the time of its appearance, New York's Harper and Brothers. In the same year, 1853, Harper also published *Liberia; or, Mr. Peyton's Experiments* by

Mrs. Hale; they had previously published both *Keeping House and House-keeping* and *Boarding Out; or, Domestic Life;* in addition, they took over Hale copyrights from Marsh, Capen, Lyon & Webb. The Harper historian, Eugene Exman, notes that *Woman's Record* was a "big book for Christmas sales" and that it "had a lead position in the 1853 catalogue" (330). But 1853 was also the year of the great fire that destroyed the entire Harper printing plant on December 10. J. Henry Harper reprints Hale's letter of condolence, dated ten days later, which conveys both sympathy and the conviction that "adversity, that tries the souls of good men . . . brings its own reward in ways that are often more really beneficial than continued prosperity would be" (103). Exman points out her adroitness in dealing with her publishers here: during the ten days prior to the fire "four new books had been dispatched to dealers to fill advance orders. Among them was *Liberia, or Mr. Peyton's Experiments* by Mrs. Hale, a fact, however, which she did not comment on when she sent a letter of condolence" (Exman 359). It was by practicing just this kind of apparent self-effacement, while busily promoting her own work and that of other literary women, that Sarah Josepha Hale maintained her position as the most famous female editor of the nineteenth century.

When viewed as a whole, Hale's writing and editorial decisions over half a century display an astonishing constancy of purpose. Imbued by a vision of woman's role in the republic and in the world, Hale used every outlet available to her to promulgate her ideology and to support women's progress toward achieving the position she envisioned for them. Her ideology was a product of American political culture and Victorian views of gender difference. Women, morally superior rather than physically strong, were charged with responsibility for the moral direction of the family and the society. When Hale opened *Woman's Record* with the claim that what the world needs is moral power, she meant the moral power of women.

However, because Hale so firmly believed that woman's moral power was rooted in her inherent, essential nature, she opposed any attempt by women to compete with men, to enter the public spheres of politics or economics, or, as her rebuke of Mott showed, to try to become like men. As American society changed, becoming urban and industrial, Hale broadened her definition of woman's role to meet the needs of the age. A single mother herself, she first identified writing and teaching as appropriate activities for women; later she became the preeminent supporter of female missionaries and physicians. After the Civil War she supported light industrial work, domestic work, and clerical work as occupations for women who needed to earn a living. As Zophy points out, Hale's careful selection of these pursuits for middle-class women unintentionally paved the way for job segregation and the accompanying low pay for women workers (176).

Although Sarah Hale continually emphasized the duties of wife and mother as paramount, even praising women with whom she differed philosophically if they fulfilled their domestic duties well, she needed to find a way for woman's influence to be spread beyond the family. She found it, of course, in her own career as writer and editor. Women could promote moral progress and Christian life far beyond their own households as authors and yet not neglect their primary responsibilities. In addition, women writers could inspire others of their sex to moral and intellectual improvement. Sarah Hale's own position as an editor gave her the resources to promote women authors and to use model biographies of outstanding women to encourage her readers in their own lives. *Woman's Record* thus stands both as an explication of Hale's philosophy and as an example of the means by which woman's influence would be felt.

Notes

1. Finley 43; she points out that the first thirteen volumes were entirely English.
2. See Welter for a full exposition of this thesis.
3. For a full discussion, see Bardes and Gossett, *Declarations of Independence* 17–37, and passim.
4. Douglas notes that a writer for the *New Englander* protested Hale's "whitewash job on Nero's mother" but that Hale defended Agrippina because she was above all a mother (86–87).
5. Hale doesn't think much of Wheatley's work: her "poems have little literary merit; their worth arises from the extraordinary circumstance that they are the productions of an *African woman;* the sentiment is true always, but never new" (553). No women of color appear in the fourth era.
6. There is a fuller analysis of this novel in Bardes and Gossett, *Declarations of Independence.*

Works Cited

Bardes, Barbara, and Suzanne Gossett. *Declarations of Independence: Women and Political Power in Nineteenth-Century American Fiction.* New Brunswick, NJ: Rutgers UP, 1990.

Baym, Nina. "Between Enlightenment and Victorian: Toward a Narrative of American Women Writers Writing History." *Critical Inquiry* 18 (1991): 22–41.

———. "Onward Christian Women: Sarah J. Hale's History of the World." *New England Quarterly* 63 (1990): 249–70.

Conrad, Susan Phinney. *Perish the Thought: Intellectual Women in Romantic America, 1830–1860.* New York: Oxford UP, 1976.

Coultrap-McQuin, Susan. *Doing Literary Business: American Women Writers in the Nineteenth Century.* Chapel Hill: U of North Carolina P, 1990.

Douglas, Ann. *The Feminization of American Culture*. New York: Avon, 1978.

Exman, Eugene. *The Brothers Harper*. New York: Harper and Row, 1965.

Finley, Ruth. *The Lady of Godey's: Sarah Josepha Hale*. Philadelphia: Lippincott, 1931.

Gossett, Thomas. *Uncle Tom's Cabin and American Culture*. Dallas, TX: Southern Methodist UP, 1985.

Hale, Sarah J. *The Ladies' Wreath*. Boston: Marsh, Capen & Lyon, 1837.

———. *Northwood: A Tale of New England*. Boston: Bowles and Dearborn, 1827; *Northwood; or, Life North and South: Showing the True Character of Both*. New York: H. Long, 1852.

———. *Woman's Record; or, Sketches of All Distinguished Women from the Creation to A.D. 1868*. 3d ed. New York: Harper and Brothers, 1872.

Harper, J. Henry. *The House of Harper*. New York: Harper and Brothers, 1912.

Hersh, Blanche Glassman. *The Slavery of Sex: Feminist-Abolitionists in America*. Urbana: U of Illinois P, 1978.

Hoffman, Nicole Tonkavich. "Sarah Josepha Hale 1788–1874 [*sic*]: Profile." *Legacy* 7 (1990): 47–55.

James, Edward T., Janet Wilson James, and Paul S. Boyer, eds. *Notable American Women, 1607–1950: A Biographical Dictionary*. 3 vols. Cambridge, MA: Belknap P of Harvard UP, 1971.

Martin, Lawrence. "The Genesis of Godey's 'Lady's Book.'" *New England Quarterly* 1 (1928): 41–70.

McCall, Laura. "'The Reign of Brute Force Is Now Over': A Content Analysis of *Godey's Lady's Book*, 1830–1860." *Journal of the Early Republic* 9 (1989): 217–36.

Mott, Frank Luther. *A History of American Magazines, 1741–1850*. New York: D. Appleton, 1930.

Walker, Cheryl. *The Nightingale's Burden: Women Poets and American Culture before 1900*. Bloomington: Indiana UP, 1982.

Welter, Barbara. "The Cult of True Womanhood, 1820–1860." *American Quarterly* 18 (1966): 151–74.

Wilson, Forrest. *Crusader in Crinoline*. Philadelphia: Lippincott, 1941.

Wood, James Playsted. *Magazines in the United States*. 3d ed. New York: Roland, 1971.

Zophy, Angela. "For the Improvement of My Sex: Sarah Josepha Hale's Editorship of *Godey's Lady's Book, 1837–1877*." Diss. Ohio State U, 1978.

3.

Print and Pedagogy:
The Career of Elizabeth Peabody

Bruce A. Ronda

Fluent in ten languages, knowledgeable in classical history, trained in philosophy, theology, and linguistics, author of essays and textbooks, teacher and educational reformer, colleague of dozens of the most influential men and women in the mid- and late-nineteenth century, Elizabeth Palmer Peabody (1804–1894) surely merits inclusion as one of Susan Conrad's "intellectual women" of the Romantic era (Conrad). Yet Peabody's gusty enthusiasms, occasional tactlessness, and inattention to personal appearance drew attention away from her intellectual achievements, creating an image of Miss Peabody the eccentric, the person who walked into a tree on Boston Common, only to say "I *saw* it, but I did not *realize* it" (Tharp 336). While these stories are entertaining and may serve to humanize this incredibly learned person, they also distract from Peabody's accomplishments and from the insights her career furnishes us into the situation of New England literary women in the mid-nineteenth century.

Our efforts to lift Peabody's reputation from the level of amusing anecdote are here focused on her involvement in the literary marketplace, the business of producing, marketing, buying, and selling words. As an educator and reformer, Peabody was deeply aware of the role of print in conveying ideas and proposals to audiences. Indeed, as this essay suggests, her involvement in the business of words mirrors her own search for a personal and professional identity. In print and in person, the key word for a deeper understanding of Peabody is *mediation*. The printed page mediates between author and audience, and Peabody herself served as mediator between the radical and original thinkers of the New England Renaissance and a middle-class, educated public committed to certain reforms within a liberal Unitarian and politically Whiggish framework. In Peabody's case, however, the role of mediator was no mere intellectual nicety. Excluded, like other New England bluestockings, from the clubs, colleges, and careers available to men, Peabody sought to win a place for herself in the reform and literary circles of Boston and to support herself as an unmarried woman with no sources of income other than her pen and her teaching ability. For Peabody,

3.1. Elizabeth Peabody, lithograph, c. 1870. The Schlesinger Library, Radcliffe College.

the production and marketing of words, her own or others, contributed to her livelihood, provided a vehicle for her considerable intellect, and offered a means of entry into the community of reflective and engaged people. As words made public through facilitators like Peabody linked authors with audiences, so words also linked Peabody with her own audiences and provided for her economic security. Still, such public display of the self, through print and personality, exposed Peabody to the gaze of others and raised the tormenting issue of reputation, no small matter for a woman who so craved the respect of her reform-minded peers.

Despite its considerable number of writers and its enormous concentration of educated readers, the Boston area did not become a publishing center until after 1850, with the credit going largely to Ticknor and Fields's relentless promotion of New England authors (Charvat 170; Brodhead 54–57). In the early years of the century, New England publishing was decentralized at best, with publishing going on in Hartford, Connecticut; Portland, Maine; and dozens of other towns and small cities throughout the region. As William Charvat points out, many early-nineteenth-century authors were also publishers of their own work, bearing the expenses of manufacturing and arranging for printing and distribution (Charvat 8). This commercial decentralization corresponded to the amateur status of many writers who, like Timothy Dwight, Joel Barlow, and Charles Sprague, had professions other than literature. Between the 1830s and the onset of the Civil War, however, a growing number of New England writers, including Emerson, Hawthorne, Longfellow, and Stowe, supported themselves and their families with their literary output. This move toward literary professionalism, says Lawrence Buell, paralleled the Romantic notion of the writer as creative genius rather than scribe of the culture's values, and was part of the shift away from local publishing toward massive publishing houses willing to bear the risks and take the profits of mass production and distribution (Charvat 169; Buell 69).

Elizabeth Peabody offers an illuminating example of this gradual but noticeable shift from amateur to professional writing and from local to more centralized publishing. She never supported herself solely from writing, nor did she consider herself a writer by vocation. Her calling, as she understood it, was teaching. But in her case teaching children and adults was inextricably linked to words spoken and printed, so we can consider her engagement in the literary marketplace as a corollary of her lifelong work as an educator.

Peabody opened her first school in 1820 at the age of sixteen. Here she followed the lead of her mother, Elizabeth Palmer, a brilliant, self-educated woman who conducted a female academy in Andover, Massachusetts, in the first years of the nineteenth century. Betsey Palmer, as she was called, was one of many young New England women who opened private schools for girls in the 1780s and '90s, teaching academic subjects such as grammar, history, foreign languages, and philosophy, as well as pursuits like dancing and music designed to make young women more appealing candidates for marriage.

Betsey Palmer married Nathaniel Peabody in 1802, and in 1804 they moved to Billerica, Massachusetts, where Elizabeth was born. In 1808 the family moved to Salem, where Mrs. Peabody set up another private school which, together with tutorials, provided Elizabeth with her first instruction in history, literature, philosophy, and theology.

Elizabeth Peabody's first school, in Lancaster, Massachusetts, took its direction from her mother's early work and was one of many such private academies and schools scattered throughout New England. While Massachusetts had provided tax-supported "public" schools since the seventeenth century, many parents preferred to send their children to private schools conducted by recent college graduates or brilliant young women like Elizabeth Peabody, settings where class distinctions would be preserved.

In 1832, Peabody returned to Boston, where in the late 1820s she had taught the children of the city's fashionable elite in a school operated by the educational reformer William Russell. Now, with her sister Mary, Elizabeth opened another school but soon found that it was not producing enough income. So in the fall she opened a discussion series for women, called Historical Conversations, or Conferences, mostly covering classical history and literature. Shortly afterward, she opened a second course, called "The Reading Party." To her friend Maria Chase, Peabody described the reading material for the first seminar: "We employed six days in reading various beautiful things about Socrates—including some manuscript translations I have of Plato—& now we are reading Herder on the Spirit of Hebrew Poetry—which is an exquisite book" (Ronda 107). She soon discovered that her adult students lacked a sense of historical continuity, something she had come to prize from her conversations with the Unitarian leader William Ellery Channing. With his encouragement, she began to write historical outlines: *Key to History, Part I, First Steps to the Study of History* (1832); *Key to History, Part II, The Hebrews* (1833); and *Key to History, Part III, The Greeks* (1833).

How much Peabody needed these adult education students may be gauged from these lines to her sister Mary written in February 1834:

> I am so poor. I have paid last quarter's board, and for my wood and lights
> for all winter. Historical school will give fifty dollars the next quarter. I
> do not know how much the reading party will give, but I hope fifty, and
> I have saved some money from last quarter which will, altogether pay in
> April for this quarter. My present prospect is to go home in May pennyless
> and prospectless, except for what I may hope from the Christian Exam-
> iner [a series of three articles on the "Spirit of the Hebrew Scriptures"
> published in that Unitarian journal in May, July, and September 1834]. . . .
> If Mr. [George] Emerson should offer me a place in his school, I would
> take it for three hundred dollars. (Ronda 123)

In 1834, Peabody's growing involvement in educational reform and in the burgeoning Transcendentalist movement, together with her pressing financial need, prompted her to become Latin instructor and assistant at Bronson Alcott's celebrated and notorious Temple School, located in the Masonic Temple on Tremont Street in Boston. Through his considerable contacts, Alcott had gathered a number of students from educated and privileged families, and he set about offering them an education that was both academically rigorous and pedagogically unconventional. He engaged the students in very little rote learning, relying instead on conversations with them, a technique that worked well in the teaching of literature and history, and less well in the sciences, with which he had very little patience.

From her notes, Peabody began writing an account of Temple called *Record of a School,* which was first published in 1835. She fully agreed with Alcott that children, like all people, possess a spiritual and immortal core, to which all true education must be addressed. Still, she disapproved of his method of encouraging introspection, which seemed to her to violate the privacy of the child in its intrusive probing into the young conscience. Boarding in the same houses with the Alcotts, Peabody experienced a growing estrangement in 1835 and 1836, not only from Alcott's ideas, but from the nosy and unconventional behavior of the Alcott family. In 1836, Alcott published *Conversations with Children on the Gospels,* a book which caused a firestorm of criticism for its discussion, however veiled and innocuous, of conception and birth. Alcott had devoted much classroom time in the fall of 1835 to a study of the Gospels, with Peabody taking notes much as she had done at previous class sessions. But when she realized his intention to publish the conversations, she insisted that he omit the offending passages from the volume. Although the sections do not appear in the body of the text, Alcott included them as "Notes," thus calling even more attention to them (Miller 151). Anxious to protect her reputation, which was already shadowed by her alliance with Alcott at Temple School, Peabody severed all ties with him and Temple School and retreated to Salem. Still, she was able to see much that was worthy in his educational experiment, defending it in a long analysis and defense published in the Boston *Register and Observer* early in 1837.

Like Peabody's *Keys to History,* the publications inspired by Temple School demonstrated the ties between education and print that were central throughout her career. *Record of a School* was a manifesto of radical Romantic pedagogy, in its defense of a child-centered educational method. *Conversations,* in which Peabody appeared as "the Recorder," was meant to illustrate further the method Alcott employed, but to Peabody and many others it violated the standards of acceptable conversation and instruction. The very means Alcott and Peabody had chosen to demonstrate and publicize Romantic pedagogy had backfired, turning against them the very people on whom such radical experiments relied. Peabody understood all too well the Victorian conventions of appropriate behavior, especially female behavior. As she wrote to Alcott,

> I should like, too, to have the remarks I made on the Circumcision omitted.
> I do not wish to appear as an interlocutor in that conversation either. . . .
> Why did prophets and apostles veil this subject in fables and emblems if
> there was not a reason for avoiding physiological inquiries, &c? This is worth
> thinking of. However, you as a man can say anything; but I am a woman,
> and have feelings I dare not distrust, however little I can *understand them*
> or give an account of them. (Ronda 181)

Elizabeth Peabody's return to Salem in 1836 following the debacle of Temple School was only a temporary retreat from the world of literary and reform politics, for in Salem she "discovered" Nathaniel Hawthorne and helped launch him on his career as a professional writer. The Peabody and Hathorne (it was Nathaniel who added the "w") children had played together in Salem in the first years of the nineteenth century, although Elizabeth only remembered there being a daughter, also named Elizabeth. When Peabody moved back to Salem and heard that some evocative stories about New England, including "The Gentle Boy," were being attributed to a son of the widow Hathorne, she assumed the author was in fact the daughter Elizabeth or perhaps some older relative. After all, Hawthorne's stories and sketches had been appearing anonymously since 1830 in newspapers, gift-annuals, and magazines like *The Token* and the *New-England Magazine.* Upon visiting the Hathorne house, she discovered her error. Peabody invited Hawthorne and his sisters Elizabeth and Louisa to visit, which they did on November 11, 1837. During a second visit, Nathaniel Hawthorne met Peabody's sister Sophia, beginning the famous romance that would result in their marriage (Hawthorne 1: 177–82; Pearson 270; Ronda 418–21; Mellow 101).

During the next year, Peabody tried to draw out the reticent Nathaniel, sometimes resorting to letters and visits to the older "intellectual" sister Elizabeth as a means to do so. This kind of well-meaning intrusiveness on Peabody's part tormented Hawthorne for the rest of his life, and since she became his sister-in-law in June 1842, he could hardly escape her except by going to Europe. Still, Peabody helped Hawthorne secure a political patronage post as measurer of coal and salt at the Boston Custom House in 1839 (foreshadowing his more famous post at Salem). She also published three of his books of children's stories—*Grandfather's Chair, Famous Old People,* and *Liberty Tree*—in late 1840 and early 1841, obtaining the manuscripts from the author, arranging for their printing by Wiley and Putnam, and placing the volumes with booksellers (Mellow 176).

By the end of the 1830s, Elizabeth Peabody was fully engaged in the Transcendentalist phase of the Romantic movement. She had come to know Emerson (her Greek tutor in the early 1820s), who invited her to attend the Transcendental Club in 1837; she encouraged Hawthorne to break out of his shell of isolation and published several of his stories; she was a key participant in the educational experiment at Temple School; she knew George Ripley and Theodore Parker, who were central to the theological arguments between Transcendentalists and Unitarians; and she was reading voluminously in the literature of European Romanticism.

For all her involvement in the heady and controversial debates of the 1830s, Peabody understood that controversy meant exposure and possible damage to reputation. In 1830 she wrote to Elizabeth Davis Bliss, "I have suffered intensely from contact with society all my life—for I chose to keep myself *unsheathed*—through fear of being selfdeceived." And yet, she continued, she aspired to the ideal of "the lady & the Christian," ideals which required reticence, self-control, and attention to culturally appropriate behavior (Ronda 94–95). But it was Elizabeth's sister Mary, a supremely conventional and rather censorious person, who most aroused her fears of the

consequences of being "different." Elizabeth's feelings burst out in this letter
to Mary from May 1836:

> *you do not confide in me because you do not think I have discretion.*—Now
> as I think *I have discretion* & as I think *discretion is an entirely essential*
> *thing*—your coming to this decision—& acting upon it—as it has ever
> been perfectly plain that you have—with the most entire confidence that
> your impressions in regard to my *indiscretion* are correct—& without mak-
> ing me either explain the cases away—or acknowledge their character—is
> *& ever has been the wound that I have felt perpetually irritated between us.*
> (Ronda 170)

Teaching in private schools and conducting classes for adults all required
sensitivity to the opinions of others, particularly of parents whose children
were entrusted to the hands of teachers like Peabody. Even writing offered
no refuge from the pressures of public opinion; Peabody was desperately
afraid that the same public that might attend her schools or buy her books
would associate her with the scandals of *Conversations* and Temple School.
Nonetheless, she persisted, staying engaged with Romantic ideas and social
reform on the one hand, and remaining attuned to the opinions and preju-
dices of middle-class, politically liberal Victorian families on the other.

Partly to put her own finances on a more solid footing, and partly to
gather her remaining family (after the deaths of her brothers Wellington and
George), Peabody rented space on West Street, a narrow block between
Tremont and Washington Streets in Boston. The family occupied the back
rooms, and in July 1840, Peabody opened West Street Bookshop and library.
Here as nowhere else in the antebellum years do we see Elizabeth Peabody
engaged so directly in the business of print.

Soon a center for literary and reform-minded readers in the city, West
Street sold domestic and foreign books and periodicals or loaned them for a
small fee. She stocked her father Nathaniel's homeopathic medicines and, at
the suggestion of Washington Allston and William Ellery Channing, sold art
supplies as well. The variety of purposes suggests something of the ama-
teurishness of literary enterprise in the 1830s and '40s, as informal and local
publication and distribution of printed matter slowly and erratically gave way
to more systematic forms of business. Still, West Street was undoubtedly
Peabody's most successful business venture and brought her into contact
with even more of the literary and political lights of the Boston area.

In fact, as Peabody herself pointed out, no one had quite organized
such a center before. "[A]bout 1840 I came to Boston and opened the business of importing and publishing foreign books, a thing not then attempted
by any one. I had also a foreign library of new French and German books"
(Cooke 1: 148). This foreign circulating library numbered 1,161 volumes,

according to its catalog (Stern 5–12). Whether buying or borrowing, readers like James Freeman Clarke and Thomas Wentworth Higginson found foreign periodicals, volumes of French eclectic philosophers, and German ballads among the bookshop's treasures (Hale 144). Presiding over all was "Miss Peabody herself, desultory, dreamy, but insatiable in her love for knowledge and for helping others to it" (Higginson 86). As a publisher of foreign books, Peabody obtained the stereotype plates or advance sheets from European or English printers and had volumes printed in the United States, which she then offered for sale in her shop.

By the early 1840s, West Street had become a gathering place for literary and reformist folk, not simply a retail business. Margaret Fuller's conversations were held in the bookshop in 1839 (even though it was apparently not yet open for business) and 1840, and once in 1841. The Peabodys' "large parlor" was also the site for conversations that led to the founding of the utopian community of Brook Farm. Peabody described the spirit of this particular group to her friend John Sullivan Dwight: "While they are so few—& the community plan is not in full operation it is unavoidable that they must work very hard—but they do it with great spirit—& their health & courage rises to meet the case—" (Ronda 250). Peabody also wrote a series of essays describing and endorsing Brook Farm, "A Glimpse of Christ's Idea of Society," published in the *Dial* in October 1841, "A Plan of the West Roxbury Community," appearing in the January 1842 *Dial,* and "Fourierism," in the April 1844 *Dial.*

Although she submitted other essays to the *Dial,* only these three appeared. The reluctance of even her friends to publish her writing suggests that Peabody's reputation as a flighty and overenthusiastic person was increasing, despite the good service she performed for the Transcendentalist cause at West Street. Emerson thought her style was too excessive: "you would think that she dwelt in a museum where all things were extremes & extraordinary" (Emerson 5: 262). Margaret Fuller echoed that judgment, and was determined that no more Peabody essays appear in the *Dial.* Peabody's reputation even extended beyond the Transcendentalist circle. James Russell Lowell's sister Mary Putnam wrote him regarding the publication of Peabody's "A Vision" in the March 1843 number of his journal *The Pioneer:* "Now with all my regard for Miss Peabody, I cannot think that her abilities qualify her to write a leading article for *any* periodical. Her name alone would be an injury to any work to which she should be a contributor—and her vision should be something very *transcendent* indeed to enable it to make head against this prejudice" (qtd. in Bradley 237).

Despite these reservations, Peabody was entrusted with the task of publishing the *Dial* from 1841 to 1843. In October 1841, Weeks, Jordan and Company, the *Dial*'s first publisher, went bankrupt, and Margaret Fuller, then the magazine's editor, suggested that publication be shifted to Peabody. This involved assembling final copies of articles, arranging for their printing and binding, marketing the product, and handling the finances. Early in 1842, Peabody and James Freeman Clarke inspected the books of Weeks, Jordan and found that there were only three hundred paying subscribers to the *Dial,* not five to six hundred as they had been told. This number would ensure an annual income of about $750, but since the costs of paper and printing amounted to $700, little money would be left to pay for Margaret Fuller's editorial services, to say nothing of payment for Peabody's work. A year later Peabody found that the income from sales would not even cover costs.

In April 1843, Peabody informed Emerson, the *Dial*'s new editor, that subscriptions were down to 220, and that people seemed to prefer to pay for single copies rather than take out subscriptions. To Emerson, this shift suggested a need for more aggressive distribution of the journal. But Peabody was not quite the person for this kind of marketing effort; she had been unable to get the April issue to the booksellers at the beginning of the month, something Emerson thought crucial for successful sales. In response to her "careless" policy, Emerson turned to his own publisher, James Munroe, to take over the publishing duties from Peabody. Still, the *Dial* continued to lose subscribers, and a year later, in April 1844, the journal published its last issue (Myerson 71, 74, 88–90).

Meanwhile, the bookshop continued to attract customers, but with the failure of the *Dial,* the energy seemed to go out of the West Street hub. In 1845 Peabody turned to teaching again, this time in a school for boys conducted by Hungarian émigré and linguist Charles Kraitsir (Ronda 236). In the last years of the decade, Peabody's energies went into her own version of the *Dial,* a journal she called *Aesthetic Papers.* Gathering contributions from Emerson, Thoreau, Hawthorne, and John Sullivan Dwight, Peabody hoped to fashion a journal that would expand "aesthetics" to mean a sense of shape and proportion in all human creation, not just in works of art. Even more, she hoped that her journal would stimulate discussion of the connection between aesthetics and society, rather than simply be an investigation of personal creativity and taste: "the word *aesthetic* is difficult of definition, because it is the watchword of a whole revolution in criticism. Like Whig and Tory, it is the standard of a party; it marks the progress of an idea. It is as a watchword we use it, to designate, in our department, that phase in human progress which subordinates the individual to the general, that he may reappear on a higher plane of individuality" (Peabody, "The Word 'Aesthetic'"4). Like the *Dial,* the contributions were serious, even memorable; Thoreau's "Resistance to Civil Government," later known as "Civil Disobedience," was first published there. But also like the *Dial,* it attracted few subscribers, and its first issue, in May 1849, was also its last (Ronda 237).

Elizabeth Peabody did not consider herself a professional writer. Still, her work as an educator necessarily drew her into the business of print. Teaching as mediation between student and material is analogous to writing or publishing as mediation between individual thought and public consumption. Indeed, all Peabody's educational efforts surveyed thus far have involved some form of writing or publishing. In the early 1850s, she continued this linkage by championing the system of Josef Bem. Bem was an exiled Polish general who had devised a system of teaching history by using charts of colored squares to indicate the succession of events. Peabody published a guide to Bem's system in 1850 called *The Polish-American System of Chronology* and embarked on a tour of the northeastern states to encourage school committees to adopt the system. Bem's system may now seem familiar in an age of multimedia education, but in the mid-nineteenth century it was outlandish and offered to amused Bostonians yet another example of Peabody's eccentricity. Theodore Parker asked artist and writer Christopher Cranch to illustrate this scene: "Elizabeth P. Peabody is looking at an expressman's slate and writing an order on it in the street. She has a bundle of Bem's Chronology under her arm, a parasol and her bonnet falling back etc., and the expressman is looking on with dire amaze" (qtd. in Myerson 279, 13n).

The mutuality of pedagogy and print that so marked Peabody's career in the antebellum years found its greatest fulfillment in the crusade that occupied her for much of the rest of her life, the kindergarten. Influenced by the ideas of German educational reformer Friedrich Froebel, Peabody saw in the kindergarten movement a perfect fusion of Romantic idealism and social reform. In its celebration of the female kindergarten teacher (or "kindergartner") as uniquely possessing those traits most suited to work with young children, and in its preference for teachers who worked out of love of children rather than out of need for money, the Froebelian kindergarten movement seemed to resolve for Peabody the daunting problem of reputation; here was a movement in which she could be assertive, even aggressive, yet which relied centrally on the Victorian assumptions about woman's nature as nurturing and caregiving.

In 1859 Peabody met Margarethe Schurz, wife of Republican politician Carl Schurz and founder of a German-speaking kindergarten in Wisconsin, and learned about kindergartens and the work of Froebel. The following year Peabody opened the first English-speaking kindergarten, on Pinckney Street in Boston's Beacon Hill neighborhood. As with her other reform projects, Peabody understood the power of the printed page, and with her sister Mary Mann quickly wrote *The Moral Culture of Infancy and Kindergarten Guide*. Within a few years, the school had attracted thirty students, taught by Peabody and Mann, two assistants, a French teacher, and a gymnasium instructor. But by 1866, Peabody was becoming dissatisfied with her kindergarten. Despite its "pecuniary success and a very considerable popularity," Pinckney Street seemed to encourage in its pupils "precocious knowledge and consequent morbid intellectual excitement quite out of harmonious relation with moral and aesthetic growth" (Peabody, "Our Reason for Being"). These words suggest Peabody's concern that Pinckney Street was becoming another Temple School, with its exaggerated emphasis on introspection.

In an 1882 essay on "The Origins and Growth of the Kindergarten," Peabody commented that her educational experiment was admirable, "but it was simply no kindergarten. What it had taken Froebel fifty years of suffering life and painful experimenting to work out of abstract first-principles, amid the confusions of a contradictory past, was not divined even by two experienced women, who had made child-culture their own life-work" (Peabody, "Origins and Growth" 523). Even more upsetting for Peabody than her own misunderstanding of the principles of the Froebelian kindergarten were the successful efforts of other kindergartners, not particularly interested in either Froebel's Romantic assumptions or his pedagogical methods, in setting up their own schools based on Peabody's *Kindergarten Guide.* In search of a better understanding of Froebel's approach, and to gain the support of the Froebelians in Germany, Peabody went to Europe in 1867. Upon her return, she issued a corrected version of *Kindergarten Guide.* Beginning in 1873 she edited and published a journal, the *Kindergarten Messenger,* and in 1877 she helped found the American Froebel Union.

Throughout the 1870s, Peabody carried the message of the kindergarten in personal tours of the eastern and midwestern United States, and in a staggering amount of written material—pamphlets, tracts, journal articles, training manuals, books, and countless personal letters. Following Froebel but also drawing on her considerable exposure to the Romantic movement, Peabody argued that all education, including early childhood education, was a "leading out," as the Latin root suggests, of the spiritual and intuitive insights that all possess. As a fusion of gentle guidance and self-exploration, education thus became a way of countering the growing naturalism and materialism evident in postwar American culture, trends Peabody recognized and deplored (Ronda 355; Beatty 39). The challenge to the educator lay in finding the appropriate means of drawing out that inherent insight. Froebel's method involved music, play, and the use of simple objects and shapes. To be avoided were rote learning, memorization, too much intrusive introspection, and too much content learning. Peabody recognized that she had succumbed to this last temptation in her early "false" kindergarten in Boston (Ronda 311). By the mid-1870s a network of kindergarten training schools had sprung up, largely through Peabody's personal appearances and her incessant barrage of print.

Under the pressure of a growing immigrant population and the increasing reputation of social science, by the end of the century responsibility for kindergartners' self-understanding shifted away from ministers and more toward professionals. As Barbara Beatty puts it, "cognitive learning and socialization rather than spiritual attunement and moral education became the goals of kindergarten pedagogy" (Beatty 45). Still, Peabody and the other Romantic educators had gotten the kindergarten word out, organized and systematized training schools, and provided a vocabulary and an ideology to explain and justify their approach.

Indeed, one of the most striking things about Elizabeth Peabody, in her linking of pedagogy and print, is her lifelong effort to provide a structure for ideas and insights which, one might say, resist structure. We have described her as essentially a mediator, and this characteristic might be phrased even more strongly and paradoxically: Peabody sought to institutionalize that which was perceived as radically free and untrammeled. She took the central Romantic insight that each person possesses, inherently and originally, divine truth, and she sought to restate and reshape it for a larger and sometimes skeptical audience. Educational reforms of various sorts, journals like the *Dial* and *Aesthetic Papers,* books like *Record of a School* and *Kindergarten Guide,* should all be seen as part of Peabody's unceasing effort to interpret, mediate, shape, and define Romantic insights for a largely middle-class and Victorian audience.

Peabody's cultural role as Romantic mediator involved her continuously in the public realm, and raised just as continuously the question of her reputation. Many of her contemporaries found her amusing or exasperating, and loved to exchange funny stories about her. She was, by most accounts, nosy, tactless, maddeningly talkative, and an undisciplined writer. Current scholarship has tended to repeat these stories endlessly. For example, in his otherwise admirable biography of Hawthorne, James Mellow describes her as "authoritative, fussing and fussy, pedantic, eager to instruct the world" (128).

No doubt Peabody could drive to distraction even the most sympathetic reformer with her ceaseless advocacy of good causes, but her personal traits should not blind us either to her distinctive contributions or to the cultural situation which partially shaped her. Like many other nineteenth-century middle-class American women, Peabody faced a Victorian patriarchal ideology which defined the genders as intellectually and emotionally distinct, assigning women the sphere of home, children, religion, and morality (Coultrap-McQuin 8–9). But Peabody was also shaped by a family heritage that demonstrated, through her mother, women's intellectual ability, by personal circumstances that left her unmarried in a culture that saw marriage as woman's supreme goal, and by exposure to a Romantic ideology that validated personal feeling and spontaneity as powerful sources of truth. In fact, eccentricity may be a perfectly understandable response in a woman caught in the midst of such conflicting cultural pressures, a way of maintaining individuality without experiencing total rejection or condemnation. Even more, the label of "eccentric" should be examined for its patriarchal assumptions. As the term suggests, the eccentric deviates from the normal course, and thereby calls attention to the assumptions that define normality. Even though Peabody was often deeply pained by the criticism she endured for her odd ways, she was perhaps despite herself demonstrating the power of an independent intellectual woman.

Standing as she did at the juncture of personal and ideological forces, and given the limited career options open to women at the time, it is not surprising that Peabody should turn to education, and particularly early childhood education, as a means of integrating these forces. In an increasingly literate society, education requires the printed word, and Peabody soon found herself writing, publishing, and marketing educational materials. And like the career of teaching, writing and publishing revealed the gradual but perceptible shift from local, amateur, and unsystematic to national, professional, and highly organized. In her advocacy of the kindergarten movement and in her effort to shape an ideology around the work of Froebel, Peabody was part of that drive toward organization. Still, she retained, in her writing as in her teaching, the core Romantic belief that spiritual truth lay at the center of each person. Such a belief was the foundation of Peabody's fusion of print and pedagogy.

Works Cited

Beatty, Barbara. "'A Vocation from on High': Kindergartning as an Occupation for American Women." *Changing Education: Women as Radicals and Conservators*. Ed. Joyce Antler and Sari Knopp Biklin. Albany: State U of New York P, 1990. 35–50.

Bradley, Sculley. "Lowell, Emerson, and the *Pioneer.*" *American Literature* 19 (1947): 231–37.

Brodhead, Richard. *The School of Hawthorne*. New York: Oxford UP, 1986.

Buell, Lawrence. *New England Literary Culture from Revolution through Renaissance*. New York: Cambridge UP, 1986.

Charvat, William. *Literary Publishing in America, 1790–1850*. Philadelphia: U of Pennsylvania P, 1959.

Conrad, Susan Phinney. *Perish the Thought: Intellectual Women in Romantic America, 1830–1860*. New York: Oxford UP, 1976.

Cooke, George Willis. *An Historical and Biographical Introduction to the "Dial."* 2 vols. 1902. New York: Russell and Russell, 1961.

Coultrap-McQuin, Susan. *Doing Literary Business: American Women Writers in the Nineteenth Century*. Chapel Hill: U of North Carolina P, 1990.

Emerson, Ralph Waldo. *The Journals and Miscellaneous Notebooks of Ralph Waldo Emerson*. Ed. William Gilman et al. 14 vols. to date. Cambridge, MA: Harvard UP, 1960.

Hale, Edward Everett, ed. *Autobiography, Diary and Correspondence of James Freeman Clarke*. Boston: Houghton Mifflin, 1891.

Hawthorne, Julian. *Nathaniel Hawthorne and His Wife*. 2 vols. Boston: Houghton Mifflin, 1884.

Higginson, Thomas Wentworth. *Cheerful Yesterdays*. 1895. New York: Arno Press, 1968.

Mellow, James. *Nathaniel Hawthorne in His Times*. Boston: Houghton Mifflin, 1980.

Miller, Perry, ed. *The Transcendentalists*. Cambridge, MA: Harvard UP, 1950.

Myerson, Joel. *The New England Transcendentalists and the "Dial."* Rutherford, NJ: Fairleigh Dickinson UP, 1980.

Peabody, Elizabeth Palmer. "The Origins and Growth of the Kindergarten." *Education* (May–June 1882): 507–27.

———. "Our Reason for Being." *Kindergarten Messenger* 1 (May 1873): 1.

———. "The Word 'Aesthetic.'" *Aesthetic Papers*. Ed. Elizabeth Peabody. Boston: EP Peabody, 1849.

Pearson, Norman Holmes. "Elizabeth Peabody on Hawthorne." *Essex Institute Historical Collections* 94 (1958): 256–76.

Ronda, Bruce A., ed. *Letters of Elizabeth Palmer Peabody, American Renaissance Woman*. Middletown, CT: Wesleyan UP, 1984.

Stern, Madeleine. "Elizabeth Peabody's Foreign Library." *American Transcendental Quarterly* 20 supplement (1973): 5–12.

Tharp, Louise Hall. *The Peabody Sisters of Salem*. Boston: Little, Brown, 1950.

4.

Josephine St. Pierre Ruffin: Pioneering African-American Newspaper Publisher

Rodger Streitmatter

By 1890, Josephine St. Pierre Ruffin had already lived a full and productive life. The descendant of an African prince had completed a proper education in Boston and New York. At fifteen she had married a young man from Boston's black elite. She had borne him five children, burying one of them and shepherding the other four to appropriate stations in life. At the same time, she had provided wifely support for her husband, standing stalwartly by his side as George Lewis Ruffin advanced from being the first African-American graduate of Harvard Law School to becoming a member of the Massachusetts State Legislature and the Boston Common Council, and finally, the first African-American judge in the North. When Josephine Ruffin's husband died suddenly three years after his appointment to the judgeship, it was expected that the widow would, in keeping with the times, live out her life surrounded by the trappings of wealth and social status to which she had become accustomed.

But Josephine Ruffin was not a woman who was satisfied with doing what was expected, nor would she be restrained by the times. Instead, she defied the conventions of nineteenth-century society and, in so doing, made history. Ruffin used her ample resources to found, publish, and edit the first newspaper created both by and for American women of African descent. Through *Woman's Era,* a Boston-based monthly established in 1890 and distributed nationally, Ruffin showcased the achievements of black womanhood. In an early issue, Ruffin wrote of *Woman's Era:* "The stumbling block in the way of even the most cultured colored woman is the narrowness of her environment. It is to help strengthen this class and a better understanding between all classes that this little venture is sent out on its mission" ("Editorial," Mar. 1894).

While boosting the status and enhancing the pride and self-worth of her black sisters, Ruffin simultaneously demonstrated her own abilities as a businesswoman, an organizer, and a leader first in publishing and then in the

4.1. Josephine St. Pierre Ruffin, n.d.,
from Booker T. Washington, *A New
Negro for a New Century* (Chicago:
American Publishing House, 1900).

black women's club movement. Her success at publishing propelled Ruffin to
found, in 1894, the Woman's Era Club, the first organization of African-American women in Boston and the second organization of its kind in the country.[1]
A year later, Ruffin convened the first national meeting of African-American
women, creating the precursor of the National Association of Colored Women.[2]

Early Years

Josephine St. Pierre was born on August 31, 1842, in Boston. She was the
youngest of six children born to Eliza Matilda Menhenick, a white Englishwoman, and John St. Pierre, the dark-skinned son of a Frenchman from
Martinique. Josephine's aristocratic ancestry has been traced to her great-
great-grandfather, an African prince who came to Massachusetts in the eighteenth century and married a Native American woman. Josephine's father
made his fortune as a Boston clothier.[3]

Josephine encountered racial prejudice early in her life. Her parents enrolled their light-skinned daughter in a private grammar school in Boston, but
six months later, when her racial background was discovered, Josephine was
forced to leave the school. The St. Pierres refused to send their daughter to the
city's segregated public schools, enrolling her instead in the integrated schools
of nearby Salem. She later graduated from Bowdoin Finishing School in Boston and completed two years of private tutoring in New York.

Two months short of her sixteenth birthday, Josephine married George Lewis Ruffin, a member of another of Boston's leading African-American families. Disheartened by the Dred Scott decision, the newlyweds moved to England because they did not want to raise a family in a nation that tolerated slavery. After the outbreak of the Civil War, the Ruffins returned to Boston and purchased a home on fashionable Cambridge Street. During the next few years, Ruffin gave birth to five children, the youngest of whom died in infancy.[4]

In 1869, George Lewis Ruffin became the first African American to graduate from Harvard Law School. He served in the Massachusetts State Legislature from 1870 to 1871 and on Boston Common Council from 1876 to 1877. Ruffin received national attention in 1883 when he was appointed judge of the municipal court of Charlestown, making him the first African-American judge in the North (Logan 236; Utterback).[5]

As the career of George Lewis Ruffin advanced, the talents of Josephine St. Pierre Ruffin also began to emerge. During the Civil War, she recruited black soldiers and worked with the Sanitary Commission, forerunner of the American Red Cross. Ruffin's first major undertaking occurred after the war when she founded the Kansas Relief Association. The need for the association developed when former slaves who had migrated to the West encountered severe economic difficulties. Ruffin cajoled wealthy Bostonians into sending clothing and money to the destitute refugees. In 1870, Ruffin demonstrated her concern for women's rights by becoming a charter member of the Massachusetts Suffrage Association.[6]

Ruffin's involvement with these various crusades brought her into contact with influential white leaders. She and abolitionist William Lloyd Garrison, who also lived in Boston, collaborated on the relief work in Kansas. Ruffin and women's suffrage leader Ednah Dow Cheney worked together on women's club projects, and Ruffin had frequent contact with Susan B. Anthony, Elizabeth Cady Stanton, Lucy Stone, and Julia Ward Howe. She also was a close friend of the Booker T. Washingtons, spending winters with them in Tuskegee, Alabama.[7]

It was not until after her husband's sudden death in 1886, however, that Ruffin made her most important contributions. She was a forty-four-year-old widow with grown children. In addition, she was financially secure and had a reputation for supporting philanthropic endeavors. Josephine St. Pierre Ruffin was poised on the brink of achievement.[8]

Groundbreaking Publisher

Ruffin began her historic work as a publisher in 1890, personally financing the creation and operation, from her home, of a national newspaper for African-American women. She handled all publishing responsibilities for *Woman's Era*—editing copy, laying out pages, and selling advertisements.

Although she wrote an editorial for each issue, she left most of the writing to upper-class club women from around the country whom she had recruited as unpaid correspondents.[9]

The newspaper measured nine by twelve inches, and varied in length from sixteen to twenty-eight pages. Each issue carried at least one photograph; some had as many as fifteen. An annual subscription cost one dollar; a single issue sold for ten cents. Most news and editorial items were organized under columns headed by the names of correspondents—women from states as distant as California, Texas, and Louisiana.[10]

Woman's Era contained substantive news. One item, based on interviews with Boston police and hospital officials, reported that a sixteen-year-old black girl had been held in slavery for four years. Another stated that a black woman, Fannie Barrier Williams, had been denied membership in the Woman's Club of Chicago. Ruffin, in keeping with the conventions of the African-American press, adopted an advocacy tone that allowed writers to add editorial comments as they saw fit. At the end of the article about Williams's rejection, for example, Ruffin stated: "Club principle made a weak surrender to personal prejudice."[11]

Editorial content was geared toward the African-American elite. There were no how-to items or reader-service articles to help the black underclass survive in white America. Instead, Ruffin aimed *Woman's Era* directly and unashamedly toward well-to-do women, the masthead stating that the newspaper was designed for women of the "refined and educated classes."

Ruffin was proud of the fact that all items in the *Era* were written specifically for it, rather than relying on reprints from other publications. She also boasted that *Woman's Era* was a publication of integrity and journalistic principle. The publisher wrote: "Personal feeling has no place in newspaper work. A good newspaper gives facts. A paper which is afraid of everybody's feelings has no call to be published" ("Editorial," Feb. 1896).

Woman's Era was a feminist publication, with content directed specifically toward the advancement of women. Ruffin made her strong support of women perfectly clear, saying of the *Era:* "Being a woman's movement, it is bound to succeed" ("Why You Should Subscribe"). She reiterated her sentiments through statements about African-American women, such as: "Our indignation should know no limit. We as women have been too unobtrusive, too little known" ("New York").

Editorial content included items from black women's clubs all over the country, and when the National Federation of Afro-American Women was formed in 1895, *Woman's Era* became the federation's official publication. Likewise, when the National Association of Colored Women was established a year later, it, too, chose the newspaper as its official voice (Josephine Ruffin, "National Association").

In addition to promoting women's rights, Ruffin encouraged her stable of writers to support racial reform. She insisted that African-American women should "think in order that they may not sit like idiots" when race questions were debated. Ruffin's editorial voice grew particularly strident in opposition to the legalization of segregation. When the U.S. Supreme Court upheld segregated transportation on trains in *Plessy v. Ferguson,* Ruffin advocated breaking the law rather than accepting segregation ("Separate Car Law").

Innovative Businesswoman

Ruffin devoted most of her energies to the business side of publishing. Although she possessed sufficient funds to launch *Woman's Era,* her savings were not sufficient to finance the venture indefinitely. She did not intend to make a financial profit from her newspaper, but she expected it to pay for itself.

In 1891, Ruffin began to supplement her savings by working full-time as editor-in-chief of the *Boston Courant,* a black weekly. After Ruffin edited both the *Era* and the *Courant* for a year, however, her doctor said her health would not allow her to continue both jobs. Ruffin then continued to publish the *Era,* while writing only an occasional article for the *Courant.*[12]

Because Ruffin had succeeded with the relief work she had initiated in Kansas, she was already experienced in financial planning, budgeting, and fund-raising. She told her readers that she could afford to continue to publish *Woman's Era* only if she amassed enough advertising and subscription revenue to allow her to double the number of pages per issue and to publish twice a month ("Editorial Notes"; "Notes").

It is from such editorial statements, along with the size and advertising content of extant issues, that information about the *Era*'s finances must be extrapolated. Specific details about the newspaper's revenue, advertising rates, and circulation have not been preserved.

Ruffin knew that attracting advertisers depended upon offering businesses high circulation. So hers was a two-pronged approach to the business of publishing—some techniques aimed at building her advertising base, others aimed at increasing circulation.

Creative Advertising Saleswoman

In the unfortunate tradition of the black press, *Woman's Era* struggled constantly for sufficient advertising revenue to remain financially solvent. Like other African-American publishers, Ruffin faced the dual problem of a dearth of large black-owned businesses and a reluctance by white-owned businesses to appeal to a black market (Pride).

In addition, the fact that *Woman's Era* was a national publication added to Ruffin's challenge to sell advertising. By the late nineteenth century, American newspapers had not yet evolved into national enterprises with national advertisers. But the *Era* was national in editorial scope, thereby needing to attract advertisers from across the country.[13]

Finally, working against Ruffin's efforts to attract advertising from the dominant segment of the business world was her defiant editorial stance in favor of racial reform. When Boston real estate agents denied wealthy African Americans the right to buy homes in the most desirable sections of the city, for example, Ruffin was less concerned about offending potential advertisers than about demanding fair housing rights. Using a haughty tone, the publisher wrote: "The position is absurd. No other class of vendors may say who shall and shall not buy their wares" ("Editorial," Dec. 1894).

The earliest extant issues of *Woman's Era,* dated 1894, contained sixteen pages, including two pages of advertising. The largest ads were placed by relatives of members of the Woman's Era Club. Ruffin's son Stanley advertised the contracting firm which he served as secretary, and her son George advertised the music lessons from which he made his livelihood. The father of Maria Baldwin, club vice president, advertised his real estate company.

Comparing editorial and advertising content of *Woman's Era* reveals that one of the first tacks Ruffin employed to broaden her advertising base was to stroke loyal advertisers in her editorial content. Casting aside the publishing principle of separation of "church and state," Ruffin used her news columns to promote advertisers. She boldly stated: "We are happy to be able to personally endorse nearly all our advertisers" ("Notes and Comments"). An item about a local baker illustrated the point. According to the item, "Ray, on Chatham Row, sells a prepared icing which is so good it is called 'Perfect Icing.' What an advantage to have an icing which does not spoil or foment, all prepared for us" ("Notes and Comments"). It was no coincidence that the Chatham Row Bakery was one of the *Era*'s most consistent advertisers.

By the end of 1894, there were indications that the tactics were reaping some dividends, as a local seamstress and wallpaper hanger both began advertising in the *Era.* The November issue expanded to twenty pages, December to twenty-four. The growth was possible because of a doubling in the number of advertising pages, with the two issues each carrying four pages of ads. Ruffin knew, however, that such modest growth was not sufficient, as the newspaper was still far smaller than her goal of thirty-two pages.

So in the spring of 1895, Ruffin took one of her most daring and, ultimately, one of her most unsuccessful steps to attract new advertisers. For the first time in the *Era*'s five-year history, the newspaper began running classified ads. The addition of a classified ad section signaled a fundamental change in Ruffin's approach. Before this pivotal moment, Ruffin's techniques had been designed specifically to appeal to women of the black elite. Ruffin's class of women had responded to her tactics, but their support had not been enough. This insufficient response may have been a result not of the failure of Ruffin's techniques, but of the small numbers of upper-class black women at the turn of the century—or, for that matter, the small number who were literate.[14]

Regardless of the specific impediments to her success, Ruffin's addition of classified ads demonstrated that she had begun appealing to the black masses as potential advertisers, as classifieds traditionally are designed largely for the use of middle- and low-income readers. In other words, Ruffin had recognized that she had to broaden her appeal. So she began to experiment with strategies designed to appeal not to a narrow audience, but to a broad one.

Unfortunately, the black masses represented a class with whom Ruffin's privileged life had not brought her into contact. This gulf is dramatically illustrated by the content of the sample "wants" that she published in order to indicate the range of services and items that readers might want to advertise. The six ads were for governesses and composition lessons—hardly representing the typical needs of the black masses of the late nineteenth century ("Wants," Apr.–June 1895). Eight months later, the classified section still consisted of only the same half dozen samples. After sustaining the effort for nearly a year, Ruffin abandoned classified advertising. The venture had failed miserably, not attracting a single ad ("Wants," Nov. 1895).

By the end of 1895, it was clear that Ruffin's efforts to sell additional advertising were not working. *Woman's Era* was not growing. The largest issue of the year contained twenty-four pages, the same as the largest issue of the previous year. The inventive Ruffin came up with a new idea, one that returned her to the more familiar territory of upper-class women. After helping to found the National Association of Colored Women, Ruffin helped plan a convention for the association in Washington, D.C., in the summer of 1896. In the months preceding the event, Ruffin created a free souvenir issue of the *Era,* boasting that it would be filled with advertisements from all over the country, indexed and grouped according to city. She had cleverly conceived of the souvenir issue as a way of introducing her national newspaper to distant businesses and, thereby, broadening her advertising base beyond Boston ("Statement").

The highly successful August–September 1896 free issue consisted of twenty-four pages, including a hefty fifteen pages of ads. What is more, the issue included, as Ruffin had hoped, advertisements from African-American businesses throughout the country, including New York, Philadelphia, Washington, Chicago, Denver, and Los Angeles.

Despite Ruffin's clever strategy and hard work, however, the non-Boston businesses that advertised in the souvenir issue did not become steady patrons. By the end of 1896, Ruffin's newspaper was declining rapidly. The August and September issues were combined, as were the October and November issues. Rather than becoming a semi-monthly, as Ruffin had hoped, *Woman's Era* had become a bi-monthly. No issue whatsoever was published in December. And the January 1897 issue consisted of only sixteen pages, reverting back to the shorter length of three years earlier.

Persistent Circulation Promoter

At the same time that Ruffin was attempting to attract new advertisers, she was also experimenting with various techniques to increase the *Era*'s circulation. Her first approach surfaced early in 1894 when Ruffin designed a subscription contest that she promoted with the bold headline: "Free! Splendid Premium Offers." According to an accompanying news article, the reader who produced the most new subscriptions would receive a year's free tuition in voice, piano, or violin at the Boston Training School of Music. Neither the advertisement nor the news article mentioned that the free lessons would be provided by George Ruffin—the son of the publisher. In short, the savvy publisher had devised a scheme that would give the winner a substantial prize while costing the newspaper very little ("Free!").

Later that same year, Ruffin introduced another very different tack to build circulation. Using the network of black women's clubs that she knew so well, she began traveling to other cities to solicit subscriptions. During her visits, Ruffin spoke to the various local clubs, strongly urging her fellow aristocrats to subscribe to the country's only newspaper designed specifically for them ("Social Notes").

Still later that year, Ruffin adopted the most aggressive of her marketing tactics: attacking the competition. In December she announced that *Ladies' Home Journal,* the largest women's magazine in the country, had refused to accept articles written by African-American women. Further, she told readers that if they were wealthy enough to afford to subscribe to the *Journal,* they should be proud enough of their race and gender to be insulted by such an affront to the educated women of the race. She then demanded that all such African-American women should cancel their subscriptions to the *Journal* and use the money to subscribe to the *Era.* Ruffin wrote bitterly: "Think of this, you colored women whose money and efforts are going to support in luxury the writers of that paper, while you hesitate to give ten cents toward the encouragement of writers of your own race! O, the pity of it!" ("Loyal Woman").

The scolding apparently did not cause the newspaper's subscription list to soar, however, as early 1895 marked a turning point in Ruffin's circulation-boosting strategy, just as it had in her advertising-boosting strategy. So, at the same time that she tried to attract classified ads from the black masses, she also departed from her efforts to attract new subscriptions from upper-class women—offering free music lessons, appealing personally to fellow club women, challenging upper-class African-American women not to support a white magazine that insulted them—and tried to appeal to women of a lower socioeconomic level.

In April 1895, the innovative publisher offered a free sample issue of her newspaper to anyone who sent her a two-cent stamp, even though the selling price of a single issue was ten cents ("Notice"). The technique indicates that Ruffin was convinced that any African-American woman, regardless of her socioeconomic status, who saw a single copy of *Woman's Era* would eagerly subscribe to it. The technique also indicates that the wealthy publisher did not know that the one-dollar-a-year subscription price was more than most black women could afford, no matter how good the newspaper.

The *Era's* editorial content demonstrated that Ruffin's perception of black women was skewed toward the wealthy. Representative was an item about a Boston seamstress, which read, "Mrs. Casneau makes and furnishes materials for a walking or visiting dress for $23.00. This hardly needs comment. A stylish, well-made cloth dress at $23.00 is a bargain, as the average woman must know" ("Notes and Comments"). The "average woman" as Ruffin defined her obviously was far different from the typical black woman of late-nineteenth-century America, who could not have afforded to spend $23 a year to clothe her entire family!

When Ruffin was forced to begin trying to appeal to middle- and low-income women as subscribers, as when she tried to attract them as advertisers, she was clearly stretching her business acumen beyond her frame of reference. And her efforts, though bold and creative, failed.

In early 1896, Ruffin's personal correspondence, for the first time, described her anguish over the pressure of financing *Woman's Era*. She wrote Ednah Dow Cheney: "I am struggling to carry along." Despite the stress, Ruffin tried to remain optimistic, telling Cheney: "It is hoped and expected that some arrangement may be made for better, more reliable support of the organ" (letter to Cheney, Mar. 24, 1896). But Ruffin could not deny that her publishing venture was in serious trouble.

Later in the year, Ruffin tried one last, desperate effort to increase circulation among the black masses. Finally acknowledging that the price of the newspaper was a problem for most African-American women, she cut the yearly subscription rate in half ("National Association"). When this drastic move failed to provide the necessary infusion of revenue from circulation, the determined publisher finally admitted defeat. She told officials of the National Association of Colored Women that she no longer could afford to produce the newspaper ("Open Appeal"; Giddings 104). The final issue was dated January 1897.

Although Ruffin had demonstrated remarkable creativity and persistence, she had been unable to overcome the lack of advertising that historically has deprived the black press of economic stability. Nor had she been able to increase subscriptions to bring more advertising and circulation revenue. Both her advertising- and circulation-building strategies had succeeded when she designed methods aimed at other black aristocrats but had failed when she was forced to expand beyond her own class. Ruffin knew black elite society; she did not know the masses that comprised the majority of black America.

When financial difficulties forced Ruffin to cease publication of her newspaper after seven years, she was neither bitter nor discouraged. Instead, she congratulated her newspaper—and herself—for helping African-American women uplift the race. In the final issue of *Woman's Era*, Ruffin confidently predicted that women would continue to progress, saying: "It is as impossible for women to turn back as for time—they are bound to march on" ("Open Appeal").

Although it is difficult to gauge the impact of any publishing enterprise, the existence of a newspaper created both by and for African-American women obviously increased the self-esteem and sense of empowerment of this long-denigrated minority. One historian has called *Woman's Era* "the most successful publication published exclusively by colored women," and another has praised it as "exerting an influence that was widely recognized" (Greener; Howe 337).

Women's Club Organizer

While Ruffin was breaking new ground as a newspaper publisher, she was also making history as a leader in the black women's club movement. Ruffin's one-hundred-member Woman's Era Club was committed to educating female members of the black elite. Meetings were devoted to topics such as civics, domestic science, literature, and race. In addition, the club provided scholarships to young African-American women and lobbied for improved city services in black residential sections of Boston. Ruffin remained president of the club until 1903. The position of "honorary president" was then created for her.[15]

A year after founding the local club, Ruffin expanded the concept to the national level. She took the action to defend Ida B. Wells and her anti-lynching crusade.[16] John Jacks, the white editor of a Missouri newspaper, had tried to destroy Wells's credibility by attacking her in a letter to the sponsors of her lecture tour. Those sponsors sent a copy of the letter, which indicted all African-American women as blatantly immoral, to Ruffin as publisher of *Woman's Era*. To create a united protest against the allegations, Ruffin called the first national convention of African-American women. When women from thirty-six clubs in twelve states gathered in Boston in 1895, it marked the first time that American women of African descent had assembled for a national meeting. By the end of the three-day convention, the women had created the National Federation of Afro-American Women. A year later, the federation merged with the Colored Women's League to become the National Association of Colored Women, with Ruffin as first vice president. Within two decades, the association included a thousand local clubs and fifty thousand members.[17]

In 1900, Ruffin attempted to desegregate the all-white General Federation of Women's Clubs. She submitted an application for Woman's Era Club to be admitted to the national federation, not volunteering the fact that members of the club were of African descent. After the application had been approved, Ruffin attended the federation's annual meeting in Milwaukee, planning to receive the club's credentials and thereby desegregate the federation. Ruffin's effort to break the color barrier became a major issue when southern delegates threatened to secede from the federation if a black club was admitted. Ruffin succeeded in securing her individual credentials because she was an elected representative of the Massachusetts Federation of Women's Clubs, which she earlier had desegregated, but officials refused to admit her Boston club into the national federation.[18]

To some degree, Ruffin accomplished her mission, however, as journalists across the country complimented her, thereby improving the nation's image of African-American women. Milwaukee newspapers described Ruffin as a "cultured lady" and "woman of fine presence," while a Los Angeles magazine characterized her as "a woman of charming manners" and a Pittsburgh newspaper said she was "very lady-like in demeanor." Newspapers were critical, on the other hand, of the white leaders of the federation. The *Chicago Tribune* stated: "The federated white-faced women of the clubs have not had the courage to recognize their sisters of the colored race."[19]

Final Years

After *Woman's Era* ceased publication in 1897 and she helped launch the African-American women's club movement, Ruffin increased her activity as a public speaker. She lectured, most frequently on the importance of moral courage, to audiences in Massachusetts, New Jersey, and several western states. She also helped found the American Mount Coffee School Association, which operated a school for Liberian children, and served as vice president of the association under Edward Everett Hale's presidency.[20]

Her organizational skills and national prominence benefited a number of civic organizations. She helped found the Boston branch of the National Association for the Advancement of Colored People and the Association for the Promotion of Child Training in the South, which supported a school for black children in Atlanta. She served on the executive board of the Massachusetts Federation of Women's Clubs.

Josephine St. Pierre Ruffin died of nephritis, a disease of the kidneys, on March 13, 1924, at the age of eighty-one. Her body lay in state in a public building in Boston. Funeral services were held at Trinity Episcopal Church on Copley Square, and she was buried at Mount Auburn Cemetery in Cambridge.[21]

Notes

1. The first local African-American women's club was the Colored Women's League, founded in Washington, D.C., in 1893. See Gatewood 242; and Litwack and Meier 312.

2. The National Association of Colored Women became a vehicle through which thousands of African-American women were able to expand beyond the limited sphere of domesticity, allowing them to gain a greater sense of independence. On the African-American women's club movement, see Angela Davis 3–15; Gatewood 210–46; Giddings 95–117, 135–42; Kolmer 178–80; Lerner, ed., 433–58; Lerner 158–67; Noble 129–43; and Wesley.

3. The St. Pierre family tree is in the Ruffin Family Papers. Biographical information about Ruffin, which focuses largely on her work as a club woman, is contained in various sketches of her life: Arroyo 994–97; Cash 961–65; Howe 335–39; James et al. 3: 206–8; Leonard 706; Lerner, ed., 440–41; Logan and Winston 535–36; Richings 371–72; and Scruggs 144–48.

4. The Ruffins were married June 30, 1858, in Twelfth Baptist Church in Boston. Their marriage certificate is preserved in the Ruffin Family Papers. The four Ruffin children who lived to adulthood all achieved success. Hubert Ruffin practiced law and served in the Massachusetts State Legislature and on the Boston Common Council. Florida Ruffin Ridley taught in Boston public schools. Stanley Ruffin was an inventor and manager of a Boston manufacturing company. George Lewis Ruffin, Jr., was organist at St. Augustine's Church and a music instructor. See Brown 151.

5. Utterback's undated article is preserved in the Sophia Smith Collection, Smith College, Northampton, Mass. Contents of the article indicate it was written in 1902.

6. See Dannett 309; Elizabeth Davis 237; and Sterling 257.

7. See letters, Josephine Ruffin to William L. Garrison; Margaret Washington 178; letters, Josephine Ruffin to Cheney; letter, Booker T. Washington to Francis J. Garrison. Ednah Dow Cheney was a Boston reformer and author who helped found the New England Woman's Club and Hospital for Women and Children; her foremost interests were women's suffrage and abolition. Susan B. Anthony and Elizabeth Cady Stanton organized and led the National Woman's Suffrage Association. Lucy Stone was a prominent leader in abolition and women's suffrage. Julia Ward Howe was an author and reformer committed to abolition, women's suffrage, prison reform, and the cause of peace; Howe lectured as a Unitarian preacher and wrote the poem "Battle Hymn of the Republic."

8. George Lewis Ruffin died of kidney disease. See "Death of George L. Ruffin"; and George Ruffin, obituaries.

9. Several historians (Brown 152; Bullock 169; Sterling 441) have stated that *Woman's Era* was founded in March 1894, the date of the earliest extant copy. Ruffin correspondence preserved in the Boston Public Library, however, documents that *Woman's Era* existed in 1890. Two letters that Ruffin wrote to Cheney, May 19 and 22, 1890, carry the printed letterhead "The Woman's Era." In the May 22 letter, Ruffin specifically mentions the "May *Era.*" The fact that *Woman's Era* predated the Woman's Era

Club, which Ruffin founded in 1894, is verified by two 1902 magazine articles that state that the club took its name from a newspaper called *Woman's Era* (see Hopkins; and Utterback). Ruffin initially may have distributed *Woman's Era* only in Boston but then expanded to national distribution in 1894.

10. General information about *Woman's Era* is contained in Bullock 396–97. Twenty-two issues of *Woman's Era* are preserved in the Rare Books and Manuscripts Department, Boston Public Library. The July 1896 issue also is preserved in the Moorland-Spingarn Research Center, Howard University Library, Washington, DC.

11. See Josephine Ruffin, "Chicago Woman's Club"; "Women in Business"; and "Slavery Case."

12. See Ridley; Mossell 15; and Josephine Ruffin, letter to *St. Paul Appeal.* The *Boston Courant* was founded in 1890; the earliest extant copies are dated 1900.

13. On the beginnings of nationally distributed publications, see Emery and Emery 169–250; and Folkerts and Teeter 255–336.

14. In 1890, 57.1 percent of black Americans were illiterate, compared to 7.7 percent of white Americans. See *Negroes in the United States.*

15. See Hopkins; Howe 338; and Booker T. Washington, *New Negro* 390–92.

16. Ida B. Wells (1862–1931) was a newspaper editor and activist who founded and led the anti-lynching campaign in the United States and England. In 1895, Wells married Ferdinand Barnett and changed her name to Wells-Barnett.

17. See Fields 63–64; Flexner 189–91; Giddings 93–95; Lerner, ed., 440–43; and Major 273–74.

18. For coverage in the *Milwaukee Sentinel,* see "Colored Club Is Barred Out by Directors," June 5, 1900: 1; "Storm Must Break Over Color Line," June 6, 1900: 1; "Mrs. Lowe for Presidency," June 7, 1900: 1; "Breach Was Avoided," June 9, 1900: 6. See also Wood 128–31.

19. "Mrs. Lowe Is Named Again," *Milwaukee Journal* June 8, 1900: 1; "Will Draw Color Line," *Milwaukee Journal* June 4, 1900: 5; Utterback; "Women's Clubs Cannot Avoid Color Issue," *Pittsburgh Dispatch* June 6, 1900: 7; "What the Woman's Federation Did," *Chicago Tribune* June 10, 1900: 36.

20. Edward Everett Hale was an author and Unitarian minister in Boston and Worcester, as well as chaplain of the United States Senate. A humanitarian, Hale advocated an international court to eliminate war.

21. See "Deaths"; and Work 422.

Works Cited

Arroyo, Elizabeth Fortson. "Josephine St. Pierre Ruffin." *Black Women in America: An Historical Encyclopedia.* Ed. Darlene Clark Hine. 2 vols. Brooklyn, NY: Carlson, 1993. 2: 994–97.

Brown, Hallie Q. *Homespun Heroines and Other Women of Distinction.* 1926. Freeport, NY: Books for Libraries P, 1971.

Bullock, Penelope L. *The Afro-American Periodical Press, 1838–1909.* Baton Rouge: Louisiana State UP, 1981.

Cash, Floris Barnett. "Josephine St. Pierre Ruffin." *Notable Black American Women*. Ed. Jessie Carney Smith. Detroit: Gale Research, 1992. 961–65.

Dannett, Sylvia G. L. *Profiles of Negro Womanhood*. New York: M. W. Lads, 1964.

Davis, Angela Y. *Women, Culture, & Politics*. New York: Random House, 1989.

Davis, Elizabeth Lindsay. *Lifting As They Climb*. Washington, DC: National Association of Colored Women, 1933.

"Death of George L. Ruffin." *New York Freeman* November 27, 1886: 1.

"Deaths." *Boston Evening Transcript* March 15, 1924: 9.

Emery, Michael, and Edwin Emery. *The Press and America: An Interpretive History of the Mass Media*. 7th ed. Englewood Cliffs, NJ: Prentice-Hall, 1992.

Fields, Emma L. "The Women's Club Movement in the United States, 1877–1900." Master's thesis. Howard University, 1948.

Flexner, Eleanor. *Century of Struggle: The Woman's Rights Movement in the United States*. Cambridge, MA: Belknap P of Harvard UP, 1959.

Folkerts, Jean, and Dwight Teeter. *Voices of a Nation: A History of Media in the United States*. New York: Macmillan, 1989.

Gatewood, Willard B. *Aristocrats of Color: The Black Elite, 1880–1920*. Bloomington: Indiana UP, 1990.

Giddings, Paula. *When and Where I Enter: The Impact of Black Women on Race and Sex in America*. New York: William Morrow, 1984.

Greener, Richard T. TS. By courtesy of the Trustees of the Boston Public Library.

Hopkins, Pauline E. "Famous Women of the Negro Race." *Colored American Magazine* 5 (Aug. 1902): 273.

Howe, Julia Ward, ed. *Representative Women of New England*. Boston: New England Historical Publishing Co., 1904.

James, Edward T., Janet Wilson James, and Paul S. Boyer, eds. *Notable American Women, 1607–1950: A Biographical Dictionary*. 3 vols. Cambridge, MA: Belknap P of Harvard UP, 1971.

Kolmer, Elizabeth. "Nineteenth Century Woman's Rights Movement: Black and White." *Negro History Bulletin* 35 (1972): 178–80.

Leonard, John William, ed. *Woman's Who's Who of America: A Biographical Dictionary of Contemporary Women of the United States and Canada*. New York: American Commonwealth, 1915.

Lerner, Gerda. "Early Community Work of Black Club Women." *Journal of Negro History* 59 (1973): 158–67.

———, ed., *Black Women in White America: A Documentary History*. New York: Random House, 1971.

Litwack, Leon, and August Meier. *Black Leaders of the Nineteenth Century*. Urbana: U of Illinois P, 1988.

Logan, Rayford W. *The Negro in American Life and Thought*. New York: Dial, 1954.

———, and Michael R. Winston, eds. *Dictionary of American Negro Biography*. New York: Norton, 1982.

Major, Gerri. *Gerri Major's Black Society*. Chicago: Johnson Publishing, 1976.

Mossell, Gertrude Bustill. *The Work of the Afro-American Woman*. 1894. New York: Oxford UP, 1988.

Negroes in the United States. Bureau of the Census. Washington, DC: GPO, 1904.

Noble, Jeanne L. *Beautiful, Also, Are the Souls of My Black Sisters: A History of the Black Woman in America*. Englewood Cliffs, NJ: Prentice-Hall, 1978.

Pride, Armistead Scott. "Negro Newspapers: Yesterday, Today and Tomorrow." *Journalism Quarterly* 28 (1951): 179–82.

Richings, G. F. *Evidences of Progress among Colored People*. Philadelphia: George S. Ferguson, 1897.

Ridley, Florida Ruffin. "George Lewis Ruffin" entry (4). Schomburg Center for Research in Black Culture. Clipping File. New York Public Library.

Ruffin, George Lewis. Obituaries. Folder 26. George Lewis Ruffin Papers. Moorland-Spingarn Research Center, Howard University Library.

Ruffin, Josephine St. Pierre. "The Chicago Woman's Club Reject [*sic*] Mrs. Williams." *Woman's Era* Dec. 1894: 20.

———. "Editorial." *Woman's Era* Mar. 24, 1894: 8.

———. "Editorial." *Woman's Era* Dec. 1894: 10.

———. "Editorial." *Woman's Era* Feb. 1896: 10.

———. "Editorial Notes." *Woman's Era* Mar. 24, 1894: 7.

———. "Free! Splendid Premium Offers." *Woman's Era* June 1, 1894: 7.

———. Letters to Ednah Dow Cheney. May 19 and 22, 1890; Mar. 24, 1896. By courtesy of the Trustees of the Boston Public Library.

———. Letters to William Lloyd Garrison. Jan. 13, 1875; Apr. 19, 1879. By courtesy of the Trustees of the Boston Public Library.

———. Letter to *St. Paul* (Minnesota) *Appeal* Nov. 14, 1891: 3.

———. "A Loyal Woman." *Woman's Era* Dec. 1894: 19.

———. "National Association of Colored Women." *Woman's Era* Aug.–Sept. 1896: 2.

———. "New York." *Woman's Era* July 1895: 3.

———. "Notes." *Woman's Era* Aug. 1894: 8.

———. "Notes and Comments." *Woman's Era* Sept. 1894: 14.

———. "Notice to Subscribers." *Woman's Era* Apr. 1895: 12.

———. "An Open Appeal to Our Women for Organization." *Woman's Era* Jan. 1897: 2.

———. "Separate Car Law." *Woman's Era* Feb. 1896: 9.

———. "Slavery Case in Boston." *Woman's Era* Sept. 1894: 14.

———. "Social Notes." *Woman's Era* Sept. 1894: 11.

———. "Statement to Advertisers." *Woman's Era* June 1896: 1.

———. "Wants." *Woman's Era* Apr. 1895: 17.

———. "Wants." *Woman's Era* May 1895: 9.

———. "Wants." *Woman's Era* June 1895: 20.

———. "Wants." *Woman's Era* Nov. 1895: 16.

———. "Why You Should Subscribe for the Woman's Era." *Woman's Era* May 1, 1894: 15.

———. "Women in Business." *Woman's Era* Mar. 24, 1894: 13. Ruffin Family Papers. Amistad Research Center. Tulane University.

Scruggs, L. A. *Women of Distinction: Remarkable in Works and Invincible in Character.* Raleigh, NC: 1893.

Sterling, Dorothy, ed. *We Are Your Sisters: Black Women in the Nineteenth Century.* New York: Norton, 1984.

Utterback, Helen Porter. "Mrs. Ruffin and the Woman's Era Club of Boston." *Los Angeles Herald Illustrated Magazine* [1902]: 7.

Washington, Booker T. Letter to Francis Jackson Garrison. Feb. 22, 1904. Booker T. Washington Papers. Library of Congress.

———. *A New Negro for a New Century.* Chicago: American Publishing House, 1900.

Washington, Margaret Murray. "Club Work Among Negro Women." *Progress of a Race.* Ed. J. L. Nichols and William H. Crogman. Naperville, IL: Nichols, 1929.

Wesley, Charles H. *The History of the National Association of Colored Women's Clubs: A Legacy of Service.* Washington, DC: National Association of Colored Women's Clubs, 1984.

Wood, Mary I. *The History of the General Federation of Women's Clubs.* New York: General Federation of Women's Clubs, 1912.

Work, Monroe N. *Negro Year Book, 1925–1926.* Tuskegee, AL: Negro Year Book Publishing, 1925.

5.

Mabel Loomis Todd, Martha Dickinson Bianchi, and the Spoils of the Dickinson Legacy

Elizabeth Horan

The Auction of the Mind

Emily Dickinson's publication history is notoriously contentious.[1] The charges of theft, fraud, and piracy that consumed four generations of women and that continue today originate in Emily Dickinson's resistance to publication.[2] When one of her poems saw print, anonymously, through the actions of another, she complained that it had been "robbed" of her. Her well-known poem beginning "Publication—is the Auction / Of the Mind of Man—" describes publication as a "disgrace" that reduces the "human spirit."[3] She also rejected the argument that she had a "duty" to publish for the "use" of "the world."[4] As a consequence her fame was entirely posthumous: only some eleven out of more than seventeen hundred poems that she wrote were published prior to her death in 1886. During her life she used correspondence to circulate her manuscripts in order to avoid the market, but as soon as her written "thought" became the property of others, the occasional unauthorized publication turned into a stream of volumes. Following Emily Dickinson's death, her friends and relatives staked out claims to the astonishing array of materials she had produced—thousands of variously divided, copied, stolen, mutilated poems and letters in every stage of composition. Legal complexities eventually overcame Dickinson's real and presumptive heirs' attempts to establish exclusive rights to the materials. Careful study of the publication correspondence reveals a previously unexamined aspect of the Dickinson industry: the publishers avoided court by building coalitions among themselves and with academics. These coalitions turned the losses of individual claimants into corporate gains by undermining all attempts to maintain the poet's legacy as an exclusive familial preserve.

The quarrels over the rights to Emily Dickinson's manuscripts can be traced to the two closest female relatives who survived her. They partially sympathized with her attitude toward publication. Susan Gilbert Dickinson, the poet's sister-in-law and closest female friend, joined in the poet's circulating poems among friends and neighbors. Lavinia Dickinson, the poet's

5.1. Mabel Loomis Todd, 1911.
Todd-Bingham Picture Collec-
tion, Manuscripts and Archives,
Yale University Library.

sister, shared Emily Dickinson's perspective on the poems as a form of property and as an extension of "thought," but Lavinia's enthusiasm for publication was the reverse of Emily Dickinson's attitude. Following the poet's death,
Lavinia wanted her sister's genius known. Taking advantage of Lavinia's enthusiasm and Susan's reservations about print, Austin Dickinson's young mistress, Mabel Loomis Todd (1856–1932), seized the opportunity. Todd worked
alongside Emily Dickinson's longtime friend, the distinguished editor, Civil
War soldier, and Unitarian minister Thomas Wentworth Higginson. Higginson
and Todd prepared some hundred poems for publication: after Todd had
copied them, they added titles, altered rhymes, conventionalized punctuation and spelling, and shaped the poems into uniform lines and stanzas.[5]
The excellent sales of this first edition led Todd to promote Emily Dickinson's
reputation and market through lecture tours and further editions, first with
Higginson's assistance, then on her own. Through these successes, Todd
gained ground in her rivalry with Susan Dickinson and established a degree
of social legitimacy. Todd and her allies used their understanding of the
market, but they underestimated the Dickinson women's tenacity in defending their proprietary interests. During the 1890s, the first and best-docu-

5.2. Martha Gilbert Dickinson (later Bianchi), c. 1890. bMS Am 1118.996, Dickinson Photo Box 2, by permission of the Houghton Library, Harvard University.

mented epoch of the Dickinson industry, Mabel Todd mapped out a path of audience development that continued into the twentieth century.[6] Todd's production and promotion of Dickinson volumes halted in 1898, following Austin Dickinson's death, when Lavinia successfully sued to recover a strip of land that she said the Todds had tricked her into deeding to them, and that the Todds said was meant to compensate Mrs. Todd for her work.[7]

Mrs. Todd's subsequent twenty-five-year "silence" on the subject of Emily Dickinson left Susan Dickinson's daughter Martha (1866–1943) with a free hand to represent Emily Dickinson as she chose.[8] Given Lavinia's mandate regarding Todd, to "Get that name off Emily's books!" Martha Dickinson initially decided in 1900 to prevent all reprints and further editions of her Aunt Emily's work.[9] No scholar has ever noted that decision, remarkable in itself and in the context of a business strategy that later went in the opposite direction. In the dimming light of her own literary career as a poet and novelist, and following Susan Gilbert Dickinson's death, Martha Dickinson Bianchi lessened her resolve. In 1914 Bianchi edited a volume of the poems that Emily Dickinson had sent to Susan Dickinson, *The Single Hound*. The new text continued the marketing approach that Todd had developed previously, presenting the poems as a "friendship" book for women buyers who would find it suitable for gift giving.[10] In her private correspondence, Bianchi indicated that she had designed the collection as an extension of what she thought her mother would have wanted (letter to Brownell, March 30, 1914). In seeking to restore Susan Dickinson's name, which Mabel and Austin had systematically scissored and erased from the poet's correspondence, Madame Bianchi (as she preferred to be called) went one step further: she repackaged the volumes of her predecessors without acknowledging their work or even their names.[11] Bianchi cut and pasted Todd's edition of the poet's letters into a biography that she issued under her own name, and she simultaneously brought the various Todd-edited Dickinson volumes into a single collection.

The public's renewed interest in the poet during the 1920s coincided with Madame Bianchi's need for ready cash and her discovery of Alfred Leete Hampson as a collaborator. Hampson sorted out poems and answered correspondence while Bianchi wrote family and childhood reminiscences at a half-century's remove. Hampson's assistance and the royalties on the newly packaged Dickinson legacy underwrote Bianchi's winters in Europe and summers in Amherst, where she received Dickinson "pilgrims" in the Evergreens, her house "within the hedge."[12] These reiterated phrases in Madame Bianchi's personal correspondence, like her self-descriptions as "the last of the Dickinsons" and "Emily's posthumous niece," evidence a pathos too easily overlooked by scholars caught up in the drama of a businesslike Mrs. Todd battling an entrenched, incompetent aristocracy.

Confident of absolute control over the Dickinson legacy as her unique birthright, isolated by her social preferences for friendships among the older members of old families, Bianchi was oblivious to how changes in the publishing industry were redefining the audience for Emily Dickinson. Market segmentation, the influence of university-based writers, and subsidiary rights and permissions to reprint especially mattered in the 1930s, following the poet's centenary. The aftereffects of the stock market crash sent the once-brisk sales of trade books into the doldrums. Publishers needed dependable markets, such as those in college texts. Little, Brown was anxious to cooperate with academics, but Madame Bianchi regarded them as potential competitors who needed to be reminded that her version of Emily Dickinson was the only authoritative one.

The 1931 comeback of Mabel Loomis Todd, aided by her daughter, Millicent Todd Bingham (1880–1968), was a nightmare for Bianchi, for it was the first sign of an alliance between publishers and critics who viewed Bianchi's claims as an obstacle to be overcome. Todd's success in publishing her collection of reedited Dickinson letters without obtaining permissions from Bianchi or her publishers led the interested parties to work behind Bianchi's back. Bianchi's own publishing firms of Little, Brown and Houghton Mifflin worked with Scribner's and Harper, Row to negotiate an exceptionally liberal interpretation of "fair use" that temporarily broke Bianchi's monopoly on the Dickinson legacy. For the last thirteen years of her life, from 1930 on, Bianchi struggled in vain to preserve her control over her Aunt Emily's estate as a new generation, "the academic literary historians," discovered Emily Dickinson as a generalized representative of the nation's relation to its past (Lubbers 184–95). The lady poet of the nineties, read for religious and sentimental reasons and for her echoing of standard themes in verse by women (Buckingham xv) was transformed, set into the center of the newly shaped canon of American literature. The prestige attached to her work grew accordingly, and with it the struggle over who was entitled to the rights to her work. Study of Dickinson publication materials from the 1930s and '40s reveals that Bianchi's publishers joined with the academics in challenging her authority. For all her business strategizing, Bianchi paid dearly for her naïve faith that her publishers and lawyers would uphold her birthright as the only authentic heir to the poet's legacy.

Bianchi died feeling betrayed, and her major competitor, Millicent Todd Bingham, did not fare much better. Even though Bingham earned the respect that the academic establishment was loath to grant to Bianchi, Todd's daughter died much as Susan Dickinson's daughter had, feeling robbed and defeated. In Bingham's case, Bianchi's hand reached from beyond the grave to prevent any of Todd's cohort from sharing in the spoils, when libraries and university corporations entered into the feud, drawn by interests in acquiring valuable manuscripts and publication rights.

Even though all the principals have died, the struggle over Emily Dickinson's property continues, embedded in her institutionalization. Dickinson scholars have long understood the centrality of the book trade in negotiating Emily Dickinson's reputation.[13] Several boxes of loosely organized Dickinson publication papers kept in the Houghton Library indicate that within the book trade, the interpretation of property rights in the poet's estate was decisive especially in the controversies of the 1920s and 1930s. Publishers working in concert with lawyers and university-based literary critics were crucial in constructing the warring parties' claims. These "outsiders" largely determined the course of the feud, for they helped redraw the principles of property on which the claimants to the poet's legacy founded their versions of the past.

Alternatives to Publication:
"The Mind Alone, without corporeal friend"

The publication strategy of sending poems in letters allowed Emily Dickinson to stay at home, as she explains to Susan Dickinson in a letter discovered in 1992: "If I do not come with feet, in my heart I come—talk the most, and laugh the longest—stay when all the rest have gone."[14] Susan Dickinson, in turn, played a key part in bringing Emily Dickinson's verses to others. The two women shared literary tastes and mutual friendships with leading editors such as Samuel Bowles and Josiah Holland, so Susan Gilbert Dickinson was chief among the friends who missed the poet's presence at parties and who regularly passed the original manuscripts and copies of her poems on to others. Because Susan had received upwards of three hundred poems and letters from Emily Dickinson, she was probably less surprised than the poet's sister and lifelong housemate Lavinia is supposed to have been on finding the hundreds of manuscripts stacked in her sister's room, following her death.

The reading aloud to guests of Emily Dickinson's poems was a regular occurrence in Susan and Austin Dickinson's household. Susan Dickinson's preference for this mode of "publication" to a select and limited audience ran at cross-purposes, however, with Lavinia Dickinson's claims on the manuscripts and, by extension, on Lavinia's plans to amplify the audience for the poems following her sister's death. Writing to Thomas Wentworth Higginson just as the first volume of Emily Dickinson poems was being issued to the general public, Lavinia complained that Susan had stood in her way: "Mrs. Dickinson . . . wished the box of poems there, constantly and was unwilling for me to borrow them for a day, as she was fond of reading them (the verses) to passing friends" (Bingham 87). Yet Lavinia was similarly fond of reading the poems aloud: Martha Dickinson Bianchi writes of how Susan had invited Amherst graduate and New York editor William Crary Brownell to assist in editing a volume of some one hundred poems. According to Bianchi, she and her brother "typed about half the number to be submitted to him, under Susan's direction, which Aunt Lavinia sent over hastily one evening for them 'to read to a caller.' We never had them back. Aunt Lavinia found Susan's method too slow: also she had always ruled and in brief, she continued to overrule" (Bianchi, autobiographical MS).

Even though the manuscript poems were returned to Lavinia, Susan still had many materials that the poet had sent her, which casts doubt on Bianchi's assertion that her mother would have finished the project if only Lavinia had not precipitously retrieved the poems. Susan Dickinson did send a few of Emily Dickinson's poems to magazines, with some small success, but it seems that she was ambivalent about bringing them into the public forum of the market. Writing to Higginson, Susan Dickinson indicates that she was inclined to keep the poems away from the market, that she had not envisioned a commercial volume, but a privately printed collection of poems and prose, with "quaint bits to my children & c." (Bingham 86). The deference of her letter to Higginson is partially motivated by a fear of publicity, which Susan, unlike Lavinia, hoped to avoid: "a market judgement I have none of, and shrank from going contrary to your practical opinion in the matter. . . . I trust there will be no more personal detail in the newspaper articles . . . she as deeply realized that for her, as for all of us women not fame but 'Love and home and certainty are best.'"

Susan's confidence and capabilities lay in criticism, correspondence, and memoirs, forms that lay outside the market. While Walsh's account of the

Dickinson-Todd feud correctly observes that the "publicity" to which Susan Dickinson's letter to Higginson alludes is a fear of having Austin Dickinson's affair with Mabel Loomis Todd brought to public knowledge, this does not address Susan's strategic self-presentation. After depicting herself as timid and deferential, she follows by representing herself as a spokeswoman for the poet and then for "all of us women" when she pointedly dismisses "fame." Given Susan Dickinson's equation of a "horror of print" and the lack of "a market judgement" with femininity, the accomplishments of her rival, Mabel Loomis Todd, are all the more remarkable.[15]

Mabel Loomis Todd:
"I covered myself feet deep in glory"

Mabel Todd was the driving force behind the popular success of the poetry of Emily Dickinson in the 1890s. The range of Mabel Todd's activity points to how women of the 1890s differed both from their predecessors and from the women of the next two generations. In contrast to the home-centered lives of Lavinia Dickinson and Susan Gilbert Dickinson, Mabel Todd was confident in regard to business and enthusiastic about public life. She relished world travel. Even if seclusion favored Emily Dickinson's independence as a poet, Susan Dickinson's letter shows how "Love and home and certainty" could and did limit a woman's scope. Mabel Todd, however, made domesticity an opportunity to develop herself as an expert in "taste"—an appreciation of beauty and its currency—and to purchase her social advancement. If the next two generations of Dickinson editors (Susan's daughter Martha and Mabel's daughter Millicent) were less original, less bold, it was not for want of worldly opportunity: they had more formal education, and were at least as well traveled as their mothers. As the daughters of women who had achieved much from relatively humble beginnings, Martha and Millicent had more to lose. They were nearly sixty and undertaking second careers when each began publishing Dickinson materials, unlike Mabel Todd, who was in her thirties and had comparably fewer opportunities when she turned to the Dickinson legacy. The women of the ensuing generations worked under the likelihood of legal action.

Mabel Todd's entry into the Dickinson stronghold was a thirteen-year love affair with Austin Dickinson, Emily Dickinson's brother, husband of Susan Dickinson, lawyer, treasurer of Amherst College, and arguably the most important man in Amherst. Lavinia Dickinson turned to Mabel Todd for help in copying the poems and preparing them for publication because Mabel's connection with Austin made her virtually a family member, even though Austin was unwilling to divorce his wife. He compensated Mabel in other ways, such as giving her and her husband, David, land adjacent to his own.

Austin's cosignature on a loan built the Todds' Queen Anne-style "cottage," where Austin visited Mabel as freely as he chose. The two lovers also had assignations in the Dickinson family house, and their three- and four-hour carriage rides were a matter of local comment.

The association with Austin Dickinson provided both Mabel and Susan with the financial means for developing "taste," but the "certainty" that Susan enjoyed as Austin's legitimate wife kept her accomplishments within the walls of the Dickinson salon. Mabel, on the other hand, was forced to look elsewhere, and to less-established venues. Her worldly activities reflect an ambiguous position of serving the wealthier classes, including the Dickinson gentry, while catering to the masses in their desire for a smattering of culture. Unlike the gentry, she needed the ready cash that the public activities brought: money and position combined to support her self-image as a woman of talent and social skills, a "lady to the core." Being such a lady required devotion to social graces, to painting, singing, and giving music lessons at the amateur level. She offered her accomplishments under the pretense of amusing herself or others rather than for the practical motive of supplementing the household income, or for her emotional need to be identified with social and literary luminaries.

Walking a tightrope between class privilege and the limitations of gender, Mabel Todd wanted to be perceived as unusual, but she could not afford to appear to be a nonconformist. Austin Dickinson cautioned her about the possibility of being soiled by success: on learning of the enthusiastic reception accorded her first public lecture on the topic of Emily Dickinson, he wrote, "If you were not so thoroughly a woman of the most womanly type, I should fear much of this experience would make you less of one" (Longsworth 345–46). Austin Dickinson's language exposes the fragility of Mrs. Todd's worldliness, given that the first requirement for being a lady is the good opinion of others. For Austin Dickinson, her "womanliness" derived from their sexual intimacy rather than from the "glory" of public accomplishments that could defeat her.[16]

The primary constraint of being a lady was that Mabel Todd had to embrace the ideal of service, presenting her literary and artistic activities under the very rubric of "giving to the world" that Emily Dickinson had rejected. The ideal of service justified editorial and promotional activities (for Dickinson texts as well as for her husband's, father's, and female friends' writings) and her activities as a community-builder (founding Amherst's Daughters of the American Revolution chapter and Women's Club, and participating in Amherst town planning). These activities corroborated Mabel Todd's feeling that she belonged to a select class; they contrast with the individualism and even eccentricity of Emily Dickinson and her sister.

Todd's genius lay in recognizing marketable ideas and persuading others to join in her enthusiasms. The publication correspondence for Emily

Dickinson's texts in the 1890s shows Todd couching her opinions in the deferential language of gentility and refinement. She urged the publishers to target the ladies' market; her deference represents her as that market's spokeswoman. Assigning to the Dickinson *Poems* a conventionally defined femininity, Todd's correspondence with the publishers cites the reviews that mention the "charm" of the book, describing it as "unique and adorable," and she played up the idea of ladies' being susceptible to their emotions: "That shade of green strikes everybody as so dainty that they buy it all at once, almost without looking inside. For a Spring book, it seems to me particularly charming."[17] The publishers took her advice in these and other observations about packaging because it corresponded to their ideas of how ladies bought books.

Every Dickinson editor has since built on the foundation that Mabel Todd laid when she cast the poems as privileged communications between poet and audience. Recognizing that a product is what it does, or what it promises to do for the purchaser, Todd stressed Dickinson as an exclusive, especially sensitive poet who would be appreciated only by a few. By contrast, Higginson, her collaborator on the first two volumes of *Poems*, stressed Dickinson's personal reclusiveness, which he recast into the fiction of the poet as modest "virgin recluse" whose "verses seem to the reader like poetry torn up by the roots, with rain and dew and earth still clinging to them" (Bingham 127). Avoiding Higginson's gentlemanly innuendo about modesty, Todd picked up on the "discriminating reader" approach implicit in the earliest critics' suggestions that Dickinson would not have a large public.[18] Her drafts of prefaces to the poems developed the idea of the self-selecting audience, the "sensitive" reader (though what that sensitivity consisted of is not entirely clear).

Higginson's reputation as a promoter of women writers and his network of contacts with opinion leaders sympathetic to women opened the door for Todd's entry into the lecture circuit. Todd was fortunate that Higginson was well regarded but overextended, for his need to attend to other projects gave Todd free rein, especially in identifying the market and creating demand for the books. Furthermore, Higginson perceived Todd's need, as an aspiring lady, for public approbation: thus his astute recommendation of Thomas Niles at Roberts Brothers as a publisher for the *Poems*. The Boston-based firm of Roberts Brothers had a reputation built on gentility. The work of women writers, such as the perennial bestseller *Little Women,* was an important element of the sales base that made Roberts Brothers the likeliest publishers to take on an unknown such as Dickinson, especially after Lavinia Dickinson had agreed to pay for the plates. Where the Dickinson family accepted Niles because of his brief correspondence with Emily Dickinson, Todd cited Helen Hunt Jackson's estimation of Niles as "the only Boston publisher who knew how to treat a lady" (Bingham 104).

Todd's entry into the lecture circuit following the appearance of the "popular" library edition gave her greater clout with the publishers, and from the libraries the publicity campaign moved on to children, a market segment strongly influenced by women.[19] Todd published individual poems in children's magazines and placed an early notice for the *Poems* in *Mrs. Logan's Home Magazine* alongside her own review (Bingham 85). Ministers were important as opinion leaders, and they could also influence women's taste, as the letters of appreciation showed. The Reverend William Hayes Ward indicates the success of marketing Dickinson as a poet to be read "at home"; his letter to Todd tells how he had read the poems "over and over at my home to my sisters," and he could have used them in the pulpit as well (Bingham 113). In his capacity as a clergyman Higginson obtained invitations for Todd to address gatherings such as the Round Table, convened by ministers and elderly ladies. Higginson also introduced Todd to Julia Ward Howe, who became a close associate in the women's club movement. That network was vital to Todd's expansion of the Dickinson market: she spoke to audiences of a hundred or more women, and followed up by sending the names of the officers of the clubs to the publisher along with instructions that these women receive leaflets after she, Todd, had lectured.[20]

In the first epoch of Emily Dickinson's fame, Higginson provided the introduction and lent his name to the enterprise, but it was Todd's demeanor that kept the publishers interested, Lavinia's cash that convinced them, and Todd's marketing campaign that promoted the books. While she maintained all her prerogatives as a "lady," she got her way because she willingly deferred to men such as Austin Dickinson, Higginson, Niles, and William Dean Howells. She was careful not to appear pushy and to take others' interests into account when she proposed new lines of action. For example, Todd approached Niles with the idea of her putting out an "Emily Dickinson Day Book," with epigrams; he responded with mild enthusiasm. After his sudden death a few months later, she wrote his successor, Hardy, saying that Niles "seemed to think it would sell largely" and adding, "If I don't do it, someone else will want to" (Bingham 311).

Social consciousness was key to the editing process: following Higginson's lead, Todd categorized the manuscripts according to her perceptions of how the public might receive them. While Todd was sketching the parameters of "taste," Higginson established his authority in grammatical matters. When the two editors disagreed, Todd initially deferred and then appealed to a "higher authority" based on kinship, that is, on her proximity to the poet's sister. When Higginson proposed Latin titles for some poems, for example, Todd responded that Latin was appropriate to an educated gentleman such as himself, but that "Lavinia also preferred to leave the titles out" (Bingham 58). In her correspondence with the publishers, she knew whose opinion mattered. In describing one dispute with Lavinia, Todd crossed out "me" and wrote "him," referring to Austin Dickinson, saying that Lavinia's "evasion of the contract matter . . . has annoyed him a great deal" (letter to Hardy, Sept. 28, 1894).

"Outsiders" and "the copyright of Emily's mind"

The deference and taste that Mrs. Todd practiced in her extensive public engagements and correspondence abetted her social advancement without paying her bills. Being a gifted amateur let her define her expertise loosely, her qualifications deriving from the personal attributes of spirit, native intelligence, and emotional depth rather than from any extensive training. The gifted amateur could not command a professional's fee: her speaking engagements paid expenses and no more. The publishers and Higginson would have appreciated her promotional work, but Lavinia Dickinson would be the one to arrange compensation. As the poet's heir Lavinia held all rights to the manuscripts and assumed the author's place as the conveyor of gifts. The editors described themselves as Emily Dickinson's friends. As a result of how Todd, Higginson, and Lavinia Dickinson defined themselves, the editors' compensation for their work on the Dickinson *Poems* came as small "gifts" of cash from Lavinia.

From the family's perspective, Emily Dickinson's long-standing correspondence and her two meetings with the unimpeachable Higginson attested to their friendship, but Todd's status was more ambiguous. She had seen the poet only at her funeral. It was Mabel's proximity to Austin that led Lavinia to bring the poems to her. In 1888, the year that the editing began, Mabel was in some sense a member of the family, and she and Austin had decided to try conceiving a child (Longsworth 297). No child resulted, but the prospect of providing for one might have led Lavinia to agree that Mabel would receive Austin's share of their paternal inheritance in the event of his death.

Since shifting the poems from a gift network to a market economy endowed with cash value anything the poet had written, Todd began planning a collection of the poet's letters within a month of the first series of Dickinson poems' appearance in print (Walsh 127). Despite the custom of burning an individual's correspondence following her death, and despite a few people's reservations about publishing the private letters of a private writer, once these good New Englanders began realizing the cash value of the poems and letters, few manuscripts were intentionally destroyed. The possibilities raised by Emily Dickinson's extensive correspondence spurred the Dickinson family on. A man calling himself Gardner Fuller claimed to have many of the poet's manuscripts that he was planning to offer for publication (Bingham 197–205). Although the Dickinsons did not buy him out, and no more was heard from "Gardner Fuller," the incident brought home the importance of securing their rights and preempting possible competitors by collecting and publishing the *Letters*.

While Lavinia later described Mabel Todd's labors as primarily those of a copyist, she acknowledged that the collaborative work involved in assembling a collection of letters, which would depend on the goodwill of the poet's correspondents, went beyond the copying of poems. Where the onus of the work in editing Dickinson poems lay in copying the manuscripts and in observing and complying with the "taste" of the time, editing the letters would begin with contacting Emily Dickinson's correspondents—the ones known to the family at least—and convincing them to give or lend letters for publication in whole or in part. It would also be necessary to create a plausible chronology, for the poet almost never put dates on her correspondence.

In the subsequent quarrel over the *Letters,* Mabel saw herself as the mediator, the public's authority on Emily Dickinson. She pressed Lavinia for compensation, but Lavinia responded by stressing Mabel's status as an outsider. "I will never give away to an outsider the ownership of my sister's brains," she declared (qtd. in letter, Bianchi to Frothingham, Apr. 19, 1932). Using the term "Mind" as the poet had, as a synonym for written texts, Lavinia averred to Higginson that "nothing would induce her to 'give the copyright of Emily's mind to any one' but herself" (Bingham 222). She took the suggestion that she share with Mrs. Todd the copyright of the *Letters* as an alienation of property, tantamount to theft: "Emily would be indignant at any attempt to rob her sister," she wrote to the publisher (Bingham 286). Eventually Lavinia did allow Mabel to share the copyright, but the concession embittered her toward her brother's mistress.

Following Austin Dickinson's sudden death in 1896, Mabel Todd had nothing to shield her from public gossip. Lavinia did not comply with her brother's request that Mrs. Todd receive his share of their inheritance from their father, but she did agree to sign a deed for a parcel of Dickinson land that fronted the Todds' property and that ran alongside her own. Mabel brought a lawyer to witness the deed, Lavinia signed, and the Todds sailed off on an excursion to observe a solar eclipse and collect ethnographic data among the Ainu, in Japan. When Mrs. Todd returned, Lavinia served her with a lawsuit for the retrieval of the property that Mrs. Todd had "obtained through misrepresentation and fraud."

The two weeks of the subsequent trial were a public spectacle in Amherst. Mr. and Mrs. Todd moved from their house by the Dickinsons a week before it began. The local newspaper printed summaries; the town's sympathies were divided; key witnesses felt unable to appear, having their depositions taken instead. After a deposition from the Dickinson family servant indicated the extent of Mrs. Todd's and Austin Dickinson's relationship, Mrs. Todd's lawyer was called away on business to Washington and Mrs. Todd had to change counsel (Longsworth 412, 416).

Reputation was key to the Dickinson lawsuit against Todd. Answering Todd's assertion that the land was payment for her work on the *Poems* and the *Letters,* Lavinia Dickinson held that Todd had begged for the job, knowing that the *Letters* would make her literary reputation, that Todd was merely the copyist while she, Lavinia, as Emily Dickinson's legal heir, owned the letters that she, Lavinia, had collected. Lavinia could not deny that she had signed the deed, but in court she took on the role of naif, describing this signature as her "autograph," thus implying that she saw herself as a celebrity by way of her sister's posthumous fame (Sewall, vol. 1, app. 2).

The very facility for promotion that Mabel Todd used on behalf of the *Poems* undid her. Todd was on trial for misrepresentation and fraud, but the trial transcript has the prosecuting attorney conclude by focusing on her public life, pointing out that Lavinia Dickinson was a "gentlewoman," as opposed to the defendant, whose lecture tours and work on the *Poems* indicated that she was "very much a woman of the world" (Longsworth 422). Public condemnation of Mabel Todd was based on her being a woman of a younger generation and a lower class than was Lavinia. Losing the lawsuit made prophetic a line she had written years earlier in an unpublished manuscript: "I care not who makes the city's laws if I may have a hand in making its beauty" (Todd, "Village Improvement"). The lady's beautifying hand was stayed by the city's unwillingness to execute its laws in her favor.

Martha Dickinson Bianchi:
"I like to feel my hand is on Emily's property"

Following Austin Dickinson's death and Mabel Todd's defeat, Lavinia Dickinson wrote to the publishers at Little, Brown and Company. When she proposed omitting the work of Higginson and Todd from future editions, Little, Brown (who had bought out the original publishers in 1898) were cautiously receptive (letter to Lavinia Dickinson, Mar. 10, 1899). Nothing came of it, for Lavinia died that August, and the thirty-three-year-old Martha, the sole survivor among Austin and Susan Dickinson's four children, came into a substantial estate that included Emily Dickinson literary rights held jointly with the publishers. For the heir to two of the finest properties in Amherst, real estate in Atlantic City and Michigan, plus considerable stocks and bonds, the income from the royalties on her aunt's poetry was, at this point, small change.[21]

Martha Dickinson's earliest communication with Little, Brown substantiates her lifelong preoccupation with subsidiary rights. In her vehement refusal of a routine third-party request for permission to quote from Emily Dickinson's *Letters*, Martha wrote:

I am entirely unwilling to have any of the letters of my Aunt E.D. reprinted in any form whatsoever. The reasons are of a distinctly personal nature. I intend now to come to Boston on business matters and shall at that time wish to have a short business interview with your representative in regard to my accounts. I wish also at this time to repeat what I directed my man of business to state some time ago—that no new editions of my Aunt's

poems are to be contemplated. Am careful to act fairly and finally as Aunt
L. D. deceased who expressed wishes before her death with all possible
conciseness and determination. (letter to Little, Brown, June 26, 1900)

Like Mabel Todd, Martha Dickinson knew whose authority mattered
with whom, and she represented her own desires as fulfilling the wishes of
another. Little, Brown pointed out that Lavinia consistently sought her sister's
fame and "did not desire that the books be withdrawn from circulation" (letter to Martha Dickinson, June 26, 1900). It was strange for Martha Dickinson
to be invoking the deceased Lavinia (even using Lavinia's phrase "my man
of business," meaning "my lawyer") and to be threatening legal action as a
means of obstructing new editions. Hammond, the lawyer whom Martha
Dickinson engaged to speak with Little, Brown, well knew the "distinctly
personal" reasons to which his client alluded, for he had been instrumental
in winning the Dickinson-Todd lawsuit, and he knew that Susan Dickinson
and her daughter would have felt particularly insulted by Todd's edition of
the Dickinson *Letters*.

Little, Brown responded to Martha Dickinson's threat of legal action to
stop the books from being sold, reprinted, or made into new editions, by
indicating, through Hammond, that they would cede all, for a price: "The
sales in the past few years have been excellent, and continue to be good, so
that the publication of the books is profitable. Rather, however, than have
any trouble in the matter, we would be willing to dispose of the above stock
and plates, and all our rights, at what we consider is a very moderate price,
viz., $700" (letter, Little, Brown to Hammond, Feb. 11, 1901). Hammond's
approach to Martha Dickinson would become standard for her legal counse-
lors in subsequent publication disputes: he cultivated her good will by as-
suring her that she was within her rights, and he worked mightily to dis-
suade her from going to court to prove them. He urged Martha Dickinson to
accept their offer, not arguing that it was just, but that "You will have constant
annoyance from this matter if you do not buy" (letter to Martha Dickinson,
Mar. 16, 1901).

Hammond was eventually right, but Martha Dickinson decided not to
buy out the publisher's holdings or go to court to prevent further publications. On January 24, 1901, she cashed her first royalties check, for $42.57,
from Little, Brown. Instead of suppressing the earlier volumes, she renewed
in her own name the copyrights on Todd's and Higginson's work, copyrights
which had belonged to Lavinia Dickinson. Aside from royalties checks that
arrived biannually, Martha Dickinson had minimal communication with Little,
Brown over the next two decades. When in 1906 Little, Brown had to decide
what to do with the unprofitable remainders of the Todd-edited *Letters,* they
followed an earlier arrangement with Lavinia rather than seeking Martha's
opinion (letters to Lavinia Dickinson, Jan. 28, 1899, and Feb. 2, 1899).

Forming the backdrop for Martha Dickinson's return to the Dickinson legacy are various personal and financial setbacks: a short-lived, ruinous marriage, the death of Susan Dickinson, an unremarkable literary career, and a tendency to live beyond her means. Although Martha Dickinson followed her aunt in writing poetry, she was no recluse who disdained print. On the contrary, she considered herself a cosmopolitan.[22] Conrad Aiken describes meeting her during one of her yearly trips to London in 1923: "'I,' she said on this occasion, 'am not in the least like my repressed Aunt Emily. I, Mr. Aiken, am burnt out!'" (Aiken 25). During one such European tour, in 1903, at age thirty-six, in Carlsbad, Bohemia, Martha Dickinson had married Alexander Bianchi, a captain in the Russian army who claimed descent from Italian nobility. Beginning in 1904 in New York, Captain Bianchi borrowed some three thousand dollars under false pretenses from a Miss Terry, a New York-based friend of his wife's.[23] When Miss Terry and her attorney successfully sued to have the debt repaid, Madame Bianchi had to sell the family Mercedes, various stocks, and the land over which Lavinia and Mrs. Todd had fought in order to pay off Captain Bianchi's debt and the lawyers.[24] The last documentable year of her marriage, or of Captain Bianchi's existence, is 1908, when Madame Bianchi's lawyers had him sign some papers while he was hospitalized in Rochester, New York.[25] The Dickinson family lawyer, Henry Field, protected some of Madame Bianchi's property from aggrieved creditors, placing it in trust under her mother's name, but Susan Dickinson died in 1913. By 1916 the Dickinson homestead and its meadow, which Martha's grandfather had worked hard to bring back into the family, had to be sold.

Madame Bianchi's legal and financial troubles correlate with her increased literary productivity from 1906 onward. First, she turned away from writing poetry, a genre not especially popular with readers of the time, but her novels with cosmopolitan themes did not fare much better.[26] In 1913 Madame Bianchi unsuccessfully sought to interest Scribner's in publishing a new edition of Emily Dickinson, a collection of anecdotes, letters, and some poems (letter to Brownell, Mar. 30, 1914). She queried the editors at Little, Brown, but because poor sales had led them to melt the plates of the *Letters,* their reply was conservative: "The interest of the critical reading public is in her verse rather than in personal anecdotes and selections from letters" (letter to Bianchi, Feb. 1914). She and the publishers managed a compromise: Madame Bianchi's first efforts in publishing the family legacy, *The Single Hound: Poems of a Lifetime* (1914), consisted of poems that Susan Gilbert Dickinson had received as letters from Emily Dickinson.

The poems published in *The Single Hound* could have introduced Emily Dickinson to a new and sympathetic audience, one open to the literary experimentation of modernism and imagism, yet the text attracted scant attention: the sales figures indicate that the poet's return to popularity did not really begin until 1924 (Lubbers 101, 119, 248n). As opposed to the many

Dickinson editions of the 1890s, fewer than a thousand copies of *The Single Hound* were printed in a single edition. In contrast to Mrs. Todd's marketing campaign of the 1890s, Madame Bianchi treated *The Single Hound* as a private, albeit published, memorial to her mother. Unlike Todd, with her knack for identifying and cultivating opinion makers and cultural gatekeepers, Bianchi sent her review copies to personal friends who had fine addresses, houses in Europe, and good social standing, but were not particularly intellectual and had no influence over the new generation of book reviewers whom Rubin describes in *The Making of Middlebrow Culture*. Unlike Todd, who had bolstered her authority with Higginson's and always maintained excellent relations with this very influential writer and editor and his family, Bianchi never cottoned to Higginson.[27] Too proud or temperamental to be anyone's protégée, Bianchi had only one relationship that could be called mentorial, with Gamaliel Bradford, and it could not have survived her attacking his work on Emily Dickinson.

In 1913, the cool responses of the editors at Little, Brown and at Scribner's only delayed Madame Bianchi's original plan to collect a prose edition of letters and anecdotes centered on her mother's friendship with Emily Dickinson. When Martha Dickinson Bianchi met and befriended Alfred Leete Hampson in 1922, the project was revived. Hampson's precise qualifications are not clear, but it is significant that he became her secretary or literary collaborator just as the copyright on Todd's edition of Dickinson letters lapsed.[28] With the expiration of any legal claims that Todd may have had, Madame Bianchi could use Todd's work as freely as she chose. Bianchi moved with unusual speed: beyond arranging with Little, Brown for the consolidation of the Dickinson volumes of the 1890s, she brought the revived proposal for an edition of letters and anecdotes to Houghton Mifflin. Even though Bianchi indicated that the former editor's mind was in a "pathological" state and it would be best not to contact her, both Houghton Mifflin and Little, Brown did contact Mrs. Todd, by now retired and living in Florida (letter, Greenslet to Bianchi, Aug. 17, 1923).

Todd had suffered a debilitating stroke in 1913, but her reply to the Houghton Mifflin editors reveals a business sense as keen as ever. She wrote that she was often asked about the book, that she believed there was interest, and that it would sell (letter, Mabel Todd to McIntyre, Sept. 17, 1923). Finally, she asked that her work be acknowledged, but when Ferris Greenslet of Houghton Mifflin wrote to Bianchi about Todd's response, he added, "I imagine you are not likely to use anything from the Todd book excepting the letters themselves, so that the 'credit' that Mrs. Todd suggests will not have to be considered."[29]

Among Martha Dickinson Bianchi's papers at Harvard lies the remains of a copy of Todd's 1894 edition of Dickinson *Letters*. Although the title page has been torn out, Todd's name still appears on the spine, and the bookplate on the inside cover identifies Amherst College Library as the owner. No overdue notice appears among Madame Bianchi's papers. This is the "working manuscript" of Bianchi's *Life and Letters of Emily Dickinson*, pages scissored and pinned with Bianchi's penciled additions and deletions throughout. Regarding herself as the sole heir to the poet's legacy, Bianchi would have found it unthinkable to buy a copy of Todd's edition. Far from covering her tracks, Madame Bianchi frequently alluded to the extensive sales of *The Life and Letters of Emily Dickinson* as the basis for the poet's subsequent fame. That the cut and paste "manuscript" still exists testifies to Bianchi's disregard for any other claim.

Madame Bianchi's editing involved taking the excerpted letters as they had appeared in Todd's text, arranged according to recipient, and rearranging them chronologically, following Todd's approximate dates, and adding previously unpublished letters that Susan Dickinson had received from Emily Dickinson. Analyses of the originals of Emily Dickinson's intense, emotion-charged correspondence with Susan Gilbert Dickinson show that Martha Dickinson Bianchi consistently deleted the most passionate expressions and deliberately misconstrued significant dates.[30]

What was published as *The Life and Letters of Emily Dickinson* is unique in Madame Bianchi's work: it bears a dedication to her primary contacts at Houghton Mifflin, editors Ferris Greenslet and Curtis Hidden Page. Bianchi records her gratitude for their work in a canny move that attaches their names to the questionable appropriation of Todd's work. Aside from Bianchi's introduction, what was new and original about *The Life and Letters of Emily Dickinson* (1924) was that the publishers marketed it as a biography and that Houghton Mifflin and Little, Brown cooperated by having the two texts, *The Life and Letters* and *Collected Poems,* appear simultaneously. The latter collection brought together in one volume the poems that Higginson and Todd had edited in the 1890s.

Todd proved correct in her prediction that the reissued letters would sell, but sales were even more spectacular five years later, on the 1929 publication of the next Dickinson volume, *Further Poems of Emily Dickinson.* Anticipating public criticism of the editors for having neglected to include these texts in the earlier *Collected Poems,* some marketing genius at Little, Brown took advantage of Bianchi's vague allusion to having come across this previously unpublished work in some previously unlooked-at papers of her grandfather's. It became a "sensational discovery" that the dust jacket spells out in the subtitle "withheld from publication by her sister Lavinia." Little, Brown's publicity in March 1929 called it "The Most Important Literary Discovery of the Century." The book was a best-seller in part because the publishing staff believed it would have excellent sales, and they marketed it accordingly, as a "blockbuster," rather than to the usual targeted audiences. Although the general public bought the sensational story that these texts

were love poems withheld by the poet's sister, reviewers were more skeptical. They questioned Martha Bianchi's editorial decisions, they wondered
about the appropriateness of describing the texts as love poems, and they
particularly reflected on how the timing of the book, just prior to the poet's
centenary, necessitated a revision of the Dickinson canon.

In 1929, with Dickinson sales at an all-time peak and the Dickinson
centenary only months away, Bianchi and Hampson were working against a
deadline to assemble the *Centenary Edition* of Emily Dickinson's poems for
Little, Brown; Bianchi was also hoping to finish her definitive biography,
Emily Dickinson Face to Face, before much longer. Because Bianchi knew
that she was a leading moneymaker for the two publishers, she managed to
evade their persistent requests; she held fast to her contractual right to deny
permissions, stating, "I like to feel my hand is on Emily's property" (letter to
Jenkins, Aug. 9, 1928). She kept promising that she would tell "the true story
of the editing and publishing the poems" in her memoirs at some later date
(letter to Linscott, Nov. 25, 1929). With Little, Brown disturbed by rumors of
hundreds of unpublished poems, and with Yale, Amherst, and Mount Holyoke
all planning commemorations of Emily Dickinson, the publishers wanted to
represent the forthcoming volume of poems as "complete" (letter, McIntyre
to Bianchi, July 11, 1930). They repeatedly asked Bianchi to take the four-
hour trip from Amherst to Boston to look over the unpublished Dickinson
poems that Higginson had given to the Boston Public Library, but Bianchi
would not consider including them. As would often be the case when Little,
Brown pressured her, her response was to ask for copies of her latest royalties statement (for the first half of 1930, when $5.00 a day was a good work-
ing wage, Bianchi received $1,167.58) and then to state that she would pub-
lish only her aunt's best work: "In regard to these unsubstantiated rumors of
hundreds of so-called unpublished poems, let me make myself plain once for
all. I speak only for myself, and of my knowledge. The few unpublished poems I have left are not up to Emily's standard. . . . I have an unsurmountable
objection to stuffing her volumes, and would prefer to discard even, to inclusion of mediocrity" (letter to Jenkins, Aug. 15, 1930). It was a statement that
she would later regret.

Bianchi's assertions that the unpublished poems from Higginson's collection were not up to Emily's quality made Little, Brown very nervous, for
she had not seen the poems in question—it was enough for her, she said,
that the Houghton Mifflin editors had. Quality aside, Bianchi had no reason
to trouble herself with texts that she could not readily copyright. Little, Brown
eventually had the unpublished Higginson manuscripts photographed and
sent to Bianchi in Amherst, an expense that they deducted from her royalties, but the damage was already done: Carl Van Doren turned down the
forthcoming *Centenary Edition* as a possible Literary Guild selection because
he had heard that there were hundreds of unpublished poems.

The carefully phrased denials in Bianchi's letters regarding the rumors of unpublished poems would not have eased the publishers' anxieties very much. "I know of no 'friend of the family,'" she wrote, "who could possess hundreds of unpublished poems of my Aunt Emily Dickinson. The original editor who intimated as such, at South Hadley last November, is the person convicted of a fraudulent land transaction in open Court" (letter to Jenkins, May 1930). Little, Brown took some comfort from their understanding that Bianchi was Emily Dickinson's sole heir, that by way of her inheritance from Lavinia Dickinson she was the only person with literary rights to her aunt's estate. Other persons who held Dickinson materials, such as Higginson's daughter Margaret Barney, or Mabel Todd and her daughter Millicent Bingham, could not publish manuscript poems without Bianchi's permission. Because Little, Brown's contracts with Bianchi required that all requests for permissions and information go through her, her publishers held up and successfully collected damages from Alfred Knopf and Company for the unauthorized use of poems in a biography by Genevieve Taggard (letter, Bianchi to Jenkins, June 23, 1930).

Bianchi's confidence in her rights grew still further as her lawyers assured her that no one could publish Dickinson letters without her permission, since owning a manuscript was distinct from owning the right to publish it. As the Dickinson Centenary approached, a more forgiving or less opportunistic person than Mabel Todd would have let Bianchi have her day. The rumors of hundreds of unpublished manuscripts were true: spurred on by Bianchi's uncredited appropriation of her work, Mabel Todd, aided by her forty-four-year-old daughter Millicent, had begun reconsidering her position in 1924, as Millicent Bingham's letter to Amy Lowell describes: "Mamma came from Boston, I met her in Amherst, and we extracted the Emily things from the barn, and today we have been looking them over. They are simply superb. . . . What an orgy we shall have when the said M.D.B. steps out someday!" (Nov. 13, 1924). Characteristically, Todd tested the waters by speaking with critics such as Robert Hillyer and Louis Untermeyer; then she spoke at Mount Holyoke's commemoration and described her role in the editing in a 1930 *Harper's Magazine* article. Because Bianchi felt certain that Todd would not publish Dickinson materials without permission, in November 1931 she sailed off for Europe just before Todd's *Letters of Emily Dickinson* hit the stores.

Todd's return to the Dickinson industry was carefully executed, and it taught Bianchi some of the law's finer points, such as that when any part of what Bianchi termed her aunt's "literary remains" entered the public domain, she could never control them again. Todd could use the material from the same edition of the *Letters* that Bianchi had appropriated. Bianchi, on the other hand, could use none of the materials held exclusively by Mrs. Todd, such as the only known photograph of Emily Dickinson, and numerous photographs of Austin Dickinson. Aided by her daughter's research, Todd capitalized on her rival's omissions, which she contrasted with her own "return to sources." As opposed to Martha Dickinson Bianchi's reliance on oral tradition and invocation of the poet's presence, Todd offered documents. To Martha Dickinson Bianchi's claim that she was, as Lavinia's sole heir, the only authorized source of Dickinson materials, Mabel responded that the family—Lavinia and Austin—had given her these materials for publication, a claim borne out by Todd's earlier work. Furthermore, the Todds were thinking of the longer term. Bianchi's sense of entitlement limited her scope whenever Dickinson materials came up for auction, for she would not dream of purchasing what she regarded as her own. The Todds, by contrast, were first in line to buy.

The timing of Todd's return was particularly disastrous for Bianchi. Todd met a sympathetic response from editors who were impatient with Madame Bianchi's monopoly. In a telling comment on how Dickinson's popularity, and the literary scene, had changed since the 1890s, it was not ministers and women's club leaders but college professors, reviewers, and editors of anthologies who were Todd's allies in the 1930s. Conrad Aiken, Louis Untermeyer, and Mark van Doren, who had worked with Bianchi in the rediscovery of Emily Dickinson in the 1920s, praised Todd's new book and criticized Bianchi's. Bianchi responded by tightening her custodianship. She required editors who wished to reprint Dickinson poems to include in their bibliographies all of her books and only "authorized and authentic sources," that is, work she and Alfred Hampson had personally overseen. Writers who questioned Bianchi's interpretation were referred to works she had approved. She controlled and usually forbade radio readings of Emily Dickinson's poetry. She tirelessly informed those correspondents who were tactless or naïve enough to mention Todd that this woman had been convicted in court of misrepresentation and fraud. Bianchi corrected the biographical sketches that appeared in the anthologies to stress Susan Dickinson's role and to minimize references to Higginson (letter to American Book Co., May 11, 1936). Bianchi's concentration on the theme of Emily's "renunciation of the love of a married man" could be read as a slap in Todd's face, but Todd had already scooped Bianchi by revealing the name of Charles Wadsworth.

"I am aware," wrote Bianchi, "of the source from which the stream of personal criticism and all but persecution flows—as are many of my friends—and am quite unmoved accordingly. I am also aware that many careerists would undoubtedly like to make a name—incidentally what money they could from my Aunt's fame. This will never be allowed by me" (letter to Jenkins, June 27, 1931). Madame Bianchi's feeling that Mrs. Todd was a liar and unprincipled thief who had been exposed in public court blinded her to the sympathetic audience that Todd found among the reviewers, editors, and anthologists. As the poet's niece and last surviving member of the Dickinson family, Madame Bianchi felt that her own authority was obvious, that Todd had been warned off Dickinson property in the trial. Bianchi's idea of what constituted her property broadened, more and more, over the years. Correspondents asking to see Emily Dickinson's house were directed not to bother the tenants, and when the *Massachusetts Guide Book* contacted her about including a photo of the house, she replied that she would permit it only if the photo included her house as well, without admitting that she did not own the Homestead, and had not owned it for many years.

Although she cultivated an appearance of imperviousness to criticism, Madame Bianchi looked for vengeance when her property rights were directly attacked. Morris U. Schappes concluded an unfavorable review in *American Literature,* stating: "The frequently offered suggestion that all available manuscripts be turned over to a group of capable scholars for scrupulous examination and editing has never been more pertinent than now. One almost wished for a state control of manuscripts such as exists in Russia, to provide scholars with the privilege of being scholars unhampered by property rights" (85). His next article enumerated the defects and revealed the unacknowledged debts of the Bianchi-Hampson text by comparing it to Todd's. Bianchi didn't reply when her editor at Little, Brown sent her the article, and elsewhere she claimed not to have read Schappes, although she pursued a vendetta in which she used her acquaintance with a Professor Ernest E. Leisy of Texas, who belonged to *American Literature*'s board, to make sure that work by Schappes, "a certain Jewish communist," would no longer be welcome in that magazine, and that her work would be "reviewed from the Anglo Saxon point of view" (letter to Jenkins, Oct. 11, 1935). When editor Harry Hayden Clark asked for her responses to Schappes's criticisms, she asked how Clark could take seriously this same Schappes, who had recently been dismissed from his job at CCNY for union organizing and was clearly a communist (letter to Clark, May 9, 1936). Bianchi subsequently requested that Clark's publisher put another editor on the job, for Clark had not proved his dedication to "Emily" when he had failed to comply with her invitation to visit her that summer in the Evergreens (letter to American Book Co., May 11, 1936).

Madame Bianchi's dependence on royalty income was key to the Dickinson publications of the 1930s: new or newly packaged volumes appeared at regular, two-year intervals. Todd's revised and enlarged edition cut to nothing the sales of Bianchi's edition of the *Letters* and the text of what Bianchi had intended as her "definitive" biography sold poorly. When sales fell off, and Bianchi and Hampson had no new product in the works, they paid closer attention to subsidiary rights and permissions fees, and were far more likely to write long letters of encouragement and direction to the editors of anthologies. Bianchi's watch on rights and permissions buoyed the sales of her editions in the short term, but her supervision worked against the long-term interests of her publishers in developing the Dickinson materials as a form of symbolic capital that would enhance their prestige within the book trade. Bianchi's refusal to answer the critics or to package her materials according to the new academic standards lowered Little, Brown's reputation among academics at the very time when the publishers most sought to raise it.

By the fourth year following the 1929 crash, publishers realized that the depression was not temporary. Retaining market share through a monopoly such as Bianchi's mattered little when the book trade was depressed. As long as sales had been high and Madame Bianchi appeared to be the single source, the publishers had treated her handsomely. As profits dwindled, so did the publisher's willingness to fight Madame Bianchi's battles against "chisellers" and "leaches" (letter to Field, Aug. 18, 1931). By 1935 the market was saturated and the kid gloves came off: when Madame Bianchi and Alfred Hampson presented the editors at Little, Brown with another "discovery," the latter made the unprecedented move of conducting a market survey and sending the manuscript text of what they sarcastically termed "further Further poems" to an outside reader, Theodor Morison (letter, Jenkins to Bianchi, Apr. 30, 1935). The contest dragged on for months, with Little, Brown's editors constantly returning to the question of past discoveries. Before Little, Brown would agree to publish the latest "discoveries" in 1935, they forced Bianchi to state in print that she had no more poems worthy of publication and to accept a rate of royalties which was the lowest she had ever received.

When as late as 1937 Madame Bianchi continued to insist on maintaining the publications as a monopoly, Little, Brown established covert agreements with other publishers and with the academics. When Scribner's sought permissions to reprint poems in George Whicher's landmark biography, *This Was a Poet* (1938), Little, Brown inquired of Bianchi, whose response was firm: no permissions to this "fundamentally unreliable" writer (letter to Jenkins, June 23, 1938). She was furious when Little, Brown went ahead without her and refused to press for additional payments for unauthorized use. Not even Madame Bianchi's old friend and lawyer Henry Field could persuade her to allow for any opinion other than her own, not even when he reiterated an earlier opinion that a controversial book, and the evidence of different perspectives, would stimulate the sales of her various Dickinson volumes in print (letter, Greenslet to Bianchi, Oct. 29, 1931).

Epilogue: The Wheels of the Law

The alliances between publishers and academics that began in the 1930s both kept Emily Dickinson's name before the public and ensured that the feud would go on. In the same year when Little, Brown indicated that they would not press Scribner's to pay additional permissions or damages for the unauthorized use of Dickinson materials in Whicher's book, Madame Bianchi drew up her will. It left everything to Alfred Leete Hampson, with the curious stipulation that "The house shall not be occupied by anyone other than said Alfred Leete Hampson, the members of his family, guests, and servants, and if said property shall be sold the house shall be razed before the transfer of title to said land."[31] Madame Bianchi's will cited "sentimental reasons" for not wanting the Evergreens to be occupied by anyone else: did she fear that Todd's daughter or friends would find a way in, after all those years of exclusion, or was it that by this time anyone but her collaborator was an outsider?

Millicent Todd Bingham was able, in 1943, to set into action the "orgy" she had anticipated "when said M.D.B. steps out some day." Although she had inherited enough materials from her mother to put together several books, beginning with a collection of unpublished poems by Emily Dickinson, she could not be sure that a publisher would risk the possibility of a lawsuit with Little, Brown. But Cass Canfield of Harper's decided that Bingham had a strong claim, "based on physical possession—a claim which dated back many years" (Canfield 188). Depressed by the prospect of a lawsuit and his own timidity in keeping the poems from the public, Canfield tells how he sat on the New York train, returning from his visit with Mrs. Bingham in Washington, when "I startled my fellow passengers by exclaiming, 'Am I a man or a mouse?' No one in the car answered 'Mouse,' so I concluded I was the former" (189).

When Harper's published Mrs. Bingham's collection of Dickinson poems, along with her account of the early editing that she had finished ten years previously, Hampson did not respond with a lawsuit. Instead, the librarian and archivist William McCarthy, a loyal friend of Hampson and Bianchi's since 1929, set to cataloguing the papers and poems in the Bianchi estate. Working for the Rosenbach Foundation, McCarthy arranged for the sale, at forty thousand dollars, of Emily Dickinson's papers and memorabilia, to Gilbert Montague, a corporate lawyer and fifth cousin to Madame Bianchi. Montague subsequently presented the collection to Harvard, and McCarthy set to work with "Dow and other lawyers . . . on a document to right the wrongs done to Lavinia and Martha" (letter, McCarthy to Hampson, Mar. 29, 1950). Harvard would own the manuscripts and a share of future royalties; Hampson and Little, Brown retained their copyrights and some control over permissions; and the sale was conditioned to exclude Whicher, Bingham, or Charles Green of the Jones Library in Amherst from working with the materials. (Green's sin had been publishing Little, Brown's sales figures on the Dickinson books up to 1930.)

Harvard's entrance was to be Mrs. Bingham's undoing: despite her physical possession of Dickinson materials, "the wheels of the law" would grind her down.[32] She wound up ceding all publication rights. McCarthy kept the Hampsons informed. In 1951, he wrote of how "Mrs. B. is being handled by Harvard's lawyers with no punches pulled"; then, in 1955, "Harper's lawyers have accepted the fact that they control no Dickinson copyrights. . . . all royalties from their former books as reprinted by Harvard go to you"; and finally, in 1960, "Mrs. Bingham had no legal rights over Emily Dickinson copyrights to pass on to Amherst."[33] In other words, Mrs. Bingham could donate the materials that she and her mother had amassed, but she could not profit from her labor or assign any Dickinson rights to another.

Bingham could publish her additional materials only after she had stated in print that Harvard University claimed ownership of them. Harvard's position led Bingham to divide between Amherst and Yale the remainder of the materials that she held at her death in 1968. With Alfred Leete Hampson's widow dead twenty years later, the publication rights—"the royal air in the parcel"—now belong entirely to Harvard and to Little, Brown, who as corporate owners bear the burden of the poet's injunction, to "Be the Merchant of the Heavenly Grace." With regard to the human spirit, the "disgrace of price" reduced the lives of four, possibly five, women in disputes over the ownership of manuscripts. When it came to the market, Emily Dickinson was right.

Notes

1. All quotations from the Dickinson publication papers kept by Martha Dickinson Bianchi and Alfred Leete Hampson, the Theodore Frothingham correspondence, the Amy Lowell papers, and Mabel Loomis Todd's correspondence with Houghton Mifflin appear by permission of the Houghton Library, Harvard University. The correspondence of Mabel Todd with Thomas Wentworth Higginson, referred to in the text, is in the Amherst College Library; the letter from Martha Dickinson Bianchi to William Crary Brownell of Scribner's appears by permission of Amherst College. Quotations from Mabel Loomis Todd's papers located in the Todd-Bingham archives of the Sterling Library are quoted with the permission of Yale University. For conversations about the Dickinson industry, I wish to thank Will Buckingham, Katie King, and Ellen Hart. This essay is dedicated to the memory of my grandfather, Frederick Malcolm Clouter (1894–1978), who worked for the publishing firm of Little, Brown and Co. during the 1920s and 1930s.

2. I use the phrase "resistance to publication" in direct opposition to the concept of "tacit consent to publication" that Dickinson editor Thomas Johnson uses (*Poems* xxviii–xxix). "Tacit consent" implies that she meant yes even as her actions, her challenges, and her letters show that she resisted and derided the publication-minded arguments of her correspondents.

3. Dickinson regarded unauthorized publication of her work as theft (Johnson, *Letters* 316) and denounced the market aspect of print (Johnson, *Poems* 709).

4. Dickinson's rejection of the "philanthropic" argument for publishing her work appears throughout her correspondence. See Johnson, *Letters* 261, 380, 444a, 937a.

5. The editing of Dickinson materials is a very complex question. A historical overview

and description of editing issues appears in Johnson, "Introduction" to *Poems,* and in Franklin, *Editing.* Following the 1981 appearance of facsimile reproductions of much of the poet's work in Franklin, *Manuscript Books,* editing Dickinson's poems and letters is once again a matter of controversy, and scholars have become highly critical of Johnson's editorial approach. For cogent discussion of current issues in Dickinson editing, see Capelluti; Ellen Hart; McGann; Shurr; and Howe, who all argue for new editions to register aspects of the poet's manuscripts that Johnson and Franklin discount, such as the importance of page layout and the ambiguous status of poems in letters.

6. Where Bingham is admittedly partisan, Buckingham puts Todd's and Higginson's business strategies in the context of the reading public and literary culture of the 1890s.

7. Varying analyses of the lawsuit appear in Bingham, Sewall, Longsworth, and Walsh.

8. Bingham's description of Todd as silent is not precisely accurate. Todd abetted the English publication of *Letters* (letter, Higginson to Todd, Mar. 13, 1905).

9. Letter, Bianchi to Greenslet, Nov. 1931; Bianchi, unpublished autobiographical manuscript; and letter, Martha Dickinson to Little, Brown, June 26, 1900.

10. The ads for Bianchi's 1914 book were the first to adopt what became a controversial approach, describing the poems as "hitherto withheld from publication" and "now given to the world by the only surviving member of the Dickinson family." The ad appears in the Frothingham-Dickinson correspondence, Mar. 1914.

11. While Bianchi memorialized the friendship between Susan and Emily Dickinson in her introduction to *The Single Hound,* the obituary of Susan Gilbert Dickinson, published in the *Springfield Republican* and surely written or approved by Bianchi in 1913, never mentions Emily Dickinson, as Sewall's handwritten note on the Houghton Library text of the obituary points out. On the mutilation of Emily Dickinson manuscripts by Mabel Todd and/or Austin Dickinson, see Martha Nell Smith.

12. *Within the Hedge* was the title that Martha Dickinson gave to her first volume of poems (Doubleday 1899). Bianchi uses the word *pilgrims* throughout her correspondence to refer to the Dickinson enthusiasts who visited her in Amherst.

13. Lubbers carefully traces how literary critics came to regard Dickinson's poetry as central to the literary canon of the United States. Myerson similarly provides useful information for studying how editors, publishers, and the reading public negotiated the reputation of Emily Dickinson.

14. This new poem and letter was bought by Amherst College in June 1992 from a private Pennsylvania collector. Ellen Hart argues that Emily Dickinson's correspondence includes poems that the Harvard editors did not recognize as such. Permission to quote from the letter is courtesy of Special Collections and Archives, Amherst College Library.

15. Judith Farr's discussion of Susan Dickinson's Victorianism explores more fully her attitude toward domesticity (9–13).

16. Letter, Todd to Austin Dickinson, Apr. 12, 1894; cited Longsworth 382.

17. *Boston Traveller,* Nov. 22, 1890; Boston paper, n.a., n.d.; letter, Todd to Hardy, Mar. 13, 1894.

18. One early reviewer judged: "That it should have a large public is not to be expected but those who are fit will read" (*Springfield Republican,* Nov. 16, 1890); Arlo Bates, Roberts Brothers' reader for the manuscript, wrote in an early review: "She has put on paper things which delight the few" (Bingham 74).

19. Todd sent a Dickinson poem entitled "The Sleeping Flowers" to be published in a child's magazine; some other poems went to be published in *The Youth's Companion* (Bingham 127). But this audience was not Todd's first choice. Earlier, Dickinson's work was rejected when she sent it to *The Century*: I thank Prof. Will Buckingham of Arizona State Univ. for reminding me of this.

20. For one such request, see letter, Millicent Todd for Mabel Loomis Todd to E. D. Hardy, Dec. 22, 1894. On Todd's addresses to women's clubs and institutions, see Bingham 178, 211–12n, 325, 333.

21. I deduce these aspects of Martha Dickinson's inheritance from the letters of Henry P. Field, Attorney, to Martha Gilbert Dickinson Bianchi, July 1, 1913.

22. Class constraints sent Martha Dickinson to finishing school (Miss Porter's in Farmington, Conn.) and coupled with ill health, may have been what kept her from college. Prior to her marriage at age thirty-six, she could not travel to Europe unchaperoned: her brother Ned trudged across Europe escorting his mother and sister even as he wrote his friend Theodore Frothingham that he would be happy never to see another cathedral again.

23. The Frothingham correspondence contains an unidentified newspaper clipping (Mar. 1907) that details the circumstances of Captain Bianchi's loan.

24. See Field's bill for legal services, July 1, 1913. For the resolution of the lawsuits, see 138 NY App. Div. Reports (215–29).

25. Letter, Bianchi to Frothingham, Dec. 6, 1914. The Bianchis were divorced in 1920 (letter, Field to Bianchi, 1920; letter, Frothingham to Bianchi, Sept. 1920. Houghton Library, Harvard U).

26. Bianchi's novels and volumes of poetry published throughout her thirties and forties apparently earned no royalties. All her novels and her collection of translations from Russian poetry were published by Duffield and Co. The Duffield correspondence may be included in Mary Landis Hampson's estate (Walsh 3–9; Levi St. Armand 11). On the public's lack of interest in poetry, see James D. Hart.

27. It may have been on Martha's behalf that Susan Dickinson attempted to befriend Higginson, inviting him to a party on July 2, 1888 (letter, Higginson to Susan Dickinson) just as Mabel Todd was about to begin work copying the poems. In 1889 Martha Dickinson asked for Higginson's comments on a manuscript book of her poems; he promised to be "perfectly frank" (letter, Higginson to Martha Dickinson, Sept. 21, 1889). His comments were kind, and no more (letter, Higginson to Martha Dickinson, Oct. 9, 1889). Letters cited here are at the Houghton Library, Harvard U.

28. Todd may have let the 1922 copyright lapse because of the difficulty of renewing it, given that nobody knew for certain in whose name the original had been made. The relevant files were lost just after Thomas Niles's untimely death.

29. Letter, Greenslet to Bianchi, Sept. 20, 1923, cited in letter, Bianchi to Greenslet, July

9, 1931. Todd's return led Madame Bianchi and Hampson to preserve systematically the publication papers from 1930 on. The precise circumstances of Bianchi's pre-1930 Dickinson publications are evident primarily from later papers. Greenslet may not have understood that Bianchi would not be consulting the originals of the letters that Todd had used.

30. Schappes concentrates on Bianchi's unacknowledged borrowings from Todd; Faderman's more recent evaluation looks at Bianchi's suppression of homoerotic elements as a modus operandi, in misconstruing dates and printing only parts of letters.

31. Will of Martha Gilbert Dickinson Bianchi, filed Jan. 19, 1944, Northampton, Massachusetts.

32. William Jackson said to Bingham, in Washington, D.C., about 1950, as Richard Benson Sewall told me in Sept. 1989: "The wheels of the law grind slowly, but they grind exceedingly fine."

33. Letter, McCarthy to Alfred Hampson, Lincoln's Birthday, 1951; letter, McCarthy to Mary Landis Hampson, Oct. 31, 1955; letter, McCarthy to Mr. Dow, Oct. 10, 1960.

Works Cited

Collections of Emily Dickinson's Poetry and Letters

Letters of Emily Dickinson. New and Enlarged Edition. Ed. Mabel Loomis Todd. New York: Harper, 1931.

The Letters of Emily Dickinson. Ed. Thomas H. Johnson; assoc. ed., Theodora Ward. 3 vols. Cambridge, MA: Harvard UP, 1958.

The Manuscript Books of Emily Dickinson. Ed. Ralph W. Franklin. 2 vols. Cambridge, MA: Belknap P of Harvard UP, 1981.

New Poems of Emily Dickinson. Ed. William H. Shurr, with Anna Dunlap and Emily Grey Shurr. Chapel Hill: U of North Carolina P, 1993.

The Poems of Emily Dickinson. Including variant readings critically compared with all known manuscripts. Ed. Thomas H. Johnson. Cambridge, MA: Harvard UP, 1951, 1955.

The Single Hound: Poems of a Lifetime. Ed. Martha Dickinson Bianchi. Boston: Little, Brown, 1914.

Unpublished Poems of Emily Dickinson. Ed. Martha Dickinson Bianchi and Alfred Leete Hampson. Boston: Little, Brown, 1937.

Other Sources

Aiken, Conrad. "The Dickinson Scandal." Yale Review July 2, 1945: 25–26.

Bianchi, Martha Dickinson. Autobiographical MS, n.d. Houghton Library, Harvard U.

———. Emily Dickinson Face to Face. Unpublished Letters with Notes and Reminiscences. Boston: Houghton Mifflin, 1932.

———. The Life and Letters of Emily Dickinson. New York: Houghton Mifflin, 1924.

———. Letter to American Book Co. May 11, 1936. Houghton Library, Harvard U.

———. Letter to William Crary Brownell. Mar. 30, 1914. Amherst College Library.

———. Letter to Harry Hayden Clark. May 9, 1936. Houghton Library, Harvard U.

———. Letter to Henry Field. Aug. 18, 1931. Houghton Library, Harvard U.

———. Letters to Theodore Frothingham. Dec. 6, 1914; Apr. 19, 1932. Houghton Library, Harvard U.

———. Letters to Ferris Greenslet (Houghton, Mifflin). July 9, 1931; Nov. 1931. Houghton Library, Harvard U.

———. Letters to Herbert Jenkins (Little, Brown). Aug. 9, 1928; May 1930; June 23, 1930; Aug. 15, 1930; June 27, 1931; Oct. 11, 1935; June 23, 1938. Houghton Library, Harvard U.

———. Letter to Robert Linscott (Houghton, Mifflin). Nov. 25, 1929. Houghton Library, Harvard U.

———. Letter to Little, Brown and Co. June 26, 1900. Houghton Library, Harvard U.

Bingham, Millicent Todd. *Ancestors' Brocades: The Literary Debut of Emily Dickinson.* New York: Harper, 1945.

———. Letter to Amy Lowell. Nov. 13, 1924. Houghton Library, Harvard U.

Buckingham, Willis, ed. *Emily Dickinson's Reception in the 1890s: A Documentary History.* Pittsburgh, PA: U of Pittsburgh P, 1989.

Canfield, Cass. *Up and Down and Around: A Publisher Recollects the Time of His Life.* New York: Harper, 1971.

Capelluti, Jo-anne. "Fading Ratios: Johnson's Variorum Edition of Emily Dickinson's Poetry." *Emily Dickinson Journal* 1.2 (1992): 100–20.

Faderman, Lillian. "Emily Dickinson's Letters to Sue Gilbert." *Massachusetts Review* 18.2 (Summer 1977): 197–225.

Farr, Judith. *The Passion of Emily Dickinson.* Cambridge, MA: Harvard UP, 1992.

Field, Henry P. Letters to Martha Dickinson Bianchi. July 1, 1913. Houghton Library, Harvard U.

Franklin, Ralph Waldo. *The Editing of Emily Dickinson: A Reconsideration.* Milwaukee: U of Wisconsin P, 1967.

Frothingham, Theodore. Letter to Martha Dickinson Bianchi. Sept. 1920. Houghton Library, Harvard U.

Greenslet, Ferris. Letters to Martha Dickinson Bianchi. Aug. 17, 1923; Oct. 29, 1931. Houghton Library, Harvard U.

Hammond, John C. Letter to Martha Dickinson. Mar. 16, 1901. Houghton Library, Harvard U.

Hart, Ellen. "The Encoding of Homoerotic Desire: Emily Dickinson's Letters and Poems to Susan Dickinson, 1850–1886." *Tulsa Studies in Women's Literature* 9.2 (Fall 1990): 251–72.

Hart, James D. *The Popular Book: A History of America's Literary Taste.* New York: Oxford UP, 1950.

Higginson, Thomas Wentworth. Letter to Mabel Loomis Todd. Mar. 13, 1905. Amherst College Library.

Howe, Susan. "Emily Dickinson." *Sulfur* 28 (1991): 134–55.

Jenkins, Herbert. Letter to Martha Dickinson Bianchi. Apr. 30, 1935. Houghton Library, Harvard U.

Little, Brown and Company. Letters to Lavinia Dickinson. Jan. 28, 1899; Feb. 2, 1899; Mar. 10, 1899. Houghton Library, Harvard U.

————. Letters to Martha Dickinson Bianchi. June 26, 1900; Feb. 1914. Houghton Library, Harvard U.

————. Letter to John C. Hammond. Feb. 11, 1901. Houghton Library, Harvard U.

Levi St. Armand, Barton. "Evergreens Preservation Plan Initiated." *Emily Dickinson International Society Bulletin* 4.1 (1992): 11.

Longsworth, Polly. *Austin and Mabel: The Amherst Affair and Love Letters of Austin Dickinson and Mabel Loomis Todd.* New York: Farrar, Straus, and Giroux, 1984.

Lubbers, Klaus. *Emily Dickinson: The Critical Revolution.* Ann Arbor: U of Michigan P, 1968.

McCarthy, William. Letter to Mr. Dow. Oct. 10, 1960. Houghton Library, Harvard U.

————. Letters to Alfred Leete Hampson. Mar. 29, 1950; Lincoln's Birthday, 1951. Houghton Library, Harvard U.

————. Letter to Mary Landis Hampson. Oct. 31, 1955. Houghton Library, Harvard U.

McGann, Jerome J. *The Textual Condition.* Princeton, NJ: Princeton UP, 1991.

McIntyre, Alfred. Letter to Martha Dickinson Bianchi. July 11, 1930. Houghton Library, Harvard U.

Myerson, Joel. *Emily Dickinson: A Descriptive Bibliography.* Pittsburgh, PA: U of Pittsburgh P, 1984.

Rubin, Joan Shelley. *The Making of Middlebrow Culture.* Chapel Hill: U of North Carolina P, 1992.

Schappes, Morris U. "Errors in Mrs. Bianchi's Edition of Emily Dickinson's Letters." *American Literature* 4 (1933): 369–84.

————. Review of *Emily Dickinson Face to Face. Unpublished Letters with Notes and Reminiscences. American Literature* 5 (1933): 82–85.

Sewall, Richard B. *The Life of Emily Dickinson.* 2 vols. New York: Farrar, Straus, and Giroux, 1974, 1980.

Smith, Martha Nell. "To Fill a Gap." *San Jose Studies* 13.3 (1987): 3–25.

Taggard, Genevieve. *The Life and Mind of Emily Dickinson.* New York: Knopf, 1930.

Todd, Mabel Loomis. Letters to E. D. Hardy. Mar. 13, 1894; Sept. 28, 1894. Mabel Loomis Todd Papers, Manuscripts and Archives, Yale U Library.

————. Letter to Alfred McIntyre of Little, Brown. Sept. 17, 1923. Mabel Loomis Todd Papers, Manuscripts and Archives, Yale U. Library.

————. "Village Improvement Association." MS, n.d. Mabel Loomis Todd Papers, Manuscripts and Archives, Yale U Library.

Todd, Millicent. Letter for Mabel Loomis Todd to E. D. Hardy. Dec. 22, 1894. Mabel Loomis Todd Papers, Manuscripts and Archives, Yale U Library.

Walsh, John Evangelist. *This Brief Tragedy: Unraveling the Todd-Dickinson Affair.* New York: Grove Weidenfeld, 1991.

Whicher, George Frisbie. *This Was a Poet: A Critical Biography of Emily Dickinson.* New York: Scribner's, 1938.

6.

Cakes and Poetry:
The Career of Harriet Moody

Susan Albertine

On March 4, 1919, the poet and editor Ridgely Torrence described the arrival of what he called an "Olympian" cake, "crowned and anointed," he recalled, "with royal orgeat and orbed with gemmy fruits of Elysian orchards." This divine concoction appeared in a "gilded barge . . . float[ing] up the stairs" of Harriet Moody's home in Chicago. And, Torrence added, "As Thoreau said of his birth, it came in the nick of time. Still I could find it in my heart to wish the barge had arrived yesterday, for Frost came here to dinner last night and he is so eminently worthy of the CAKE and the CAKE so deserving of him that I'm sorry they couldn't have met. A King of men and of poets (and he is both) should know the Queen of Cakes" (qtd. in Dunbar 39–40). Torrence implies, doubtless unintentionally, that like Robert Frost (King of men and of poets), the Queen of Cakes also had a double identity—the Queen of Cakes signified, metonymically, the Queen Maker of Cakes herself. If she was not a poet, in Torrence's language she stood in queenly maternal relation to the artists who came to her for nurturance. And this double identity is precisely what has interested me in Harriet Moody's career.

I happened upon Harriet Moody's life writings in the same way I have learned about other long-forgotten lives. In my search for archival records of independent, unconventional women's careers—those often seen, paradoxically, as threatening to the social order—I habitually ask in research libraries for underused collections of papers by or about strong-minded women who flourished before 1920 and who made their own livings. Without fail I find someone: examples include Bertha Cates, manager of a coal business; Harriet Morehead Berry, the Mother of Good Roads in North Carolina, responsible for bringing asphalt pavement to the state; and Harriet Strong, irrigation pioneer of Southern California.[1]

Some years ago I asked the same question at the University of Chicago and was shown three neglected boxes of remarkably diverse materials: recipes for chicken salad; letters from Rabindranath Tagore, Edwin Arlington Robinson, Amy Lowell, Robert Frost, Vachel Lindsay, and Marie Curie; art deco advertising booklets for Pied Piper Chocolates; printed flyers for the

Swift Company, featuring recipes for inexpensive cuts of beef; exquisite settings of Shakespearean sonnets on laid paper; clippings of articles by Jane Addams on Hull House and the campaign for universal suffrage; glossy advertising photos of cakes, pies, bonbons, and recipes for cakes and more cakes. It was irresistible.

After a second, longer trip to Chicago, my work on the career of Harriet Converse Moody (1857–1932) has come to depend on the convergence of cakes and poetry.[2] Poets, like all of us, must eat, and it is interesting to consider that what they eat and who provides their sustenance has a bearing on their art. "To have poetry you must first have cookery. Put it the other way round, however, . . . To have cookery you must first have poetry," wrote a reviewer of Harriet's last cookbook (Wilber). A talented entrepreneur, Harriet Moody found fulfillment, in large part, by providing food and a nearly indescribable range of services to poets and other artists. For a woman to do this, and to do it with such glorious success, to be nurturing and influential in such a conventional, stereotypical way, bears discussion in itself. Standing at the margins of renown—quite by choice, Harriet would have said—she played a central role in the Chicago Literary Renaissance and the *Poetry* magazine circle. It might be argued that Harriet Moody reached the center by being so effectively marginal. She was a self-effacing patron, salonière, and friend of the arts whose career resists any naming, and in this, I have found, she is typical of many self-supporting middle-class women—both white women and women of color—who flourished before 1920.

A career of this kind raises a number of questions for critical assessment. Was Harriet Moody engaged in the "dirty," low-status work that Joan Brumberg and Nancy Tomes have described as typically "professional" for women, that is, professional work requiring the closest human contact (287)? Is it warranted to locate her career at both the margins and the center of print culture? If, indeed, we conceive of print culture as a network in which all points are vital, rather than exclusively as a hierarchy surmounted by high-cultural writers, then an assessment of Harriet Moody's career, in addition to bringing her work from obscurity, can make greater claims for her achievements. I find it helpful to refer to Robert Darnton's communications circuit, an analytical schema for the history of the book in which positions are assigned to authors, publishers, printers and suppliers, shippers, booksellers, binders, and readers, all relating in a complex but consistent manner (27–32, 47). If, in the myriad services they perform, mentors or facilitators of writing are brought into the circuit at a point between the author and publisher and again as readers and critics, then their importance becomes apparent. To locate Harriet Moody's career within such a network is precisely my intent. Her career may then be seen as exemplary, both admirable and representative of other women's work.

Harriet Converse Tilden came of age a few years before the New Woman became a recognizable type, and in many ways she appears to be a model of fin de siècle female independence.[3] She was born to an intellectually brisk mother and a father who became a successful livestock broker in Chicago—both strong abolitionists, Harriet was proud to say, both to be admired and resisted.[4] A tomboy and the object of her father's "excessive idolatry," according to Olivia Dunbar (Mrs. Ridgely Torrence), who published a memoir fifteen years after Harriet's death, Harriet insisted, despite parental objections, on attending Cornell University, where she graduated in 1876 with a degree in English literature (Dunbar 18–23). After a year of medical school, which her parents reluctantly allowed her to begin, she returned to Chicago and made her debut, with the understanding that she would then continue with medical school. Instead, however, she chose to marry a prosperous young lawyer named Edwin Brainard, once more against parental will (Dunbar 27–30). The marriage was not a success, and the Brainards were soon divorced. Harriet scrupulously returned her $100,000 marriage settlement (Dunbar 34). After the death of her father, she assumed financial responsibility for her invalid mother (her father having lost his fortune and her two brothers unable to help), and once more despite her father's predictions—"my father had often assured me that I had no business sense"—began her career ("My First Business Efforts" 6).

She became first a schoolteacher in the Hyde Park neighborhood of Chicago, and to all reports, a gifted teacher and lifelong friend to many of her students, including Alice Corbin (later Henderson), who became associate editor of *Poetry* magazine, and Elizabeth O'Neill, who eventually took charge of Harriet's household (Dunbar 35, 46). Her first ventures in publishing were struck from the Windtryst Press, set up in her home to print her students' work. She also became a graduate fellow in the department of English at the University of Chicago.

Satisfying as teaching was, it could not possibly support a large home and a mother accustomed to luxury. At the suggestion of a friend, in 1889 she experimented with gingerbread until she found a recipe that would suit the Marshall Field tea room. "Being minded, as Hamlet says, 'to fly at anything I saw,' I accepted the commission," she later wrote ("My First Business Efforts" 2). Chicken salad soon followed, and the Home Delicacies Association (HDA) began its work, first in a basement, then on the spacious top floor of her home, and later in a building to itself.[5] Harriet was from the outset determined to cook homestyle food of the highest quality, regardless of expense. Essentially conservative in outlook, she saw moral responsibility in her work. The HDA sought to restore the honor of the modern home by providing proper sustenance: food lovingly prepared for dining as ritual and ceremony. It "stiffen[ed]" the "morale" of customers, reminding them "of the time before the world had gone quite madly kitchenetted" ([Kellogg], "Mrs. WVM" 41).

Although Harriet marketed her elegant restaurant and catering services to the privileged classes, she would eventually make a more democratic ap-

6.1. The Home Delicacies Association, Christmas 1896 or 1897. Special Collections, Regenstein Library, University of Chicago.

peal in *Delineator Institute* booklets, for example, and advertising brochures directed to the lower middle class. For women who had to do their own cooking, and for those with inadequately skillful cooks, Home Delicacies products, along with Harriet's restaurants and advice, won a devoted following. Her success may indicate a host of common assumptions about the disruptive force of modernity: that a more ethnically diversified labor force meant "less accomplished" domestic workers; that women's greater mobility meant less time for the home fires (in the kitchenette); that middle-class homes should function ever more efficiently, with fewer servants; that advancing technology meant a cheapening of commodities and values. For nearly forty years, until she closed the business in 1929, the Home Delicacies Association was a Chicago institution. Home Delicacies products were sold at Marshall Field and Company, at the Field Museum cafeteria, at the tea room of the Chicago Little Theatre, and at an impressive array of clubs and corporations. She stocked the dining cars of many rail lines that passed through the city. She maintained a branch at Selfridge's in London. Her restaurant, Le Petit Gourmet, on North Michigan Avenue was among the "smartest" in the city; her catering services were patronized by Chicago society.[6]

For at least a decade, Harriet maintained two careers, continuing her teaching as she established the HDA, managing her mother's household and her own as well. "I thought of myself then as an unassailable fortress," she recalled (Dunbar 44). After her classes finished, she went to HDA and then took a daily drive with her mother. In 1899, her life changed dramatically when at a dinner party she was introduced to the poet William Vaughn Moody, then a professor of English at the University of Chicago.[7] They soon became deep, fundamental, and "totally unsentimental" friends, sharing a profound commitment to poetry, spirituality—both thought the visible world an illusion—individualism, and an idealized vision of gender in each other (Dunbar 50–53; Brown 131, 135). For several years they were lovers. On April 4, 1904, Will wrote Harriet from the Grand Canyon: "My longing to have you here increased three-fold the moment I felt a horse's sinewy back between my legs. We must ride!" Yet although Will pressed the issue, they put off marriage. Harriet's mother objected to the match; it may be because Harriet was eleven years older than Will. Their unedited correspondence suggests that Harriet herself did not wish to remarry, for reasons that do not survive. "Dearly Beloved, let us hesitate no longer. . . . We must be together, and we must be so in peace, with freedom from the corrosion of intrusive comment, in the only way in which our mutual life can be gently fostered and moulded as we would have it," he wrote on July 26, 1906.[8] A week later, Will noted that Harriet said no, "with a gentle firmness which leaves me nothing to say" (Aug. 2, 1906). Olivia Dunbar recalls, "She once said, laughing at herself, that she could love a dozen men at once and that no one man could completely respond to her in kind—she was at the same time the very spirit of constancy. She did not, she could not, waver however slightly in her allegiance to her supreme friendship" (69).

Perhaps more practical reasons were a factor. Will needed freedom of movement and seclusion in order to write; Harriet's business and responsibility for her mother tied her to Chicago. It is important to remember, of course, that she paid taxes through most of her career without being able to vote, and that for many self-supporting women of the period, marriage under sexist property laws was a genuine threat to financial independence. She and Will managed to be a couple in their own manner, traveling together to New York, Virginia, and Mackinac Island. She always kept a room for him at her home (Dunbar 61–63). It seems entirely possible that Harriet did not wish to bear the social burdens of marriage, burdens she as a divorcée and an arbiter of taste well understood.

In May 1909 they did marry, a decision coinciding with an alarming decline in Will's health. After he died of brain cancer in 1910, Harriet devoted herself absolutely to poetry and the HDA. In part she wished to advance Will's reputation and manage his literary estate; in part she had to be self-supporting. Yet her subsequent activities to promote the arts served a deep, personal desire and commitment that cannot adequately be explained by her devotion to Will. Remarkably, she was able to conceive of her work for the arts and for the palate as a unified whole. No poet herself, in a strict sense, though a brilliant conversationalist, she could cook for art and as art.

Harriet's contribution to modern poetry was multifaceted and complex. She joined *Poetry* magazine as one of its original financial backers, a "personal friend" among the original one hundred donors who gave fifty dollars per year for five years (Monroe, *Poet's Life* 243–44). But Harriet presented far more than a sum of money. Before the first issue came out, a Boston journal threatened to use the same title. Editor Harriet Monroe had to rush the first number into print in October 1912, although she had few valuable poems and only fourteen pages of text: "So Mrs. William Vaughn Moody came to the rescue, as in various later emergencies she so often did, by permitting us the first printing of her dead husband's poem 'I Am the Woman'" (Monroe, *Poet's Life* 285). It was a revealing and in some senses an ironic rescue, for "I Am the Woman," ostensibly a poem on the emancipation of women, essentializes Harriet herself as the type of what was then called the strong feminine ideal, a female force, in Henry Adams's phrase for it, a mother-goddess familiar in Columbia, the Statue of Liberty, and the heroic figures displayed in robust majesty in public architecture and statuary of the period.[9] The final lines suggest the poem's slanted tribute to emancipation, written in a florid, mythopoetic style that *Poetry* would soon repudiate:

> I am the Woman, ark of the Law and sacred arm to upbear it,
> Heathen trumpet to overthrow and idolatrous sword to shear it:
> Yea, she whose arm was round the neck of the morning star at song,
> Is she who kneeleth now in the dust and cries at the secret door,
> "Open to me, O sleeping mother! The gate is heavy and strong.
> Open to me, I am come at last; be wroth with thy child no more.
> Let me lie down with thee there in the dark, and be slothful with
>   thee as before!" (W. Moody, *Poems and Plays* 1: 132)

The image of primal sloth as characteristic of the eternal feminine seems hardly fitting to either Harriet. In a carefully diplomatic letter written on August 27, 1911, before the poem was published, Edwin Arlington Robinson told Harriet that much as he admired the poem, he thought *slothful* sounded "a false note" (*Selected Letters* 73). Yet the content of the poem may have mattered less than the name of the poet, for Will Moody's reputation was then very sound, and the appearance of the poem would have conferred a certain stature on the first number of *Poetry*. That two such strong-minded women should have chosen this particular poem, moreover, provides further evidence that the stereotype of woman as primitive force had been thoroughly naturalized in the discourse of the period.[10]

If spiritually Harriet could accept such a vision of female essence, in the mundane world she was unconstrained by a narrow conception of gender. A talented businesswoman, Harriet gave financial help and advice to an astonishing array of artists. This included material sustenance in the form of room and board at her large, sparsely furnished, "almost masculine" home on the near South Side, where several guests were usually present (Dunbar 9). She arrived regularly with her chauffeur Anton at Union Station to welcome new artists to town. Her dinner parties became legendary. Given in her drawing room, where she sat in a settee suspended from the ceiling, the parties broke with convention in that each guest was seated in an easy chair and served at an individual table.[11] The food, of course, was the best HDA could provide, the ambience carefully set to encourage good conversation. When her visitors left, they took richly provisioned hampers of food and other gifts with them. "I never dreamed of such perfect subordination of food," wrote Zona Gale. "Usually it wig-wags at you, and gives you a new common denominator by herding you into the next room. But you combine delicious food with no emphasis. And how gracefully it takes its place! As if it knew all the time where it belonged, if only we would not insist on so much ceremony and accent and silver. You are a new wonder to me" (Dec. 26 [1913?]).

Harriet did not flatter her guests, but warmed up quickly to intelligence and humor. Her evenings ran late. It was her practice to sit up for poetry readings and other artistic performances. "I wish I was sitting at your hearth again, listening to your remarkable readings from the pen of the great soul who was called from you into the great Silence," Edwin Markham wrote. "Those readings at your hearth are among the joyous memories. The hours in your house have afforded me some of those beautiful moments, which belong to the most precious things of our existence" (December 30, 1923). Harriet enjoyed making plans with new friends, especially young people in need, helping them to solve financial problems, writing letters of recommendation, and scheduling engagements for them (Dunbar 10–14). Among the writers whose careers she helped to promote and shape were Edwin Arlington Robinson, Edna St. Vincent Millay, Countee Cullen, Richard Eberhart, Amy Lowell, Robert Frost, Vachel Lindsay, Hart Crane, Rabindranath Tagore, Carl Sandburg, Yone Noguchi, Zona Gale, Padraic Colum, Edgar Lee Masters, James Stephens, John Masefield, and Walter de la Mare.

Harriet also established a series of poetry readings, which she called Les Petits Jeux Floraux, after the Académie des Jeux Floraux, founded by troubadours in Provence in 1323. The readings began late in 1920 at Le Petit Gourmet, a restaurant she owned on North Michigan Avenue. Managed and staffed by women, Le Petit Gourmet had a splendid reputation as a gathering place for luncheon, tea, and supper. Approached through a courtyard, it had quaint low-ceilinged rooms with stenciled walls of French blue, and it offered unpretentious, carefully prepared food served on provincial French earthenware (Atkinson 3–5). On Sunday evenings, the place was given over to poetry. The guest poet stayed at Harriet's home; she handled publicity for the reading; the audience paid one dollar for admission, the total handed over to the artist; and of course, Harriet served refreshments. Her friendships with poets and her various connections in the art world guaranteed a good turnout. Frost, Lindsay, Sandburg, and Colum came yearly; other readers included Maxwell Bodenheim, Countee Cullen, Alfred Kreymborg, Percy MacKaye, Edna St. Vincent Millay, Amy Lowell, Harriet Monroe, Ridgely Torrence, and Margery Swett (Dunbar 176).

Other enterprises followed naturally from this work. She arranged readings at the University of Chicago, Northwestern, and other universities, including Cornell, where she served from 1912 to 1922 as the only female trustee (W. Moody, *Letters* 436). She maintained an apartment at 107 Waverly Place in Greenwich Village, a farm in West Cummington, Massachusetts, and a summer retreat at Mackinac Island, at which all doors were open to visiting artists. If she had a salon, it was movable: "She herself really occupied a personal territory of wide area. Its center shifted with her movements; that was all. A day after leaving Groveland [Ellis] Avenue cosharers of her territory would group themselves about her in New York. A week later the same thing would happen in London. The background seemed in her case to be almost negligible" (Dunbar 151). In short, at a time when artists' colonies were hardly known and public and foundation grants not yet available, she provided the material means for artistic work.[12] In 1927, for instance, Yvor Winters wrote her "again" to help out a young artist, this time Otis Polelonema, a Hopi painter who needed to raise money for treatment of an eye problem (Sept. 30, 1927). She offered assistance to an international assemblage of artists and students without regard to nationality, ethnicity, or race. What sets her apart from other philanthropists is the fact that she was a self-made, self-supporting woman who earned her money largely to give it away. Hers was, as Olivia Dunbar put it, an "almost irrational unselfishness" (152).

There is much to admire in Harriet Moody's achievement. Certainly, her work provides more evidence—if more were needed—that modernism, once defined mainly by the works of white male writers, deserves the feminist revision it is now receiving. The movement was itself a creation of an international community sustained by the work of women like Harriet Moody, Harriet Monroe, Margaret Anderson, Winifred Ellerman ("Bryher"), Sylvia Beach, and Caresse Crosby—to name representative publishers, editors, and patrons—as well as by writers like Gertrude Stein, H.D., Marianne Moore, Mina Loy, Alice Corbin Henderson, Djuna Barnes, and Amy Lowell.

Perhaps Harriet Moody's most pronounced talent was her ability to make connections. She had a genius for networking—and I mean the term in the sense I have ascribed to Darnton: a talent that, in addition to sound critical judgment, put her in a strong position to advance a friend's career. Robinson sent her "Eros Turanos" and asked her to forward it to Harriet Monroe for publication in *Poetry,* suggesting that her endorsement might encourage acceptance (Nov. 6, 1913). Vachel Lindsay had almost filial relations with Harriet, bringing to her not only his poetry but also his political activism, including vigorous efforts on behalf of the anti-lynching campaign in 1917 (Dunbar 120, 142). Harriet's close attention and encouragement were invaluable to his career. She first brought him into New York literary society—Robinson, for example, agreed to meet him in 1914 (July 23, 1914)—and she introduced him at Cornell (Dunbar 110–11). When he experimented with choreography for his poems, he asked Harriet to introduce Pavlova to him. Pavlova was beyond her reach, but the dancer Eleanor Dougherty, whom Harriet knew, soon joined Lindsay in performances at the Chicago Little Theatre, beginning in 1916 (Ruggles 244–45). Harriet wrote letters of introduction for Padraic Colum to Cornell, to the Universities of Chicago, Illinois, and Wisconsin, and to a number of Chicago clubs. On meeting Padraic and Mary Colum in 1916, Harriet Monroe wondered, "were they pro-German . . . when we met them, a very bedraggled pair of insular Celts, in Mrs. Moody's drawing room?" (*Poet's Life* 427).

Robert Frost and Carl Sandburg, her close friends, treated her as critic, peer, adviser, and confidant. Sandburg saw her often in Chicago, and so there are few letters from him. One suggests the tone of their relationship:

> We have lost our dog. If you get hold of a setter, sheep dog, collie, German police dog, mastiff, Danish bloodhound, or any dog spotted or unspotted that growls at strangers and is good to children—bring him along. Don't let dog thoughts interrupt your vacation. Of all the teeming millions in Chicago you deserve an uninterrupted vacation. But if anybody says to you careless like that they got a good dog you can have, and it does look to you like a good dog, call their bluff, copper the hund, nail the dog, sign a contract there will be the best of care.

This was followed by some comments about a children's collection he was writing, along with a request for her to read fifteen or twenty "babies of literary destiny." The note was signed, "Your black-heart renegade, Carl" (Sept. 8, 1921; Mitgang 199).[13]

Robert Frost's letters suggest a complex affiliation and friendship that extended to the entire Frost family. Sometimes relentlessly jocular ("Dear Mrs Moody: We get a sense from your pranks of your being all around us but at the same time invisible like a deus ex machina" [Frost, *Selected Letters* 227]), he also wrote with requests for advice:

> Unless I put off writing awhile longer I can no longer conceal from you that when you are in West Cummington and we are in Franconia the distance that separates us is almost hopeless. It is not for a practical-poetical like me to teach geography to a poetical-practical like you but by the map I should

6.2. Carl Sandburg, with dogs, possibly from Harriet Moody. Stereopticon photograph 5:18, Carl Sandburg Coll., University of Illinois Library at Urbana-Champaign.

say that one of us would have to set at naught some two hundred miles to reach the other. (Let it be said in contraction that they are beautiful miles) It seems to me you ought to be the one to do the setting at naught—you with your automobiles and your superannuated horses. Come to Franconia and adopt the rest of the family as you adopted me in Chicago. We can't feed you because we haven't learned to feed ourselves yet in the right caterer's sense of the word, but we can surround you . . . with one continuous smile of welcome. I require of you that you shall come as an act penitential for not having come to West Cummington before we left Amherst. . . . I am past the help I particularly wanted of you in June, namely, advice against a step I was about to take, because I have taken the step. There is nothing left but to help me not to think too hardly of myself. (Aug. 12, 1917)

Frost almost certainly means here his decision to return to teaching at Amherst instead of supporting himself by writing (Thompson 110–11); it was an appropriate occasion to turn to a "poetical-practical" like Harriet. He was seeking advice on an issue much larger than the choice of farming or academia: he worried about existing as an outsider, though his reputation as a poet partly depended on it. Who better to consult than Harriet Moody? She routinely conducted herself along the boundary between literary outside and inside, and her reputation had been wholly built on just such difficult decisions as Frost now faced.

Harriet often made arrangements for Frost's readings and put him up at her home, saving him expense and effort (Thompson 158). On the subject of Harriet's assistance, Elinor Frost wrote to her daughter Lesley in April 1918:

I guess I haven't written to you about Mrs. Moody having arranged readings for him at 3 State Universities out there. Then he will go to Cornell on the way back. If all goes well, he will clear $175 and that will buy a Liberty Bond and settle up our bills here that are getting rather too many for us. It isn't much money for such a lot of hard work but there will probably be some advantage to his reputation in his getting acquainted with certain professors and critics out there. (Grade, ed. 24)

The Frost family was so fond of Harriet that when Robert thought Lesley needed a change from Ann Arbor ("my line of talk isn't calculated to make her like any institution"), he asked Harriet if she would invite the young woman to Chicago "for the good you would do her" (Feb. 21, [1922]; qtd. in Dunbar 189).

Practical matters took a large share of their correspondence, but Robert Frost also valued Harriet's opinions enough, for instance, to argue literary nationalism with her. She was entirely too much an Anglophile, in his view, though even as he made the accusation, he had to take it back: "But of course I'm not an American. Let's go back on America together" (Thompson 165). This was in 1919; in 1921 he was still writing on the subject: "Don't you know it's provincial to look up to England? So is it to brag about America" (Thompson 165). Other letters are confessional: "But you won't understand because you have no ambition. You have got over that last infirmity of noble minds grown nobler" (Feb. 21, [1922]); "To you alone I will confess I am still looking for a home. . . . My present agony may be homesickness for the home I've left behind me rather than for the home that never was on land or sea" (Dec. 28, 1920). The correspondence lasted at least through March 30, 1926, the date of the last extant telegram from Robert Frost to Harriet.

In her relations with Rabindranath Tagore, later Nobel laureate, Harriet appeared to be conscious of approaching an ideal of friendship. Their connection began when she invited Tagore to visit in 1912, before he was known in this country. As their friendship developed, it became deeply spiritual, for Harriet an epiphany, the first since Will Moody had died (Dunbar 94). Having been introduced to mysticism at Cornell (a professor at whose home she lived was a friend and student of Madame Blavatsky, founder of the theosophical movement), and later a Christian Scientist, Harriet was unusually receptive to Tagore's Hinduism. The spiritual communion she had shared with Will, which allowed her to believe in his constant presence, was to Tagore an article of faith. Tagore's letters to Harriet speak of walking as if together on "God's broad path to the emancipation from the narrowness of self, to the dedication of our lives to His love and service, and feel[ing] that we are walking side by side" (Apr. 16, 1913). In a subsequent letter he added, "I do not know if we shall ever meet again—but we *have* met—and that meeting can never be over—and the distance will make it all the deeper and truer by leaving out all trivialities that tend to overcrowd it" (Sept. 1913 [?]). They did meet again, and their friendship continued over the years. She was instrumental in arranging readings and making connections for him; she accompanied him to Harvard, copied his manuscripts and sent them to publishers, and shared her flat in London with him (Dunbar 101). Tagore responded with great affection, from himself and his family, and he dedicated *Chitra* to her. His last extant letter, offering condolences on her financial problems, is dated December 5, 1930.

Like most of her widely scattered correspondence, Harriet's letters to Tagore may not have survived. She left no account of their friendship aside from his letters and various newspaper clippings and photos, and a few undocumented remarks reported by Olivia Dunbar (93–106). Only a brief account survives in the papers of Harriet Monroe, at whose suggestion Harriet Moody had first written to Tagore. At his first visit, the guests sat up all night at Harriet Moody's fireside, "as if at the feet of Buddha, and listen[ed] to his tenor chanting of his Bengali rhythms" and his commentary "with singular half-satiric precision, on the intricate phenomena of our occidental civilization; opposing to its rush and roar the silent motionless absorption of his three-hour meditations at dawn."[14]

Tagore's otherworldliness was particularly attractive to Harriet. Although she was successful at her work and certainly made an art of her livelihood, she often expressed private misgivings about the realm of getting and spending. If, as Olivia Dunbar maintains, Harriet was constitutionally unselfish, she occupied an uncomfortable position as self-made woman. Tagore would have understood. Writing to Harriet after receiving the Nobel Prize, he said,

6.3. Harriet Moody,
1913, with the Tagore
family. Special Collec-
tions, Regenstein
Library, University of
Chicago.

"I am still suffering from Nobel Prize notoriety and I do not know what
nursing home there is where I can go and get rid of this my latest and my
greatest trouble. To deprive me of my seclusion is like shelling an oyster"
(Jan. 22, 1914). In a subsequent letter, containing an invitation to meet in
Japan ("Why not meet your poet in the land of the rising sun? We can follow his fiery track till the East and West become one somewhere in the
neighbourhood of Groveland Avenue"), Tagore half-seriously admonished
Harriet *not* to "plead business": "Business should never be one-sided—it
must not fix your mind to its profits only, there must come times when you
should recklessly rush to losses and be glad. The element of loss is the element of poetry in business. Business would be deadly to the spirit of man if
it were wholly successful. There should be at least one poet among your
business advisers to represent this side—the freedom from the tyranny of
desire for success" (Feb. 18, 1915).

It was a freedom Harriet must have fervently desired: "to salvage for
poetry's sake as much time as she could from the 'world of bread, pie, and

cake' that she once ruefully spoke of herself as living in" (Dunbar 253). She knew her talents lay elsewhere. As Carroll Brent Chilton wrote to her,

> You seem to me to have a kind of genius for sharing your life with your friends. . . . It is evidently a form of religion with you, or shall we say, your genius for poetry (for we all have genius implicit, only in most of us it is stopped down) has taken the path of friendship *as a worship*, instead of the way of metrical verse. . . . You tell these stories in a way that reveals worlds about yourself which does not escape the perceiving: the setting, the reticence; the chance adjective thrown out; the lifted eyebrow awaiting recognition of an inference; the pause to allow the inference to sink in. . . . I should say you are a born oral novelist. . . . (Nov. 28, [1913?])

Will Moody had thought as much: "You quarrel with me for not answering your letters, but to answer these would be like 'talking back' to sunlight and brook water" (June 2, 1902; qtd. in *Letters* 121 as June 3). Like a figure in a Virginia Woolf novel, Harriet can now be seen in fragmented glimpses only, from many points of view, without one's knowing precisely who she is and indeed seldom hearing her voice. The wonderful group portrait of HDA and friends, made at Christmas 1896 or '97, is absent Harriet (fig. 6.1). Yet it is redolent of her subjectivity. (Indeed, perhaps she was taking the picture.) The heterogeneous arrangement of Harriet's cohorts—an intriguing, attractive mixture of poets, chefs, backers, and waifs—seems consciously designed to strike the viewer as an incomplete (and thus untraditional) whole. It, and much else in the archive, bears signs that Harriet knew what new image of the self was entailed in playing the role just described. It is appropriate, in short, that just such a career should have been dedicated to modern art.

Because Harriet's gift was, as Percy MacKaye put it, "native to air, not to ink" (W. Moody, *Letters* 9), it is difficult to discover what she thought of herself or to answer complex questions about her life. Her self-awareness as a woman who could both exploit and flout her femininity remains largely undiscernible. Like other successful women of her generation and more than her white male counterparts, she had to be open to change—a shape changer, a maker of belief, even in a sense a benevolent con artist. Nina Auerbach has noted a similar pattern in the careers of professional women of the theatre. Like them, Harriet was disadvantaged because of her sex, but she learned indeed, to borrow Auerbach's words, "to assume many selves. . . . a variety of personae with which to blend into" a society inhospitable to strong, independent women (155). She became so adept at this blending that we may sometimes have trouble seeing her now. Surely this is yet another reason why such women's papers go unread.

Harriet's sexual freedom, living for years with Will Moody while refusing to marry him, stands out in sharp contrast against her public attitude, displayed in her work at HDA. A good part of her income depended on catering to weddings, so that one must read her refusal to marry against, for instance, an article in the *Ladies' Home Journal* about marriage etiquette and the proper way to decorate and serve the bride's and groom's cakes (Beem). A compromise between personal morality and public behavior because of the sexual double standard could not have been easy for her to make. Dunbar speaks of Harriet's idealization of marriage and motherhood "to an extreme degree" (29). If she idealized motherhood, it was to create her own version of the *mutterrecht*—to regenerate society by inspiring men. She sought to be a higher influence, a Muse or "Mother Postulate."[15] "I wish that, like God, you were imminent [sic] in the vast world," James Stephens wrote, "so that one could drop round and see you anywhere" (August 6, 1925). Will Moody referred to the four mystic fountains of Harriet's heart, on which were carved "sister, wife, mother, child" (July 16, 1902).

Autonomous as Harriet was in fact, she appeared to many as a person who defined herself only in relation to others. Some, mostly men, used her as a mirror. In addition to her quick artistic sympathy and extraordinary generosity, her clearsightedness, wit, and warmth in conversation made her presence a catalyst for creative interaction. Some, like Vachel Lindsay, Hart Crane, and the youthful Richard Eberhart, quite literally depended on her presence and her encouragement: "You have materially helped me toward my next month of writing," Lindsay wrote (Apr. 28, 1918); "I must thank you all over again. I have taken you too much for granted, like the sun and the stars" (May 11, 1917). The problem, of course, is that Lindsay's letters are so entirely self-absorbed that Harriet herself can be discerned in them only as a reflective surface. Only with difficulty can one infer her side of the correspondence. Whatever the rewards for the womanly guardian angel, the dangers of this kind of behavior include invisibility.

Harriet's position on feminism is by no means clear. She was thought, in fact, by some to be more interested in men than in her own sex:

> Harriet Moody's charm lay in her conversation. A first-rate repartee could transform her, lighting her somber face and infusing her voice with gaiety and challenge. She had a woman's gift for assembling around her—the word "collected" would be invidious—men of creative genius and in her drawing room would slight a scholar for an artist any day—also, it must be confessed, a woman for a man. Between her and Harriet Monroe, of the wrenlike plumage and eagle heart, there was little love lost. (Ruggles 225)

If, privately, Harriet Moody and Harriet Monroe did not get along, they treated each other cordially. "Come over and lunch with me soon again. It is a good way to get a little undisturbed talk with you. à deux is always best—

a luxury I seldom enjoy. Yours with affection, Harriet Moody," she wrote, concluding an otherwise businesslike letter on the divorce case of Edgar Lee Masters (April 23, 1922). At Moody's death, Monroe wrote a generous eulogy for *Poetry,* praising Harriet as "indomitable," her hospitality "lavish . . . and friendly beyond all expectation," especially to "impecunious youngsters" and old friends in trouble ("News Notes"); Monroe's autobiography is likewise respectful.

Harriet left no written sign that she would have wished to be thought a feminist. Yet she surrounded herself with women. Many of her senior HDA employees were female. Alice Corbin and University of Chicago professor Martha Foote Crow (both in the HDA Christmas photo) lived with her. As a trustee at Cornell, she devoted herself to women's concerns (Dunbar 147). She occasionally worked with Hull House and participated actively in fundraising for Marie Curie's research. She treasured her niece Alice Harriet and was proud of her strong maternal line (Dunbar 15).[16]

If Harriet saw her many enterprises as liberating for women, she made no comment that survives. Certainly her work appears to be a modernization of the cult of domesticity, or domestic feminism brought into the twentieth century; she pushed domesticity beyond its boundaries, shrewdly offering home comforts—good, home-cooked food—from a source outside the home, a woman's business largely employing female workers. It was a concept more traditional than, but nonetheless akin to, Charlotte Perkins Gilman's idea for communal kitchens, promoted in *Women and Economics* (1898). Like other forms of domestic feminism, however, whether consciously enacted or not, Harriet's work did little to bring men into the domestic sphere or to question the nature of the spheres themselves. She was not about changing the status quo. Allowing her name, for example, to be used in advertising campaigns by the Swift Company and for Royal Baking Powder (she claimed it was the ingredient that made her first gingerbread a success), she staunchly promoted middle-class values and a slightly widened scope for women's action. If her private life departed from her public values, she could well have seen the discrepancy as the price she had to pay for her freedom.

In 1929 the Home Delicacies Association folded. Perhaps, as hinted by several who knew her, there was treachery at HDA, for Harriet was too trusting, too unconcerned, finally, with financial contingencies. Writing to Padraic Colum in February 1928, she wryly mentioned some problems: "disruptions . . . due to the usual forming of cliques for underground work, and I finally had a strike, and shots fired, but my own unparalleled courage and decision brought me through with secret qualms disguised by smiles" (Dunbar 239). The qualms must have intensified. In a letter to Elizabeth Wallace, formerly of Romance Languages at the University of Chicago, she wrote sometime in 1929, "I think it would be well for me to take to the lecture platform, advising all women to keep out of business. I suppose you remember Daudet's little story of the lamb in the mountain, and its pathetic conclusion, 'but in the morning he was eaten.' This seems for the moment to be the curtain on my own life" (Dunbar 253). Yet in the same letter she said she wanted to live "indefinitely." She tried to eke out a living in her last three years by teaching deaf women to cook for themselves. She also planned a cookbook combining her own recipes with essays by her poet friends. Problems intervened, and the cookbook came out without the essays. It was successful, but not on a large enough scale to ensure her comfort (Dunbar 262). Still, she managed. An anonymous female donor gave her a yearly income; another anonymous former student bought her house and asked her to stay in it (Dunbar 262–69), which she did until she died of asthma in February 1932. Her individualism seems to have remained intact. In 1929 she wrote to her friend Ferdinand Schevill, a professor at the University of Chicago: "I am longing with heart and soul for adventure . . . anything where there are heights to look out from, and where there is also a little danger" (Dunbar 15n). "A little danger" and "enthusiasm enough to comrade my own," as she had written in 1924, would suffice when business failed (Dunbar 205).

Moody's was an anomalous and self-effacing career. To say that she created an artistic community or salon only partly conveys what she accomplished. To call her mainly a womanly influence, a fabulous cook and entertainer, an enabler and patron of poets, does injustice to the range of her work. She was a powerful language artist in her own right—as much a critic as a creator of atmosphere, as much "poetical" as "practical." She made art and artists circulate, made it materially possible for such circulation to happen. Her gift of conversation, her forceful presence, the tangible power that she wielded in the literary marketplace, and her genius for networking made her a substantial shaper of careers, including her own. A picture of modernism is incomplete without her.

Notes

1. The Bertha Cates and Harriet Morehead Berry papers are at the University of North Carolina; see also Albertine, "Self Found in the Breaking," for an analysis of the Harriet Strong Collection at the Huntington Library.
2. I am grateful for a Faculty Development Grant from Susquehanna University, which has enabled me to work with the Harriet Brainard Moody Papers at the University of Chicago.
3. See Jordan on the New Woman; for a comprehensive study of typecasting of American women, see Banta.
4. Letter to Tagore, Jan. 1924, qtd. in Dunbar 203.
5. Unpublished memoirs can be found in Moody, "My First Business Efforts"; and [Kellogg], "Mrs. Wm. Vaughn Moody" and "The Home Delicacies Association."

6. Records of Harriet Moody's Home Delicacies Association are held in the Harriet Brainard Moody Papers (Box 3), U of Chicago. On the Chicago Little Theatre, see Kramer 193.

7. Alice Corbin Henderson later wrote an account of the meeting for Olivia Dunbar Torrence. See Henderson.

8. Will Moody's love letters are published, heavily edited, in *Letters to Harriet.* The original letters are at the Huntington Library.

9. Banta discusses variations on the strong feminine ideal; see esp. chapters 11 and 12. On "female force," see Adams, *Mont-Saint-Michel and Chartres* and *The Education of Henry Adams.*

10. See Halpern on Will Moody's idealization of Harriet, who is figured as the female force in *The Fire-Bringer,* a verse drama, and in the poem "The Death of Eve" (Halpern 141–42); see also Brown 131–32. Harriet wrote summary notes, describing a verse drama planned by Will but never written, on the new spiritual awakening of Eve and return to the Garden ("In the unfinished trilogy" 2–3).

11. The sofa swing was significant, for Harriet's serious relations with Will began on an evening when she fell down an embankment and smashed her ankle so badly that doctors advised her to have the foot amputated. The psychological complexities of the incident are intriguing. Will's attachment to Harriet suggested maternal desire; his own mother had been an invalid, which, for a year, Harriet became (see Brown 132; and W. Moody, *Letters* 415). For her part, Harriet could not bear to be an invalid confined to a sickroom and so had the swing constructed. An unidentified newspaper article by Hi Simons, himself active in Chicago literary circles, describes dinner in Harriet Moody's drawing room.

12. See Dunbar 5; Harriet knew and admired Marian MacDowell (Mrs. Edward MacDowell), whose Colony she thought a "great enterprise." The two women cooperated in providing services to poets (Dunbar 206).

13. Mitgang has "black-hearted"; the original, at the University of Chicago, reads "black-heart."

14. "On Being an Editor" 5. A similar version of the account appears in Monroe's "Tagore in Chicago" and *Poet's Life* 320.

15. Rudnick describes the *mutterrecht,* as Mabel Dodge Luhan, and other turn-of-the-century women, enacted it. On the *mutterrecht,* Rudnick cites Green's study of the von Richthofen sisters; the phrase "Mother Postulate" is Max Eastman's (Rudnick xii). John Newkirk called Harriet a "tenth Muse" (Dec. 19, 1899).

16. Evidence of Harriet's close affiliations with women can be found throughout the Harriet Brainard Moody Papers, U of Chicago.

Works Cited

Adams, Henry. *The Education of Henry Adams.* Boston: Houghton Mifflin, 1918.

———. *Mont-Saint-Michel and Chartres.* Boston: Houghton Mifflin, 1913.

Albertine, Susan. "Self Found in the Breaking: The Life Writings of Harriet Strong." *biography: an interdisciplinary quarterly* 17.2 (1994): 161–86.

Atkinson, Eleanor B. "Le Petit Gourmet: A Bit of France in the Rush and Tumble of Chicago." Clipping from unidentified magazine. Harriet Brainard Moody Papers, U of Chicago.

Auerbach, Nina. "Engorging the Patriarchy." *Feminist Issues in Literary Scholarship.* Ed. Shari Benstock. Bloomington: Indiana UP, 1987. 150–60.

Banta, Martha. *Imaging American Women: Idea and Ideals in Cultural History.* New York: Columbia UP, 1987.

Beem, Marjory Oliver. "Cakes for the Bride and Bridegroom." *Ladies' Home Journal* Oct. 1929: n. pag. clipping. Harriet Brainard Moody Papers, U of Chicago.

Brown, Maurice F. *Estranging Dawn: The Life and Works of William Vaughn Moody.* Carbondale: Southern Illinois UP, 1973.

Brumberg, Joan Jacobs, and Nancy Tomes. "Women in the Professions: A Research Agenda for American Historians." *Reviews in American History* 10 (1982): 275–96.

Chilton, Carroll Brent. Letter to Harriet Moody. Nov. 28, [1913?]. Harriet Brainard Moody Papers, U of Chicago. By permission of the University of Chicago.

Darnton, Robert. "What Is the History of Books?" *Reading in America: Literature and Social History.* Ed. Cathy N. Davidson. Baltimore, MD: Johns Hopkins UP, 1989. 27–52.

Dunbar, Olivia Howard (Torrence). *A House in Chicago.* Chicago: U of Chicago P, 1947.

Frost, Robert. Letters to Harriet Moody. Aug. 12, 1917; Dec. 28, 1920; Feb. 21, [1922]; Mar. 30, 1926. Harriet Brainard Moody Papers, U of Chicago. By permission of the University of Chicago and Peter A. Gilbert, Trustee of the Robert Lee Frost Estate.

———. *Selected Letters of Robert Frost.* Ed. Lawrance Thompson. New York: Holt, Rinehart, and Winston, 1964.

Gale, Zona. Letter to Harriet Moody. Dec. 26, [1913?]. Harriet Brainard Moody Papers, U of Chicago. By permission of the University of Chicago.

Grade, Arnold, ed. *Family Letters of Robert and Elinor Frost.* Albany: State U of New York, 1972.

Green, Martin. *The von Richthofen Sisters: The Triumphant and the Tragic Modes of Love.* New York: Basic Books, 1974.

Halpern, Martin. *William Vaughn Moody.* New York: Twayne, 1964.

Henderson, Alice Corbin. Letter to Olivia Dunbar Torrence. Sept. 23, 1942. Alice Corbin Henderson Coll., Harry Ransom Humanities Research Center, U of Texas at Austin. By permission of the Alice Corbin Henderson Estate.

Jordan, Ellen. "The Christening of the New Woman: May 1894." *Victorian Newsletter* 63 (1983): 19–21.

[Kellogg, Edith.] "The Home Delicacies Association." Unpublished TS. Harriet Brainard Moody Papers, U of Chicago. By permission of the University of Chicago.

———. "Mrs. Wm. Vaughn Moody." Unpublished TS. Harriet Brainard Moody Papers, U of Chicago. By permission of the University of Chicago.

Kramer, Dale. *Chicago Renaissance: The Literary Life of the Midwest, 1900–1930.* New York: Appleton-Century, 1966.

Lindsay, Vachel. Letters to Harriet Moody. May 11, 1917; Apr. 28, 1918. Harriet Brainard Moody Papers, U of Chicago. By permission of the University of Chicago.

Markham, Edwin. Letter to Harriet Moody. Dec. 30, 1923. Harriet Brainard Moody Papers, U of Chicago. By permission of the University of Chicago and the Edwin Markham Estate.

Mitgang, Herbert, ed. *The Letters of Carl Sandburg.* New York: Harcourt, Brace, and World, 1968.

Monroe, Harriet. "News Notes." *Poetry* 40 (Apr. 1932): 53.

———. "On Being an Editor." Personal Papers of Harriet Monroe, U of Chicago. By permission of the University of Chicago and the Harriet Monroe Estate.

———. *A Poet's Life: Seventy Years in a Changing World.* New York: Macmillan, 1938.

———. "Tagore in Chicago." Personal Papers of Harriet Monroe, U of Chicago. By permission of the University of Chicago and the Harriet Monroe Estate.

Moody, Harriet Converse. "In the unfinished trilogy." Unpublished TS. Harriet Brainard Moody Papers, U of Chicago. By permission of the University of Chicago.

———. Letter to Harriet [Monroe]. Apr. 23, 1922. Edgar Lee Masters Papers, Harry Ransom Humanities Research Center, U of Texas at Austin.

———. *Mrs. William Vaughn Moody's Cook Book.* New York: Charles Scribner's Sons, 1931.

———. "My First Business Efforts." Unpublished TS. Harriet Brainard Moody Papers, U of Chicago. By permission of the University of Chicago.

Moody, William Vaughn. Letters to Harriet C. Brainard. June 2, 1902; July 16, 1902; Apr. 4, 1904; July 26, 1906; Aug. 2, 1906. William Vaughn Moody Coll., Huntington Library, San Marino, CA. By permission of the Huntington Library.

———. *Letters to Harriet.* Ed. Percy MacKaye. Boston: Houghton Mifflin, 1935.

———. *The Poems and Plays of William Vaughn Moody.* 2 vols. Boston: Houghton Mifflin, 1912.

Newkirk, John. Letter to Harriet Moody. Dec. 19, 1899. Harriet Brainard Moody Papers, U of Chicago. By permission of the University of Chicago.

Robinson, Edwin Arlington. Letters to Harriet Moody. Nov. 6, 1913; July 23, 1914. Harriet Brainard Moody Papers, U of Chicago. By permission of the University of Chicago.

———. *Selected Letters of Edwin Arlington Robinson.* Ed. Ridgely Torrence. New York: Macmillan, 1940.

Rudnick, Lois Palken. *Mabel Dodge Luhan: New Woman, New Worlds.* Albuquerque: U of New Mexico P, 1984.

Ruggles, Eleanor. *The West-Going Heart: A Life of Vachel Lindsay.* New York: Norton, 1959.

Sandburg, Carl. Letter to Harriet Moody. Sept. 8, 1921. Harriet Brainard Moody Papers, U of Chicago. By permission of the University of Chicago.

Simons, Hi. "Each Guest Gets a Table." Clipping from unidentified newspaper. Harriet Brainard Moody Papers, U of Chicago.

Stephens, James. Letter to Harriet Moody. Aug. 6, 1925. Harriet Brainard Moody Papers, U of Chicago. By permission of the University of Chicago.

Tagore, Rabindranath. Letters to Harriet Moody. Apr. 16, 1913; [Sept. 1913?]; Jan. 22, 1914; Feb. 18, 1915. Harriet Brainard Moody Papers, U of Chicago. By permission of the University of Chicago and S. Bhattacharya.

Thompson, Lawrance. *Robert Frost: The Years of Triumph, 1915–1938*. New York: Holt, Rinehart, and Winston, 1970.

Wilber, Susan. Review of *Mrs. William Vaughn Moody's Cookbook*. *The Chicagoan* May 1931: n. pag. clipping. Harriet Brainard Moody Papers, U of Chicago.

Winters, Yvor. Letter to Harriet Moody. Sept. 30, 1927. Harriet Brainard Moody Papers, U of Chicago. By permission of the University of Chicago.

7.

Form Follows Function:

The Construction of Harriet Monroe and *Poetry, A Magazine of Verse*

Ann Massa

Reviewing, for the *New Republic,* Harriet Monroe's posthumously published autobiography *A Poet's Life* (1938), William Carlos Williams commented, "She conceived a brilliant plan for the encouragement of the art of poetry in America. *Poetry, A Magazine of Verse,* will remain her greatest claim to distinction" (375). Monroe, essayist, art and architecture critic, experimental poet and playwright, had founded a magazine devoted solely to the publication and criticism of poetry, the first magazine of its kind in America. Excitingly and uniquely, *Poetry* was committed not to editorial whim but to an "Open Door" for "the best English verse which is being written today, regardless of where, by whom or under what theory of art it is written."[1] Nevertheless, Williams continued, "the most important part of her biography [*sic*] may possibly be the least interesting" (375). He was touched by the confessional intimacy of *A Poet's Life.* Monroe's text revealed a woman whose career was shaped not merely by her love of poetry, her determination to help put Chicago on the cultural map, and her ambition to make, somehow, a significant contribution to American literature, but also by a complex familial and sexual conditioning.

Unpublished materials expand and clarify the autobiography's hints at a combative and unhappy home in which Monroe reacted against a beautiful, sensuous, illiterate mother in favor of an intellectually dynamic and civic-minded father. Curious heterosexual relationships, with Scottish novelist Robert Louis Stevenson, Chicago architect John Root (Monroe's brother-in-law), and an unnamed third man, caused Monroe to conclude she was a failure in conventional female terms. Encouraged by her contacts with Chicago's impressive and diverse community of women, which ran the gamut from Jane Addams, lawyers, journalists, politicians and writers through Mrs. Potter Palmer, Monroe sought other forms of self-expression. Yet, if her career constituted an effective rejection of gender stereotyping, and it did, Harriet Monroe seemingly remained convinced, as she stated in *A Poet's Life,* that "moth-

7.1. Harriet Monroe,
1892, from *A Poet's
Life: Seventy Years in
a Changing World*
(New York: Macmillan,
1938).

erhood . . . has always seemed to me the grandest, most complete of all
human experiences" (58).

To write a confessional poem about Stevenson when she was sixty-six;
to lament a star-crossed love life in "The Spinster Tells Her Story" at sixty-
eight; to relive her emotions in frank and analytic detail in her autobiography in her seventies: clearly Harriet Monroe was conscious of her romantic
and sexual makeup and less than content with what she called "a spinster's
comparatively narrow lot." "Deprived of the love life's supreme fulfilment,"
she wrote, the spinster "tries to fulfil herself in other ways, and faculties
unused become gradually less insistent" (Monroe, *Poet's Life* 60). She herself
came nearest to this "supreme fulfilment" in the context of the extramarital
relationship described in *A Poet's Life* as a "hidden source of power, the
deepest and highest experience of my life . . . the rapture and agony of an
emotion shared in perfect sympathy and complete the incompleteness of
inevitable separation; a feeling which united for years a man and woman
who rarely saw each other, yet whom even death, when at last the blow
struck, was powerless to separate utterly—so long as the other lives and

remembers. A few lyrics and sonnets may have told the story—if not, it can never be told" (185–86). The sequence of nine sonnets, "To One in Exile," unpublished until 1935, sketches her mixture of dependence and frustration: "Your lips on mine restore life's arrogance" (Monroe, *Chosen Poems* 116). The 1890s lyric "I Love My Life" debates her willingness to give all and give up all, even her ambition to write, for her love:

> I love my life, but not too well
> To give it to thee like a flower,
> I love my life, but not too well
> To sing it note by note away.[2]

The opening line of "The Spinster Tells Her Story" reads, "Why have I never married, you may ask," and although the poem is not altogether specific about dates, it allows for the inference that her lover's death occurred close to 1912, the year she founded *Poetry*. It would be simplistic to call *Poetry* her lover or her child, but arguably the magazine filled a void and gave her life a kind of passionate center.

Issues of conditioning, gender, and role were at the forefront of Monroe's experience from her early years. Although she was well educated at the Moseley public school on Michigan Avenue and the Academy of the Visitation in Georgetown, Washington, D.C., she believed that her "most memorable and effective education" (Monroe, "Biography") came from the "free thinking, free roving, questioning mind of [Henry] Stanton Monroe," her father, who was both her idol and a genuinely interesting man. A doctor-farmer's son and a law graduate of Hobart College in Geneva, New York, in 1852 he left his practice to satisfy his curiosity about that "energetic growing town" Chicago, and to try his fortune there (Monroe, *Poet's Life* 4). The diversity of litigation in a city of polarized privilege and deprivation appealed strongly to him. One day he might act for a tycoon, another for a victim of the less scrupulous of that species, and yet another for a courtesan: for anyone, in fact, who could satisfy him that a legal or moral right was at stake. Integrity coupled with ability won him respect in Chicago's legal circles, and together with his boxing skills made him a hero of mammoth proportions to his imaginative daughter. In civil cases he sometimes acted as his own excellent amateur detective—so successfully that the Chicago Pinkerton agency tried to recruit him; sometimes he conducted his own physical defense. On one occasion, Monroe proudly noted, a "discredited witness [was] preparing to strike when he was landed on the side-walk from a blow in the forehead which shattered Papa's hand, so that one of the fingers is still a little crooked. . . . At such times Papa is as swift and agile as the forked lightning."[3]

Two factors in Stanton Monroe's life meant that a part-time career at least was necessary for any of the Monroe girls who did not marry. The first was the Chicago fire of 1871, in which he lost his office premises and a valuable law library; the second his subsequent refusal of a partnership in an eminent firm of lawyers in New York City. A man of social conscience, a reforming Chicagoan, he chose to act more for the needy and less for the affluent; he increasingly forgot, or forbore, to bill his clients. It seemed to Monroe that he never regretted his commitment. As a realist, a progressive, and a humanist he could not exchange the actuality of Chicago, the sometimes brutal power that abused but proved human ingenuity, for what he saw as the artificiality of the East. He relished the vindication of seeing "the city of his early choice grow into a metropolis" (Monroe, *Poet's Life* 21). Monroe sustained his commitment to Chicago through journalistic campaigns for the city beautiful and through *Poetry,* propaganda for the city cultural. She demonstrated her commitment to "the people" through her work at Hull House, her agit-prop poems—"A Workman's Song"; "The Working Girls' Song"; "The Shadow-Child"; "The Sweaters' Lament"—and through her support for such populist poets as Lindsay, Masters, and Sandburg.

Monroe did not admire her mother. While Stanton was widely read and interested in all the arts, Martha Monroe was almost illiterate. Her widowed and impoverished mother thought boys' education mattered, but not girls', and kept Martha from school to help with housework and with raising her brothers and sisters. Stanton fell in love with Martha's lustrous brown eyes, her beautifully rounded figure, her warmth, and at first saw no problems in the intellectual gulf between them. After their engagement he enrolled her in school; but he did not have the heart to send her back when she confessed her misery at being the oldest pupil in her class, and the marriage went ahead. "Manifestly, their tastes were not alike and it might have been wiser to break the engagement" (Monroe, *Poet's Life* 8), Monroe commented; for it seemed to her that her parents had nothing but a physical compatibility. "He had a quick temper and was careless and disorderly in his habits; and she was thoughtless, impatient and wholly unaware that it is a woman's business to manage her man without his suspecting it, and make the rough places smooth for him. . . . They lived more or less at cross-purposes" (Monroe, *Poet's Life* 23). Martha even blunted her own power to attract: "She possessed no trace of coquetry, and her intuitions were weak, especially as to the nature and moods of the opposite sex" (Monroe, *In Memory* 7). Stanton loved natural beauty and hated the distorting fashions that frizzed and crimped the rich, wavy hair of his wife, her greatest beauty. As for her mother's clothes, which were equally in vogue and unflattering, Monroe remembered that "all these displays of fashion were an agony to Stanton, but he did not know what to do about it. However, every new bonnet brought a crisis, with tides of wrath rolling high, and Mother prostrate under them, submerged in tears" (Monroe, *Poet's Life* 16–17). Martha's incapacity to break fashion's decrees riled Stanton, and perhaps inclined Monroe, for whom her father could do little wrong, both to query accepted forms and to show, when she grew up, that she was a leader, not a follower.

Her parents' uneasy relationship almost certainly made her wary of marriage. From the age of five she began to understand and not merely to observe "the continual drama" (Monroe, *Poet's Life* 16). *In Memory of Martha Mitchell Monroe,* a memoir which Monroe wrote and had privately published after Martha's death in 1892, was more critique than tribute. Martha emerged as tactless if honest, self-pitying if warm, and full of grudges. Significantly, the memoir caused no rifts; apparently the whole family shared Monroe's feelings. Many years later when she sent her draft autobiography to her sister for comment, Lucy criticized the section beginning, "my father's history was a tragedy . . . the most thrilling of any I remember" (Monroe, *Poet's Life* 22) as "not vivid enough."[4] She had no criticism to make of Monroe's unflattering picture of their mother, which imagined such symptomatic scenes as "one dinner when my mother impatiently sent back her plate twice to the carver for the particular cut she wanted; she got it, but I was frightened at the expression on his face. . . . [Father] narrowly escaped throwing her plate across the table [and] . . . she dissolved in tears" (Monroe, *Poet's Life* 26).

For the Monroe children, one productive result of their father's frustrating marriage was that he turned to the arts for compensation: "He took refuge in beautiful books, he even patronized the early art dealers and bought paintings. Before the Fire our house was cluttered with books, and the next year, in spite of heavy losses, he hired an architect to make the place over and add a real library with high black-walnut bookcases fitting its four walls." He and the children were "crowding in and taking possession" of the library. For them, but not for Martha Monroe, who felt excluded and jealous, it was "a room to live in happily, to talk and dream in" (Monroe, *Poet's Life* 17). Here Monroe began to read more voraciously than ever: Shakespeare and Shelley, Dickens and Thackeray, Byron and Scott, and Shakespeare again. She was taken to see "every new play of any importance and every wandering star" (Monroe, *Poet's Life* 37) who came to Chicago, and in later years recalled that her "approach to great poetry . . . was through the theater . . . our way of sailing to Byzantium, and I could not have been more than six or eight when Edwin Booth and the other Shakespearean actors first took me there. Their utterance of the richly rhymed verse was honey on the tongue for me, and it sent me to the printed page whence I could pluck out the lines, and learn some of them by heart, and make them sound their fateful music in my enchanted ears as I said them over to Lake Michigan or to the willow tree in our back yard" (Monroe, "Editorial").

From such experiences and from the encouragement of her Georgetown English teacher, Sister Paulina, Monroe began to specify the nature of a longstanding general ambition. "From earliest childhood I used to tell myself and God that I was to be 'great and famous.'" Now she wanted "to be a great poet, a great playwright" (Monroe, *Poet's Life* 55), though she also proposed, half-jokingly, to study law ("how would Papa like to have a second H. S. Monroe in the profession?").[5] But her literary ambition was not elitist. "Poetry is in the heart of the race. . . . When that poetry comes, it will be heard inevitably in the play-house, for the play-house is the people's house of dreams. . . . See," she admonished herself, "see that you make ready the house of dreams. See that you welcome all attempts of our poets, however slight and experimental, to interpret there . . . the beauty of our time" (Monroe, "House of Dreams"). Ironically, the role she saw for herself and finally enacted in *Poetry* owed something to the fact that theater was Martha Monroe's one cultural interest: "There she need fear no demand to enter the arena. There she could watch and feed her imagination." Monroe's ultimate justification of "theatre" was that "for thousands of men and women the theatre is the only place where they live in the imagination" (Monroe, *In Memory* 10).

Concurrently with the formation of Monroe's literary ambition, she was being shaped into the single woman whose status facilitated a full-time career; though, if she is to be believed, that career was no substitute for marriage and, even more importantly, for motherhood. "The Spinster Tells Her Story" ends:

> . . . loneliness is difficult—
> Some other woman's child may bring
> A pang too bitter to be borne.
> Nothing can heal that stabbing sting.[6]

"Every woman so honored makes her journey to Bethlehem . . . and brings forth miraculously a divine infant," she wrote of childbirth in 1923 (Monroe, "Nativity" 157); and at the end of her life she still asserted that "motherhood . . . has always seemed to me the grandest, most complete of all human experiences in its combination of anguish and ecstasy both physical and spiritual" (Monroe, *Poet's Life* 58). Perhaps William Carlos Williams was right when he described her as consistently "full of repressions, dreading the genus male," but her writings suggest a real sense of deprivation in being childless (Williams 376).

Clearly she was as sexually aware as she was sexually timid. "Unconsciously I gave up the problem [of courtship and marriage] and retired from the great game which I had no talent for; indeed I was even a rather dull spectator, quite unaware of its fine parts," she wrote in *A Poet's Life* (61), and added, "I was a girl wholly ungifted and uneducated in the art of sex" (57). Her adolescence had been punctuated by "unaccountable" physical sensations, which at the time she had put down as digestive upsets; not unlikely in view of the overeating which went on in middle-class midwestern homes at that period: breakfasts of chops, potatoes, and buckwheat cakes;

"heavily delicious lunches" and suppers. But in retrospect she believed it had been her ignorance about sex, and her painful, bewildering, orgasmic sensations—"deep upward surgings of the blood, tidal waves of life not to be controlled or explained"—that led to "illnesses" variously and inaccurately diagnosed as lassitude or pernicious anemia:

> If ever a child or young girl was sex-inhibited that was my fate, shut up as I was in an impenetrable shell of self-consciousness. The subject was secretly whispered around by older girls. Boys became mysterious, inhuman, remote repositories of dread whom I could never meet on simple and natural terms. If involuntary emotional feelers rose to their allure I crushed them back as shameful, pernicious and would rather have died than confess them. Thus I always played wrong in the game of sex and ran away emotionally from boyfriends; thus through the flowering years I grew up afraid of love. (Monroe, *Poet's Life* 35–36)

Such confused sexual consciousness, a romantic vision of marriage to a major man, her adoration of her father, her observation of a marriage that failed in spite of sexual compatibility—her parents were "united only by the close tie of flesh"—seem to have made her attractive to and attracted by ineligibly older men (Monroe, *Poet's Life* 23). Her first experience of "masculine allure" came with a friend of her father's (Monroe, *Poet's Life* 54). Two consistent suitors, Chicago businessman Joseph Russell Jones (she wrote unpublished love poems to him) and Washington judge Martin Ferdinand Morris (in 1903 he was still hoping she would marry him), were both born in 1823.[7] Monroe was born in 1860. Her complex of attitudes determined that the kind of men for whom she formed deep emotional attachments were inaccessible and unattainable.

Robert Louis Stevenson is a case in point. In April 1886 she wrote to him of her pleasure in his books, particularly *The Arabian Nights,* with its middle-aged and masterful hero, Prince Florizel of Bohemia. (The boy heroes of Stevenson's adventures were not for her: "Boy lovers could not climb past zero," she admitted in "To R.L.S.") He answered, and asked for a photograph; she sent back a poem as well. In June his photograph arrived. After eighteen months of only mildly flirtatious correspondence on his part—he often mentioned his wife in his letters—he came to New York en route to the South Seas; she came up from Chicago to meet him. She was "shattered"; it was a "horror"; a horror which initially stemmed from her shocked sense of Stevenson but which ultimately stemmed from her shocked sense of self.[8] For the invalid Stevenson, in the flesh, was to her unvirile, prematurely aged, a man whose body bore no relation to the attractive compelling personality of their correspondence and his books; not "my hero" but "Death's invalid," she wrote in a later poem ("To R.L.S."). Recalling their relationship in

A Poet's Life, she still showed bitterness about the way in which she had
bought a flowery spring hat specially for the occasion, arranged her hair
under it with unusual care, and rouged her cheeks. She was still cruel, to
herself as well as Stevenson, about their encounter at St. Stephen's Hotel,
11th Street. Stevenson had called on her, but she had been out; she returned
the visit to his hotel with an anticipation which quickly turned into foreboding,
and then into dread:

> The room was so large and dark, with high blinded windows shuttering
> out the sun, that I could scarcely see the tall, thin fellow—portentously tall,
> ominously thin—that was faintly outlined against the opposite wall. As he
> advanced to greet me the shock was terrific,—my romance collapsed like a
> house of cards. Not this man for me—this ghostly creature of the curved-in
> sloping shoulders, the body wasted and shrunken to the width of the mold-
> ing behind him, and the voice, when he spoke, hardly more audible than a
> whisper. In that stark moment never a thought of his genius, his growing
> fame, the long heroic fight against disease, of the letters he had magnani-
> mously written from his sick-bed to a faraway foolish young girl, never a
> generous emotion of pity at finding my hero so ill; just the tragic shock of
> finality of knowing that something beautiful was tarnished and gone.
> (Monroe, *Poet's Life* 72)

Years later she assessed the long-term significance of the meeting harshly
and sadly. She felt it showed her incapacity to love in any effective and
unselfish sense: it made her doubt not just her sexuality but her womanliness. "A truly feminine woman would have felt her heart warming instead of
turning to ice," she wrote condemningly in *A Poet's Life* (76); and in "To
R.L.S." she set out her cruelty to him:

> Poor sufferer!—you must have known
> What shock had made me pitiless.
> Love should grow soft to raise and bless
> The stricken—mine stiffened like a stone.

Stevenson had no real influence on Monroe's intellectual development
or her choice of career; he never read anything of hers except the 1885
poem to himself. But if the encounter between them was as crucial as she
was to claim, their "relationship" contributed significantly to her fatalistic belief that she was to be denied full sexual identity and must seek fulfillment
elsewhere. John Root was to influence both Monroe's intellectual development and her choice of career.

From the first year of their acquaintance, 1879, Monroe regularly entered (and later indexed) John Root's sayings and doings in her diaries: when

he came to dinner, what jokes he told, what he gave her for her birthday (December 1881, a book of sonnets), whom he entertained (March 1883, Oscar Wilde). She transcribed his philosophical, political, and artistic beliefs. She had also to describe her second disappointment at not becoming Mrs. John Root. On the first occasion "my hushed heart cried, 'I am yours / If you ever want me—to the end.' / We talked an hour, and then I learned / He was affianced to my friend" (Monroe, "Spinster"). When Minnie Walker died, Root proposed to Monroe's elder sister Dora. Monroe's diaries poignantly render Minnie's death and funeral, the new engagement, and her role as confidante to the couple when Mrs. Walker protested Root's swift marriage.

In 1891, aged forty-one, Root died a tragically early death from pneumonia, soon after his appointment as chief consulting architect for the Chicago World's Fair, planned for 1892 to mark the four-hundredth anniversary of Columbus's discovery. Monroe had talked so much and so widely about him to her friends and acquaintances that in the weeks after his death she received almost as many expressions of sympathy for *her* bereavement as if she were Root's widow. In New York Elizabeth Stoddard clipped the announcement of his death from the *Times* and wrote Monroe: "I know what trouble you are in, for it is not so long ago you wrote me so enthusiastically of him." Monroe's elderly admirer and sponsor, poet and critic E. C. Stedman, who had met Root through her, was "inexpressibly grieved by the sudden taking-off in his superb prime of manhood and achievement, of your gifted brother-in-law." Vague literary acquaintances like J. W. Bridgman, editor of the *Western Magazine,* and F. D. Sherman, of Sherman, French & Co., wrote to commiserate with her. Eugene Field sent condolences to Monroe as well as to Dora Root. It was Monroe, not Dora Root, who in 1893 took up the cudgels over what she considered to be an unflattering portrait of Root in the *National Cyclopedeia,* "a coarse little woodcut not worth a dollar . . . so false to the photograph from which it was taken and such a libel upon the man it was supposed to stand for."[9] Proprietorial feelings were aroused in both sisters over the question of royalties on Monroe's *John Wellborn Root* (1896), which Dora expected to share. Harriet Monroe fought unsuccessfully to patent her unique understanding of Root and to own the essential man. She was as proprietorial with her younger sister Lucy's husband, William J. Calhoun, U. S. Minister to China. On visits, in articles, and in her sponsorship of imagism, she appropriated the role of ambassadorial partner in her propagation of Chinese culture.

Root's death had an ironically creative effect on Monroe's life. It led her to write her "Columbian Ode" to celebrate the World's Fair to be held in Chicago, 1892–1893, a poem which in style and theme she intended to be uniquely New World and which would include a central reference to Root, whose death, she felt, had deprived Chicago and Columbus of an outstanding architectural tribute. Root's partner, Daniel Burnham, oversaw the construction of an imitative, neoclassical city; Root had wanted the Fair to put over "the dominant note in our [American] civilization . . . its youth, its newness, crudeness . . . creative energies . . . sumptuous conquering enthusiasm" (Monroe, *Root* 243). These qualities were manifested by a brazen Harriet Monroe as she sold the Fair's authorities a 2,200-line verse epic, persuaded them to have it set to music, and to have parts of it performed on opening day by elocutionist, massed choirs, and orchestra. "It was during the struggle for the Ode that she learned and showed her winning qualities: determination, entrepreneurial flair, a commitment to Chicago's culture, and the ability to enhance it. Then, and again in 1911 [soliciting support for *Poetry*] she was able to sell her sponsors two products: poetry and herself" (Massa, "Columbian Ode" 69).

As well as bringing about a dry run for *Poetry,* Root's death led Monroe to write his biography, a finely illustrated volume, which, whatever its emotional bias as a personal text, in professional terms does its subject justice and constitutes the only place where many of Root's notes, lectures, and other writings can now be found. This part of the text demonstrates Monroe's substantial cultural indebtedness to Root. Her parallel articulation of his ideas on the arts and America is striking. Root's argument ran:

> Now, in America we are free of artistic traditions. Our freedom begets license, it is true. We do shocking things; we produce works of architecture, sculpture, and painting which are wholly, irremediably bad; we try crude experiments which result in disaster. Yet somewhere in this mass of ungoverned energies lies the principle of life. A new spirit of beauty is being developed and perfected, and even now its first achievements are beginning to delight us. This is not the old thing made over; it is new. It springs out of the past but is not tied to it; it studies the traditions, but it is not enslaved by them. It is doing original work, and it will do more. (Monroe, *Root* 192)

Monroe wrote two comparable editorials on "The New Beauty" in 1913, and echoed Root (and later Pound's "Make-It-New" philosophy) in the introduction to her *New Poetry Anthology.* "The significant movement [in the arts] is toward greater freedom of spirit and form. . . . As part of such a movement, even the most extravagant experiments, the most radical innovation is necessary" (Monroe and Henderson, eds. xlv). Root believed that "if architecture was to give a vital answer to the demands of modern life, it must not merely repeat the formulae of the past" (Monroe, *Root* 61); Monroe recorded that "the battle which *Poetry*, from its first issue, fought . . . was for a more vital relation with the poet's own time and place" and asserted "modern cathedrals are second rate—mere imitations—I would rather build a first rate skyscraper" (Monroe, *Poet's Life* 362, 397). "Art attains its full expression only by following the natural law of utility or fitness," Root argued, anticipating

Louis Sullivan's influential dictum "Form Follows Function" (Monroe, *Root* 207). Monroe took up Root's point when she wrote of another of *Poetry's* battles "for the freedom of the creative spirit in the authentic and individual achievement of beauty through the fit expression of its ideas" (Monroe, *Poet's Life* 217). After Root's death she acceded to Sullivan's advice.[10]

Chicago's women as well as Chicago's architects provided fertile ground for the germination of Monroe's ambition.[11] Female talent proliferated. This was the era when Chicago was its women, some of whom gave tangible and ostentatious expression to the city's titanic affluence. Mrs. (Harold) Edith Rockefeller McCormick, one of Chicago's great eccentrics, who in her last years devoted herself to planning a new town, Edithton, solely for millionaires, provides a good example of ludicrous hauteur and ceremony. She was run a close second in social bravura by Mrs. (Potter) Bertha Honoré Palmer, the wife of a multimillionaire property manipulator. Bertha Palmer considered her time so valuable—and other people's worth so little—that twenty-seven flunkies screened visitors and their cards before they were admitted to her presence in the Palmer mansion, an imitation Rhenish castle. From a world famous collection of jade to a Louis XVI bed ten feet high, Mrs. Palmer indulged her whims and tastes to the full. Such was the splendor of her collection of diamonds that if she arrived (intentionally?) late at the opera or the theater, the blazing sight of her had literally been known to stop the show. But these were also women of culture and informed patrons of the arts. Mrs. McCormick financed the Chicago Opera and amassed a fine collection of medieval tapestries. Mrs. Palmer made one of America's first collections of impressionist paintings and was an articulate and well-read propagandist for women's rights. Such women were among the first guarantors of *Poetry*.

Monroe's friend Jane Addams was even more extraordinary. Taking as her model London's settlement house Toynbee Hall, she founded Hull House, on Halsted Street, a five-mile slum area, teeming with Germans, Russians, Italians, and Poles, saloons, pawnshops, brothels, poverty, despair, and degradation. She gave the immigrants nurseries and kindergartens; coffee bars and courses in home economics; tuition in the language and customs of America. Jane Addams's work attracted as residents and associates of Hull House a group of remarkable women who became some of the first practically qualified American sociologists: experts in the needs of Chicago and the national urban sector, they put pressure on the authorities to remedy urban problems. Louise de Koven Bowen bullied the Chicago council into setting up juvenile courts; Dr. Alice Hamilton's industrial medicine practice helped her contribute to the diagnosis of typhoid fever and to preventive industrial hygiene; Julia Lathrop and Florence Kelley worked crucially for the abolition of sweatshops and child labor. The Hull House women consolidated their pioneering work by coaching those on the shop floor to organize; one such "trainee," Mary Anderson, became the head of the Women's

Bureau in the Federal Department of Labor. These women found time to encourage Harriet in the enterprise of *Poetry* and to solicit from her "propaganda" poems. Harriet in turn gave of her time, money, and furniture to Hull House, while in times of stress and decision both she and Jane Addams would consult the sympathetic and radical Mary Wilmarth, a leading suffragist whose daughter Anna married Harold Ickes.

In the professions, too, women were making history. Chicago could boast doctors like Sarah Hackett Stevenson, member of the International Gynecological Society, the Pan-American Medical Association, the Chicago Medical Society, and the Illinois State Board of Health, Professor of Obstetrics at Northwestern University, and consultant to innumerable hospitals; Frances Dickinson, an outstanding ophthalmic surgeon and the first woman member of the International Medical Congress of Physicians and Surgeons. Educator Ella Flagg Young was in effective partnership with John Dewey. In law there was Catherine Waite, a practicing lawyer as well as editor of the *Chicago Legal Times* and author of two books on Mormon society; Catherine McCulloch, a national suffrage leader; and Myra Bradwell, who in 1869 sought, and was denied, the right to practice law, but who then founded and edited the *Chicago Legal News,* such a comprehensive and accurate set of weekly law reports that the Illinois legislature, which had denied her the right to practice, passed an act making copies of the *News* containing the laws of the state and the opinions of the state Supreme Court admissible evidence of such laws and opinions. By 1882 she got the Illinois legislature to grant to all persons, irrespective of sex, freedom to select and practice any profession. She was surely an inspiration to Harriet Monroe the journalist and suffragist who had once thought of being a lawyer. Mrs. M. R. Wallace, founder-organizer of the Chicago Industrial School for Girls, extended the sphere of women to finance and property; so did Mrs. Matilda Carse, who turned the Women's Christian Temperance Union Press into a company, floated its shares on the Chicago exchange, and raised money to have John Root build a Woman's Temple, a large office building owned and managed by the WCTU. Its president, Frances Willard, commanded in the Union a million-strong female pressure group which was also becoming a force in third-party politics. Militant black women, most notably Ida B. Wells, were campaigning against racial discrimination; Fannie Barrier Williams, too, campaigned for the representation of black women at the World's Fair (Massa, "Black Women").

There was another species of talented and articulate women in Chicago at this time: women writers. Few of them were trying to give Chicago soul, not consciously at any rate, though the incidence of talent did just that. Journalists like Margaret Sullivan (young Harriet Monroe's patron), editorial writer, and literary editor of the *Chicago Herald,* and Elia Peattie, literary editor of the *Chicago Tribune,* later a contributor to *Poetry;* founder-proprietors like Helen Starrett and Antoinette von Wakeman, who edited their own weekly news/literary journals (Did they influence the often topical content of *Poetry* editorials?): first and foremost these were self-assertive, professionally ambitious women. Novelist Edith Wyatt, one of three members of *Poetry*'s first advisory board, did not feel "literature" lent itself to causes and so wrote about democracy as a free-lance journalist. Art was art, not a message; an end in itself, not a means to an end: an attitude typified by Margaret Anderson, who, in the summer of 1911, camped on Chicago's Lake Front in a tent lined with oriental rugs, and planned a future of intellectual self-indulgence. Anderson was making the kind of proposition that the city could not countenance: a magazine that only a tiny minority could comprehend, and a permissive magazine at that. The *Little Review* could only reinforce its critique by leaving Chicago for New York in 1916.

Mary Borden the novelist also left Chicago, to settle in England; Mary Austin went to California, where she studied Indian dialects, translated Indian songs and poems, a number of which appeared in *Poetry*, and used the West coast as the setting for her fiction and the subject of her history. A few women writers did stay in the city, and some of them wrote about it: two sisters from Harriet's social world, Margaret Ayer Barnes, novelist and playwright, who won the 1938 Pulitzer Prize for *Year of Grace,* the story of a Chicago matron caught up in the Jazz Age, and Janet Ayer Fairbank, who set topical novels in Chicago. Mary Catherwood came to Chicago from Ohio via New York, and spun a series of historical romances about the city.

As a prolific minor poet and an obscure dramatist, Harriet Monroe was a member of the women's literary community, and she was heartened by the liveliness of that community. But she differed crucially from other members in that her own artistic fulfillment was inextricable from her sense of altruistic citizenship; she believed in art for society's sake, and particularly for Chicago's. Like the editors of the *Little Review,* she refused to prostitute art to Chicago's narcissistic demands; but unlike them she was prepared slowly, tactfully, deviously if necessary, to educate Chicago to the arts; to transform the city's complacent knowledge that it fascinated writers as subject-matter into an understanding of the intrinsic value of art, which would develop into a response to its contents and an interest in its forms. She undertook what was, in its own way, a task almost as difficult as Jane Addams's: to touch not Chicagoans' consciences but their consciousness of the relationship between civilization, maturity, and culture. She attempted to make out a permanent place in the city's priorities for the visual arts and the written word. She was an integral, conditioned part of a city where, in her own words, "among the women as well as the men, one finds the same love of conquest, the same desire to attain the impossible, for nothing is impossible" (Monroe, "Chicago").

In 1893 Monroe completed a thirty-six page unpublished essay on Chicago. She surveyed the history and speculated on the psychology. "Why should growing ambition fix upon a swamp for its seat of power?" she asked, and answered, "because thus it was left to the heroic, the imaginative in the westward marching army of American youth, to become the founders of Chicago. The place has been called the very seat and center of materialism—never was characterization more obtuse. The young men, wanderers from many states, who settled here during the thirties and forties, were inspired by an epic love of conquest." (A fine distinction, this between materialism and conquest.) Inside every speculator was an individual whose spirituality developed into culture consciousness, who made "at first humble efforts to keep in touch with the world's thought—collecting books, building theaters and opera houses, founding literary societies." And so, Monroe announced, climactically, "gradually appreciation ceased to be a matter of individual taste and became a public duty" (Monroe, "Chicago"). She idealized Chicago as "doer and dreamer / And doer of the dream" (Monroe, "Chicago dreams").

It is difficult to overestimate the importance of Chicago—the reality, the idea—in shaping the Harriet Monroe who founded *Poetry* in large part to demonstrate Chicago's cultural identity and who was able to found *Poetry* only because, by 1911, a hundred Chicagoans agreed to put up a total of $5,000 a year for five years. Monroe had already unsuccessfully tried to persuade one Chicagoan, George Armour, to found an experimental theater in Chicago.[12] By 1911 she had revised her career plans. Her 1903 volume of plays, *The Passing Show,* had fallen flat. In Chicago, playwrights outnumbered theaters and Monroe had competed unsuccessfully with Ben Hecht, Floyd Dell, Francis Hackett, William Vaughn Moody, and George Ade. Except for *The Troll's Holiday,* which she wrote for Hull House children, only one of her plays, the unpublished *Man-Eagle,* was performed, by the Chicago Theater Society. She had fared better with such experimental free verse as "The Hotel," "The Telephone," and "The Turbine," which had been prominently published in *Time* and the *Atlantic.* However, her status in Chicago depended less on her creative writing than on her entrepreneurial image and her vibrant civic identity as the *Tribune*'s art and architecture critic since 1909. She had worked intermittently as a journalist for the *Tribune,* the *American,* the *Evening Post,* the *Evening Examiner,* and the *Herald* since 1888. Now she expanded her brief to review not just major exhibits but also to argue, for instance, about the locations of new shops and apartments; the design of household objects; the unoriginal architecture of the University of Chicago (and, in 1913, the highly original art of the Armory Show).

To make her pitch to potential sponsors, she had to downplay her outrage that she, Ezra Pound, and other new poets found it so difficult to get published in America. Instead, she emphasized her high Chicagoan profile:

"I felt that I should be well enough known in my home town to have won my right to a hearing" (Monroe, *Poet's Life* 207). The Swifts, Palmers, McCormicks, Pullmans, Glessners, Kohlsaats, and Blaines signed up; so did less well-known bank presidents, wholesale grocers, and paint manufacturers. Their conservative taste as well as their financial support kept the magazine afloat: they counteracted any tendency Monroe may have had to publish only the avant-garde, too specialized to appeal to sufficient sponsors and readers.

But entrepreneurial common sense, unflagging public relations campaigns, and Monroe's personal popularity with the sponsors could not of themselves have sustained *Poetry*:

> Two other elements were necessary for that: a supply of significant poetry and an effective editorial policy. Both were forthcoming. Her researches and canvassing, Ezra Pound's contacts (he was *Poetry*'s foreign editor from 1912 to 1917), and, quickly, *Poetry* itself, generated a list of contributors which by 1920 included Eliot, Stevens, Williams, Frost, Sandburg, Masters, Lindsay, Amy Lowell and Marianne Moore. By 1912 Harriet Monroe herself had matured in her discrimination of poetry and her ability to write it. Her lectures on poetry at the Newberry Library, her columns for the Chicago papers and her experimental free verse demonstrated an informed and enthusiastic commitment to new poetry. She was equally determined in each issue, or at least over a year's run of issues, to publish a representative mixture of poems [alongside William Carlos Williams the "Victorian lyrics" of Clark Ashton Smith; as well as T. S. Eliot the "old fashioned" poetry of Madison Cawein (Monroe, *Poet's Life* 273, 295)]. As editor (from the first monthly issue of *Poetry* in October 1912 until her death, aged seventy-five, in 1936), she infuriated many with the catholicity of her taste. . . . But in retrospect, the wisdom and the skill of her policy and her choice proved manifest. . . . *Poetry* has always published poems, not poets; *Poetry* has survived, while more partisan publications have gone under. (Massa, "Columbian Ode" 68–69)

A recent editor of *Poetry* has argued that its conception was "not propitious. *Poetry*'s founder editor, Harriet Monroe . . . was at the time of the first issue a strong-minded literary spinster . . . virtually unknown outside her native Chicago" (Hine and Parisi xxxv). The very elements here so chauvinistically diminished made for Monroe's success. She was irresistibly determined, compulsively literary, thoughtfully single, and appreciatively known in pragmatic Chicago. She constructed a form that evolved from and expressed her culture, place, and sexual history. Form follows function, Sullivan argued; "it must evolve from and express the environment in addition to expressing its particular form" ("Louis Sullivan"). The dictum holds good for the complexly appropriate evolution of Harriet Monroe.

Notes

1. Editorial, Nov. 1912, quoted in Harriet Monroe, *A Poet's Life* 243.
2. Harriet Monroe Personal Papers. Regenstein Library, University of Chicago. Hereafter HMPP. All quotations from HMPP are made by permission of the University of Chicago and the Harriet Monroe Estate.
3. Monroe, "Notebook of Anecdotes, Conversations etc." See also Wilkie 75.
4. Marginal comment on Monroe, "A Poet's Life," autograph draft 1, HMPP.
5. Monroe, letter to family, [1879].
6. Monroe, "Spinster." Twenty unpublished short stories and many of her plays address issues of marriage, love, extramarital love.
7. Monroe, "Do I Love thee still the same?"; Lucy Monroe, letter to Harriet Monroe.
8. Monroe, letter to family, June 3, 1888.
9. Monroe, letter to James T. White & Co. Many drafts of this letter exist.
10. Sullivan, letters to Monroe.
11. For details about the women cited in the next five paragraphs, see James et al.
12. Armour, letter to Harriet Monroe.

Works Cited

Armour, George. Letter to Harriet Monroe. Aug. 2, 1905. Harriet Monroe Personal Papers. Regenstein Library, U of Chicago. Hereafter cited as HMPP.

Hine, Daryl, and Joseph Parisi, eds. *The* Poetry *Anthology, 1912–77.* Boston: Houghton Mifflin, 1978.

James, Edward T., Janet Wilson James, and Paul S. Boyer, eds. *Notable American Women, 1607–1950: A Biographical Dictionary.* 3 vols. Cambridge, MA: Belknap P of Harvard UP, 1971.

Massa, Ann. "Black Women in the 'White City.'" *Journal of American Studies* 8 (1974): 319–37.

———. "The Columbian Ode and *Poetry, A Magazine of Verse:* Harriet Monroe's Entrepreneurial Triumphs." *Journal of American Studies* 20 (1986): 52–69.

Monroe, Harriet. "Biography." [1917]. HMPP.

———. "Chicago." [1893]. HMPP.

———. "Chicago dreams under the sun." HMPP.

———. *Chosen Poems.* New York: Macmillan, 1935.

———. "Do I Love thee still the same?" HMPP.

———. "Editorial." *Poetry* 39 (1930–31): 288–89.

———. "House of Dreams." HMPP.

———. "I Love My Life." HMPP.

———. *In Memory of Martha Mitchell Monroe.* Chicago: privately published, 1892. HMPP.

———. *John Wellborn Root.* Boston: Houghton Mifflin, 1896.

————. Letter to family. [1879]. HMPP.

————. Letter to family. June 3, 1888. HMPP.

————. Letter to James T. White & Co. Feb. 11, 1893. HMPP.

————. "The Nativity in Art." *Poetry* 23 (1923–24): 157.

————. "Notebook of Anecdotes, Conversations etc." Vol. I [Aug. 1882]. HMPP.

————. Personal Papers [HMPP]. Regenstein Library, U of Chicago.

————. "A Poet's Life." Autograph draft 1. HMPP.

————. *A Poet's Life.* New York: Macmillan, 1938.

————. "The Spinster Tells Her Story." HMPP.

————. "To R.L.S." Mar. 14, 1921. HMPP.

————, and Alice Corbin Henderson, eds. *The New Poetry.* 1917. New York: Macmillan, 1932.

Monroe, Lucy. Letter to Harriet Monroe. May 22, 1917. HMPP.

Stedman, E. C. Letter to Harriet Monroe. Jan. 19, 1891. HMPP.

Stoddard, Elizabeth. Letter to Harriet Monroe. Feb. 11, 1891. HMPP.

"Louis Sullivan." *Encyclopedia Britannica.* 1989 ed.

Sullivan, Louis. Letters to Harriet Monroe. Apr. 5, 10, 1905. HMPP.

Williams, William Carlos. "Harriet Monroe." *New Republic* 94 (Apr. 26, 1938): 375–76.

Wilkie, F. B. *Sketches and Notes of the Chicago Bar.* Chicago: Henry A. Sumner, 1872.

8.

Ida B. Wells-Barnett:

About the Business of Agitation

Barbara Diggs-Brown

> Agitation, contentions, ceaseless unrest, constant aspiring—a
> race so moved must prevail. There is no half-way ground
> between right and wrong. This one or the other must obtain
> and prevail.
>
> Mental inertia is death. Indifferent acquiescence in
> wrong is death. Tamed submission to outrage is death. Agita-
> tion, constant protesting, all these standing up to be counted
> to be heard, or to be knocked down, this spirit breeds re-
> spect and dulls the edge of tyranny.
>
> —T. Thomas Fortune, editor,
> *The Globe*, New York, August 18, 1883

With these words, T. Thomas Fortune, African-American editor of the New
York *Globe,* characterized the editorial philosophy of the early black press
in the United States.[1] He shared the belief of many African-American journalists that African Americans had to agitate to ensure the freedoms so long
denied them. His challenge to his people for agitation and defiance in the
face of outrage did not go unheeded.

Ida B. Wells-Barnett was an African-American publisher, journalist,
and crusader who took up the clarion call for agitation. Through her entrepreneurial skills, journalistic talents, and activism, she campaigned successfully against lynching, one of America's most heinous crimes against African
Americans. An aggressive and courageous activist for the human rights of
her race and gender, Wells-Barnett knew the value of the newspaper editorial and worked to possess the freedom of expression that only print culture
could provide.

As the publisher and editor of four newspapers, she adeptly combined
business sense with journalistic talents to support viable publications that
served as instruments of advocacy. Wells-Barnett risked her life to witness
and report racial disturbances, riots, and lynchings throughout the country.
As a political militant, she was relentless in her appeal to national and world

public opinion about human rights violations in the United States. At the same time, she fostered the creation of national organizations of African Americans and women.

During the final decade of the nineteenth century, Wells-Barnett employed modern business practices to buy part ownership in African-American newspapers in the South and North, purchasing shares in some and exchanging her subscription lists for ownership in another. In 1889, she bought a one-third interest in the Memphis *Free Speech and Headlight*.[2] By 1891, she and one of her partners had bought out the third partner, and she held 50 percent ownership until the newspaper's destruction at the hands of a violent Memphis mob (Duster 39).

In 1892, Wells-Barnett used her *Free Speech* subscription lists to purchase one-fourth ownership of the *New York Age* (Duster 63). Before her 1895 marriage to Chicago *Conservator* editor Ferdinand L. Barnett, Wells-Barnett bought that newspaper from him and his partners (Duster 242). After the turn of the century, prior to 1913, although the exact dates have not been recorded, she published "a little paper called the *Fellowship Herald*" (Duster 359).

When she needed to finance publication of booklets important to her causes, she developed innovative, politically informed fund-raising techniques. She convinced renowned African Americans of the period, such as abolitionist and journalist Frederick Douglass, to join her on the lecture circuit. These efforts resulted in publication of *The Reason Why the Colored American Is Not in the World's Columbian Exposition—The Afro-American's Contribution to Columbian Literature,* an eighty-one-page booklet on America's oppression of black people. Ten thousand copies were circulated to international visitors at the 1893 World's Fair in Chicago (Duster 117).

Similarly, she financed publication of the findings of her investigations into lynchings in America. Lecturing in Chicago, she raised funds from every possible source. In 1895, she published *A Red Record: Tabulated Statistics and Alleged Causes of Lynchings in the United States, 1892–1893–1894*. This hundred-page booklet was a detailed record and history of the lynchings of African Americans in the United States.[3] She wrote in the first chapter: "It becomes the painful duty of the Negro to reproduce a record which shows that a large portion of the American people avow anarchy, condone murder and defy the contempt of civilization" (Duster xxi).

An anomaly as a black woman agent, she traveled through Arkansas, Mississippi, and Tennessee in the late 1800s, securing subscriptions to one of her papers to increase circulation. She wrote in her autobiography:

> At Greenville, Mississippi, I attended the state bar association, made a short appeal to them, and came out with the subscription of every man present. In Water Valley, Mississippi, the state grand master of the Masonic lodge

8.1. Ida B. Wells-Barnett, n.d., from I. Garland Penn, *The Afro-American Press and Its Editors* (Springfield, MA: Willey and Co., 1891).

suspended the session for a half hour to let me appeal to them for sub-scriptions. When I came out of that meeting I was weighted down with silver dollars and had to go straight to the bank. (Duster 39)

When sales of one of her newspapers were threatened by railway em-ployees who frequently sold illiterate passengers another newspaper when they asked for hers, she employed a marketing strategy—packaging. She printed the newspaper on pink paper so that her readers recognized and asked for the *Free Speech* (Duster 41–42).

Wells-Barnett transcended oppression and dual discrimination as a black woman and became a respected editor and businesswoman. She quickly gained the recognition of the men of the black press, who ultimately crowned her the "Princess of the Press" (Dann 63). In 1889, early in her career, she was elected secretary of the National Press Association, the first woman officer of that association.

In addition, Wells-Barnett was probably the first African-American woman to challenge white violence against freed African-American men. She insisted that the cry of rape, habitually charged against black men, was merely an excuse to justify murder in retaliation for the white southerner's loss of slave property. The stereotype of the African-American savage loosed on the white southern belle was one she challenged and undermined successfully.

Finally, driven by a desire to create an organization that responded to human rights violations against African Americans, Wells-Barnett began a movement led by African-American and women's clubs, a precursor to the modern civil rights movement. She was among the first to advocate political activism among African Americans, convincing her race to use the ballot and economic pressures to gain full civil rights. Indeed, in 1930 she ran for public office (Duster xxix).

That Wells-Barnett was one of the first African-American women to own and edit a newspaper in the United States and that she actively crusaded nationally and internationally for the human rights of African Americans and women in this country, is more than enough to guarantee her place in history. While the history of journalism acknowledges her contribution, her accomplishments as a businesswoman have not been recognized.[4]

From Slavery to Journalism

Ida B. Wells was born into slavery, the oldest of eight children, on July 16, 1862, in Holly Springs, Mississippi (Duster 7).[5] Her parents, Jim Wells and Elizabeth Warrenton, were married as slaves but, like many freed slaves, remarried after attaining full freedom and independence following the Civil War.[6]

Jim Wells was an experienced carpenter, apprenticed at the age of eighteen by his white slave-master father. Elizabeth Warrenton Wells was a cook who worked in the city. The Wells family lived in a home built by Jim Wells. Following emancipation, the Wellses wanted their children to be educated. Ida Wells wrote in her autobiography: "Our job was to go to school and learn all we could. The Freedmen's Aid had established (in 1886) one of its schools in our town—it was called Shaw University then, but is now Rust College. My father was one of the trustees and my mother went along to school with us until she learned to read the Bible" (Duster 9).

Yellow fever hit the Mississippi Delta in 1878, taking the lives of Jim and Elizabeth Wells and their baby son, Stanley. This tragedy forced Ida Wells to make a decision that radically changed her life. Family and friends met to decide the fate of the orphans, agreeing to divide them among various households. Fourteen-year-old Wells refused to have the children separated, and she became the head of the family of six children. Wells became a country schoolteacher and, with the three hundred dollars in cash her father left them, began to care for the family, hiring a local woman to help her. Wells began the grueling routine of traveling by mule each Sunday to the country classroom and returning on Friday nights to do chores and cook for the week.

In 1882 or 1883, Wells left Mississippi for Tennessee at the urging of an aunt who lived in Memphis (Duster xvi). She found a school in Shelby County with an opening for a teacher and began to study at Le Moyne Institute for the city's teachers' examination (Giddings 22). On May 4, 1884, while traveling on the railroad, Wells was subjected to an act of racial discrimination that proved another turning point in her young life. One of the train's conductors refused to accept the ticket young Wells held out to him in the ladies' car. He simply said he could not take her ticket and continued to take tickets from other passengers in the car. When he returned from the opposite end of the car to where she was sitting, he demanded she leave her seat and move to the smoking car. She refused. When the conductor attempted to move her by force, she bit his hand and sent him scurrying for help. The conductor returned with two men and together they ejected her from the car. Wells left the train at its next stop (Duster 18).

Outraged by the treatment she received, Wells sued the Chesapeake and Ohio Railroad. The case was tried in circuit court in 1884, and Wells was awarded five hundred dollars in damages (Duster 19). The railroad appealed to the state Supreme Court and the finding of the circuit court was overturned in April 1887. Wells paid two hundred dollars in court costs. She acknowledged in her autobiography that the dream of justice for African Americans was most certainly deferred. She wrote: "The supreme court of the nation had told us to go to the state courts for redress of grievances; when I did so I was given the brand of justice Charles Sumner knew Negroes would get when he fathered the Civil Rights Bill during Reconstruction" (Duster 20).

Wells was discouraged but settled into life in Memphis, teaching and taking teachers' training courses at Fisk University (Giddings 22). She became active in church life and at a lyceum, which had its own newspaper, the *Evening Star,* of which Wells quickly became editor. Her writing for the *Star* was popular, and a Baptist minister who also published a weekly, the *Living Way,* asked her to begin writing for his paper. These small beginnings were to become the start of a lifetime of journalistic writing. Journalism became an outlet for the frustrations Wells harbored after her court loss. She wrote in what she called "a plain, common-sense way on the things which concerned our people" (Duster 24). Adopting a nom de plume, she signed her pieces "Iola."

Becoming an Editor and Newspaper Owner

By 1889, the "Iola" byline was found in the leading African-American newspapers of the time, including the *New York Age,* the *Detroit Plaindealer,* the *Indianapolis World,* the Kansas City *Gate City Press,* the *Little Rock Sun,* the

Louisville *American Baptist,* the *Memphis Watchman,* the *Chattanooga Justice,* and *Our Women and Children Magazine.* It was during this period that she became known as the "Princess of the Press" (Dann 63; Giddings 24).

Wells was happy in her work as a journalist, but like many African-American writers, she could not make her living as a journalist, so she continued to teach school. While teaching was not her greatest joy, it paid a salary. "Although I made a reputation in school for thoroughness and discipline in the primary grades, I was never promoted above the fourth grade in all my years as a teacher. The confinement and monotony of the primary work began to grow distasteful. The correspondence I had built up in newspaper work gave me an outlet through which to express the real 'me' and I enjoyed my work to the utmost" (Duster 31).

She soon wanted to own a newspaper. In 1889, Wells was asked to join the Memphis *Free Speech and Headlight,* a newspaper owned by two men. Wells refused the offer to join the staff as a writer but offered to buy into the enterprise. She became one-third owner and editor, and subsequently, shortened the paper's name to *Free Speech* (Giddings 24).

Historical circulation and fiscal records for "marginal" media have not been preserved, but Wells left a reference to the fiscal condition and management structure of the *Free Speech and Headlight* at the time she became part-owner: "Mr. Fleming was business manager (collecting upward of two hundred dollars a month from the white businessmen of the city for advertising), and Rev. Nightingale was sales manager. Since he was pastor of the Beal Street Baptist Church, with the largest congregation in the state, about five hundred copies were sold every Sunday in this church" (Duster 35).

Her summer vacation from teaching provided an opportunity for the new editor of *Free Speech* to begin the work of entrepreneurship. Ever defiant of restrictions placed on women and African Americans, she traveled throughout the Mississippi valley, increasing the circulation of the newspaper (Duster 37).

Her editorial stances soon precipitated another major change in her life. She vigorously criticized the discriminatory practices of the authorities of the city of Memphis, including the board of education. In 1891, Wells wrote about the deplorable conditions of educational facilities for African-American children and the questionable character of some of the teachers in the schools. Angered by the article, the Memphis school board refused to reappoint Wells after seven years as a teacher in the system. She knew that dismissal might be the result of publication of the article and had asked Nightingale to sign it. He refused and Wells released the piece with her signature; she felt principle demanded its release (Duster 37).

Faced with unemployment, Wells turned to the only work she truly enjoyed. She became the full-time editor of the *Free Speech* and eventually became 50 percent owner of the paper. She continued her efforts to increase the circulation of the paper and was quite successful:

Building on the start of the summer before, I went to most of the large towns throughout the Delta, across the Mississippi River into Arkansas, and back into Tennessee. Wherever there was a gathering of people, there I was in the midst of them, to solicit subscribers for the *Free Speech* and to appoint a correspondent to send us weekly news.

In nine months time I had an income nearly as large as I had received teaching and felt sure that I had found my vocation. I was very proud of my success because up to that time very few of our newspapers had made any money. (Duster 39)

The *Free Speech* was rapidly becoming an influential medium in the Mississippi Delta region. In less than one year, its circulation increased from fifteen hundred to four thousand subscribers. These figures are based on the subscriptions held by the newspaper; they do not allow for the total exposure or penetration of the newspaper. There is no doubt the *Free Speech* had a life beyond its subscribers. The newspaper was read and passed along to countless others. Many who could not read had the paper read to them: "We printed the *Free Speech* on pink paper to make it distinctive to a great many people who could not read. I afterward learned that some butchers were selling copies of the *Police Gazette* to many of the poor illiterates who wanted the *Free Speech*—they could not read for themselves, so they got to asking for the pink paper" (Duster 41–42).

Wells was pleased with her work. As an editor, she wielded her pen with the strength and impact of a double-edged sword. While she wrote about racial discrimination, she also brought prominent African Americans to task. The *Free Speech* criticized Isaiah Montgomery, who served as the only African-American member of the Mississippi Constitutional Convention in 1890 (Duster 37–38). Although Montgomery tried to justify his vote for the Mississippi constitution's "Understanding Clause," which essentially nullified the right to vote for African Americans in the state, Wells never agreed with his stance and wrote that he should not have acquiesced in this matter.

Booker T. Washington also received the ire of Wells, the editor.[7] During his work at Tuskegee Institute, Washington was critical of what he saw as a lack of African-American leadership. In an article for the *Christian Register,* he complained about what he saw as the low moral and intellectual caliber of the African-American clergy of the South. Wells took offense that such criticism was aired in a white publication and wrote an editorial telling her readers and Washington just that. They eventually became good friends, but she continued to differ with his conservative viewpoints (Duster 41).

Traveling, writing, reporting, and editing, Wells felt she had at last found her "real vocation" and found kindness and support for her work (Duster 41).

The New and Defining Crusade

The post-Reconstruction years were a chaotic period in United States history. Ku Klux Klan activities and white mob violence against African Americans were commonplace. Often the violence was supported by the legal authorities, and African Americans had little redress for the crimes committed against them. Although African Americans had managed to establish modest economic success in Memphis, the city was not immune to the acts of racial hatred pervasive in the country.[8] One such act took place on March 9, 1892, and shocked the black citizens of Memphis. It was a particularly personal tragedy for Wells. She acknowledged in her autobiography that this incident marked a significant point in her life: "While I was thus carrying on the work of my newspaper, happy in the thought that our influence was helpful and that I was doing the work I loved and had proved that I could make a living out of it, there came the lynching in Memphis which changed the whole course of my life" (Duster 47).

While Wells was away in Natchez on business, three successful African-American grocers, who were competitors of a neighboring white grocer, were taken from their store, jailed, and subsequently lynched by a white mob in Memphis. Thomas Moss, a full-time postman and one of the grocery store owners, was a personal friend of Wells. Indeed, she was the godmother of his only daughter.

The details of the events that precipitated this lynching involved a quarrel between young white and black boys over a game of marbles. Soon after the quarrel, the fathers of the youngsters scuffled. That night, three white men were injured by black men when they attempted to enter the back entrance of the People's Grocery Company. More than a hundred African-American men were taken from their homes and jailed following the incident. Three days of racial tension, brought on by exaggerated press reports, resulted in the lynchings. Wells believed the deaths of the grocers went well beyond retaliation for the injuries to the three white men:

> This mob took possession of the People's Grocery Company, helping themselves to food and drink, and destroyed what they could not eat or steal. The creditors had the place closed and a few days later what remained of the stock was sold at auction. Thus, with the aid of the city and county authorities and the daily papers, that white grocer had indeed put an end to his rival Negro grocer as well as to his business. (Duster 51–52)

Wells began writing about this tragedy as soon as she returned from Mississippi. Her writing took on a very personal tone:

The city of Memphis has demonstrated that neither character nor standing avails the Negro if he dares to protect himself against the white man or become his rival. There is nothing we can do about the lynching now, as we are out-numbered and without arms. The white mob could help itself to ammunition without pay, but the order was rigidly enforced against the selling of guns to Negroes. There is therefore only one thing left that we can do, save our money and leave a town which will neither protect our lives and property, nor give us a fair trial in the courts, but takes us out and murders us in cold blood when accused by white persons. (Duster 52)

Encouraged by these words and the last words of Thomas Moss, "Tell my people to go West—there is no justice for them here," six thousand African Americans began leaving the city of Memphis for Oklahoma (Duster 51). During this exodus, the African-American citizens took the advice of Wells and the *Free Speech* and saved their money in order to move. For many, frugality meant walking instead of riding the city's streetcars. Subsequently, Wells was visited at her newspaper office by executives of the City Railway Company. They were alarmed by the decline in ridership by African Americans and asked Wells to encourage the citizens to begin patronizing the streetcars again. Wells wrote an article about the meeting and an editorial encouraging the black community to continue its quest. Also, she went to black churches and urged the congregations to continue to walk. Her act was a calculated political one. Recognizing the impact of the unorganized boycott, Wells encouraged her people to put economic pressure on the white businesses of Memphis.

Prior to the Memphis incident, Wells had read of many lynchings, and she assumed the stories told were fact. Most of the official newspaper accounts reported lynchings of African-American men for the charge of rape. But Wells knew that her friend Thomas Moss and his associates were not lynched for rape. She became obsessed with finding out the details of lynchings that were taking place across the country:

Like many another person who had read of lynching in the South, I had accepted the idea meant to be conveyed—that although lynching was irregular and contrary to law and order, unreasoning anger over the terrible crime of rape led to the lynching; that perhaps the brute deserved death anyhow and the mob was justified in taking his life.

But Thomas Moss, Calvin McDowell, and Lee Stewart had been lynched in Memphis, one of the leading cities of the South, in which no lynching had taken place before, with just as much brutality as other victims of the mob; and they had committed no crime against white women. (Duster 64)

For three months, Wells investigated the reports of every lynching that came to her attention. She visited the scenes of lynchings and interviewed eyewitnesses; in all, she investigated 728 murders (Giddings 28). Her investigations showed that regardless of the initial facts surrounding the accusations leveled at African-American men, the final charge, usually leveled just before mob law required a lynching, was the charge of rape. She wrote: "I stumbled on the amazing record that every case of rape reported in that three months became such only when it became public" (Duster 64–65).

In May 1892, before leaving Memphis for her visit to the North, Wells wrote the editorial that spurred a Memphis mob to destroy her paper and necessitate her exile:

> Eight Negroes lynched since last issue of the *Free Speech*. Three were charged with killing white men and five with raping white women. Nobody in this section believes the old thread-bare lie that Negro men assault white women. If Southern white men are not careful they will over-reach themselves and a conclusion will be reached which will be very damaging to the moral reputation of their women. (Duster 65–66)

This editorial, Wells believed, provided the white leaders of Memphis with the impetus to do what they had always wanted— to destroy the *Free Speech*. On the Monday following her Saturday *Free Speech* editorial, the white Memphis newspaper, the *Commercial Appeal,* reproduced her editorial in the first column of its editorial page with the response of the *Commercial Appeal:* "The black wretch who had written that foul lie should be tied to a stake at the corner of Main and Madison streets, a pair of tailor's shears used on him and he should then be burned at the stake" (Duster 66).

News from Memphis met Wells when she reached New York City. A mob had destroyed the *Free Speech* offices and press. Wells had anticipated a violent reaction to her editorial, but she expected it to happen when she was in Memphis. An avowed militant, she bought a pistol to protect herself in case of attack: "I had bought a pistol the first thing after Tom Moss was lynched, because I expected some cowardly retaliation from the lynchers. I felt that one had better die fighting against injustice than to die like a dog or a rat in a trap. I had already determined to sell my life as dearly as possible if attacked. I felt if I could take one lyncher with me, this would even up the score a little bit" (Duster 62).

Exiled: A Second Newspaper and a Refined Theory

After the destruction of the *Free Speech,* Wells never returned to Memphis to live. She became a contributor to the *New York Age* and began to "tell the world for the first time the true story of Negro lynchings, which were becoming more numerous and horrible" (Duster 63).

The consummate businesswoman, Wells soon bought one-fourth interest in the *Age,* negotiating her share in the paper for her subscription lists
from the *Free Speech*. Business owner and editor, she continued to exhort
African Americans to support a black press. Faced with reducing the *Age*
from eight to four pages, on November 19, 1892, she wrote in her weekly
column, "Iola's Southern Field":

> Eight million Afro-Americans without a national organ reaching in all quar-
> ters of this country, and representing every phase of race life, are without
> one of the strongest weapons of defense. To sustain such a journal is to
> sustain themselves and provide a champion to fight their battles. Here
> again, the doctrine of self-help must be practiced. The white journals will
> not give space to our defense and for lack of race support, our own can-
> not do so. (2)

Time away from Memphis allowed Wells the opportunity to reflect on
the series of events that occurred following the lynching of Thomas Moss
and his business associates. She investigated and thought about the other
lynchings she had heard about in the country. This reflection resulted in the
development of a theory that led her on a mission to expose the truth about
the lynching of black men in America.

The facts of the antebellum South are that white masters often raped
slave girls and women. Depending upon many variables, the masters kept
the children of these liaisons as their property, sold them or sent them away
to live independently (Lerner 45–47). Wells believed that southerners remained resentful of the loss of the African American as slave, property, "play-
thing," and source of income.

"Lynch law," Wells theorized, was the southern white man's authority to
strike back at the "inequity" of losing the enslaved African American. She
felt that as long as he could claim chivalry and defense of the white woman,
he was justified in his actions. In fact, Wells believed, the white man had
discovered a new tyranny. He had found a way to terrorize African-American people, to keep them submissive, and strike enough fear to thwart the
upward mobility of an entire race (Duster 70–71).

Now exiled in New York, Wells turned her journalistic skills to telling the
story as she knew it. She wrote a seven-column article published in the *New
York Age,* providing names, dates, and places of lynchings that resulted from
charges of rape. Ten thousand copies of this issue were published and circulated nationwide. The readers of Memphis alone bought one thousand copies.

While Wells was pleased with the response from such notables as
Frederick Douglass, she was disappointed that the article was not acknowledged by the white press.[9] After nearly a year of traveling and writing about
lynchings, she had not been able to reach the white readers of the country,

who she knew were the only hope for molding public opinion and up-
holding the rights of her people. She knew she needed a wave of righteous
indignation from the white public to secure the rights of fair trial and hearing for the victims of mob violence.

Frustration overcame Wells and she began to feel the solitude of her
crusade, but she was undaunted. Still another set of circumstances converged
to assist her in her campaign. On October 5, 1892, Wells was honored at a
testimonial given by two New York schoolteachers. She wrote a very moving paper for that occasion, which brought her and the audience to tears. As
a result, she received invitations to lecture to black audiences throughout
the East Coast. She read and reread the paper she wrote. Her public speaking brought her to the attention of many prominent African Americans, including Josephine St. Pierre Ruffin, William Still, and Mary Church Terrell.[10]

Finally, in the fall of 1892, Wells addressed a white audience in Boston,
and the *Boston Transcript and Advertiser* reported her appearance. It was
the first account of her story of lynchings and her anti-lynching crusade to
appear in a "white northern newspaper" (Duster 81).

An International Appeal and Third Newspaper

In February 1893, newspaper reports of a lynching in Paris, Texas, reached
Europe, and Wells's international appeal began. Scottish author and reformer
Isabelle Fyvie Mayo, appalled by the accounts of the most brutal lynchings
reported in the United States, sought someone to come to England and tell
the story of the violence.[11] She sent a letter to Frederick Douglass asking
who could best bring the message to the British Isles. Douglass, who was
too old to go himself, insisted Wells make the trip. Wells spent the spring of
1893 talking to audiences in England, Scotland, and Wales. Press accounts
of her tour appeared in London's *Society* and *Ladies Pictorial,* the *Peterhead
Sentinel and Buchan Journal,* the *Edinburgh Evening Gazette,* the *Newcastle
Leader,* the *Birmingham Daily Gazette,* the *Birmingham Daily Post,* and the
Manchester *Guardian* (Duster 95–101).

Wells returned to the United States in 1893, just in time to keep a promise to Frederick Douglass. America was celebrating the four-hundredth anniversary of its discovery, and the world was invited to its 1893 World's Fair.
The federal government had denied petitions for participation from black
organizations and individuals, an injustice Wells could not endure. She and
Frederick Douglass decided before she went abroad that a book exposing
this slight and the oppression of black people in America had to be published. But during Wells's absence, Douglass had been unable to raise funds
for publication of the book, and he was prepared to give up the idea of the
project. Wells refused to be defeated by financial constraints. She knew the

importance of a continued campaign abroad in order to get action at home. She solicited the help of Chicago women and through her newly found skill as a public speaker, she raised the funds. She and Douglass spoke to several groups in Chicago, and Wells published *The Reason Why the Colored American Is Not in the World's Columbian Exposition—The Afro-American's Contribution to Columbian Literature.* The preface of this booklet was addressed "To The Seeker After Truth."

Wells returned to England in early 1894 at the invitation of the Society for the Brotherhood of Man. William Penn Nixon, editor of the *Inter-Ocean,* a Chicago daily, asked her to serve as correspondent to the newspaper while she was there. She became the first African-American woman to correspond from abroad for a daily paper in the United States (Duster 125).[12] Wells spent six months in England, speaking and organizing anti-lynching committees wherever she traveled.

Distribution of the World's Fair booklet and international travel brought Wells national attention, and she began to see the fruits of her labors. Public debate over Wells and her charges against the United States was heated in England. While the English found the lynchings disturbing, charges that America's liberals ignored the atrocities were dismaying. When asked by the British about the responses of Reverend D. L. Moody and Frances Willard to the lynchings in America, Wells's response was incredible to the British.[13] She wrote in her autobiography: "My answer to those queries was that neither of those great exponents of Christianity in our country had ever spoken out in condemnation of lynching, but seemed on the contrary disposed to overlook that fashionable pastime of the South" (Duster 111).

Wells now had what she wanted. England, the leading importer of southern cotton, had reached the point of moral indignation, and if no one else, American enterprise would pay attention. Lynchings decreased in 1893 and continued to decline. So marred was the image of the city of Memphis, the world's leading exporter of cotton, that city officials became vigilant about the murders (Giddings 92).

Returning to the United States in July 1894, Wells was met in New York City by reporters from every local newspaper (Duster 218). She announced she would dedicate a year to "carrying the message across the country." This she did and continued her crusade against lynching.

In 1895, she moved to Chicago where she published *A Red Record: Tabulated Statistics and Alleged Causes of Lynchings in the United States, 1892–1893–1894.* She continued lecturing and organizing anti-lynching committees across the country. Also in 1895, at the age of thirty-three, Ida B. Wells married Ferdinand L. Barnett, founder of the *Conservator,* the first black newspaper in Chicago. They were married on June 27 after numerous postponements caused by the bride's speaking schedule. Wells-Barnett had purchased the *Conservator* from her fiancé and his business associates before their marriage. She went back to work as a publisher on the Monday following their wedding.

Club Life and Political Involvement

Wells-Barnett was a founder and member of several African-American and women's clubs throughout her career. The clubs were designed to give an organized voice to the issues and concerns of her race and gender. While traveling in England, she was impressed with women's involvement in civic groups, and when she returned to the United States, she encouraged women to organize civic clubs to fight for enfranchisement. In 1893, she organized the first black woman's club in Chicago, which became the Ida B. Wells Club.

Soon thereafter, black women began to organize in response to published attacks on their character and the character of Wells-Barnett. In direct response to one of these attacks, the National Federation of Afro-American Women was formed in July 1895 in Boston under the leadership of Josephine St. Pierre Ruffin:

> Rising to the defense of the white South, James Jacks, president of the Missouri Press Association, wrote to the British society in a widely publicized statement that "the Negroes in this country were wholly devoid of morality, the women were prostitutes and all were natural thieves and liars." This statement was the last straw for black club women, who had endured similar slanders in silence. (Lerner 436)

By 1896 the federation united with the National League of Colored Women in Washington to form the National Association of Colored Women. According to Paula Giddings, black women's historian, Wells-Barnett was instrumental in bringing "Black women into the forefront of the struggle for Black and women's rights" (94).

Wells-Barnett had always envisioned an organization that could investigate and respond to the charges that led to lynchings. She remained frustrated by the fact that no such organization existed. Efforts toward a national movement began in New York with the organization of the Afro-American Council in 1899, but Wells-Barnett continued to travel and single-handedly investigate riots, lynchings, and racial disturbances throughout the country.

Finally, the solitude of the crusade would have relief. In 1909, as the country prepared to celebrate the one-hundredth birthday of Abraham Lincoln, Wells-Barnett and others prepared to demonstrate African-American discontent with the violations of their rights in America. The participants signed a written appeal to the United States government to rid the country of these conditions in celebration of Lincoln's birthday. The document was distributed to the press. This effort resulted in a three-day conference of the signers, culminating in the establishment of the National Negro Committee. This group appointed an organizing committee of forty to initiate the development of a national organization. The committee of forty, of which Wells-Barnett was a member, became the organization that was to be known as the National Association of Colored People.

Throughout her life in Chicago, Wells-Barnett and her husband were actively involved in Republican politics. Candidates for city and state offices consulted Wells-Barnett, and she negotiated support of the black vote in return for agenda items important to the black community (Duster 349). In 1913, when the Illinois legislature opened for the session, Wells-Barnett was publishing *Fellowship Herald,* a small Chicago newspaper she used to report on state political issues. The legislature began with consideration of four bills against the intermarriage of black and white citizens of the state and three additional bills that Wells-Barnett characterized as "anti-Negro." One, a labor bill, she felt would virtually eliminate the existence of Negro railway porters. Wells-Barnett used the *Herald* and women's club membership to lobby the legislature to defeat these measures (Duster 360).

In the fall of 1915, Wells-Barnett served as a member of a committee commissioned to inform President Wilson of the segregation enforced in the federal government (Duster 375). In 1930, when the Republican party of Illinois became fractious and Wells-Barnett could not support the candidate of her party, she ran as an independent for state senator.

The Legacy

Wells-Barnett was an astute businesswoman who used contemporary business practices to establish and manage four newspapers in the United States. The newspapers not only proved to be successful business ventures but were also invaluable vehicles in bringing international attention to the struggle for human rights. Her innate entrepreneurial spirit prohibited her from settling for offers of mere employment. Rather, every chance she got, she leveraged these offers into equity investments in publishing organizations. She applied advanced business concepts to market her newspapers nationwide. Her marketing skills were demonstrated by personal sales of subscriptions throughout the South to increase circulation. Most impressive was her creative use of packaging techniques to distinguish the *Free Speech* from her competitors. At the same time, she was a proficient fund-raiser who used her public speaking skills to finance her newspapers and other publications. Her lectures, at home and abroad, on the treatment of African Americans resulted in funding to keep her written voice of outrage alive.

Wells-Barnett was a militant political leader who dared to say she would "sell her life as dearly as possible" in defense of her rights and the rights of her people. She was an efficacious politician who understood the power of public opinion and economic pressure. She admonished African Americans and women to organize and use the force of the ballot for justice. She not only launched the modern civil rights movement, but a verbal racist attack on Wells-Barnett also provided the catalyst for the black women's political movement.

Her accomplishments are magnified by the enormity of the barriers she overcame. Her determination to succeed in her human rights crusade and in her business is all that stood between her and a society that was completely averse to the notion of a successful African-American woman. She endured solitude, discrimination, character assassination, and threats on her life, and she prevailed.

In spite of these obstacles, and the odds against an African-American woman's establishing a successful enterprise in the late 1800s, Ida B. Wells-Barnett not only sustained her newspapers' successes, but more important, she accomplished her lifelong objective. She forced change for her people. As a direct result of her efforts, murders of African Americans by lynch mobs were significantly reduced. Her desire and determination to sustain publication because of the contribution her newspapers made cannot be separated from her commitment to writing on the subject about which she felt most passionate. Both motivations led to success.

When the framers of the United States Constitution assured freedom of expression, they gave birth to a free press, democracy's most powerful weapon. While the free press has served, from its inception, as a voice against tyranny, women and African Americans were not expected to wield this most powerful of weapons. Indeed, the free press has often excluded them. Clearly, the authors of the Constitution did not envision the likes of Ida B. Wells-Barnett. She seized the power of the press, forcing change and contributing significantly to print culture. It was her knowledge that the power of the press could bring an end to the crimes against African Americans that led her to express her outrage through the print medium. When she died on March 25, 1931, she left a legacy rich with her commitment to the acquisition and preservation of justice for her race and gender.

Ida B. Wells-Barnett is one of many African-American women who refused mental inertia, indifferent acquiescence, tamed submission, and silence in the face of injustice. She chose, instead, a life of contention and ceaseless unrest: a process of constantly aspiring, protesting, and standing up to be heard or knocked down. Clearly, her actions resulted in respect and dulling the edge of tyranny.

Notes

1. In 1879, Timothy Thomas Fortune became owner of the New York *Rumor* along with William Walter Sampson and George Parker. Fortune soon changed its format from magazine to newspaper format and the name from *Rumor* to *Globe*. In November 1884, the *Age* was discontinued. Fortune was the first African-American man to work for a mainstream newspaper, joining the staff of the New York *Sun* in October 1887. See, for example, Penn 90. On editorial philosophy, see, for example, Dann 33.

2. Much of the information contained in this chapter is from the autobiography written by Ida B. Wells-Barnett before her death and edited by her daughter. See Duster 35.

3. For excerpt, see Lerner 196–205.

4. The first black woman journalist in North America was Mary Ann Shadd Cary, who founded the *Provincial Freeman* in 1854 in Ontario, Canada. See Brown 92–96. Emery and Emery's standard journalism history textbook provides the highlights of Wells-Barnett's journalism career (309). A few paragraphs are given to Wells-Barnett in a book about women journalists (Mills 27–28). One paragraph about Wells-Barnett appears in Marzolf 25. Wells-Barnett is not mentioned in Ross.

5. The autobiography notes only that Wells was born before the close of the Civil War. Duster determines the date, July 16, 1862, from Wells-Barnett's diary entry of July 16, 1887: "This morning I stand face to face with twenty-five years of life."

6. Prior to emancipation, slave marriages were not legal and slave unions were not protected by law. Many ex-slaves had learned what it was like to have marriages not protected by law. It is likely that remarriage and legal registration of marriage were among the newly freed African American's most important social decisions. See, for example, Gutman 417.

7. Booker T. Washington (1856–1915) is best known as founder and principal of Tuskegee Institute, Tuskegee, Alabama. As an educator, Washington believed that African Americans could achieve more with vocational education than with college education. This conservative philosophy was criticized by W. E. B. DuBois. Wells-Barnett was a militant follower of DuBois. See Whitman 851–53.

8. Memphis was the site of one of the bloodiest riots of this violent period in May 1866. See, for example, Foner 261–62.

9. Frederick Douglass was born a slave in 1817 or 1818. He became America's greatest orator, author, journalist, and abolitionist. Douglass was greatly influenced by William Lloyd Garrison, abolitionist and journalist, who helped educate him and encouraged him to write. Douglass was editor of *Frederick Douglass' Paper, Douglass' Monthly,* the *New Era,* and *New National Era*. See Wolseley 32–36.

10. Josephine St. Pierre Ruffin (1842–1924) was an activist and suffragist in Boston, Massachusetts. An important force in the creation of a national organization for black women, St. Pierre Ruffin organized one of the country's first black women's clubs, the New Era Club, and became editor of its journal, *The Women's Era*. St. Pierre

Ruffin was involved in the organization of the National Association of Colored Women in 1896. See Giddings 30; and Lerner 440. William Still was an abolitionist and author. Before the Civil War, he was active in assisting runaway slaves and author of *Underground Railroad*. See, for example, Low and Clift 809. Mary Church Terrell (1863–1954) was a leading suffragist and first president of the National Association of Colored Women. A member of the National American Suffrage Association, she was a close friend of Susan B. Anthony and Jane Addams. She was one of the few African-American women who gained recognition and honors from whites. See Giddings 22; and Lerner 206–7.

11. Isabelle Fyvie Mayo was a Scottish novelist and author. She wrote under the nom de plume "Edward Garrett." See *Who Was Who, 1897–1915* 484.

12. The first African-American woman to write on a part-time basis for a mainstream newspaper was Delilah Beasley, who corresponded for the *Cincinnati Enquirer* in the late 1800s and wrote a column for the *Oakland Tribune* from 1923 to 1934. See Davis 188–95.

13. D. L. (Dwight Lyman) Moody (1837–1899) was an American evangelist who traveled throughout the United States and Britain conducting evangelistic campaigns. He dedicated most of his adult life to Sunday-school and YMCA activities. Frances Elizabeth Caroline Willard (1839–1898) was among the most prominent reformers of the 1800s. She founded the National Woman's Christian Temperance Union and, as its president for eighteen years, urged the WCTU to participate in political activities. She was the first president of the National Council of Women. In 1892, she left the United States for a four-year trip and was living in England during Wells-Barnett's visits. See Whitman 885–86.

Works Cited

Brown, Hallie Q. *Homespun Heroines and Other Women of Distinction*. 1926. Freeport, NY: Books for Libraries P, 1971.

Dann, Martin E., ed. *The Black Press, 1827–1890*. New York: Capricorn Books, 1971.

Davis, Elizabeth Lindsay. *Lifting as They Climb*. Washington, DC: National Association of Colored Women, 1933.

Duster, Alfreda M., ed. *The Autobiography of Ida B. Wells*. Chicago: U of Chicago P, 1970.

Emery, Michael, and Edwin Emery. *The Press and America: An Interpretive History of the Mass Media*. 7th ed. Englewood Cliffs, NJ: Prentice-Hall, 1992.

Foner, Eric. *Reconstruction: America's Unfinished Revolution, 1863–1877*. New York: Harper and Row, 1988.

Giddings, Paula. *When and Where I Enter: The Impact of Black Women on Race and Sex in America*. New York: William Morrow, 1984.

Gutman, Herbert G. *The Black Family in Slavery and Freedom, 1750–1925*. New York: Pantheon Books, 1976.

Lerner, Gerda, ed. *Black Women in White America: A Documentary History*. New York: Vintage Books, 1972.

Low, W. A., and Virgil Clift, eds. *Encyclopedia of Black America*. New York: McGraw Hill, 1981.

Marzolf, Marion. *Up from the Footnote: A History of Women Journalists*. New York: Hastings House, 1977.

Mills, Kay. *A Place in the News: From the Women's Pages to the Front Page*. New York: Dodd, Mead, 1988.

Penn, I. Garland. *The Afro-American Press and Its Editors*. Springfield, MA: Willey & Co., 1891.

Ross, Ishbel. *Ladies of the Press*. New York: Harper and Brothers, 1936.

Wells, Ida B. "Iola's Southern Fields." *New York Age* Nov. 19, 1892: 2.

————. *The Reason Why the Colored American Is Not in the World's Columbian Exposition—The Afro-American's Contribution to Columbian Literature*. Chicago: Donohue and Henneberry, 1895.

Whitman, Alden, ed. *American Reformers*. New York: H. W. Wilson, 1985.

Who Was Who, 1897–1915. London: Adam & Charles Black, 1962.

Wolseley, Roland E. *The Black Press, U.S.A.* 2d ed. Ames: Iowa State UP, 1990.

9.

Marketing the American Indian:
Mary Austin and the Business of Writing

Karen S. Langlois

In 1932 the American western writer Mary Hunter Austin published her autobiography with Houghton Mifflin Company. Heralded by her publishers as the greatest autobiography since Benjamin Franklin's, Austin's book was chosen as a Literary Guild selection and became the capstone of her writing career. The title, *Earth Horizon,* was a reference to an Indian rain symbol. Included in the autobiography were Austin's memories of her life in California at the turn of the century and her experiences with the Owens Valley Paiute Indians. It was during this period, she confessed, that she first discovered "there was a part for her in Indian life." As she explained, "she entered into their lives . . . the strange secret life of the tribe" (289).

Austin's claims about her familiarity with Indian culture were frequently met with disdain. Among her severest critics were various friends and professional associates who thought she fabricated her expertise. As Ina Cassidy, a member of the Santa Fe, New Mexico, artists' colony, observed: "It is very amusing to me and to others who know the Pueblos and the Navajos, to hear Mary claim to be an authority . . . for we know from personal observation and intimate knowledge that she knows very very little, at first hand" (Nov. 4, 1933). Nevertheless, Austin had largely built her career on her claims as an expert on Native American life. Her writing on Indians made up one-third to one-half of her oeuvre. Without any formal training in anthropology or ethnology, she repeatedly managed to disarm her critics and market her work to the American reading public.

Austin was born in 1868 in Carlinville, Illinois. In 1888 she graduated from Blackburn College, a small Presbyterian institution. She moved west with her widowed mother and brother to homestead in Fort Tejon, California, once the site of a large Indian reservation. After her marriage to Wallace Stafford Austin, a speculator, she lived in a series of small desert towns in the shadow of the Sierra Nevada.[1] These frontier communities were in close proximity to scattered Indian camps where the remaining Paiute Indians lived. At the turn of the century there were four to five hundred Paiutes in the Owens Valley. Their chief art was the weaving of baskets to store food-

9.1. Portrait of Mary
Austin, dated 1922
[1921]. Album 296,
Folder 3 (37.1), by
permission of the
Huntington Library,
San Marino, CA.

stuffs such as pine nuts, roots, and berries. They lived in conical structures
made of willows and sealed with mud, called "wickiups."

Although burdened with her responsibilities as a frontier housewife and
the care of her retarded daughter, Austin aspired to a life as a professional
writer. But in the desolate town of Independence, where she and her husband finally settled, there seemed little hope of a literary career. Bored by
the usual round of small-town activities, she became interested in the life of
her Paiute housekeeper and "a handful of Paiute Indians" living nearby. As
she later confessed, she become acquainted with Indian culture because
there was literally nothing else to be interested in. During a trip to Los Angeles she met Charles Lummis, a former "Harvard man" who had come west
and established himself as a nationally known authority on the Indians of
the Southwest and as the editor of the California periodical *The Land of Sunshine*. A poem Austin submitted for publication in his magazine reveals her
attraction to Indians as a potential literary subject. However, the conventional verse, "Little Light Moccasin," indicates a naïve, superficial notion of

Indian life. The following is a short excerpt from the poem, which appeared in April 1899:

Little Light Moccasin swings in her basket
     Woven of willow and sinew of deer
Rocked by the breezes and nursed by the pine trees
     Wonderful things are to see and to hear.

At the Lummis home Austin met Dr. Frederick Webb Hodge, an experienced ethnologist, who told her how to collect information about Indians. (The Bureau of Ethnology, a division of the Smithsonian Institution, had been created in 1879.) He also furnished her with an "alphabet" to use in the study of Indian languages. With this rudimentary instruction in the elements of field research, Austin pursued her interest in Indian culture. She attended the Indian celebrations, or "fandangoes," as they were called, at Fort Independence and recorded two Paiute war chants on a wax cylinder with an Edison home phonograph. She quickly informed Hodge that she had collected some "scraps of information" about Indians, including a "pretty fair account of their myths and domestic economy, incomplete accounts of their dances and secret rites, and a translation made by one of their number of some songs." In addition, she added, "I can give some description of their artifects [sic]." She hoped to utilize the material for her literary work and "in that way . . . make my bread and butter" (letter to Hodge, Nov. 5, 1899).

We have only Austin's word for how intimately she knew Indians, and her later claims differ significantly from the statements she made during this period. Unlike her contemporary James Mooney, the "Indian Man," and other white Indian experts of her day, Austin never submerged herself in Indian culture by living like an Indian or among the Indians.[2] Rather, she lived for a portion of her life in frontier areas where Indians were. She was not a professional ethnologist or anthropologist. Although she claimed to have mastered some Indian sign language, she knew no Indian languages or dialects. She was an aspiring professional writer in search of good marketable material.

Austin used some of her impressions in her first book, *The Land of Little Rain* (1903), a well-received collection of picturesque essays about the California desert. It contained two sentimental sketches that reflected her idealized notions of primitive life and her belief in the nobility of Indian character. Utilizing the Paiute women's reputation for basketry, she wrote an essay on Seyavi, an aged basket maker, who like "every Indian woman [was] an artist" (168).[3] A second sketch focused on Winnenap, a tribal medicine man, who, after his death, went to "no hymn-book heaven, but the free air and free spaces of Shoshone Land" (101). The Indians in *The Land of Little Rain* are virtuous and high-minded and have lost much of their "savageness" (Austin's term). Her next work, *The Basket Woman* (1904), a collection of folktales for children, also contains variations on the image of the "good Indian."

Austin's early work was easily marketed to an eastern audience because of its picturesque natural charm and romantic aura. However, her writing was not without its critics. Playing the role of the mentor, Lummis addressed a problem which would plague her literary career—her scattered attention to detail and her disregard for "factual" knowledge. He chastised her ("Dear Child" as he called her) for not giving the reading public what he called "a fair bargain." While complimenting her on her "great gift," he admonished her not to "swindle" her readers by writing about things she was ignorant of, or in his words, not to "feather your nest with stolen plumage" (letter to Austin, Nov. 24, 1904).

In 1905 Austin left her husband, placed her daughter in an institution, and abandoned the borders of Death Valley for the seaside literary colony of Carmel, California. As a budding Indian faddist, she appears to have "gone native" to some extent. Her professional activities were accompanied by a penchant for wearing the beaded leather gown of an "Indian Princess," and arranging her knee-length chestnut hair in long Indian braids (Genthe 75).[4] Exhibiting a Victorian affectation of Indian ways, Austin typed her manuscripts and received her guests in a studio built in a tree, which she called her "wickiup," and wrote to her friends and associates on personalized stationery monogrammed "Mary Austin, The Wickiup, Carmel by the Sea." It was an early expression of Austin's unique myth of the self as Indian expert.

Austin had a theatrical personality and a flair for the melodramatic. She perceived Indians as romantic figures despite the harsh realities of Indian life. She was fascinated by their "mystical" religion, a spiritual orientation in stark contrast to the midwestern Methodism in which she had been raised. After eighteen years in the California desert, she craved novelty and stimulation. Her identification with Indians was a way to escape the restrictive mores of white middle-class life. It was also an opportunity to enhance her literary persona and to advance her professional career. Having lived for years on the fringe of civilization, she could turn her isolation into an asset. She could exploit the ways in which her experience set her apart.

Austin's next effort was a contemporary California novel, *Santa Lucia* (1908). But she returned to her Indian material in a collection of regional short stories entitled *Lost Borders* (1909). It contained three tales about Paiute and Shoshone women and their ill-fated relationships with white men. Possessed of some stereotypical Indian traits, Austin's Native American heroines are Anglicized, romanticized figures, as is frequently the case in her writing. They have many of the qualities representative of the traditional "Indian Princess" motif—beauty, grace, and a childlike devotion to their white lovers. For example, Turwhasé, the "gray-eyed" Shoshone in "A Case of Conscience," is described as being "never weary nor afraid. She was never out of temper, except when she was jealous, and that was rather amusing. Saunders himself told me how she glowed and blossomed under his caress, and wept when he neglected her. . . . Turwhasé had the art to provoke tenderness and the wish to protect, and the primitive woman's capacity for making no demands upon it" (31).

Austin also began to collaborate on an Indian play, *The Coyote Doctor,* with the dramatist Elmer Harris. Its melodramatic storyline concerns a Paiute woman and her lover, who are forced into exile by the tribe after he is accused of practicing "coyote" witchcraft. (Plays with Indian themes were a popular form of entertainment. Donald MacLaren's *The Redskin* had been successfully produced in New York in 1906.) Negotiations to place *The Coyote Doctor* were unsuccessful, although the actress Florence Roberts had tentatively agreed to play the female lead. Nevertheless, Austin astutely saw the commercial possibilities of an Indian play, and without any technical knowledge of stage craft or dialogue, plunged forward as an aspiring playwright on her own.

By 1910 she had completed her own play, *The Arrow Maker,* which was accepted for production at the New Theatre on Broadway.[5] Her overly poetic story of "primitive domestic life" centers on the plight of a Paiute medicine woman, or "Chisera," who loses her spiritual power when she is scorned by her lover, the tribal arrow maker. Although the drama was mounted by the producers as an Indian extravaganza, all of the parts were played by white actors. To lend authenticity, costumes and properties were copied from artifacts in the Metropolitan Museum of Natural History. Photographs of the play, with its spectacular stage settings, were featured in the Sunday *New York Times* (Pictorial section, Mar. 12, 1911). However, the production closed early amid harsh reviews which criticized it as "ridiculous" and "pretentious" because of its phony dialogue and unimaginative plot. As one critic lamented, the play "belong[ed] to the a b c's of dramatic art" ("New Play" 106–7).

Nevertheless, the publicity surrounding *The Arrow Maker* boosted Austin's reputation as "an authority on the red man of the Southwest" ("To Produce Indian Play"). Catering to the public's interest in the vanishing frontier (Buffalo Bill Cody was still touring the country with his Wild West Show), she found new ways to add to her status as an Indian expert. This included lecturing on one of her favorite topics, "primitive woman." Taking every opportunity to, as she phrased it, "talk Indian," she found ample occasion to exploit her acquaintance with Native American life and to cultivate a unique identity in New York.

As part of her self-promotion, Austin was given to fictionalize or exaggerate certain aspects of her past. In an imaginative recreation of her own experience, she embellished her reputation as an Indian expert in *Christ in Italy* (1912). In a little bit of nonsense, she claimed to have studied with Tinnemaha, a Paiute medicine man, and announced that she had drunk from

Hassayampa, a secret river in California that gives Indians visionary powers (x–xviii, 68–69).[6] Austin may have been inattentive to details, or she may have been deliberately manipulating her readers' ignorance of the West. In either case, Hassayampa is a well-known river located approximately fifty miles west of Phoenix, Arizona. Austin's eastern publishers, who were primarily interested in marketing her writings as light entertainment, seldom questioned her claims or her accuracy. Her work had artistic merit, whether or not it was authentic.

In the next few years Austin supported herself on an unsteady income as a professional writer. However, the First World War undermined the sale of her work, including her California novel *The Ford* (1917), and she despaired over the poor sales of her books during wartime. Hard-pressed, she proposed a collection of Indian legends for children, entitled *The Trail Book,* arguing that the subject matter of American Indian trails was appropriate to the patriotism the war had engendered. She explained that she had begun her children's book because of "the lack of imaginative material with the American stamp." The "time was ripe," she proclaimed, for a literary movement back to "American sources" (letter to Greenslet, Sept. 29, 1917).

Austin had established herself as a creative writer and essayist. In addition, she decided to try her hand at academic nonfiction, to "capture . . . the intellectual audience" (letter to Van Doren, July 14, [1921]). For example, she accepted an assignment from Carl Van Doren to contribute a six-thousand-word essay on "Aboriginal Non-English Writings" to the *Cambridge History of American Literature* (1921). The other contributors were an illustrious group of male university professors, and Austin was clearly out of her depth as a professional writer and nonacademician. Her numerous book and magazine deadlines left her little time to pursue original research. She wrote in desperation to Frederick Hodge for suggestions on what she might read, and pored over the information he sent her, which included his own scholarly papers. Commenting later on her practice of availing herself of other people's hard-won expertise, he privately complained that she was "always a sponge" (Gordon 181). Nevertheless, Austin met her deadline. Ever mindful that writing was a business, she sent off a letter reminding Van Doren to send her a check.

Partly as a result of her association with Hodge, in 1918 Austin was given an appointment at the School of American Research in Santa Fe, New Mexico, as an associate in Native American literature. She was confident that the appointment would add stature to her reputation as an authority on Native American life. She had exhausted her material on California Indians, and would now be able to gather information about Indian tribes of the Southwest. One wonders about Austin's sensitivity in setting an Indian prayer-meal bowl on the desk in her office to hold her pencils and pens. Soon she began to hold "friendly court" with the local Indians and to investigate the Indian pueblos near Santa Fe. It was reported by the local press that she was touring the region, getting "local color" for a series of stories.

Austin's diverse interests soon focused on the translation of Indian songs or poems, an interest she shared with many amateur and professional ethnologists. Beginning in 1911 she published several "transcriptions" or "re-expressions" of Indian poems or songs, which appeared in *McClure's, Harper's,* and *Poetry.* She was dependent on bilingual translators, and the ethnographical authenticity of her Indian material was frequently questioned. For example, she identified "A Song in Time of Depression," one of two "Medicine Songs" which she published in *Everybody's Magazine,* as a Paiute poem "transcribed from the Indian Originals." However, the lines "Return and sing, O my Dreams, / In the dewy and palpitant pastures" suggested Austin's own penchant for florid language (415). As she admitted, some publications, such as the *Atlantic Monthly* and the *Century,* refused to publish her Indian material unless she "confessed that I had made it up, but never on the assumption that they were Indian" (*Earth Horizon* 333). In stark contrast to its rejection of Austin's "re-expressions," the *Century* had published the translations of the anthropologist Alice Fletcher as early as 1894.[7]

Although highly imaginative, Austin often exhibited a limited capacity for careful, analytical thinking. At Blackburn College she had taken classes in the natural sciences, but she lacked training in modern social science research methods. Hindered by her inadequate academic background, she depended on her creative instincts and "feminine intuition." She sometimes drew unwarranted conclusions on the basis of inadequate evidence and frequently paraded her theories as fact. Concerning the results of her research on Native American songs, she explained: "Then I made some further inquires into Indian song forms with a view to local influences. I find them derived very largely from dramatic forms, and had [sic] some new light on drama in relation to the food quest. That in turn threw light on the so called 'sex drama' which turned out to follow a food curve" (letter to MacDougal, Jan. 28, 1919).

Despite the dubious nature of her "re-expressions," Austin became a leading pioneer in the burgeoning field of "Amerind" verse. Proclaiming her theory that poetic cadence is a function of the environment, she completed an abstruse if imaginative introduction to accompany her collection of Indian poems. She submitted *The American Rhythm,* as it was called, to Ferris Greenslet, her editor at Houghton Mifflin, who had previously assured her that his company wanted the rights to all of her Indian material. Expecting something romantic and picturesque along the lines of her earlier work, Greenslet was put off by her theorizing. He expressed his doubts that his company could successfully market the book, and rejected it for publication.

Published by Harcourt, Brace and Company in 1923 and reissued by Houghton Mifflin Company in 1930, Austin's idiosyncratic "criterion of American rhythms" caused an outcry in some circles, as represented by the poet Arthur Davison Ficke, who accused her of making it all up. Dismissing the legitimacy of his concerns, she made the sweeping observation that she was the final authority on the study of Indian poetry as "my own field, first staked out and preempted by myself" (letter to Ficke, Mar. 27, 1930). Nevertheless, Ficke noted, as a poet he "simply [did] not believe a word of it" and was "absolutely stumped" by her assertions. Referring to her well-known reputation for attacking her critics, he taunted, "if you want to print this somewhere, and slay me in your reply to my objections, you have my permission."[8]

His response was, to Austin's way of thinking, a manifestation of traditional male superiority. As she complained, "my men readers in particular seem pent [sic] on taking me down a peg or two" (letter to MacDougal, May 16, [1923]). Indeed, she had received "a number of long letters from College professors . . . pointing out that . . . I would have written [the book] quite differently if I had not been a woman."[9] She was criticized for her blatant disregard of academic methods and her obliviousness to the proper use of facts. Outraged by questions concerning the scholarly value of her work, she combated her critics with charges of sexism. She defended her intuitive approach as perfectly sound, and lashed out at the chauvinism of male experts who relied on "formal intellectualization" and an "ivy league education."

Austin may well have been right in her charges of gender discrimination, but she was also guilty as charged. The issue was the extent of her expertise. By way of illustration, in 1907 the musicologist Natalie Curtis had published *The Indians' Book,* a well-received collection of Native American songs. Curtis had studied at the National Conservatory of Music in New York and abroad and had collected her translations by traveling by train, wagon, and horseback to visit Indians in remote locations across America. Obviously Austin was self-taught, but how much did she know? Had she exploited her intuitive understanding of Indians, a superficial acquaintance with their culture, and the borrowed expertise of more knowledgeable people to develop a career as an Indian savant?

By the 1920s Indians were Austin's stock in trade. She kept her name before the public with a steady stream of articles and book reviews about indigenous American culture. There was growing popular interest in the subject of Native Americans, and Austin was indefatigable in persuading editors to accept her expertise on practically every aspect of primitive life and to give her space in their periodicals.[10] She also continued to publish her Indian short fiction. In 1922 she contracted with Harry Payne Burton, the editor of *McCall's,* to write three stories with an Indian theme for $750 each, an extremely high fee in that day. Caring less about the authenticity of her work than its exotic appeal to his female reading audience, Burton instructed her to "seize every opportunity that you artistically can" to add "touches of glamour" and alleviate a "grim atmosphere."[11] In the world of commercial magazine publishing, as in the commercial theater, the marketing of Native American life was a white person's game that frequently had little to do with real Indians. As a market product they were irrelevant.

Austin's name was sufficiently linked with Indians in the popular mind that she was invited to become consulting editor to the Camp Fire Girls, an organization whose symbols were derived from Indian lore. Her appointment included the likelihood that some of her stories would be serialized in their publication, *Everygirl's Magazine*. Sizing up the matter from a strictly commercial point of view, her publisher noted that he could envision "widespread publicity for your books in your connection" with the periodical (Houghton Mifflin, letter to Austin, Feb. 18, 1922). Unfortunately, Austin was never inclined to reject opportunities that enhanced her visibility, no matter how ludicrous. She agreed that the venture would be good publicity for her Indian work, although she was a little dubious about using "my position in Camp Fire to sell my own books" (letter to Pratt, Feb. 15, 1922).

In order in increase her income and professional recognition, Austin also attempted to sell the motion picture rights to her Indian work. The "celluloid Indian" was the new fashion. D. W. Griffith had successfully adapted *Ramona,* Helen Hunt Jackson's romantic novel about the California mission Indians, into a popular silent film starring Mary Pickford. As Austin confided to her publishers, she had already received a "number of nibbles" on her play *The Arrow Maker.* As Austin explained, "I do really mean to make a serious effort to get my Indian stories on the screen. Nobody living is so well prepared to do this authoritatively." Noting that the Santa Fe area was "crammed with movie people," she hoped to place a story that would "go over big." She pinned her highest hopes on her 148-page manuscript "Thinking White," the tale of an educated Navajo Indian who marries a white woman. Convinced that it was "a good screen story," she hoped to tie the film rights in with book publication, and to reap the agent's selling commission and the screenwriter's fee (letter to Greenslet, Apr. 5, 1927).

To broaden her sources of income, she also exploited her flair for the dramatic in a career as a public lecturer with the Louis J. Alber World Celebrities Lecture Bureau, which promoted such well-known personalities as Harry Houdini. She saw lecturing as a useful way to "try out" her Indian material on the public. Her standard fee was two hundred dollars for her presentations at Chautauqua meetings, women's clubs, Rotary associations, literary and poetry societies, and university forums. Among her lectures, which included talks on Native American dance, drama, and literature, the most popular was that on aboriginal poetry, accompanied by readings from her own Indian verse. Bewailing the impossibility of trying to type on passenger trains, she crisscrossed the country on her annual winter lecture tour. On occasion her lectures were simultaneously broadcast to a radio audience. To increase her financial return, she tried to organize her tours in conjunction with the publication dates of her books, and to arrange for extra promotion and bookstore displays in all the cities and towns on her itinerary.

In addition, Austin attempted to curry favor with important people who could help advance her professional career. Besides copies of her books, she frequently sent gifts of Indian cornmeal, pottery, and jewelry, including rings that her New York acquaintances nearly "pried" off her fingers. Exhibiting her penchant for Indian religious symbols, she also sent fetishes, sometimes with mixed results. She mailed the writer Louis Adamic "the foot of a little furred animal," with instructions that he should carry "Mokiach, my Lord Puma" on his person to release his "subconscious forces." As Adamic recalls in his autobiography, *My America,* he wondered if Austin was a "vague folk-cultist" or a "crackpot" (479).

"The country has almost seemed to go *indian* [*sic*]," the apologist Mabel Dodge proclaimed in 1922, and Austin was in the vanguard.[12] As a leading enthusiast, she was frequently criticized for her flamboyant "Amerindian airs." Indeed, there appears to have been considerable playing for effect in her appearance at a publisher's banquet in her honor at the National Arts Club in New York City. Her choice of companion for the evening was the well-known young Chickasaw Indian artist Overton Colbert, who wore quill-embroidered buckskin, a full-length black, white, and flamingo feather Indian headdress, and a necklace made out of alligator teeth. The middle-aged woman writer and Native American escort were a variation of the popular Indian sidekick motif.[13] Capitalizing on her reputation as an authority on Indians, Austin was creating something more than her writing to be noticed. She was producing and aggressively promoting a highly marketable image.

In a review of one of her books, Van Wyck Brooks reflected on what he perceived as the decline of Austin's serious career and the ascendance of her personal psychodrama. In an account that seemed straight out of a silent film, he described how, while researching *The Trail Book,* she would go to the Museum of Natural History at midnight,

> and, standing among the Indian relics, fall into a trance that placed her in a mystic communion with the Great Spirit and the souls of the dead. And once, by daylight, to the alarm of the guard who supposed for a moment that she had designs on the collection, she took several relics from a case that had been opened for her and placing them in her bosom fell into a state of silent ecstasy. Great was the guard's relief when, after a few minutes, she returned the relics to the case and explained that she had been in communion with the gods of the red men. (310–11)

Austin was indignant at Brooks's review, and lashed out at the story as "false and discrediting" (letter to editor, June 8, 1920). While admitting that she had gone into the museum at night with a lantern, taken Indian artifacts and costumes out of the cases, and, in some instances, tried them on, she was outraged at seeing her actions belittled in print. Yet she often engaged in what was perceived as odd behavior. It was another aspect of her creative approach to expertise—a kind of Aristotelian mimesis. As she explained in the *American Rhythm:* "I have naturally a mimetic temperament that draws me toward the understanding of life by living it. . . . So that when I say I am not, have never been, or offered myself, as an authority in things Amerindian, I do not wish to have it understood that I may not, at times, have succeeded in being an Indian" (37–41).

Putting aside the issue of Austin's outrageous denial of having ever claimed to be an authority, her comment sheds new light on her work as an Indian expert. Her understanding of Indians was, in part, an imaginative journey. She believed that she knew about Native American culture because she perceived it intuitively and had tried to imitate it. In so doing, she had entered into the "Indian consciousness." Is it possible to find value in such a nonintellectual approach? If so, Austin was a creative artist who tried to achieve a perfect fusion of art and life; if not, she was a classic example of the "wanna-be Indian" only too well known to the Native American community.

For example, in preparation for her book *The Land of Journeys' Ending* (1924), Austin undertook an automobile trip across the Southwest. Temporarily inconvenienced by a sandstorm, she left her car, wrapped herself in an Indian blanket, and after positioning herself under a large rock, made "good medicine" to improve the weather (Fink 227). One wonders at Austin's acting out the traditional "blanket Indian" stereotype. As an Indian faddist, she freely adopted religious and cultural aspects of "Indianness" that she believed were superior to those of Western civilization. However, she may have been guilty of more than a little arrogance when she self-servingly co-opted only those practices which particularly intrigued her. As she once observed (in a comment that was hardly to her credit), she liked to "play" Indian.

Austin was frequently guilty of a similar offense in her writing. As she observed, she was not interested in the "exactitudes" of the ethnologist.[14] She freely blended factual information, descriptive phrasing, Indian stereotypes, and the workings of her imagination to create her own conception of Native American life. The following passage is taken from *The Land of Journeys' Ending,* published by the Century Company and serialized in *Century* magazine:

> The evening meal at the pueblo is taken before the fire, with the smoking food-bowl in the middle, the platter of bread beside it, the swinging cradle within reach, the children leaning on their parents' knees and taking their portions by the only rule of table manners the pueblo knows, with slowness and dignity. After supper the sack of native tobacco and the heap of soft corn husks, and the quiet stealing away of one or another of the house

group for the hour of meditation and the last salute to the Sun Father; then the voice of the *pregonero,* sounding from the housetop, with directions for to-morrow's labor. If it should be evening at Taos, you will hear the young men, ghostly in their white sheets, on the bridge between the north and the south houses, singing their wordless moonlight melody, or at Zuni they will foregather on the terraces to moan melodiously until the protest of some sleepy elder cries them silence. (243)

Obviously, the above passage gave a romantic picture of the beauty and humanity of Pueblo culture, but it also belied its complexity. Her descriptions were frequently idealized and impressionistic, crafted for the white imagination. Generally speaking, she did not write for professionals. She popularized a primitive, indigenous culture for a middle-class, mass-market audience. As a self-proclaimed intuitionist she advocated those aspects of life that were nonrational, nonscientific, and nonanalytical. As an outspoken neoprimitivist she promoted certain features of Native American culture that she found absent in white civilization and that she perceived to be of value.

In 1925 Austin permanently relocated to New Mexico. She built a house with her royalties and the money from her lecture tours, outfitted it with the latest innovation in Santa Fe—gas heating—and decorated it with Native American baskets and rugs. Santa Fe was the center of a thriving tourist trade, and she devoted much of her time to the preservation of Indian arts. As she observed in an unguarded moment, such activities also vindicated her against her critics. "The easterners used to be afraid of me," she explained, "afraid that I might be mistaken [about Indians]. . . . And, of course, the part I play in the new museum and the Indian Arts Foundation at Santa Fe make a difference" (letter to Greenslet, Feb. 1, 1929). She was soon active in a variety of reforms to ensure the preservation of Indian arts and the protection of Indian lands. Her impressive efforts on behalf of Native American rights inspired the *Los Angeles Times* to dub her "Little Mother to 350,000 Indians."[15]

Regrettably, Austin also spent a lot of time promoting herself in innumerable newspaper interviews. As her interest in Indians became legendary so did her grandiosity. One of her more outrageous statements was that all Americans would eventually look like Indians—"flat back, high chest, square chin" (a comment guaranteed to reinforce stereotypes).[16] Alluding to Austin's pompous habit of making visionary, "prophetic" declarations, her friends snidely referred to her as the Chisera, the Paiute name for a medicine woman. In a pointed criticism regarding her divine self-importance, a writer for the *Forum* compared her overbearing manner to that of the priestess at Delphi delivering the oracles. As one reviewer dryly concluded, Austin's pretentious observations might "be important without being quite all-important."[17]

Austin's unbounded enthusiasm for Native Americans was no doubt motivated in part by spiritual, aesthetic, and cultural values. But throughout her life she also evinced a habitual pattern of excessive emotionality and flamboyant, self-dramatizing behavior. As she frequently complained, her own life "bored" her. She was driven by an insanely intense need to be noticed and to be associated with grand causes. Often neglecting her writing, she was distracted by her various roles as Indian enthusiast, propagandist, and reformer. As she informed an editor at Bobbs-Merrill who asked about acquiring one of her manuscripts, "I have no time for a mere publisher" (letter to Chambers, June 9, 1928).

Nevertheless, Austin wanted her Indian books to be "money makers" and was frequently disappointed in her royalties. On occasion, she reprimanded her publishers for their inexcusable "stupidity" in marketing her Indian books, claiming that they could have "gotten [more] out of them, if you understood them and the rapidly increasing interest in the subject" (letter to Greenslet [Feb. 3, 1929]). Periodically, she hounded them to expand the consumer interest in her work by trying to exploit the British market and by obtaining German and French editions. Overwhelmed by the endless list of her suggestions and complaints, the editor Ferris Greenslet cast her career as an Indianist as a mock-heroic play, and offered to convene "a grand pow-wow on your future work as a whole" (Greenslet, letter to Austin, Oct. 24, 1927).

Despite her efforts at promoting her work, Austin remained financially insecure throughout much of her career. She added to her income by republishing her Indian poems in anthologies, giving second serial rights on magazine stories to newspapers, and pocketing twenty-five-dollar royalties from various university and little theater productions of *The Arrow Maker* and a second Indian play, *Fire*. Her determination to make her work profitable is illustrated in the publication of *Taos Pueblo* (1930), completed in collaboration with Ansel Adams. His twelve original black and white photographs of the pueblo were accompanied by Austin's text, which was completed in one week without her ever having seen his photographs. Although the country was in the midst of the depression, the work was published as an expensive art book by San Francisco book designer John Henry Nash. Lamenting that a costly book could not possibly stay in print, Austin took her personal copy to New York on her annual lecture tour to show to her publishers, in the vain hope that they would publish a less expensive edition. In a dogged attempt to make more money, she asked Adams if he had any leftover photographs that could be marketed with her inscriptions. She also inquired if he had any moving pictures of Taos or "any other Indian movies" for which she could supply the text. As she observed, her agent, Ann Watkins, could "sell anything" (letter to Adams, Mar. 13, 1931).

Austin frequently seemed to want a monopoly on Native American material. Although she was generous in offering help to her friends, she damned many of her competitors as "ignoramuses." As she complained, some of the authorities on Native American culture had never been closer to an Indian than a cigar store. Faced with an avalanche of important new books on Indians, she resorted to making exaggerated, even fantastic, claims about her own work. In an application for a Guggenheim to help pay for a typist and a translator, she grandly observed, "One possible objection to my getting the award this time is that I do not know any authorities on Indian Art to refer to, I being the only authority who has written anything on that subject" (letter to Hodge, Oct. 24, 1932). It was hardly the kind of statement that would endear her to other white experts or to Native Americans. Unfortunately there is no record of what Indians thought of Austin.

Although Austin wrote in a wide variety of genres on a vast array of subjects, she consistently promoted herself as *the* authority on Indians. "Practically everybody at work in this field refers to me sooner or later," she noted. Somewhat as an afterthought, but perhaps more to the point, she also admitted that "the public seems to be willing to accept me on this subject with less criticism than on any other" (letter to Greenslet, Nov. 10, 1926). Nevertheless, for all her extravagant claims, she could not silence her critics. Responding to some of her writings, Franz Boas, the leading academic anthropologist, "gave me an unpleasant quarter of an hour," she complained, "attacking my personal integrity" (letter to Dear Friend, Apr. 13, 1930). Her former mentor, Charles Lummis, was one of her most avid detractors. At first sympathetic to her efforts, he was now appalled, and he condemned her "oracular impudence" and "incalculable nerve." Contrary to her claims of expertise, he observed, "she never would study anything for it all comes to her by divine revelation" (Fiske and Lummis 106). In his comments on *The Land of Journeys' Ending,* he berated her for her careless use of language, in particular, her use of the word *Puebl6ño* to refer to the "inhabitants of the Indian towns of New Mexico and Arizona" *(Land of Journeys' Ending* 456). "There is no such word in any language, and there can not be such a word in Spanish. A skilled writer is entitled to make words in his own language, if he gives them the parentage of Clarity and of Legitimacy. But 'Puebleño' isn't even a bastard word" (Lummis, "Pueblo Myth" 171).[18]

In 1934, the last year of her life, Austin published *One-Smoke Stories,* a collection of piquant Indian tales. She described the work as "one of my pet books the only genuine book of Folk Tales, in the Folk manner that has yet appeared in America" (letter to Bender, Jan. 27, 1934). However, she was quickly forced to refute charges that her "authentic" Indian tales were "worthless to the student interested in exact observation." In response to yet another expert, she angrily threatened to "remove [his] scalp and wear it in my belt." However, she was given to privately admit that not only was her work in *One-Smoke Stories* not original, but that "in forty years I have published but two tales not previously published by other collectors" (letter to Canby, Apr. 1, 1930).

In a second book published that same year, *Can Prayer Be Answered?* Austin attempted to silence her detractors forever by asserting that she had "Indian blood," an imaginative embellishment on her earlier claim of a "somewhat mythical Indian ancestor" (*Can Prayer* 12; *Earth Horizon* 267). As Ina Cassidy caustically observed, Austin no longer needed to "talk to Indians, or to be with Indians in order to *know them.*"[19] A claim of Indian ethnicity automatically confers knowledge and power. There is no way to document the truth of Austin's statement, but clearly she had become her own art. Nevertheless, non-Indians cannot be Indians. If it were simply the case of an individual adopting an Indian persona, it would be a relatively harmless matter. However, it becomes more problematic if Austin made such a claim to enhance her status as an Indian expert. Then again, perhaps she had half-begun to believe it herself.

Throughout her career Austin's association with Indians made for good publicity and for good copy. Her work as an Indianist brought in money and advanced her professional life. The country's continued infatuation with Native Americans provided a receptive market for a commercial product—her literary output. She was selling something that the general public was willing to buy, and with some effort she was always able to place her work. Austin's writing contributed to a certain idea of Native Americans—a variation of the "Noble Savage." Her Indians were artistic and spiritual, living in harmony with nature, in stark contrast to the usual "cowboys and Indians" motif. Thus, she stressed a vastly more positive image. She accomplished a great deal in fostering sympathetic, popular interest in indigenous culture and in giving added legitimacy to a part of western life that was largely neglected and unknown. Nevertheless, a large part of her writing was in the tradition of Euro-American ethnocentrism, whites creating and imagining the American Indian. Her work, when compared to photographs and ethnological reports, evidences cosmetic "improvements" on real Indians.

Austin's infatuation and identification with a picturesque, romanticized idea of Indian life reveals as much about her creative temperament as it does about Native American culture. Indians, as America's resident exotics, provided the richness and drama her own life lacked. They served her artistic and psychic needs. Through them she made her professional career more colorful. They became projections of her personality and her artistic alter ego. Austin was a gifted writer with an absolute genius for self-promotion. While she had a certain knowledge of primitive life, she was also something of a charlatan. Nevertheless, her imaginative self-mythology as the leading authority on Indians was unusually successful by any standards of her day. If her work was criticized by more knowledgeable experts and others of her contemporaries, it was accepted by most publishers and by the American reading public.

Notes

I would like to thank Terry P. Wilson of the University of California at Berkeley for his comments on an earlier version of this paper, presented at the Annual Meeting of the American Historical Association in Cincinnati in 1988.

1. For additional information on this period of Austin's life see Austin, *Earth Horizon;* Fink; and Stineman.
2. For a discussion of ethnology, professionalism, and field research, see Moses.
3. For a discussion of the marketing of Austin's western work, see Langlois, "Mary Austin and Houghton Mifflin."
4. See also Ted Gale's cartoon of Mary Austin in her Indian braids, *Los Angeles Times* [1910], Braun Research Library, Southwest Museum, Los Angeles, CA. In response to Austin's identification with Indians, as well as her stubborn personality, her Carmel associates nicknamed her Sitting Bull.
5. For additional information see Langlois, "Mary Austin and the New Theatre."
6. See also Austin, *Can Prayer Be Answered?* 3–6.
7. See Alice C. Fletcher, "Indian Songs—Personal Studies of Indian Life," *Century* Jan. 1894: 421–31.
8. Ficke, letter to Austin, Mar. 11, 1930, qtd. in Pearce 241–42.
9. Austin, letter to Luhan, May 16, [1923]. For additional comment on Austin's expertise on Native American poetry, see Howard; and Castro 5–45.
10. For a list of Austin's publications, including those on Native Americans (books, journalism, short stories, essays, poetry, and contributions to collections), see bibliographies in Stineman 249–52; and Wynn 399–412.
11. Burton, letter to Austin, Sept. 23, 1922. In 1925 Austin won the O. Henry Memorial Prize for "Papago Wedding." For a selection of Austin's short stories, see *The Land of Little Rain; Lost Borders; The Basket Woman; The Trail Book; One-Smoke Stories;* and *Western Trails.*
12. Luhan, letter to Austin [Dec. 1922], qtd. in Pearce 172.
13. Alice Fletcher was frequently accompanied by her collaborator and adopted son, the Omaha head chief's son and ethnologist Francis La Flesche. For an illuminating discussion of their relationship, see Mark 307–9.
14. Austin frequently described herself as a "folklorist" as opposed to an "ethnologist," as in her letter to Canby, Apr. 1, 1930. This distinction was frequently, if incorrectly, employed to validate both her status as an "authority" on Indians and her right to make unsubstantiated claims regarding their life and culture.
15. "Mary Austin Little Mother to 350,000 Indians, Says Coast Paper," Oct. 31, 1933, unidentified newspaper clipping, Bancroft Library, U of California, Berkeley. Among Austin's many activities on behalf of Native American rights were her efforts to defeat the Bursum Bill, which threatened Pueblo land rights. She also organized the Indian Arts Fund, bequeathing it her home in Santa Fe following her death in 1934.
16. "Race of Future Like Indians." One example of Austin's numerous stereotypes occurs in her depiction of Turwhasé, the Shoshone heroine in "A Case of Conscience" (*Lost*

Borders 32–33). Following the birth of her first child Turwhasé is described as being "hopeless. She had never left off her blanket, and like all Indian women when they mature, had begun to grow fat." Another example appears in *Earth Horizon* 246, wherein she refers to a Paiute baby as a "beady-eyed brown dumpling."

17. "Miss Austin Defines One Hundred Per Cent American Poetry," unidentified newspaper clipping, Cassidy Collection, Bancroft Library, U of California, Berkeley.

18. For a defense of Austin see T. M. Pearce 35–40.

19. Diary, Jan. 19, 1934. Cassidy also noted that she had never seen an Indian in Austin's home, with the exception of Tony Luhan, who was married to Austin's friend and confidant, Mabel Dodge.

Works Cited

Adamic, Louis. *My America, 1928–1938.* New York: Harper, 1938.

Austin, Mary. *The American Rhythm.* New York: Harcourt, Brace, 1923.

———. *The Basket Woman.* Boston: Houghton Mifflin, 1904.

———. *Can Prayer Be Answered?* New York: Farrar and Rinehart, 1934.

———. *Christ in Italy.* New York: Duffield, 1921.

———. *Earth Horizon.* Cambridge, MA: Houghton Mifflin, 1932.

———. *The Land of Journeys' Ending.* New York and London: Century, 1924.

———. *The Land of Little Rain.* Boston: Houghton Mifflin, 1903.

———. Letter to Ansel Adams. Mar. 13, 1931. Huntington Library, San Marino, CA.

———. Letter to Albert Bender. Jan. 27, 1934. Mills College Library, Oakland CA.

———. Letter to Henry S. Canby. Apr. 1, 1930. Huntington Library, San Marino, CA.

———. Letter to D. L. Chambers [Bobbs Merrill Company]. June 9, 1928. Lilly Library, Indiana U.

———. Letter to Dear Friend. Apr. 13, 1930. Braun Research Library, Southwest Museum, Los Angeles, CA.

———. Letter to Arthur Davison Ficke. Mar. 27, 1930. Huntington Library, San Marino, CA.

———. Letter to editor [*The Freeman*]. June 8, 1920. Van Pelt Library, University of Pennsylvania.

———. Letters to Ferris Greenslet. Sept. 29, 1917; Nov. 10, 1926; Apr. 5, 1927; Feb. 1, 1929; [Feb. 3, 1929]. Houghton Mifflin Co., Boston.

———. Letters to Frederick Webb Hodge. Nov. 5, 1899; Oct. 24, 1932. Braun Research Library, Southwest Museum, Los Angeles, CA.

———. Letter to Mabel Dodge Luhan. May 16, [1923]. Yale U Library.

———. Letter to Daniel Trembly MacDougal. Jan. 28, 1919. Arizona Historical Society, Tucson.

———. Letter to Daniel Trembly MacDougal. May 16, [1923]. Huntington Library, San Marino, CA.

———. Letter to Mr. Pratt [Houghton Mifflin]. Feb. 15, 1922. Houghton Mifflin Co., Boston.

———. Letter to Carl Van Doren. July 14, [1921]. Princeton U Library.

————. "Little Light Moccasin." *Land of Sunshine* Apr. 1899: 261.

————. *Lost Borders.* New York: Harper, 1909.

————. "Medicine Songs." *Everybody's Magazine* Sept. 1924: 413–15.

————. *One-Smoke Stories.* Boston: Houghton Mifflin, 1934.

————. *The Trail Book.* Boston: Houghton Mifflin, 1917.

————. *Western Trails: A Collection of Short Stories by Mary Austin.* Ed. Melody Graulich. Reno and Las Vegas: U of Nevada P, 1987.

Brooks, Van Wyck. "A Reviewer's Notebook." *Freeman* June 9, 1920: 310–11.

Burton, Harry Payne. Letter to Austin. Sept. 23, 1922. Huntington Library, San Marino, CA.

Cassidy, Ina. Unpublished diary. Bancroft Library, U of California, Berkeley.

Castro, Michael. *Interpreting the Indian: Twentieth-Century Poets and the Native American.* Albuquerque: U of New Mexico P, 1983.

Fink, Augusta. *I Mary: A Biography of Mary Austin.* Tucson: U of Arizona P, 1983.

Fiske, Turbese Lummis, and Keith Lummis. *Charles F. Lummis, the Man and His West.* Norman: U of Oklahoma P, 1975.

Genthe, Arnold. *As I Remember.* New York: Reynal and Hitchcock, 1936.

Gordon, Dudley. *Charles F. Lummis: Crusader in Corduroy.* Los Angeles: Cultural Assets P, 1972.

Greenslet, Ferris. Letter to Mary Austin. Oct. 24, 1927. Huntington Library, San Marino, CA.

Houghton Mifflin Company. Letter to Mary Austin. Feb. 18, 1922. Huntington Library, San Marino, CA.

Howard, Helen Addison. "Mary Hunter Austin (1868–1934)." *American Indian Poetry.* Boston: Twayne, 1979. 67–86.

Langlois, Karen S. "Mary Austin and Houghton Mifflin Company: A Case Study in the Marketing of a Western Writer." *Western American Literature* 23.1 (1988): 31–42.

————. "Mary Austin and the New Theatre: The 1911 Production of *The Arrow Maker.*" *Theatre History Studies* 8 (1988): 71–87.

Lummis, Charles F. Letter to Mary Austin. Nov. 24, 1904. Braun Research Library, Southwest Museum, Los Angeles, CA.

————. "Pueblo Myth and Ritual." *El Palacio* Mar. 3, 1928: 171–72.

Mark, Joan. *A Stranger in Her Native Land: Alice Fletcher and the American Indians.* Lincoln: U of Nebraska P, 1988.

Moses, L. G. *The Indian Man: A Biography of James Mooney.* Urbana and Chicago: U of Illinois P, 1984.

"The New Play." *Theatre Magazine* Apr. 1911: 106–7.

Pearce, T. M. "The Literary Idiom of Mary Austin." *Mary Austin: A Memorial.* Ed. Williard Hougland. Santa Fe, NM: Laboratory of Anthropology, 1944. 35–40.

Pearce, Thomas Matthew, ed. *Literary America, 1903–1934: The Mary Austin Letters.* Westport, CT: Greenwood, 1979.

"Race of Future Like Indians Seen by Author." New York *Herald* Nov. 13, 1932.

Stineman, Esther Lanigan. *Mary Austin: Song of a Maverick.* New Haven, CT: Yale UP, 1989.

"To Produce Indian Play." *New York Times* Nov. 14, 1910.

Wynn, Dudley Taylor. "A Critical Study of the Writings of Mary Hunter Austin (1868–1934)." Diss. New York U, 1939.

10.

The Trials of Margaret Anderson and Jane Heap

Holly Baggett

The 1921 obscenity trial of *Little Review* editors Margaret Anderson and Jane Heap, for the publication of James Joyce's *Ulysses,* provides us with a look into the political, sexual, and literary maelstrom which characterized the transition from Victorianism to modernism. In this court case we can see how the twentieth-century struggle to acknowledge female sexuality profoundly affected the political context of a literary trial. Anderson and Heap were politically radical lesbians who tried to fight censorship while bringing the best of modernist literature to America in their magazine the *Little Review*. Their defense attorney, John Quinn, was a conservative known for his generous patronage of modern art and literature. Quinn was also a homophobic misogynist whose comments about Anderson and Heap in his private correspondence reveal how, in the words of Carroll Smith-Rosenberg, "sexual language functions as political metaphor" (246).

The *Ulysses* trial was played out in the paradox of America in the late teens and early twenties, where social liberation in matters of sexual behavior and norms coexisted with the political conservatism of the postwar Red Scare. The debate over censorship was transformed as the prudery of late-Victorian vice-societies gave way to more enlightened public discussions of sexuality. Under the influence of "sexologists" such as Havelock Ellis and the popularized work of Freud, society now viewed women as sexual beings. While this awareness of female sexuality was liberating for some women, it created dangerous conditions for others. Intense, intimate, and lifelong friendships between women, previously seen as asexual in the Victorian ideology of "separate spheres," were now viewed as something altogether different—lesbianism.

The general anxiety about lesbians, and by extension, Anderson and Heap, had a political component. The *Ulysses* case was certainly an example of the effort to suppress literature considered to be "obscene," but as the dynamics of the trial illustrate, it was also very much about the attempt to silence the "New Woman" of the twenties. The novel *Ulysses* itself raises many questions about sexuality and sexism; interpretation of "Nausicaa," the

10.1. Margaret Anderson, 1918. Special Collections, University of Delaware Library, Newark, Delaware.

chapter which led to the *Little Review*'s conviction, is still debated among Joyce scholars. During the real-life courtroom discourse, the fictional theme of female sexual desire in *Ulysses* was read in clearly misogynist terms. John Quinn's discovery that his clients were lesbians brought forth an explosion of fury, which to a certain extent accounted for his self-defeating legal strategy in the courtroom. The episode shows how the convergence of the New Woman and the sexuality of modernism could produce explosive results. In the prosecution of Anderson and Heap, truth had become stranger than fiction.

* * *

Margaret Anderson was a beautiful woman. Few autobiographies or letters mentioning her fail to include this impression. Her enthusiasm, idealism, and passion meant, in the words of one colleague, that "anyone who could resist Margaret Anderson was made of granite and cold steel" (Tietjens 64). A rebellious youth, she spent her early years confronting adults about everything from the quality of her handwriting to the nature of God. Dissatisfied with the stupefying intellectual climate of bourgeois life in Indiana, she broke free to Chicago, where against tremendous odds, she founded the *Little Review*, a literary journal which would publish the most important modernist writers of the twentieth century.

Anderson's leadership in the Chicago Literary Renaissance extended beyond an attack on the genteel in literature to include a politically and philo-

10.2. Jane Heap, 1918.
Special Collections,
University of Delaware
Library, Newark,
Delaware.

sophically radical agenda. Her heroes were Friedrich Nietzsche, Emma
Goldman, and Margaret Sanger, all of whom she lauded in the pages of the
Little Review. Her defense of anarchism, with such editorial comments as "Why
didn't someone shoot the Governor of Utah before he could shoot Joe Hill?"
("Toward Revolution") led to a government file which the FBI refuses to re-
lease seventy years after the fact.[1]

She was equally uncompromising about her lesbianism both personally
and professionally. Beautiful and feminine, she attracted many men, but their
admiration often dissolved into condescension when they discovered her
immunity to male magnetism. In 1915 Anderson wrote an editorial in which
she criticized Edith Ellis (wife of Havelock) for failing to comprehensively
discuss homosexuality in her husband's research. She ended with an attack on
the legal system's persecution of men and women "crucified and tortured for
their love" ("Mrs. Ellis's Failure"), which has been identified as the earliest militant defense by a lesbian of homosexuality in the United States (Katz 363–64).

In 1916 Anderson fell in love with Jane Heap, a Chicago artist originally
from Kansas. Their meeting, Anderson would write decades later, led to "a
new unexpected life that to me was like a second birth" ("Conversation" 6).

Heap surpassed Anderson in her unabashed public statements about her own sexuality. Heap was a cross-dresser, a practice mentioned just as frequently as Anderson's beauty in the autobiographies and letters of their acquaintances. This contrast of style led to unwarranted assumptions about gender roles within their relationship, as demonstrated by Malcolm Cowley's remark that "Anderson was beautiful, the woman of the couple; Jane Heap wore tailored clothes and had savagely bobbed hair" (Feb. 5, 1964). Heap, of course, was not the only female member of the avant-garde who cross-dressed. Clothing for many women in the early twentieth century was the key to emancipation in both a literal and a figurative sense. Adopting male attire gave them simultaneously physical and symbolic freedom from the narrow definition of gender.[2] Heap's public image was that of the "mannish lesbian" identified by early sexologists. As an example of this masculine woman, Heap was particularly a symbol of dangerous sexuality.[3]

Anderson and Heap were a study in contrasts beyond their external appearance. Anderson was optimistic and enthusiastic by nature; Heap was prone to dark moods. A droll sense of humor served to mask some of her despair, as did her immersion in art and poetry as a young woman, which, she stated, was an attempt to rob "the Real" of "some of its power to stun one's soul" (letter to Reynolds, Aug. 18, 1908). There can be little doubt that Heap's childhood, spent adjacent to the grounds of the Topeka State Insane Asylum, where her father worked and where she often played, had a tremendous impact on her sensibilities. Both her published essays and private letters express the empathy she felt with the isolation and anguish of the asylum's patients. Heap carried into adulthood an intuitive kinship with those who felt they never belonged; "We are all foreigners," she wrote Florence Reynolds, "and long for someone to talk our language" (Aug. 29, 1908). After graduating from high school in 1901, she left Kansas to study at the Art Institute of Chicago.

When the two women met in the office of the *Little Review* in Chicago's Fine Arts Building, Anderson was mesmerized. Here she wrote, "was my obsession—the special human being, the special point of view." Her "mind was inflamed" by Heap's ideas: "this was what I had been waiting for, searching for, all my life" (*Thirty Years' War* 107–8, 122). Anderson soon begged Heap to become coeditor of the *Little Review,* a move Heap initially resisted. Relenting but determined to remain in low profile, Heap signed her contributions to the journal with the lowercase initials *jh.* Because of Heap's self-effacement (Anderson by contrast wrote three autobiographies), she has remained somewhat mysterious to historians of the American avant-garde, and her contribution has been underestimated.[4]

The association of Anderson and Heap with Ezra Pound, the antifeminist expatriate in London, as their foreign editor might seem peculiar. Pound, after all, had fashioned a theory arguing that thought and logic were funda-

10.3. Jane Heap and
Margaret Anderson, 1922.
Special Collections,
University of Delaware
Library, Newark, Delaware.

mentally masculine processes and were analogous to sperm entering the
"female chaos." In addition to his general condescension toward women,
Pound persistently attempted to take over literary magazines founded and
edited by women.[5]

Pound's sexism was not straightforward, however; he also had a record
of encouraging female poets such as H.D. and Marianne Moore. Yet his support was partial and self-serving. He often misread their work as examples
of his theory of logic in verse and was, in the words of one literary critic,
"blind to the ways in which an awareness of gender informs their work"
(Burke 104). When Pound expressed interest in acting as the *Little Review*'s
foreign editor, Anderson was delighted. Earlier that year Anderson and Heap
moved the *Little Review* to New York to make the magazine "an international concern"; hence Pound's suggestion seemed especially fortuitous. In
addition, their agreement promised to realize Anderson's ambition to widen
the scope of the *Little Review*. In exchange for a guaranteed amount of space
each month, Pound would solicit material from T. S. Eliot, Wyndham Lewis,
and James Joyce, among others. When their agreement was settled, Pound

lost little time collecting work from authors abroad, as well as assuming a proprietary attitude toward the *Little Review,* which he described to Joyce as "my magazine" (*Pound/Joyce* 103).

Yet the assertion of one scholar that "Pound so dominated the magazine during his two years he was London editor that the presence of Margaret Anderson and Jane Heap could have easily been overlooked" is just one of the more strongly stated distortions of the alliance among the three editors (Alpert 234–35). Anderson and Heap were anything but pushovers when it came to the material Pound sent them. Anderson wrote the poet about work she considered inferior, including some of his own contributions, and she received his grudging concession that she was right—about the others' work, of course, not his own (*Pound/Little Review* 61–69).

In addition, Heap's playful response to *Little Review* readers who were concerned that Pound's arrival had changed the magazine into a vehicle for foreign writers to the detriment of American modernists illustrated that she was not threatened by her foreign editor. "Fear not, dear ones," she admonished the *Little Review* faithful. "We have learned to be penny wise; we will not be Pound foolish" ("Reader Critic" 1917).

When Pound's ritual sarcasm, attacks on American artists, and merely general misanthropic observations resulted in further outcry, Heap took a position which clearly demonstrated her independence and her desire to publish the best material available: "We have let Ezra Pound be our foreign editor in the only way we see it. We have let him be as foreign as he likes: foreign to taste, foreign to courtesy, foreign to our standards of Art." She continued that as long as Pound sent them "work bearing the stamp of originality and permanence—we have no complaint of him as an editor." Any other problems concerning Pound's eccentric style, Heap proclaimed, would be taken care of "outside the magazine." She concluded, "We need no commiseration for our connection with Mr. Pound. We are not blind deficient children" ("The Episode Continued" 35–37).

Anderson and Heap published writers Pound specifically told them not to, as well as producing two "All-American" numbers of the *Little Review.* Although standard literary histories commend the *Little Review's* publication of the "men of 1914"—Pound, Joyce, Lewis, and Eliot—Anderson and Heap were responsible for making an audience for the foremost female modernists—Djuna Barnes, Gertrude Stein, Dorothy Richardson, and Mina Loy.

Despite its successes, however, the *Little Review* was plagued by financial problems. In the Chicago period, subscriptions, advertisements, and donations barely kept the magazine afloat. Anderson's espousal of anarchism caused a great loss of revenue; at one point she camped on the beach of Lake Michigan for lack of rent. Pound's arrival was, then, a happy event because he had secured a patron who would pay for the literary contributions solicited by Pound. This man was John Quinn, a New York lawyer and art collector. Quinn's private collection of modern art was massive. In *My Thirty Years' War*, Anderson recalls dining with Quinn in his Central Park West apartment, where "Every inch of space from baseboard to ceiling was covered with modern sculpture. Brancusi's Child in the World stood out grotesquely in the confusion" (207). If Anderson's observation brings to mind the Victorian love of conspicuous consumption, it is because Quinn was in many respects a transitional figure between Victorianism and modernism. The son of an Ohio baker, he collected art in the same way many Gilded Age tycoons did, as an expression of status. His parents having been Irish immigrants, he was interested in sponsoring Irish authors; he served as James Joyce's agent in America and much of the money he relayed to Pound was meant to pay Joyce for work published in the *Little Review*.

Quinn was very much a social conservative, whose interest in "modern" art did not necessarily endear him to radical thought—particularly concerning political rebellion or sexual freedom. In a revealing letter to Pound, Quinn expressed his disgust with "the pseudo-Bohemianism of Washington Square": "It is a vulgar, disgusting conglomeration of second and third rate artists and would be artists, of I.W.W. agitators, of sluts, kept or casual, clean and unclean, of Socialists, of poetasters and pimps, of fornicators and dancers and those who dance to fornicate—But hell, words fail me to express my contempt for the whole damn bunch" (qtd. in Reid 285). Not only did Quinn attack "agitators" and "sluts," but he was also clearly making a connection between political radicalism and sexual promiscuity.

When he began his association with the *Little Review*, Quinn was unaware that it was edited by two lesbians. After his first visit to Anderson he wrote Pound, "Miss Anderson is a woman of taste and refinement and good looking." He did, however, have his suspicions about Heap, whom he described as "a typical Washington Squarite." "I only saw her once," he wrote, referring to Heap, "and if she has not got bobbed hair it should be" (June 2, 1917).

Several months later, Quinn was still impressed with Anderson and even included Heap in his praise of their work. Anderson, he gushed, was "a damn attractive young woman, one of the handsomest I have ever seen, very high spirited, very courageous and very fine. And I think it is all to their credit that they are making this uphill fight decently and almost alone. I don't know that I have seen any two women who were less maudlin, less sentimental and slushy about it, and more courageous." Quinn was not celebrating female autonomy; he doubted, he wrote Pound, that any two women could make a success out of a magazine like the *Little Review*. Rather, the scenario Quinn created evoked the world of a Victorian novel with Anderson and Heap as two helpless heroines of fine and upright character. Anderson, the beauty, required a hero in his romantic story to save the magazine. When Quinn introduced the hero, however, he was a Freudian modernist intent upon mixing business with pleasure. "Miss A is a very beautiful woman," he wrote in the same letter; "I have no doubt that she could get a good 'backer,' if she was willing to have him be a 'fronter first'" (Oct. 31, 1917).

For their part Anderson and Heap expressed doubts about Quinn. They had serious misgivings about his abilities as a literary critic, in addition to the annoyance they felt with his propensity to give them constant advice (Reid 288). Pound, who was the receiver of each party's summation of the other, became worried that the entire arrangement might be jeopardized by "personal bickerings with sexual undertones" (Wilhelm 194). His concern was justified; when Quinn discovered that Anderson and Heap were lesbians, and that as Joyce's agent he must defend them against obscenity charges, sexual undertones burst forth with a violent intensity.

* * *

The first episode of *Ulysses* would appear in 1918, but the events of 1917 established the politics of its publication. America had entered the First World War in April. Two months later Emma Goldman and Alexander Berkman were tried in New York City for encouraging resistance to the Conscription Act. Anderson and Heap attended Goldman's trial every day and released a letter to New York newspapers calling on people to protest both the trial and the draft law. The letter, signed by Anderson but actually written by Heap, argued passionately on behalf of Goldman and Berkman. "The Government will have its way with them unless something is done at once. This is not an anarchist issue: it is the fight of every individual. . . . remember that this means prison and deportation and other delicacies of the law for the hideous crime of free speech. PROTEST!" (letter to Reynolds, June 23, 1917). As a result Anderson and Heap were evicted from their *Little Review* studio office.

In October of 1917 the *Little Review* was confiscated by the U.S. Post Office because of a Wyndham Lewis short story, "Cantleman's Springmate." The story is the tale of a soldier bitterly awaiting deployment to the front; he seduces a young girl, then ignores her letters telling him she is pregnant. The issue was confiscated under Section 211 of the Penal Code of 1913, which forbade "obscene, lewd, or lascivious" material from circulation in the mails. Enraged by the action, Pound wrote an editorial in the *Little Review,* stating, "I confess to having been a bad citizen to just the extent of having been ignorant that at any moment my works might be classed with the invention of the late Dr. Condom" ("The Classics Escape" 32–33). In a suit for an injunction against the postmaster of New York, Quinn argued that the antiwar sentiment of the story was the reason for confiscation. The passage of the Espionage Act banning treasonable material from the mails led to the suppression of fifteen magazines, the most famous case being that of the *Masses.* Quinn used his brief to argue, "There is nothing under the Espionage Act involved here. There is nothing disloyal in the number of the magazine in question. No question is presented here similar to the Masses case" (U.S. District Court, *Anderson v. Patten* 32). Privately, however, Quinn thought differently. He was sure Anderson and Heap had brought scrutiny from the authorities because of their antiwar statements and support of Goldman (Reid 290).

The connection of sexual lewdness and political radicalism in the minds of both Quinn and the postal authorities sheds light on the meaning of First Amendment rights in the early twentieth century. As Paul Murphy tells us, the protection of civil liberties in this period was believed to be only for "good people" who conformed to prevailing social standards. Racial and religious minorities, immigrants, women, "or people espousing radical and destructive economic and political theories, clearly were not ready for the full utilization of their constitutional liberties" (40–41).

The "Cantleman" case foreshadowed the issues which emerged from *Ulysses*. In late 1917 Pound received the first three chapters of *Ulysses* from Joyce. Although he immediately feared censorship, he was in favor of publication. In spite of the suppression of their magazine that same year, Anderson and Heap were also willing to risk printing *Ulysses*. Anderson wrote years later that when she came across the sentence "Ineluctable modality of Being, seasprawn, sea-wracked signature of all things I read," she said to Heap, "This is the most beautiful thing we'll ever have. . . . We'll print it if it's the last effort of our lives" (*Thirty Years' War* 175). To *Little Review* readers she announced, "WE are about to publish a prose masterpiece" ("Joyce" 2).

When Quinn saw the first installment, he was livid. Although he was a patron of Joyce's, he thought that *Ulysses* was "toilet room literature, pissoir art" and that certain passages would "subject it to damnation in thirty seconds by any court or jury" (Mar. 14, 1918). In the same letter to Pound, Quinn indicated that he was aware of Anderson's lesbianism. Anyone reading the entire issue "would say that the person or persons responsible for the selection of that number suffered from sex mania or the obsession of sex, or that they were taking out on paper and in type what they should have taken out between some man's or woman's legs. . . . those who are sexually satisfied don't take it out on paper. *Vide* Havelock Ellis works *passim*." Quinn's mention of Havelock Ellis is a clue here; the British sexologist spent much of his career studying homosexuality, and specifically lesbianism. In this letter Quinn pinpointed one of the central stereotypical responses to lesbians in the early twentieth century. Lesbians were simultaneously seen as sexually insatiable and frigid.[6]

What angered Quinn throughout his association with Anderson and Heap was their frequent dismissal of his opinions. He complained to Pound that Anderson was like most other women in not appreciating free advice, and wrote, "I don't give a damn for her morals or lack of morals, but I object to her lack of politeness" (Mar. 14, 1918). Their sexuality in his mind became an integral part of their indifference to authority. Similarly, female autonomy expressed in feminism became interrelated with lesbianism in the thinking of physicians during this same period; one doctor warned that "the driving force in many agitators and militant women who are always after their rights, is often an unsatisfied sex impulse, with a homosexual aim" (Simmons 57). This doctor was not alone in his preoccupation with militant women and their possible deviance. George Chauncey tells us, "The sudden growth in the medical literature on sexual inversion was part of the general ideological reaction by the medical profession to women's challenge to the sex/gender system during this period" (122–32). Havelock Ellis, who in certain respects called for an understanding of homosexuals, asserted that the feminist movement was leading not only to a rise in female homosexuality, but also to crime and insanity. It is not surprising, given these pronouncements from "experts" on human sexuality, that Quinn felt fully justified in equating Anderson's lack of respect for his views with her "deviant" sexual orientation. Quinn in fact would come to see her sexuality as the reason for her next confrontation with the law—her "abnormality" had forced the issue. Quinn wrote Pound he "was through" with Anderson and Heap, and by the end of that year he informed them he would no longer pay contributors to the *Little Review*. One of the reasons he stated to Anderson was his expenses for war-related projects such as Liberty Bonds and the Red Cross (Dec. 3, 1918).

With Quinn's subsidy gone, and smarting from the attacks of *Little Review* readers, Pound resigned as foreign editor. Anderson and Heap continued to publish *Ulysses* without any assistance from Quinn or Pound. In early 1919 the post office suppressed two issues (January and May 1919) of the *Little Review* for obscenity. There is no evidence that anything from the *Ulysses* chapters of the confiscated issues had any political content, but the fact that it was seized during the most intense months of the Red Scare of 1919 may have accounted for heightened scrutiny by the authorities.

The postal inspectors were not the only people disgusted by *Ulysses;* many *Little Review* subscribers also registered their disapproval to Anderson and Heap. One reader asserted that the two women had become advocates for "abnormal art . . . sexual perverted cheap Bowery vileness" (R.McC.). Others complained they could not understand the novel. "Really now Joyce! What does he think he is doing? I swear I've read his *Ulysses* and haven't found out yet what it is about, who is who or where. Each month is worse than the last" (S.S.B.). Another subscriber argued it was not prudery that led her to dislike the novel, but the description of "natural functions" which were better left alone (Bishop). Heap dryly responded, "Yes, I think you must be right. I once knew a woman so modest that she didn't wear underwear; she couldn't stand its being seen in the wash" ("Reader Critic" 1920). The controversy brought to a halt the revenue from publishing houses who advertised in the magazine; some specifically cited the legal troubles of *Ulysses* for the termination of their accounts. Anderson fought back by writing "To the Book Publishers of America," an angry editorial in which she defiantly observed, "we have managed to keep alive in spite of an unsympathetic and ignorant public, a jeering press, and a censor that expects the worst of any effort dedicated to the best" (65).

The reaction of Anderson and Heap to both advertisers and readers demonstrated their self-image and priorities as editors. They were determined to publish what they wanted, regardless of the criticism they received. They realized this stance was financially dangerous. But their commitment to the *Little Review* was to publish what they personally valued. It was this highly focused self-confidence that enabled them to defy Pound and infuriate Quinn.

Following Pound's departure, Heap wrote directly to Joyce for the first time and expressed concern over his slow delivery of chapters, rather than their possible obscenity. In January 1920 Heap wrote she felt "much like a robber in starting this letter . . . there has always been such a note of ownership in Ezra Pound's attitude toward you and your work that we have held back, with a little amusement, from breaking in even when there has been a necessity for us to express our pleasure and pride in printing you or our anger and disgust at the suppression." She informed Joyce that the May issue had been burned by the post office, which also threatened to permanently suppress the *Little Review* if they did not "stop pulling that stuff" (Jan. 9, 1920). The same month Heap was writing Joyce, another issue was confiscated. When she wrote to inform him, Heap admitted, "We laughed so much reading proof on that episode that we forgot to think 'obscenity.' The flowery passages are too good—I shall be sorry when Bloom finishes this day" (Feb. 1920). Leopold Bloom, however, would never complete his day in the pages of the *Little Review*.

* * *

In the summer of 1920 the *Little Review* was confiscated again and this issue led to formal obscenity charges and a trial. The focus of the *Ulysses* chapter "Nausicaa," which led to the legal attack on Anderson and Heap, has been of interest to feminist Joycean critics; its subject contributed to the ironies of the sexual politics which emerged in the courtroom. Suggesting that the themes of *Ulysses* cannot be divorced from the attack upon its publishers, one critic tells us, "the early chapters of *Ulysses* all present the pressures of gender in a late Victorian patriarchal Irish social system that divides the sexes, abides by Catholic principle and economics of gender, and suppresses sexuality" (Scott 199).

The action of "Nausicaa" includes the encounter of Leopold Bloom and the young Gerty MacDowell on Sandymount Beach. Joyce fashioned Gerty's character as a parody of both Victorian womanhood and fiction written for a female audience. He employed a nineteenth-century novel, *The Lamplighter* (1854) by Maria Cummins, to serve as a basis for his own parody. Cummins's heroine, not so coincidentally named Gertrude, is a genuine exemplar of Victorian heroines: self-sacrificing, patient, and pure. While some critics have taken

Joyce's parody at face value, others argue he was attempting implicitly to criticize the Victorian values which suffocated the young Gertys of the world. Kimberly Devlin asserts that Gerty MacDowell "tries to follow the standards of selflessness and gentility endorsed in *The Lamplighter*, but a subversive voice keeps mocking these ideas." Joyce's use of voice is crucial to understanding his complex design in "Nausicaa"; it "comically subverts the possibility and desirability" of the virtue of the traditional Victorian heroine ("Romance" 386, 383).

Central to Gerty's unhappiness with the social role prescribed to her is the denial of female sexuality. The key incident within the chapter which led to obscenity charges is Bloom's masturbation as he looks at Gerty, who is purposefully leaning back to expose herself. The sexual charge of the scene is not confined to Bloom's orgasm, but extends also to the satisfaction Gerty experiences. "Gerty may try desperately to suppress her erotic impulses," writes Devlin, "but she is ultimately unsuccessful. She recognizes with pleased composure the pleasure Bloom gains from his voyeurism, she is more hesitant to acknowledge the voyeuristic titillation *she* derives from surreptitiously watching Bloom watch her." This "counter female voyeurism" belies the Victorian tenet of woman's innate asexuality ("Female Eye" 136).[7] Just as Anderson's lesbianism disqualified her for Quinn's Victorian model, Gerty MacDowell failed the requirement of purity that defined her nineteenth-century fictional sisters.

The New York Society for the Suppression of Vice, under the leadership of John Sumner, formally pressed charges against Anderson and Heap for circulating obscenity through the mails.[8] And despite his lack of affection for Anderson and Heap, John Quinn defended the *Little Review* for the sake of Joyce. When Anderson and Heap met with Quinn in his office shortly after the charges were filed, the lawyer exploded in a fit of rage and told them *they* belonged in jail. Anderson was somewhat nonplussed by Quinn's outburst and suggested the *Little Review* would get another lawyer, despite "knowing that no power on earth could have wrested that power from him." "One didn't argue with John Quinn," she wrote in *My Thirty Years' War;* "one enjoyed his performances too much. He was better than a prima donna. No woman would throw such obvious scenes, or look around so hopefully for the applause of her audience" (215).

Quinn's letters to Pound during this period make constant and increasingly vitriolic statements connecting Anderson's and Heap's sexuality to the trial. "I have no interest at all," he wrote in the fall of 1920, "in defending people who are stupidly and brasenly and Sapphoistically and pederastically and urinally, and menstrually violate [*sic*] the law, and think they are courageous." In essence Anderson and Heap brought this trial upon themselves. "THEY ARE BORES. They are too damn fresh. They stand for no principle. They are cheap self-advertisers. All pederasts want to go into court. Bringing libel suits is one of the stigmata of buggery. The bugger and the Lesbian constantly think in terms of suits and defenses" (Oct. 16, 1920). In his view Anderson and Heap had deliberately and wantonly broken the law. The equation of lesbianism with litigation underlined Quinn's basic conviction that the real offense was their sexuality.

One of the most fascinating elements of Quinn's language both in objecting to *Ulysses* and in describing Anderson and Heap was his use of bodily images strikingly similar to what one critic has called Leopold Bloom's "fetishistic concern" with "feces, menses, urine, and other physical secretions" (Henke, *Joyce* 106). In one tirade against Anderson and Heap he wrote, "I don't mind the aberrations of a woman who has some openness and elasticity of mind, who may be mentally as well as physically plastic, in whose excretions there may occasionally be cream; but, by God! I don't like the thought of women who seem to exude as well as bathe in piss, if not drink it or each other's." In this same letter Quinn said he thought the *Little Review* was on a "blacklist" because of "the general devotion" to articles on "urine and feces and sweat and armpits and piss and orgasms and masturbations and buggeries and Lesbianisms and God knows what." In fact whatever references there were to these elements in the *Little Review* were largely contained in *Ulysses*. Quinn, however, associated them not with Joyce, but with Anderson and Heap. "These people," he wrote, "seem to sweat urine and probably urinate sweat. At any rate, they look as though they would stink piss if you got close enough to smell them" (Oct. 16, 1920).

By the time of the pretrial hearing, Quinn's attitude had become one of pure misogyny. In writing to Pound a description of women who had come to the hearing in support of Anderson and Heap, he said, "There was Heep [*sic*] plus Anderson, plus heaps of other Heaps and Andersons. Some good looking, some indifferent. The two rows of them looking as though a fashionable whorehouse had been pinched and all its inmates hauled into court, with Heap in the part of the brazen madame." The women, he continued, "seemed about as interested and excited about what was going to happen as though they expected to be raped. Nothing but a rape could excite them so much" (Oct. 21, 1920).

While Quinn's previous comments were crude, by the time of the hearing they had degenerated into violence. He suggested that any woman in court was there as a result of prurient interest in Anderson or Heap or the sexual aspects of *Ulysses*. Legal, literary, or intellectual concerns could not account for their participation; hence they were branded whores or lesbians. The women who attended in support of Anderson and Heap, and were by implication endorsing resistance to the male-dominated legal system, had constituted a powerful presence in the courtroom. This galled Quinn, who responded with an attempt to reimpose male authority—his own—through the invocation of rape. Reduced by his own fury, Quinn lashed out in what came to be a sexual war, where his enemies and clients were one and the same.

Forced to defend Anderson and Heap, Quinn tailored his legal strategy to emphasize misogynist and homophobic arguments. In the hearing he asserted the judge should distinguish between two types of "filth." There was, he argued, "the strong hard filth of a man like Joyce" compared to the filth produced by "a soft flabby man like Wilde." The filth of Joyce, he continued, was a deterrent to sexual indulgence, while Wilde's unquestionably led to "corruption." Quinn additionally argued that *Ulysses* could not corrupt anyone who could not understand it. Those who could understand it (implying Anderson and Heap) could do so only because they were already corrupted. The judge disagreed, however, and replied no one could misunderstand "the episode where the man went off in his pants," and the *Little Review* went to trial (letter, Quinn to Pound, Oct. 21, 1920).

Even though he had left the *Little Review*, Pound, responding to a request from Quinn, wrote Joyce and asked him to tell Anderson and Heap not to publish any further chapters. In this letter Pound described Anderson and Heap as incompetents who "messed and muddled, never to their own detriment" (*Pound/Joyce* 184–85). Joyce, however, remained unmoved. Quinn's assertion that lesbians were obsessed with lawsuits was actually more applicable to Joyce. His biographer has written that the author "had a penchant for litigation" and was dreaming of "a trial of *Ulysses* as successful as that of Madame Bovary" (Ellmann 502). Anderson, Heap, and Joyce were determined to proceed regardless of the consequences; Quinn and Pound found fault only with the two women. In spite of the obscenity charge, Anderson and Heap published the next installment of *Ulysses*. In the December 1920 number they launched an attack against the notion that art could be judged in a courtroom. "The heavy farce and sad futility of trying a creative work in a court of law appalls me," wrote Heap in her article "Art and the Law." "The society for which Mr. Sumner is agent, I am told, was founded to protect the public from corruption. When asked *what public?* its defenders spring to the rock on which America was founded: the cream puff of sentimentality, and answer chivalrously 'Our young girls.' So the mind of the young girl rules this country?" The *Ulysses* case was "truly ironical," Heap pointed out, because the *Little Review* was being prosecuted "for printing the thoughts in a young girl's mind." The acknowledgment of female sexuality, whether in twentieth-century America or in the character of Gerty MacDowell, was the crux of male anxiety and the resulting sentimental cant about the purity of women.

The trial was held in February 1921, in a special sessions court before three judges (two of whom, according to Anderson, slept through the entire proceedings). The initial proceedings demonstrated both an attempt to silence women as well as a refusal to acknowledge the right of women to view sexually explicit material. Quinn did not permit Anderson or Heap to testify, a strategy Anderson saw as an attempt to render them "inconspicuous, meek, and silent." When the assistant district attorney announced he was going to read the offending passage out loud, one of the judges objected. He thought the passage should not be read in the presence of a young woman such as Anderson. The judge, Anderson later wrote caustically, regarded her with "a protective paternity" and "refused to allow the obscenity to be read in my hearing." When Quinn informed him she was the publisher, the judge responded he was sure she "did not know the significance of what she was publishing" (*Thirty Years' War* 219–21). The offending passage was read, and the court recessed for a week to enable the judges to read the entire chapter.

When the trial resumed, Quinn repeated his argument that the lasciviousness of *Ulysses* was a deterrent to filth rather than a corrupting influence. In addition he argued that only those familiar with the city of Dublin could understand what was really happening in the book, and the erratic punctuation, which he attributed to Joyce's poor eyesight, made it incomprehensible to everyone else. Finally, Quinn argued that he did not understand *Ulysses* and offered the opinion that "Joyce has carried his method too far in this experiment." "Yes," responded one judge, "it sounds like the ravings of a disordered mind. I can't see why anyone would want to publish it." After this exchange Anderson began to stand up and respond to the judge's statement. She was stopped, however, by Heap, pounding her in the ribs with the admonition "don't try and talk, don't put yourself in their hands." Anderson sat down ("Ulysses in Court" 24–25). Heap's remark to Anderson indicates that the two editors decided to remain silent for their own reasons. They faced a hostile prosecution, indifferent judges, and a defense attorney who thought they were in fact guilty. It went against the grain of Anderson's nature, but she agreed with Heap not to speak. In "Ulysses in Court," written during the trial, Anderson stated, "I am determined, during this unnecessary hour in court, to adopt the philosophy of self-preservation. I will protect my sensibilities and my brain cells by being unhearing and untalkative" (23–24). The two women were found guilty of obscenity, fined one hundred dollars, forced to promise not to publish any further chapters, and fingerprinted.

* * *

The American experience in the 1920s had alienated many intellectuals; the end of the Great War, the failure of Versailles, the Red Scare, and the advent of Harding, Coolidge, and Hoover all left thoughtful Americans with a sense of estrangement. The reemergence of nativism and fundamentalism led to two other significant court cases of the decade—Sacco and Vanzetti and the Scopes "Monkey Trial." The migration of American writers and artists to Europe was symptomatic of this disaffection. Life abroad was, among other things, much more amenable for gays and lesbians. It is no coincidence that when *Ulysses* was published as a book in France, it was by another lesbian, American expatriate Sylvia Beach.

The political character of modernism, which expressed anger and anxiety over the upheaval of the early twentieth century, has been the subject of much debate. Did the literary experiments reflecting a fragmented and disharmonious world, random in the representation of space and time, and creating a fractured, symbolic, and inner language, serve reactionary retreat or revolutionary attack? In *Rich and Strange,* Marianne DeKoven argues that these "simplistic dualisms" cloud and misrepresent the issue. Holding that modernists shared a great deal of ambivalence toward feminism and socialism, DeKoven believes that both men and women sought the destruction of the hierarchical status quo, but at the same time feared the results. "Male modernists," she asserts, "generally feared the loss of hegemony implicit in such wholesale revision of culture, while female modernists generally feared punishment for their dangerous desire for that revision" (20). Anderson and Heap not so much feared punishment for change as despaired of its arrival. "No doubt," Heap wrote in the *Little Review,* "all so-called thinking people hoped for a new order after the war. This hope was linked with the fallacy that men learn from experience. Facts prove that we learn no more from our experiences than from our dreams" ("Lost" 5).

John Quinn was clearly an individual fearful of the consequences of change. His vitriolic outbursts against Anderson and Heap, when all three of them were supposedly engaged in the same struggle—to promote James Joyce in America—exposed the sexual politics of the modernist endeavor. Quinn spent a great deal of money, time, and effort in supporting artists such as Joyce and Pound. In addition, in the course of his life he purchased over two thousand works of modern art. But Quinn was also deeply in sympathy with the conservative political culture of the decade. This strange alliance of radical lesbian and conservative homophobe underscores DeKoven's contention that modernism is more multifaceted in its political implications than most critics would have us believe. The *Ulysses* trial shows modernism not as a revolutionary or reactionary movement, but as an amalgam of conflicting artistic, political, and sexual attitudes.

Sylvia Beach published *Ulysses* in France in 1922, one year after Anderson and Heap's trial. Announcing this to *Little Review* readers, Jane Heap simply commented, "We limp from the field" ("Ulysses Again" 34). The consequences of the trial were profound for the *Little Review.* Anderson felt that *Ulysses* was "the epoch's supreme articulation" and wanted to cease the publication of the journal. Feeling pessimistic about the future of art in America, worn down by financial strain, and ending her relationship with Heap, Anderson left for France in 1924. She relinquished control of the *Little Review* to Heap, who guided the magazine in the direction of increasingly avant-garde and European artistic movements. Dada, surrealism, and Russian constructivism, in addition to theater set design, de Stijl architecture, and machine age aesthetics all graced its pages. Published sporadically, the *Little Review* became a quarterly after the *Ulysses* trial and finally ceased publication in 1929.

By then it was clear that Heap had joined Anderson in her dismissal of the state of modern art and letters. In her farewell editorial, entitled "Lost: A Renaissance," Heap wrote, "We have given space in the *Little Review* to 23 new systems of art (all now dead), representing 19 countries. In all of this we have not brought forward anything approaching a masterpiece except the Ulysses of Mr. Joyce." Both Anderson and Heap saw the decline in art and literature as a reflection of, in Heap's words, "an ailing and aimless society." The arts, Heap wrote in her last editorial, had "broken faith" with their origin and purpose. "Perhaps," she continued in the closing paragraph, "the situation is not so hopeless as I have described it. Perhaps it doesn't matter. Or perhaps it would be more than an intellectual adventure to give up our obsessions about art, hopelessness, and Little Reviews, and take on pursuits more becoming to human beings" (6).

Notes

I would like to thank Patricia Thatcher for her thoughtful criticism and encouragement in the formulation of this essay.

1. The FBI acknowledges having a file on Anderson as a result of her pronouncements during this period but refused a request under the Freedom of Information Act to obtain the file.

2. Gilbert and Gubar explore the relationship between cross-dressing and modernism in chapter 8 of *No Man's Land,* vol. 2.

3. See Newton 281–93.

4. For an exception to this see Platt. Recently discovered Heap correspondence has filled in many of the gaps in the biography of her early life.

5. See Barash; and Monroe 268.

6. For references to lesbian "nymphomaniacs," see Faderman 51; and Simmons 57–58.

7. Gerty has been a topic of lively debate among Joyce scholars; see Baym; Hart and Hayman; Henke,"Gerty McDowell"; and Laws.

8. The original complaint did not come from the society, but from an attorney whose daughter received an unsolicited copy of the *Little Review* at home. The attorney complained to the New York district attorney who pressed Sumner to file charges. This was first uncovered by Jackson R. Bryer.

Works Cited

Alpert, Barry. "The Unexamined Art: Ezra Pound and the Aesthetic Mode of the Little Magazine." Diss. Stanford U, 1971.

Anderson, Margaret. "Conversation." *Prose* 2 (1971): 5–21.

———. "James Joyce in the Little Review." *Little Review* Jan. 1918: 2.

———. "Mrs. Ellis's Failure." *Little Review* Mar. 1915: 16–19.

———. *My Thirty Years' War*. 1930. Westport, CT: Greenwood, 1970.

———. "To the Book Publishers of America." *Little Review* Dec. 1919: 65.

———. "Toward Revolution." *Little Review* Dec. 1914: 5.

———. "Ulysses in Court." *Little Review* Jan.–Mar. 1921: 22–25.

S.S.B. "Reader Critic." *Little Review* June 1918: 57.

Baggett, Holly. "Aloof from Natural Laws: Margaret C. Anderson and the *Little Review,* 1914–1929." Diss. U of Delaware, 1992.

Barash, Carol. "Dora Marsden's Feminism, the *Freewoman,* and Gender Politics of Early Modernism." *Princeton University Library Chronicle* Autumn 1987: 31–56.

Baym, Nina. Introduction. *The Lamplighter*. By Maria Cummins. New Brunswick, NJ: Rutgers UP, 1986.

Bishop, Helen. "Reader Critic." *Little Review* May–June 1920: 73–74.

Bryer, Jackson R. "Joyce, *Ulysses,* and the *Little Review." South Atlantic Quarterly* 66 (Spring 1967): 148–64.

———. "'A Trial Track for Racers': Margaret C. Anderson and the *Little Review."* Diss. U of Wisconsin–Milwaukee, 1965.

Burke, Carolyn. "Getting Spliced: Modernism and Sexual Difference." *American Quarterly* 39 (1987): 98–121.

Chauncey, George. "From Sexual Inversion to Homosexuality: Medicine and Changing Conception of Female Deviance." *Salmagundi* 58–59 (1982–1983): 114–46.

Cowley, Malcolm. Letter to Jackson Bryer. Feb. 5, 1964. Private collection of Jackson Bryer.

DeKoven, Marianne. *Rich and Strange: Gender, History, Modernism*. Princeton, NJ: Princeton UP, 1991.

Devlin, Kimberly. "The Female Eye: Joyce's Voyeuristic Narcissists." *New Alliances in Joyce Studies*. Ed. Bonnie Kime Scott. Newark: U of Delaware P, 1988. 135–43.

———. "The Romance Heroine Exposed: 'Nausicaa' and *The Lamplighter." James Joyce Quarterly* 22 (Summer 1985): 383–96.

Ellmann, Richard. *James Joyce*. New York: Oxford UP, 1959.

Faderman, Lillian. *Odd Girls and Twilight Lovers: A History of Lesbian Life in Twentieth-Century America*. New York: Columbia UP, 1991.

Gilbert, Sandra M., and Susan Gubar. *No Man's Land: The Place of the Woman Writer in the Twentieth Century*. Vol. 1. *The War of the Words*. New Haven, CT: Yale UP, 1988.

———. *No Man's Land*. Vol. 2. *Sexchanges*. New Haven, CT: Yale UP, 1989.

Hart, Clive, and David Hayman., eds. *James Joyce's* Ulysses: *Critical Essays*. Berkeley: U of California P, 1974.

Heap, Jane. "Art and the Law." *Little Review* Dec. 1920: 5–6.

———. "The Episode Continued." *Little Review* Nov. 1918: 35–37.

———. Letters to James Joyce. Jan. 9, 1920; Feb. 1920. Courtesy of the Department of Rare Books, Cornell U Library.

———. Letters to Florence Reynolds. Aug. 18, 1908; Aug. 29, 1908; June 23, 1917; July 1917. By permission of Jane Purse and Special Collections, U of Delaware Library.

———. "Lost: A Renaissance." *Little Review* 1929: 5–6.

———. "Reader Critic." *Little Review* June 1917: 28.

———. "Reader Critic." *Little Review* May–June 1920: 73–74.

———. "Ulysses Again." *Little Review* Autumn 1922: 34.

Henke, Suzette. "Gerty MacDowell: Joyce's Sentimental Heroine." *Women in Joyce.* Ed. Suzette Henke and Elaine Unkeless. Urbana: U of Illinois P, 1982. 132–49.

———. *James Joyce and the Politics of Desire.* New York: Routledge, 1990.

Joyce, James. *Ulysses.* New York: Random House, 1965.

Katz, Jonathan. *Gay/Lesbian Almanac: A New Documentary.* New York: Harper and Row, 1983.

Laws, Jules David. "'Pity They Can't See Themselves': Assessing the 'Subject' of Pornography in 'Nausicaa.'" *James Joyce Quarterly* 27 (Winter 1990): 219–39.

R.McC. "Reader Critic." *Little Review* June 1918: 65

Monroe, Harriet. *A Poet's Life: Seventy Years in a Changing World.* New York: Macmillan, 1938.

Murphy, Paul. *World War I and the Origin of Civil Liberties in the United States.* New York: Norton, 1979.

Newton, Esther. "The Mythic Mannish Lesbian: Radclyffe Hall and the New Woman." *Hidden from History: Reclaiming the Gay Past.* Ed. Martin Bauml Duberman, Martha Vincinus, and George Chauncey, Jr. New York: New American Library, 1989. 281–93.

Platt, Susan Noyes. "Mysticism and the Machine Age: Jane Heap and the *Little Review.*" *Twenty/One* Fall 1989: 19–44.

Pound, Ezra. "The Classics Escape." *Little Review* Mar. 1918: 32–33.

———. *Pound/Joyce: The Letters of Ezra Pound to James Joyce.* Ed. Forrest Read. New York: New Directions, 1967.

———. *Pound/Little Review: The Letters of Ezra Pound to Margaret Anderson: The Little Review Correspondence.* Ed. Thomas Scott, Melvin Freidman, with the assistance of Jackson Bryer. New York: New Directions, 1988.

Quinn, John. Letter to Margaret Anderson. Dec. 3, 1918. *Little Review* Papers, Golda Meir Library, University of Wisconsin–Milwaukee.

———. Letters to Ezra Pound. Oct. 16, 1920; Oct. 21, 1920. By permission of the Special Collections Department, Northwestern U Library.

———. Letters to Ezra Pound. June 2, 1917; Oct. 31, 1917; Mar. 14, 1918. By permission of the John Quinn Memorial Collection, Rare Books and Manuscripts Division, New York Public Library, Astor, Lenox and Tilden Foundations.

Reid, B. L. *The Man From New York: John Quinn and His Friends.* New York: Oxford UP, 1968.

Scott, Bonnie Kime, ed. "James Joyce." *The Gender of Modernism: A Critical Anthology.* Bloomington: Indiana UP, 1990. 196–204.

Simmons, Christine. "Companionate Marriage and the Lesbian Threat." *Frontiers* 4 (1979): 54–59.

Smith-Rosenberg, Carroll. *Disorderly Conduct: Visions of Gender in Victorian America.* New York: Knopf, 1985.

Tietjens, Eunice. *The World At My Shoulder.* New York: Macmillan, 1938.

United States District Court Southern District of New York, Margaret C. Anderson, complainant against Thomas G. Patten, Postmaster of the City of New York, Defendant. IN EQUITY No. E-14-379. Yale Collection of American Literature, Beinecke Rare Book and Manuscript Library, Yale University.

Wilhelm, James J. *Ezra Pound in London and Paris, 1908–1925.* University Park: Pennsylvania State UP, 1990.

11.

Sylvia Beach: Commerce, Sanctification, and Art on the Left Bank

Noel Riley Fitch

> Book [ME. boke, book; AS. boc, pl. bece. >same base as Engl.
> beech (see Beach): prob. so called because runes were first
> carved on beech.]
>
> *Oxford English Dictionary*

Sylvia Beach fled the Presbyterian parsonage of Princeton, New Jersey, to create a life for herself abroad. After working in journalism, volunteer farming during World War I, and the Red Cross in Serbia, Beach founded a bookselling and lending business called Shakespeare and Company on the Left Bank of Paris. Through this business she was able to support herself both vocationally and avocationally, for she was an avid reader. By applying the missionary zeal of her ancestors to a life of service beyond personal aggrandizement and financial profit, she gained a kind of secular sainthood.

The literary and spiritual achievements of Sylvia Beach (1887–1962) and her Shakespeare and Company bookshop (1919–41) have been documented in a biography (Fitch's *Sylvia Beach and the Lost Generation,* 1983), in histories (Benstock's *Women of the Left Bank,* 1986; Ford's *Published in Paris,* 1975), and in the numerous memoirs and autobiographies of this century. More attention has been paid to her work as publisher of James Joyce than to the means of her sanctification, her career as bookseller—or to choose a better word—bookkeeper, the only English word with three consecutive double letters. What follows is a more detailed look at the specifics of her business and how it corresponded to her view of gender roles.

Though Sylvia Beach created what may be the most famous bookshop in history, she was not the only American woman of business devoted to the arts in Paris. There were a number of "bookkeepers" who wrote, printed, published, sold, distributed, reviewed, and publicized books. Among these were four other publishers: Nancy Cunard, an Englishwoman who hand-set books for her Hours Press; Barbara Harrison, who elegantly printed books for her Harrison of Paris; Caresse Crosby, who with her husband, Harry, published books for their Black Sun Press; and Alice B. Toklas, who with

11.1. Sylvia Beach, Shakespeare and Company, 8 rue Dupuytren, Paris, 1919. Noel Riley Fitch Collection.

Gertrude Stein sold a Picasso and founded Plain Editions to publish five of Stein's books. Among the founders of little magazines were Florence Gilliam (*Gargoyle*), Ethel Moorhead (*This Quarter*), Margaret Anderson and Jane Heap (*Little Review*), and Harriet Weaver (*Egoist*). Adrienne Monnier, Beach's life-partner, was the French writer, publisher, and owner of La Maison des Amis des Livres bookshop. Janet Flanner reviewed books in the *New Yorker*, and Natalie Barney and Gertrude Stein had weekly salons that brought writers, translators, and editors together. Thus, perhaps at no other time in history have women so actively participated in the business of art and the art of business. Morrill Cody said, "it was the women among us who shaped and directed and nourished the social and artistic and literary life of the Anglo-American colony" (Cody and Ford 11). Benstock calls it "literary midwifery" in the birth of modernism (20).

Among all these accomplished American women, Beach was the most successful businesswoman and entrepreneur, for she founded and operated for twenty-two years the first English-language bookshop and lending library on the Left Bank. She had no formal training for this career. As a bookworm who dieted chiefly on French parchment, her only stock in trade was a love of books and writers. Whatever she learned about operating a business came from Adrienne Monnier, who had founded her House of the Friends of Books in 1916. It was Monnier who found the location for the first shop for Beach on rue Dupuytren and, when two years later a shop opened across the street from her own shop on rue de l'Odéon, who helped Beach move around the corner. There they could face each other across this little street and create what Monnier called "Odéonia," that spiritual place for book lovers. Monnier helped her learn to deal with the landlord, carpenter, plumber, tax man, and government bureaucrats. She also helped to arrange for the publication of Joyce's *Ulysses* with her own printer in Dijon, Maurice Darantière. Beach and Monnier were lovers, friends, and business associates. In a sense they divided the literary trade, Monnier handling the French-language books, Beach the English.

The true business of Shakespeare and Company was threefold: lending books, selling books, and publishing books. All the literary readings, private teas with authors, apartment referrals, check cashing, translating, and editing were in addition to these. Book lending (virtually unknown in Paris bookstores then) was the chief activity of the shop, because paperback publication for English-language books had not yet come into existence. Thus books were too expensive, especially for struggling writers. Ernest Hemingway, Archibald MacLeish, Katherine Anne Porter, and all the other members of Shakespeare and Company borrowed and returned books.

Beach was a casual librarian who had no cards in the books. When a member—she called them "bunnies" after the French word for subscriber, *abonne*—paid from five to twelve francs per month (depending on the number of books), she wrote the name at the top of a card and beneath that, the titles of the books borrowed. To the left was the date of borrowing; to the right the date of return. She gave free subscriptions to Henry Miller, Virgil Thomson, Porter, and others who did not have money at the time. These cards, which remain in the Sylvia Beach Papers at Princeton University Library, are a valuable resource for today's scholars, for they reveal the reading habits of the leading writers between the wars. For example, a look at the cards reveals that Stein read all of William Dean Howells; Hemingway read Turgenev over and over; and in the 1930s Simone de Beauvoir read Hemingway and Faulkner. Beach's process for lending books was simple and designed for the ease of the reader, but its simplicity made it difficult for the librarian if she had to remember who had borrowed what book. Then she had to search each card for the title. Monnier called this "le plan américain"— not because it *had* a prescribed plan, but precisely because it did not: no call numbers, no catalog, no index cards.

The fact that subscribers to the lending library could purchase flexible membership from one to twelve months made it convenient for artists who were short of change or just planning a short stay in Paris. But Beach had a steady clientele of foreign residents in Paris. Only once did she record the average length of subscription, on the back of an address book for the mid-1930s. During this period the lending library had a monthly average of thirty-four one-month members and fourteen twelve-month members. There were always at least eight or ten people who held free memberships. The average of eighty-nine paying members a month (about a third of them new members) during the spring of 1936 was undoubtedly a record number, because during the next months membership fluctuated from a low of fifty-four in July to a high of eighty-six in October of 1936, and from a high of eighty-seven in February to a low of sixty-eight in July of 1937. These records of the 1936–37 year, the only records preserved of the number of library subscribers, were probably kept during the drive by the Friends of Shakespeare and Company to save the shop from financial crisis in the mid-1930s. The Friends was founded by André Gide, who took out his first membership, for a year, on December 1, 1919, and borrowed a book entitled *Minor Elizabethan Drama.*

To facilitate the return of overdue library books, Beach ordered printed postcards from Darantière, on the back of which was sketched William Shakespeare seated behind an open book, tearing out his hair by the roots. Below the drawing was printed "please return," with space for the book title. At the bottom was printed the bookshop name and address. A careful look at the record books at Princeton University reveals that only a few, including Joyce and Hemingway, forgot to return their books.

The bookselling side of the business was just as casual as the lending library, but it had more potential to add money to the cash drawer. Sales fluctuated seasonally and annually. Predictably, more books and journals

SHAKESPEARE   AND   COMPANY
— Sylvia Beach —
BOOKSHOP   LENDING   LIBRARY
PUBLISHER
12, RUE DE L'ODÉON, 12
Tél. : Littré 33-76
PARIS VIe

R. C. Seine : No 284.402

11.2. Business card, Shakespeare and Company. Noel Riley Fitch Collection.

sold during the tourist months every year. There were days in the late 1930s when few if any books sold. No books sold during the opening days of World War II, when the Germans occupied Paris. The "sales department" of the shop, said Beach in an early draft of her memoirs, "was practically non-existent" during the depth of the Depression (Sylvia Beach Papers, Box 166). During the 1920s sales fluctuated between five and twenty books and journals a day, including *Ulysses*. In 1923, for example, she averaged (beyond Joyce's novel) eight sales of books and journals a day in January, eleven a day in June. Although no one has studied all the specific titles that she sold, a brief look at her sales books reveals that she sold chiefly modern works, the nineteenth-century classics, and Shakespeare, her patron saint.

Because she sold to French students, professors, and authors, she made a considerable contribution to introducing American literature to the French.[1] The sales of more costly American book titles for one year, 1926, reflect her interests. It was the year that Beach held a special exhibit of Walt Whitman manuscripts and books, which were more popular with the French writers than with the visiting American writers; the year that American composers were featured in a special concert given by their teacher Nadia Boulanger; and the year that George Antheil unveiled to raucous audiences his *Ballet mécanique*. American words and music were everywhere in 1926.

1926 Sales of American Books
at Shakespeare and Company

AUTHOR AND TITLE	COPIES SOLD
Anderson, Sherwood	
Dark Laughter	2
Poor White	3
Winesburg, Ohio	2
Beasley, Gertrude	
My First Thirty Years	3
Bird, William	
French Wines	5
Cabell, James Branch	
Jurgen	2
cummings, e.e.	
Enormous Room	2
Tulips and Chimneys	1
XLI Poems	2
Is 5	2
ML	1
Dickinson, Emily	
Selected Poems	1
Dreiser, Theodore	
An American Tragedy	1
Eliot, T. S.	
Sacred Wood	10
Poems	12
Emerson, Ralph Waldo	
Complete Works, Vol. 1	1
Heart of Emerson's Journal	1
Fitzgerald, F. Scott	
All the Sad Young Men	2
The Great Gatsby	1
H.D.	
Collected Poems	2
Hemingway, Ernest	
In Our Time	7
The Sun Also Rises	3
Torrents of Spring	3
Herrmann, John	
What Happens	1
James, Henry	
The Ambassadors	1
The Awkward Age	1

The Tragic Muse	1
What Maisie Knew	1
Untitled books	3
Lewis, Sinclair	
Babbitt	3
London, Jack	
untitled	1
Sea Wolf	1
Loos, Anita	
Gentlemen Prefer Blondes	2
McAlmon, Robert	
A Hasty Bunch	1
Distinguishing Air	1
Village	1
O'Neill, Eugene	
Emperor Jones	1
Poe, Edgar Allan	
Poems	2
Pound, Ezra	
Antheil and the Treatise of Harmony	3
Cathay	2
Lustra	5
Poems 1918–21	2
Ripostes	1
Sandburg, Carl	
Poems	3
Stein, Gertrude	
Composition as Explanation	1
The Making of Americans	3
Twain, Mark	
Huckleberry Finn	3
Tom Sawyer	1
Van Vechten, Carl	
Nigger Heaven	1
Wescott, Glenway	
Apple of the Eye	3
Whitman, Walt	
Leaves of Grass	10
Williams, William Carlos	
In the American Grain	3
Spring and All	2

Note: Miscellaneous sales included a life of Herman Melville, ten copies of untitled books listed as "Modern Library," and more than a dozen unidentifiable titles.

At least a fifth of these books, including those by Bird, cummings, and Pound, were published by little presses operating in Paris. The range and author representation of this American list (which does not include journals) does not differ considerably from the books that she sold during the first and last months of operation. In fact, Pound's *Cathay* was the first book she ever sold, followed soon by Whitman's poetry.

A closer look at the American authors that sold the most during the year 1926 shows that the titles of T. S. Eliot, who lived in London but came to Paris for events such as the Whitman exhibit and the Antheil concert, sold more (twenty-two) than any other author. After Eliot there followed, among the American authors: Hemingway with thirteen, Pound with twelve, Whitman and Sherwood Anderson with ten each, cummings with eight, and James with seven. All except James and Whitman (both dead) were regular members of the company. This fact illustrates one reason the avant-garde writers were in Paris: their readership was here. Prominent on the Left Bank was Hemingway, whose *The Sun Also Rises* and *In Our Time* had just been published by commercial publishing companies; all the temptations of success—or so he would remember it—were breaking up his marriage to Hadley, his wife of five years. The Whitman sales reflect the combined impact of both Beach's exhibition (April 21 through June 30) and the March issue of Monnier's journal *Le Navire d'Argent,* an all-American issue with translations of short works by McAlmon, Hemingway, Williams, cummings, and others, and an essay by Whitman translated by Beach and Monnier. The sales of cummings's books may reflect the fact that he received the *Dial* poetry prize for 1926. Several titles in addition to the Hemingway books were newly published works, including those by Van Vechten, Wescott, H.D., Pound, and Loos. (James Joyce bought one of the Loos books and read it in three days during November, according to Beach.) Loos aside, the avant-garde bought and sold their works at the shop, where their lives and works were intertwined.

Ten years later (1936), according to her ledgers at Princeton, Eliot's titles were still selling more (twenty-three) than any other except Joyce. Nine Hemingway titles sold, along with the other authors on the 1926 list. But by this time there were more titles of the premodern classics, probably a reflection of the disappearance of the little publishing companies in Paris. The last full year of operation for Shakespeare and Company was 1941, when the biggest sellers, with fourteen each, were Hemingway (nine copies of *Farewell to Arms*) and Pearl Buck's *The Good Earth.* Joyce, Eliot, and Whitman were still selling, but readers during this war year preferred realistic fiction.

A close analysis of her book sales reveals the fluctuating interest in British and American literature in Paris between the wars. Her preference for Whitman, Eliot, Hemingway, and, of course, Joyce is reflected in the steady sale of their titles over a twenty-year period. Among these, only Whitman, because he lived in the previous century, was not her friend. Other titles sold perennially, including *Mother Goose* and *Little Women,* the Oxford dictionary, Cassell's French-English dictionary, and Frazer's *The Golden Bough.* There were obvious trends; for example, several books on Spain were sold in 1926 following the appearance of Hemingway's *The Sun Also Rises.*

English literature accounted for the bulk of book sales in the earliest months of the bookshop. Joseph Conrad and Shakespeare were the most popular, followed by Rudyard Kipling and Samuel Butler. During the mid-1920s, sales increased for poetry by Blake, Yeats, and Keats and for novels by Jane Austen and Virginia Woolf. During 1926 there were sold, among the English titles, works by Bernard Shaw, W. H. Hudson, E. M. Forster, Katherine Mansfield (three copies of *The Garden Party*), and Norman Douglas (four copies of *South Wind*). The big seller for 1929 and the few years that followed was D. H. Lawrence's *Lady Chatterley's Lover,* which Beach had declined to republish despite the urging of Lawrence. His books sold steadily through the 1930s. The all-time best-selling author was, of course, James Joyce. Often the same customer bought several books by Joyce—*Exiles, Chamber Music, Dubliners, Portrait of the Artist as a Young Man,* and *Ulysses*—whose sales were listed separately at the bottom of the ledger each day. Often beside the record of a sale of the novel, Beach would write "1 Frenchman," "3 tourists," or "1 red-headed American." On September 10, 1924, she recorded "repaired copy to Eleanor Wilson," her Princeton friend and the daughter of the former U.S. President. By the middle of the 1920s, she was also selling Joyce criticism, such as Herbert Gorman's *James Joyce* and Stuart Gilbert's *James Joyce's Ulysses,* a key to the novel.

The little artistic magazines from which modern literature was launched made up an important element of her sales. With rare exceptions (for example, Fitzgerald), authors of the early twentieth century first published in little magazines—magazines that were either censored or ignored by the U.S. market. The bookshop was their major distribution point. Some of these little magazines were published in America (*Little Review* and *Poetry*) and England (*Egoist*), but most came from Left Bank expatriates: *Gargoyle, transatlantic review, This Quarter, transition.* Poor patrons could borrow a copy of one of these magazines.

The expense for commercially published books was enormous, for all the English-language books had to be imported. The exceptions were the little expatriate press books printed in France: Robert McAlmon's Contact Editions, William Bird's Three Mountains Press, Edward Titus's Black Manikin, the Crosbys' Black Sun Press, Stein and Toklas's Plain Editions, Cunard's Hours Press, Harrison of Paris, and Beach's own editions of Joyce's works. For all these small presses, she was the major distributor because many of the titles were censored in Britain and America or were not imported because their chief audience was the avant-garde in Paris. But the books from large English and American presses were expensive, and import duty high.

Beach had to juggle bookkeeping in three currencies, a task that probably frustrated her more than any other, for she had no aptitude for mathematics. On more than one occasion a friend tried to teach her the fine points of bookkeeping, to no avail.

The business of selling books was complicated by the international system of selling, mailing, importing, and taxing books; it was simplified by Beach's casual approach. She was anything but casual in choosing and reading the books, of course, but once they arrived, she did not put prices in them. She encouraged people to look through, even read them in the shop, and often gave informal lectures on the author and work for her English-speaking French patrons. Through the years the sales of her books, as revealed in her records, reflect her interests and enthusiasms. She had "all the theories that many booksellers would like to have but sacrifice for financial interest," said Morrill Cody in *Publishers Weekly* (1262).

As a publisher, Beach gained fame but lost financial security. Her publishing of Joyce's *Ulysses* may not have made money for her, but it did help her achieve international fame. If business success is equated with income, the venture was a failure, in part because Joyce took more money from the till than any "advance" would have warranted. Also, Beach violated almost every tenet of a successful publishing house, according to Michael Joseph, especially the rules that say "all firms unable to operate on a steady margin of profit should sink their individualism and . . . cut down on unnecessary costs"; "economic considerations alone will determine the prices" (198–99). But history judges her a truly great publisher because she intervened with Darantière for months in order to get him to print proofs over and over until Joyce had written fully a third more of *Ulysses* on the proofs themselves. She indeed "enabled" the greatness of this novel.

In her study of alternative publishing, Sally Dennison points out that the printing of books was originally done by booksellers, before publishing companies existed: "Milton's *Paradise Lost,* Bunyan's *Pilgrim's Progress,* and all of Shakespeare's works were originally published by booksellers." Alternative publication keeps control with the writer, and when the alternative publisher is a bookstore, she adds, their means of distribution and promotion are great advantages (77). Joyce was indeed fortunate. Because Monnier took over the publication of the French translation of *Ulysses,* he was able to work for several years with the translators to ensure an authoritative translation of the difficult novel.

The full story of getting the chapters typed, preselling subscriptions to the book in order to pay the printer, and selling and smuggling the books has been fully told in *Sylvia Beach and the Lost Generation* (Fitch). The final word should be Beach's: there were "dreadful problems" involved in the publication, she wrote in an unpublished speech she delivered in Brussels not long before her death (Sylvia Beach Papers, Box 180). For a decade she reissued the novel, through eleven printings or editions. *"Ulysses* was her trial, her torture, and finally her triumph," said Hugh Ford in *Published in Paris,* his history of expatriate publishers. "It brought Shakespeare and Company a second celebrity, a living bard, who turned the shop into a literary shrine. It burdened our literature with a work of extraordinary versatility. It canonized Sylvia Beach" (33).

She also published two other titles for Joyce: *Pomes Penyeach,* his second volume of poetry, and *Our Exagmination round his Factification for Incamination of Work in Progress,* a collection of essays on the book that would later be published as *Finnegans Wake.* She designed the cover of the volume, a circular wheel, with the name of each contributor forming a spoke. Because the novel was still being written and portions of it were appearing serially in *transition, Our Exag* (as they called it) sold poorly and remained in boxes in the shop for years. Poor business judgment, Michael Joseph might say.

Beach handled all the business of translations of Joyce's work, paid his bills, arranged his appointments, and handled the press—a decade of service to Joyce, his work, and his family (Fitch). Brenda Maddox, the biographer of Nora Joyce, has since concurred that Joyce "exploit[ed] everyone around him while [remaining] convinced that he was being persecuted." For the entire Joyce family, Maddox adds, Shakespeare and Company was bank, "ticket agency, post office, secretarial service, and customs house" (234–35). The personal and professional Joyce business was nearly a full-time job, but Beach also helped edit two French journals; ran her daily lending library, bookstore, and salon; offered visiting writers an informal tea room, rental agency, post office, and bank; and presented her French customers with informal lectures on American literature.

The banking and taxes involved in selling, lending, and publishing were solely Beach's responsibility, and one for which she was not temperamentally suited. She learned to keep the tax man at bay, in typical French fashion, by keeping two sets of books. When she faced a new printing of *Ulysses,* she borrowed from her sister Holly or her mother. As her ledger books reveal, she kept operational expenses very low; she paid small amounts for errands, shutter raising, window washing, carpentry, stove repair, taxi, and stamps. She used an old-fashioned copper balance for weighing books for postage. In addition to her own records, she kept the finances for her mother, when she was visiting Europe, and for George Antheil, the American composer who rented one of her upstairs rooms and for whom she collected funds. She was also sales agent for a number of writers, including Lawrence and McAlmon.

Shakespeare and Company was also a salon and meeting place, a service that obviously encouraged business. When she presented a reading, she incurred printing costs for the announcements (except for the reading by Hemingway, who vacillated about his performance until it was too late to print formal announcements), the renting of chairs, and the food and drink that Monnier prepared for the reception afterward in their apartment. Edith Sitwell came from London for the first reading, Eliot for one of the last. Most of the readings were given by and for French writers—including Gide, Valéry, and Romains. The readings were infrequent, except during Gide's campaign to save Shakespeare and Company in the 1930s, but the small informal discussions and meetings were spontaneous and frequent. Herbert Lottman claims that both Beach and Monnier held "nonstop open house" in their shops at rue de l'Odéon (29). Beach had a facility for being a hostess that stemmed from both parsonage life and early feminine training, but she could be very prickly when her hard work was interrupted by fools.

To the idealistic observer, running a bookshop and library may seem romantic, a high calling. In reality, it is dirty, hard work. Beach was no dabbler in the arts or salon life; she had to support herself. The business was a necessity. Using a small legacy from her mother, she opened her own business on November 17, 1919. She never expressed a desire to marry—the shop would provide her living. She preferred the company of women, who allowed her her freedom. She was completely responsible for her own business. Lifting books was backbreaking; opening boxes cut up her hands; riding her bike across town to customs kept her face ruddy; tying string, pasting labels, dusting books, typing letters, and building fires in the stove dirtied her body and clothes; calculating the finances in three currencies and typing dozens of letters a week strained her eyes and exacerbated her migraine headaches. Jean Henley, an assistant who worked for her in the 1930s, remembers how heavy were the boxes of cheap books that had to be hauled outside to the front windows in the morning and carried back in at night. In short, it was monotonous, lonely, and fatiguing work. Hugh Ford says that her success was "five percent accident and ninety-five percent hard toil." It was, he adds, "sheer donkey work" ("Publishing in Paris" 66). Monnier called their work "drudgery [la corvée]" (13).

In addition to intuition and hard work, she had at her command a generous portion of common sense and pragmatism. Sisley Huddleston said she was "eminently practical" (208). This pragmatism—and her creative mixing of English and French idioms—endeared her to the French; for many, she was the quintessential American. Both a feminist and a practical Yankee, she needed little, and would have worn the same suit for years if her family and friends had allowed it. No trailing skirts or thin-soled shoes would hobble her. She wore short skirts (for that day) with pockets—a businessman had to have pockets, she explained (Herrick)—sensible shoes, and a large hat to protect her from the elements. She had expressed scorn for the delicate women wearing impractical shoes during her Red Cross days in Serbia (and later in internment camp in World War II). As a girl she had subscribed to *Suffragette* magazine and expressed outrage and admiration for the English suffragettes who endured torture.[2] As she had roamed through Spain and Italy in the years prior to World War I, so she rode her bicycle (maybe the first instrument of emancipation for women) around Paris on her errands—enjoying the freedom allowed her as a foreigner, proud to be a productive and independent woman.

Perhaps her greatest asset in business was her strong and charismatic personality, unrecognized by male historians and critics such as Ezra Pound, Malcolm Cowley, Richard Ellmann, and Hugh Kenner, who have portrayed her as a passive handmaiden to the great James Joyce. Those who knew her well testified to her energy, stubborn will, playful but sharp wit, and loyalty (the latter a parsonage trait). "She left one with a memory of solid exhilaration," says Leslie Katz (Aug. 1, 1977). She had a way of talking intimately that made one feel the center of her universe. As early as 1929, Wambly Bald said in the Paris edition of the *Chicago Tribune* that "the charming personality of Sylvia Beach" was the "chief asset" of the "Left Bankers' Trust Co. [that is, the 'unincorporated' Montparnasse artistic life]," and her bookshop he called "the favored social club of the literati" (2). Jackson Mathews and Yves Bonnefoy said that friends collected her quips and multilingual coinages. Glenway Wescott said she, like Hemingway and Picasso, had "a rather light, pointed, winged, toxic, and quotable way of talking" (196).

Although Beach was born into what her friend Bryher called "the last group to grow up under the formidable discipline" (203) of the Victorian era and was reared in a Protestant parsonage with all its attendant traditionalism, she did not have a traditional view of women. Several factors made her receptive to early-century feminism. She was the middle of three sisters, with no brothers to contend with for attention. Her mother, married at a very early age to an older minister, soon resented her marital and parsonage roles and took refuge in Europe and the art world. She encouraged her daughters to do the same. Two of the girls (Sylvia and Cyprian, an actress) were lesbians who had long-term relationships. The oldest (Holly) married late in life and lived a traditional bourgeois life in Greenwich, Connecticut. Sylvia's closest friends were always women, including Monnier, with whom she lived, and Bryher, the English novelist Winifred Ellerman, who lived with the poet H.D. (Nearly half a century of letters between Bryher and Beach reveal their deep loyalty and shared feminist views.)

Beach had no husband or family wealth behind her. She was the boss, with all the freedom and responsibility that title implies. Not surprisingly, she frequently referred to herself in the masculine gender as a hardworking "businessman" or "the tired working man" in letters to her family. Educated to a polarized view of gender roles, she chose what she called "man's work" (Sylvia Beach Papers, Boxes 6, 9, 12). In her world only men worked hard in business and took sole responsibility for their lives. Yet in an early draft of her memoirs, she also compares her endless responsibilities to a female occupation: There is "no harder life than the bookseller's," she says, it is "as bad as the housewife's with its ramifications and continual interruptions" (Sylvia Beach Papers, Box 166).

Both Beach and Monnier supported themselves solely by their businesses, though the Beach family occasionally rescued one of their daughter's publishing projects and the Monnier family sent food from their farm near Chartres. Beach may have referred to Shakespeare and Company as a "business," but she began it on faith and operated it as a calling. Her business differed from others for two reasons: she was a woman and she was a minister's daughter. Thinking of her nine generations of pastoral and missionary ancestors, she regarded her work as literary missionary work. Monnier, who referred to herself as a *religieuse ancienne* and wrote eloquently about the calling of the seller of books, testified that Beach had "aimed at the kingdom of God, the rest was given to me as a surplus" (13). Beach, the minister's atheist daughter, rarely used such explicit spiritual references. Yet she lived ascetically, as Benstock notes, and "exuded . . . missionary zeal" (206). "Business, for us, has a moving and profound meaning," wrote Monnier in 1920. A bookseller must have an "immediate and intuitive understanding" of the persons who enter her shop and a union with "a soul made up of all ideas and all images" (69–70). This "soul" lived in Odéonia.

Unlike such male bookshop owners as Edward Titus on the Left Bank and what she called the "big junk shops"—Brentano's, W. H. Smith's, and Galignani's—on the Right Bank, she did not stock expensive leather-bound editions of the classics. Readers, not collectors, were drawn to her door. She could work as hard as they, probably harder, but her driving motive was not financial. Hers was a selected stock. "I got everything I liked myself to share with others in Paris" (21). She dismissed one book, with characteristic wit, because it was "totally lacking in vitamins." Contrary to the rules of success, she specialized in poetry and the avant-garde, and her choices helped to form critical opinion. She had "scorn for the standardized predilections" of the masses, said Herbert Gorman, and she kept the "chaff of letters" from her shelves. All her books and periodicals, he added, had "good intentions" (285).

Though she once compared the business of selling books to selling shoes, her business was more an art form, more personal and intuitive. And to the surprise of young assistants Eleanor Oldenberger (now Herrick) and Hélène Moschos, she did not try very hard to sell her stock. She encouraged browsing and borrowing. Occasionally, according to Herrick, she tried to talk a customer out of buying a book—as if she hated to part with it. Such behavior indicates that her intentions were not primarily financial or characteristically masculine.

She chose to be both elitist and amateur. "The amateur, the true amateur," wrote Monnier in "Number One" of her *Gazette,* "follows only his taste. His acquisitions enrich not his pocketbook but his person, they bring him happiness in the true sense of the word." Monnier, like Beach, did not want to speculate financially on books or make her shop a "stock exchange for books" (141–42).

Though a literary success—in getting the word printed, sold, and distributed—Shakespeare and Company was almost a financial failure. She barely kept it afloat as she sailed between two world wars; and she did not franchise any branches—except spiritually. Since her death, five shops with that name have opened to carry on the spirit of Shakespeare and Company in cities around the world: Rome, Vienna, Paris, Manhattan, and Berkeley. In fact, she skirted bankruptcy frequently, for Joyce took every loose franc. The small loans from her mother and sister and, finally in the 1930s, a fund-raising campaign by André Gide and a quarterly endowment by Bryher kept the doors open. The shop was, in fact, a nonprofit enterprise—literary charity work, as she liked to call it, acknowledging the work often designated for women, but work that, in her case, she chose. Hers was a kind of Bohemian sainthood and she a desanctified saint, the self-defrocked progeny of nine generations of ministers. Though she called herself a businessman, she qualified the role—which was both gender-based and secular—by caring nothing for money, success, fans, or bores—all of which a businessman must cultivate and endure if he is to "succeed." Physically perhaps she was a Geneva Protestant—combining business and living in the same building—but without the profit motive or the head for business. An amusing illustration of her casual business practices is evident in the following message from the Irish-born Frank Harris, best known for his controversial (and unreliable) autobiography, *My Life and Loves,* in three volumes: "Dear Miss Sylvia, business and you are poles apart: thank God! You've sent me accounts with no years marked, and you discover 50 of my books in a 'cobbler's remise' and you've lost only 3 and you mean to pay me for them! forget it—please." Several months later, he added: "I am more content to be in your hands and I hate ordinary business people" (Sylvia Beach Papers, Box 120).

"The person who can bring to an 'ordinary' profession a sense of dedicated vocation, restores to that profession its genius," says Katz in his tribute to Beach. "Lincoln was a politician, Melville a seaman, Thoreau a camper. She was a bookseller" ("Meditations" 82). Katz is describing an "artist"—one who restores to a profession its genius—"one who," says the *OED*, "makes of his craft a 'fine art.'" She was an artist in part because she wrote her memoirs and translated Henri Michaux's *A Barbarian in Asia* and other works by Eliot, Valéry, McAlmon, and Bryher. But more important, she was a creative artist of the environment and an artist of relationships. Her greatest creative expression was a *place* called Shakespeare and Company, for like an architect or sculptor she expressed the beautiful in visible form. It was her greatest work of art, from the fabric on the walls, the antique furniture, the Serbian rugs on the hardwood floors, the photographs over the fireplace, to the warmth of the little stove—a creative space illuminated further by the artist's personality. Dressed in velvet jacket and neck scarf, she looked like a character from a Colette novel. Katherine Anne Porter gives this description of the artist of this place:

> When I first saw [Sylvia], in the early spring of 1932, her hair was still the color of roasted chestnut shells, her light golden brown eyes . . . were . . . acutely attentive, and they sparkled upon one rather than beamed, as gentle eyes are supposed to do. She was . . . a delightful presence not accountable to any of the familiar attributes of charm. Her power was in the unconscious, natural radiation of her intense energy and concentration upon those beings and arts she loved. She loved her hundreds of friends, and they loved her . . . each sure of his special cell in the vast honeycomb of her heart. . . . Her genius was for friendship; her besetting virtue, generosity . . . and courage that assured even Hemingway. (54)

Among the two dozen women who actively created or ran businesses or salons for the arts in Paris during the first four decades of this century in Paris, Beach worked the hardest and had the most contacts. The salons of Stein and Barney were active before Beach arrived in Paris, but they served only artists and, then, only limited circles. Because Shakespeare and Company was open long hours (9 A.M.–12:30 P.M. and 2–7 P.M.), all international groups, even warring factions, could find a time to enter its doors. One of the rare exceptions was Stein, who withdrew her library membership during the Joyce years of the bookshop, but returned in the 1930s to have her Plain Editions books sold there. Beach outlived the other businesses, operating the company for twenty-two years—even longer unofficially, for she lent books from her apartment and continued translating and corresponding with writers around the world until her death in 1962. In comparison, the little presses of Cunard and Harrison and the little magazines of Gilliam, Anderson, and Heap were short-lived. Some of the women (and all of the expatriate men) fled Europe during World War II.[3] Only her French partner, Monnier, ran her business longer than did Beach. Monnier died in 1955; Stein had died in 1946, long after she had stopped her regular salon; and among all these expatriate women, only Toklas (1965), Barney (1972), and Gilliam (1979) outlived Beach in Paris.

Since the 1983 publication of the biography of Beach and her bookshop, there have been several books about this period that reassess the contributions of women, including Beach, to modernism. Benstock and Maddox, in particular, pay serious attention to Beach. Also, Bonnie Kime Scott, in *Joyce and Feminism,* places Beach among the "new free women . . . mature and capable" whom Joyce knew (115). There remains an occasional condescending remark that echoes the earlier male critics of the modernist period. Mary

Lynn Broe, for example, links Beach with Monnier, Crosby, and Cunard, as women who were "assigned" the "niche" as "the women muses and enablers of male modernism . . . the handmaidens to James Joyce, Henry Miller, and other male Modernists" (59). Words such as *enablers* and *handmaidens* might imply a criticism of their efforts to publish the work of men. Had they published, edited, and translated only women, however, they would have been turning aside both art and business.

Beach reconciled the seeming dichotomy between art and business. It is not just that poets and novelists need publishers, bookstores, and readers—as composers need players, and painters their galleries. She did more than perform a service; she linked the word to the marketplace. Thomas Mann, in tribute to his American publisher, Alfred Knopf, acknowledged in 1940 the lofty role of this intermediary between art and commerce: "The publisher is not a soloist of spiritual exertion, but the conductor of the orchestra, whereas the author, in his public loneliness, with only himself to rely on, hemmed in of necessity by his ego, struggles to do his best. . . . What a glorious occupation, this mixture of business sense and strategic friendship with the spirit!"

Beach was the conductor of the orchestra, to use Mann's metaphor, for she directed her business activities in the service of the literary spirit.

Notes

1. Sales of English titles, which constituted two-thirds of the sales, are more difficult to ascertain because many sales notations simply say "Tauchnitz"—the cheap German editions of the classics that she kept in the outside window box.

2. Sylvia and Eleanor (later called Cyprian) Beach exchanged enthusiastic letters and articles about what they called the "Votes for Women" movement (Sept. 26, 1913, and Feb. 26, 1914). Sylvia Beach Papers, Box 1.

3. In the first half of this century, the foreign women were the first to come to Paris (Barney arrived in 1902, Stein in 1903, Edith Wharton in 1906, Beach in 1916) and the last to leave. They were, Glenway Wescott remarked to Kay Boyle, "more completely abroad than the rest of us" (Cody and Ford 169).

Works Cited

Bald, Wambly. *On the Left Bank, 1929–1933*. Ed. Benjamin Franklin V. Athens: Ohio UP, 1987.

Beach, Sylvia. Papers. Firestone Library, Princeton U. Published with permission of Princeton U Library.

———. *Shakespeare and Company*. New York: Harcourt, Brace, 1966.

Benstock, Shari. *Women of The Left Bank: Paris, 1900–1940*. Austin: U of Texas P, 1986.

Bonnefoy, Yves. Personal interview. June 23, 1978.

———. "The Voyage de Grece." *Mercure de france* 349 (Aug.–Sept. 1963): 28–33.

Broe, Mary Lynn. "My Art Belongs to Daddy." *Women's Writing in Exile*. Ed. Mary Lynn Broe and Angela Ingram. Chapel Hill: U of North Carolina P, 1989. 41–86.

Bryher. *The Heart to Artemis: A Writer's Memoirs*. New York: Harcourt, Brace & World, 1962.

Bryher Collection. Beinecke Library, Yale U.

Cody, Morrill. "Shakespeare and Company—Paris." *Publishers Weekly* 105 (April 12, 1924): 1261–63.

———, with Hugh Ford. *Women of Montparnasse*. New York: Cornwall Books, 1984.

Dennison, Sally. *(Alternative) Literary Publishing: 5 Modern Histories*. Iowa City: U of Iowa P, 1984.

Ellmann, Richard. *James Joyce*. Rev. ed. New York: Oxford UP, 1982.

Fitch, Noel Riley. *Sylvia Beach and the Lost Generation: A History of Literary Paris in the Twenties and Thirties*. New York: Norton, 1983.

Ford, Hugh Douglas. "Publishing in Paris." *Women, the Arts, and the 1920s in Paris and New York*. Ed. Kenneth W. Wheeler and Virginia Lee Lussier. New Brunswick, NJ: Transaction Books, 1982. 65–73.

———. *Published in Paris: American and British Writers, Printers, and Publishers in Paris, 1920–1939*. New York: Macmillan, 1975.

Gorman, Herbert. *James Joyce*. New York: Farrar & Rhinehart, 1939.

Harris, Frank. Letters to Sylvia Beach. July 17 and Nov. 12, 1924. Sylvia Beach Papers. Princeton U. Published with permission of Princeton U Library.

Henley, Jean. Letter to the author. Oct. 25, 1977.

Herrick, Eleanor Oldenberger. Personal interviews. Jan. 1979 and Feb. 14, 1980.

Huddleston, Sisley. *Paris Salons, Cafés, Studios: Being Social, Artistic and Literary Memories*. Philadelphia: Lippincott, 1928.

Joseph, Michael. *The Adventure of Publishing*. London: Allan Wingate, 1949.

Joyce, James. James Joyce Collection. Lockwood Memorial Library, State U of New York at Buffalo.

Katz, Leslie. Letter to the author. Aug. 1, 1977.

———. "Meditations on Sylvia Beach." *Mercure de france* 349 (Aug.–Sept. 1963): 82–85.

Kenner, Hugh. *The Pound Era*. Berkeley: U of California P, 1971.

Lottman, Herbert R. *The Left Bank: Writers, Artists, and Politics from the Popular Front to the Cold War*. Boston: Houghton Mifflin, 1982.

Mathews, Jackson and Martheil. Personal interviews. May 1969 and June 18, 1978.

Maddox, Brenda. *Nora: The Real Life of Molly Bloom*. New York: Houghton Mifflin, 1988.

Monnier, Adrienne. *The Very Rich Hours of Adrienne Monnier*. Trans. with Intro. Richard McDougall. New York: Scribner's, 1976.

Moschos, Myrsine. Personal interview. June 22 and 24, 1978.

Porter, Katherine Anne. "Paris: A Little Incident in the Rue de l'Odéon." *Ladies' Home Journal* 81 (Aug. 1964): 54–55.

Scott, Bonnie Kime. *Joyce and Feminism*. Bloomington: Indiana UP, 1984.

Wescott, Glenway. "Memories and Opinion." *Prose V* (1972): 177–202.

12.

"Yes, no, peut-être": Caresse Crosby
after the Black Sun Set

Mary Lynn Broe

She rode to the Ritz atop a vegetable cart in the Latin Quarter, shot pheasants from her bathtub in Ermenonville, Rousseau's old mill. She staged bacchanals for the "flaming youth" of the twenties at the old gun armament at Etretat, and in the "Pompeian" bathtub for four on the rue de Lille. She emerged from the mouth of a papier-mâché dragon as a flesh-colored Inca princess ("my figure was as evident as the prow of a ship"), while Harry, clad only in a necklace of dead pigeons, wielded a bag of live snakes (*Passionate Years* 143). "I've never been out on the town with Eliot," she once wrote, "he's not that sort of poet" (*Passionate Years* 265). In later years Douglas Fairbanks swung from her rafters at Hampton Manor, the Jefferson farm in Virginia. Salvador Dali floated a piano in her lily pond, played chess and drank liqueur in her parlor . . . in the company of a cow. At Le Moulin du Soleil, she hired a Cordon Bleu cook for the occasional visits of Count Armand de la Rochefoucauld, but more to prepare lunches for twenty other "guests": Soucoupe, a little white goat, two handsome cockatoos, a donkey, several carrier pigeons and ducks, Siamese kittens, an "unpredictable cheetah," a screaming macaw, and "one elegant ferret" (*Passionate Years* 179).

Mary Phelps Jacob Peabody Crosby (1892–1970)—whose mellifluous name "Caresse" was minted to form a cross-shaped anagram with her husband Harry's—had married two millionaires and brushed tempers with Back Bay Boston as well as with New York and international aristocracy. *The Passionate Years,*[1] her only published memoir, details a sybaritic childhood replete with more anecdotal details, like flies in amber. She had her picture painted by Charles Dana Gibson. In her teens, Cole Porter escorted her to a circus. At her debut, King George V chased her hat at a royal garden party. Caresse was even the first American Girl Scout. Commenting on this breathless social register of arts and society, she wrote: "We never went boating without white gloves and a veil" (*Passionate Years* 42).

In later years, when Caresse exchanged her ermine-lined baby carriage for a civet-cat coat, she moved from the syntax of hermetic poetry and limited editions to the transnational vocabularies of *Portfolio, An International*

12.1. Caresse Crosby, with *Portfolio,* n.d. The Caresse Crosby Photo Collection, Special Collections, Morris Library, Southern Illinois University at Carbondale.

Journal of the Arts (1945–58)[2] and to two Washington art galleries. She reinscribed public space with the visionary macropolitics of a plan for World Citizenship, a movement of Women Against War, and a two-hundred-acre Peace Center at Delphi. Caresse even devised a "thirty-year plan" to mesh the crafts of the Abruzzi artisans at Roccasinibalda, her castle near Rome, with the talents of intercontinental artists and writers. The forty years from Harry Crosby's suicide (1929) until her death in Rome (1970) describe Caresse's dedicated transgression of aesthetic, national, and geographic boundaries. As she moved from solipsism to humanistic expansion and regeneration, she abandoned those red and gold sunbursts on the Black Sun's Editions Narcisse (1925) for symbolic World Passports, hundred-page manifestos, and world peace centers at Cyprus and Delphi. Did she truly move in that "ecstasy of vagueness," as her friend Harry Moore claimed?[3] Was she merely, as Ezra Pound pee-vishly charged, a "kind heart, curious collections of erronious [sic] notions," but not "a pillar to lean on" (CColl 140: 64/10)?[4]

As early as 1913, Caresse Crosby rebelled against conventional strictures, casting off the whalebone corset that imprisoned women from the knees to the armpits: she invented the brassiere for her debut. In 1944, she flouted Washington segregation laws by bringing Canada Lee to the stage and African Americans to the audience of her art gallery. Yet in Geoffrey Wolff's book, *The Black Sun,* Caresse gets merely a postscript. And in *Exile's Return,* Malcolm Cowley links the private symbolism of Harry Crosby's early death to the shared internal decay of all those Left Bank refugees of art: "his [Harry's] life had a quality of a logical structure. His suicide was the last term of a syllogism; it was like the signature to a second rate but honest and exciting poem" (72).

When asked in 1949 to comment on Caresse Crosby's autobiography, Cowley responded superfluously, if not condescendingly: "Try hard to get a few more general values into your story. . . . You should explain something more of your (and Harry's) dreams and ideals; I know you had them even when you didn't talk about them. Try a little more for the sense of history . . . mention a few titles of favorite songs, if you remember them, to fix the era" (letter to Caresse Crosby).

A virtuoso adventurer, Caresse Crosby hardly needed song titles to "fix a life" that, with the energy of its narration, read like a Hearst headline. As the sensational life of Harry Crosby—egotist, neurotic, womanizer, sun devo-tee, and poetaster—has been resurrected, revised, and mythologized every few years since Cowley published his memoir, over forty years of Caresse Crosby's radical achievements in the world of international publishing and the arts (1929–70) remain virtually unknown to literary history.

Caresse Crosby was one of a number of American and British women who, at least initially, founded or managed small presses and magazines in Paris (1914–30).[5] These bold bookwomen had unique technical means and conceptual control—economic as well as critical power—to reshape modern-ism. Powerful as well as different, their literary enterprises anticipate Benedict Anderson's suggestion that "communities are to be distinguished . . . by the style in which they are imagined" (15). Jane Heap, for example, carried on a sharp-witted dialogue on the changing nature of art and culture in her "Reader Critic" column of the *Little Review*. Raffish Nancy Cunard redefined the workplace with an experimental literary aesthetic. Using an old Mathieu press, she hand-set her own type in her Norman farmhouse. She published new authors such as Alvaro Guevara, making sure that all authors realized one-third of her proceeds after cost. Barbara Harrison's exotic designs used the aprons of Auvergne schoolgirls for the cover of Aesop's *Fables*. Sylvia Beach, known chiefly as publisher of the 730 pages of *Ulysses* in 1922, also organized international as well as local lists for financing the printing of books. Likewise, she mounted an international protest against the pirating of unprotected book rights. Other courageous bookwomen such as Kay Boyle, Maria Jolas, Florence Gilliam, and Ethel Moorhead challenged the previous generation's training in "domestic economy" as they shaped and revised modern literature with what in 1929 Margaret Anderson called their "creative opinion":

> I began the *Little Review* because I wanted an intelligent life. By intelligent I didn't—and don't—mean: 1) the capacity to follow an argument; 2) the capacity for documentation; 3) the gift of erudition, authority, strong physical vibrations, or any of the other primary signs by which people seem to get labelled intelligent at the moment when I am finding them particularly uninteresting. By intelligent I meant—creative opinion. (*Little Review Anthology* 350)

It was in such a shared creative spirit that Caresse Crosby transformed the Black Sun from a limited-editions press, whose lavishly bound volumes were dedicated to the "aesthetics of romance" between husband and wife, into a commercial press that specialized in low-cost reprints and avant-garde paperbacks (*The Devil in the Flesh; Le Grand Meaulnes; Vol de Nuit*). Black Sun had published private memorials to the Crosby marriage in titles as revealing as *Impossible Dreams* or *Sleeping Together*. Like a missal, colored tapes held together the sides of D. H. Lawrence's beautiful red and gold manuscript of *Sun,* while marble papers, beautifully laid vellums, and calfskin bindings marked Black Sun's volumes of Hart Crane's *The Bridge,* Archibald MacLeish's *Einstein* and *New Found Land,* Kay Boyle's short stories, and Georg Grosz's lithographs for *Interregnum*. Black Sun's epigraphs, much as the titles do, tell the story. "To My Harry," Caresse wrote:

> Your way lies through the bright mists of morning
> I fear to lose you in their shining depths.
> So, swift, I bathe in moonlight, and hair flying
> I follow you, with winged shoes for my steps.
>   (*Crosses of Gold,* May 11, 1925, n.p.)

"Life," another of Caresse's earliest poems in *Crosses of Gold,* reads: ". . . is a picture puzzle / Of a thousand silly bits. / Of every shape and color / Yet how lovely when it fits." And in *Painted Shores* (1927): "To HC: Yours is the music for no instrument, / yours is the preposterous color unbeheld," to which Harry responded in *Sonnets for Caresse* (1927):

> So hath the boon been given by the
> poets of old time (Dante to Beatrice—

And I profane not), yet with my lesser
powers, shall I not strive to give it thee? (n.p.)

Throughout her career, Caresse would weave those tiny, scattered bits of mosaic into a harlequinade of brilliant color, a radical publishing experiment, traveling to Berlin to buy special colored inks for her Continental Editions: "The colors of the titles should match the countries—Red for Russia, Blue for Peru, but Green for 'Torrents of Spring' [Hemingway] in honor of Diana and the woods of Michigan" (*Passionate Years* 283). Fifteen years later *Portfolio,* an intercontinental review of art and literature, would radically challenge the sacrosanct notion of the little "parish" magazine by making a folder from outsized and loose printers' leaves, gathering a rainbow of colors and textures and sizes from old scraps of paper left on shop floors. At the same time that Eugene Jolas led the "revolution of the wordists" in a campaign against monotonous syntax and the tyranny of time, Caresse uttered her own bold manifesto for a new literary and personal world order in Crosby Continental Editions: "I am going to publish books that I like, that have merit and that interest or amuse me personally . . . books that will express the genius of every country in the language we all understand at a price we can all afford" ("Open Letter to Hemingway" vi). Writing to Kay Boyle, she called a moratorium on nostalgia and backward thinking, summing up her Paris years before Harry's suicide in this way: "I am done in by those persistent six or seven years . . . they have stood in my way too long. I want to project and remember anew or not remember at all—write about the new world *that is all about me*" (undated letter).

From 1930 to 1935 Caresse Crosby offered the world of letters international literature in a new format—the Crosby Continental Editions (CCE). Four years in advance of Penguin, she distributed paperbacks—what she called "remakes of really good books"—in a bold publishing venture in direct commercial competition with the German publisher Tauchnitz (*Passionate Years* 274). Far in advance of most thirties' markets, CCE appeared six years before the Pelican "Adult Education" books, prompting André Maurois's comment in advertising copy: "Paul Valéry has rightly said: 'The real League of Nations should be a League of Minds.' But how create this when Anglo-Saxons and Latins misunderstand each other? To widely diffuse—as does the CCE—the best books of the two civilisations, is to lead towards the formation of a new Europe." As Jean Cocteau quipped about CCE's little twelve-franc/one-shilling railroad-kiosk reprints of avant-garde and classical literature by such writers as Kay Boyle, René Crevel, Raymond Radiguet, Alain-Fournier, Dorothy Parker, and Ernest Hemingway: "The Crosby Continental Collection fits easily in the pocket, can be carried everywhere, ready to give life and hope—in fact, the opposite of a revolver" (advertising copy).

Revealingly, Caresse Crosby was unaware that her first CCE manuscript, Hemingway's *Torrents of Spring,* was a lively satire about Sherwood Anderson.[6] Caresse thought she had commissioned a work in progress on toreadors for which she had bartered return passage to New York for Hemingway and his family. After a long wait for the manuscript, she received five pages of "mostly one-word lines of four-letter words" (*Passionate Years* 297). Politely, she returned the copy to him (to his horror), only to learn that his seven-hundred-dollar advance money had already been cashed in on transatlantic tickets. Using her "Open Letter to Ernest Hemingway" as introduction to the CCE *Torrents of Spring* (Paris, 1932), she was able to conceal, yet reveal, her acerbity:

> I wanted to do something as you two [Hemingway and Chaplin] had done something . . . make something out of all this Anglo-Saxon alertness and zest for discovery of new things in ancient lands. The barrier that separates us and always will . . . is the difference in language. Local color, bulls and blood are all very well, but one wants to know what the people are saying and thinking . . . good fishing, and again, many thanks. (CColl 140: 5/4 and 50/11; *Passionate Years* 298–300)

In the spring of 1931, Caresse solicited the imprimatur of former Black Sun editors, famous men of letters such as Stuart Gilbert, Eliot, Lawrence, and Pound, to introduce four volumes of Harry's posthumously collected poems. Curiously, it was Pound's introduction to *Torchbearer,* his praise for Harry's vitality and "direct perceptions into a totality" far beyond the scholar-pedagogues who were, in his words, "subsidized to collect washlists," that struck the right chord for Caresse in her new literary and artistic ventures. For it was not that these little CCE paperbound editions were so momentous and enduring in their own right: the truth was, they were rather short-lived, and not very lucrative. After six months, they had netted only $1,200 in profits. By mid-1933 she wrote to Kay Boyle that the CCE "had not one cent of working capital" (undated letter). As Caresse said, "The CCE took a big loss at the end of the year [1930], and by 1935 had quite eaten itself up—but it brought me back onto the literary scene not with a whimper but a bang!" (*Passionate Years* 315). It was she, not Harry, who deployed that "excess vitality" that Pound had praised. It was Caresse, not Harry Crosby, who truly cast a "vote of confidence in the cosmos" (Pound, Introduction to *Torchbearer* vii).

Of major significance, however, is the literary correspondence with Lawrence, Pound, Kay Boyle, and Jacques Porel. As with Hemingway, who was portrayed elsewhere by Caresse as someone "never young," and a writer whom she, contrary to Paris newspaper headlines, most definitely "had not invented" ("Who in the World"), the epistolary exchanges and introductions surrounding the origins of CCE and *Portfolio* tutored Caresse in publishing savvy and in the technical pedagogies for which Pound so condemned the modern writer. With little formal education, Caresse was a grassroots initiate to the publishing industry and to what Ezra Pound called the "art of the deal." The letters fashion a rare "Guidebook for the Aspiring Publisher," as they also provide a glimpse into the construction, dissemination, and economics of a literature in direct challenge to high modernism. Virtually hundreds of letters—from which the following is a representative, if brief, selection—document the haggling, theorizing, strategizing, and even sentimentalizing that comprised the education of a literary sensibility, as they highlight some of the transatlantic influences on the small-press publishing industry during a rich, experimental time in the shaping of modern literature. In my opinion, Caresse Crosby learned as much from the margins, from misreading and rejecting ideas and publishing directives about CCE and *Portfolio,* as she did from direct translation of advice.[7] I want to look briefly at selected correspondence and then move on to her unique wartime journal, *Portfolio,* Caresse Crosby's cultural Baedeker for a world at war.

"Frankly, what I saw alarmed and shocked me. It was writing that I could not grasp at all and therefore could not enthuse over as a work of importance—not a lack of daring on my part, for had the *Tropic* excited or beguiled me I would have dared 100%. To me it was rude and unpalatable."[8] It was clear in 1932 that Caresse Crosby did not like Henry Miller's manuscript of *Tropic of Cancer,* which was shown her by the infamous Jack Kahane of Obelisk Press. Yet not long before, the stocky, bristly Hart Crane ("he was rather like a young porcupine . . . [with] a lot of gusto and a Rabelaisian laugh") had beguiled her at Le Moulin (*Passionate Years* 246), despite his midnight prowlings and nocturnal pickups, which the maid reported in this way:

> "Oh, Madame," she said, "quel malheur, quel malheur." . . . Hart had already departed . . . but he left behind him traces of great activity. On the wallpaper and across the pale pink spread, up and down the curtains and over the white chenille rug were the blackest footprints and handprints I have ever seen, hundreds of them. . . . he had brought a chimneysweep home for the night. (*Passionate Years* 246–47)

In order to bribe him to finish *The Bridge,* Caresse had to ply him with Cutty Sark and writing paper—and then steal his trousers and shoes.

If we compare the letters exchanged by Harry and D. H. Lawrence with those that Lawrence sent to Caresse after 1929, we see the emergence of a practical, fiery side of Caresse. Lawrence's letters to Harry (1928–29) were comradely and deferential. Lawrence seemed grateful for the hundred dollars in gold nuggets that Harry had delivered to him in a Queen of Naples snuffbox in exchange for the *Sun* manuscript. Wrote Lawrence on May 26,

1928: "What right have I to receive these things? . . . Perhaps one day we can square it, somehow." His letters were full of praise for their shared bond of "sun-sensitiveness," the "direct, phallic, nocturnal connection of men with the sun"; also with aesthetics—much talk of sun fauns, sun nymphs, Zuni, and Aztec suns (letter to Harry Crosby, Aug. 28, 1928). On April 1, 1928, Lawrence wrote, "How beautiful the gold is! Such a pity it ever became currency. One should love it for its yellow life, answering the sun." Even Lawrence's ideas for a stock edition of *Sun* for a hundred francs, penned to Harry in January 1929, are undercut by "But I don't know why I bother you . . ."

Perhaps the best example of this cavalier, "save-a-little-sunspot-of-insouciance" relationship comes from an October 20, 1928, letter from Lawrence to Harry: "Do a little *de luxe* or *di lussissimo* edition of *Sun* if you like. But *you'll* have to decide how many copies you're going to print. And you give me twenty-five percent or thirty percent profits, as the commercial deluxers do: if there is any profit. If not, we'll consider it wine spilled to Phoebus Apollo!" (CColl 140: 5/4).

Lawrence's correspondence with Caresse, on the other hand, is neither so genial, nor so magnanimous. At Le Moulin in Ermenonville, she recalls riding a donkey cart with him in search of spring daffodils, finding him "fugitive, strung taut and full of wisdom." As they returned to the mill, Lawrence proceeded to break a gramophone record over Frieda Lawrence's head. He felt, Caresse insisted, "insouciante" (*Passionate Years* 231–32). In the letters to Caresse, Lawrence talks of his fleecing by the pirates of Lady Chatterley ("I lost at least $15,000") (Aug. 12, 1929). He warns Caresse about Harry Marks (U.S. bookseller) and the lucrative business of U.S. retailing, tutoring her in strategies for getting suspicious books past the U.S. censors: his scheme was to send the book in parts, unbound, loose sheets, forwarding the binding separately, then the frontispiece, so that the book might be bound up in New York. At one point in the correspondence, Lawrence chides Caresse for her sale of *The Escaped Cock:* "Did you really sell the whole edition for $2,250? It seems absurd, for Marks was retailing it at $25 a copy. . . . But did you sell the whole edition, *including the vellums,* for $2,250? If you did you are not the good business woman I should expect you to be" (Feb. 14, 1930).

Writing to Caresse only a few months after Lawrence's death, Frieda Lawrence had the final word about this venture, a canny summary of their epistolary exchanges. Frieda wanted *The Escaped Cock* manuscript back in Bandol. On June 6, 1930, she wrote: "Are you *only* a business woman? With the usual tricks? No, my dear, Harry was a different sort. He was not *that* kind—No! I won't give you another word of Lawrence to print if I don't get the manuscript of *The Escaped Cock.* Yours in disgust, Frieda."

Caresse was hardly "a business woman, up to the usual tricks," though she was clever enough to turn many of her mistakes into triumphs. After the

Hemingway fiasco with *Torrents of Spring,* she traded the money she had advanced Ernest for the continental rights to an even better work, *In Our Time* ("Here was a fine gambit," she admitted of the deal), nevertheless taking the opportunity for a few swipes at his abrupt one-word style ("Swell") (*Passionate Years* 297).[9]

Yet at other times, her literary tastes, formative and immature enough, were impounded, as she was challenged: "I must think of something more interesting for you to do next—in fact, have already done so," Pound wrote from Rapallo in May 1930 (CColl 140: 5/5, 64/10, 64/11). What followed this announcement was a virtual encyclopedia of letters (CColl 64/10) in which Pound tried, among diatribes and hectoring, to get Caresse to take over the fifty-six pages of his translation of Guido Cavalcanti from the bankrupt Aguila Press. Typically, he offered Caresse a thirteen-page itemized literary menu of specific fare for translation in the CCE series, from *Tre Croce* to Frobenius. In this monumental letter, dated only September 7, no year specified, from Fondamenta Sorenzo, he dictated long, opinionated, but crackling annotations on what was dull, skillful, or salable in British and American fiction at the time: Hardy's *Mayor of Casterbridge,* anything by Ford Madox Ford, Joyce's *Dubliners,* James Farrell's *Low Life,* and Mike Gold's *Jews Without Money.*

Ironies abound in Pound's correspondence: "I'll never recommend a lot of books because there are never such a lot worth reading or readable" (letter from Venice, Sept. 7, no year). Yet later, after he had anticipated all technical or aesthetic questions that might be raised about his prescriptions: "If you want any more yawp from me, go ahead and ask questions" (letter from Rapallo, Aug. 2, no year). His lively literary opinions correctly earned him the title of "romantic scatologist" from Edward Dahlberg, particularly for comments such as the following: "I think Rimbaud is good when he is using the equivalent to 'howling bird shit,' and not redundant phrases such as screams and *excrement* or *clamorous birds"* (letter from Rapallo, Aug. 25, 1930). And of Paul Morand, Pound wrote that he was "a pig who wrote 3 good books—or at least 2" (letter from Venice, Sept. 7, no year). What Pound invaluably provided Caresse was not only an odd tutoring in marginalized writers, a race and class consciousness, but an often conflicted set of publisher's ethics: "I don't believe in anthologists who refrain from paying originators"; yet on February 5, 1931, he wrote: "Thanks for the cinq mille. Most opportune. Ruin staved off, wolf kicked in the jibletts [*sic*]." Still he continued, in the same sampling of advice, to qualify his egalitarian economics by urging Caresse to "squeeze our minor figures who derive advance value from the distinguished company and approval of the selector," or "If you can't get anything else, you might do a volume of my prose cut down from *Divigations* and elsewhere" (letter from Venice, Sept. 7, no year).

Continuing his gratuitous "practical advice," Pound emphasized the ethics of soliciting translations and the importance of timing—his belief that "a quick turnover (in publishing) allows one to get on with the next job sooner" (Aug. 25, no year). After recommending Basil Bunting as translator of *Tre Croce,* he wrote: "I can't be held even indirectly responsible for having authors insulted. You *can't* ask people to go translating great chunks of books for nothing" (Nov. 10, no year). Never above blackmail or "barter," as he called it, Pound announced: "Anything I could say as blurb depends wholly and utterly on whether the few books I want to see printed are going to be included on a definite and agreed-upon list with a certain percentage of [my] recommended material." Pound feared, of course, that Caresse Crosby would ignore his advice, which, in literal prescription, she did. So he continued: "There it is. Very hard not to be made a damn fool of by feminine charm. Will try to keep my sense of literary values immune" (Nov. 10, no year).

Lastly, Pound suggested to Caresse that she might treat a publisher's reader and tutor (Pound himself) more respectfully: "He gets a fee for advice, and that ends it. It's either taken or dropped. He is not expected to use the arts of persuasion" (Nov. 15, 1930). Pound's letter from Rapallo cannily sums up much of his mentoring of Caresse in the book world:

> Sorry, but manners that are above criticism are almost useless to produce thought. Put it this way / you go to a doctor, he gives you a prescription. You go to another doctor who gives you another prescription, *more or less* like the first, that is to say just different enough to be (in the first doctor's opinion) worthless. Then you come round and ask the first medico to sign the second prescription. Both prescriptions look pretty much alike / etc. . . . Put the question up to Porel [Caresse's lover and business partner in the founding of CCE]. In the case of the medico nothing is *en jeu* save the medico's professional reputation . . . and in questions of literature? (Nov. 15, 1930; Pound attaches a letter)

Years of letters exchanged with Jacques Porel (CColl 140: 64/3–4) finally prompted Caresse to write: "Although Jacques knew all the jeunesse doree and the jeunesse douee of Paris, he was no better at finance than I was" (*Passionate Years* 274). When this son of the famous French actress Rejane was not railing about American women ("born spoiled, living spoiled, dying spoiled"), or lamenting hopelessly dull American types (Mar. 5, 1932), he did urge Caresse to include in CCE "in the first six months, the three best young writers: Hemingway, Dos Passos and Faulkner" (Jan. 13, 1932). Writing to her in the United States from the press on rue Cardinale in January 1932: "Please have the right for one book of each—and it will be perfect."

Porel had rather formulaic tastes, yet he offered some sound advice: e. e. cummings's *Enormous Room* was impossible to print ("too long"); the first CCE volume was not pleasing because it was smaller than the Tauchnitz editions and bore, according to Porel, the unmistakable touch of Caresse, the spoiled American ("too 'luxe' looking from a commercial point of view") (Jan. 13, 1932). In her autobiography, Caresse does admit that it was Porel who brought to her attention "such lovely books as *Grand Meaulnes, Diablo au Corps* and *Vol de Nuit*" (*Passionate Years* 274).

In Porel's last letters to Caresse, he chided her for her "infernal lack of taste" in literature, slandering her growing business skills, "something hard under all your sweetness." He accused her of frivolity, of "making terrible confusions between people." Most revealingly, he disliked the "new woman" she had become, one who said, all too readily, "yes, no, peut-être."

Perhaps the most satisfying correspondence in the Crosby archive are the letters of forty years that Caresse exchanged with Kay Boyle (CColl 140: 5/4 and 33/6–14).[10] Together the letters provide a remarkable document of literary mentoring, of "professional networking" (Boyle introduced Caresse to William Carlos Williams and Alfred Steiglitz, among others), and of candid artistic judgment, but also, and more important, they show unbounded nurturance and support. "I send you my heart very palpitating and warm," Kay Boyle wrote to Caresse Crosby on January 14, 1930, shortly after Harry's suicide pact with Josephine Rotch Bigelow. Throughout numerous illnesses, dire poverty, love affairs, and difficulties with family and children, Boyle expressed to Crosby thanks for the latter's "giving new impetus to [my] work" (Jan. 14, 1930). In a letter of September 26, 1930, she tried to persuade Caresse to visit Midi: "We would read little things together and you would sing. I feel strangely out of place in a leisurely world. I want so much to see you—the little tents around your eyes and your hands and your prancing legs." In October 1930: "You are doing a rare and fine thing with Black Sun Press—and there isn't anyone else, as far as I can see, who is doing anything. Your sense of beauty and appropriateness is certainly not shared by Nancy Cunard or other disinterested printers." And again, as late as January 27, 1956, Boyle wrote: "Thanks for the manifesto on legislation for World Citizenship. I think you are wonderful to have entered into this body and soul and I love you for it." Shortly after this letter, Caresse sent Kay unexpected money from her previous translation of Raymond Radiguet's *Devil in the Flesh,* a few prized Matisse lithographs, and a standing invitation for residency at Roccasinibalda.

In addition to the unqualified support shared by the two women over most of a lifetime, Kay Boyle offered significant literary advice to Caresse, the aspiring publisher. In a September 3, 1931, letter, Boyle thought the CCE should include a work by Colette for a "beginning," for "craft and inspiration." She thought, too, that CCE should publish André Breton's *Nadja*—not only because it is the "very best that has come out of sur-realism [*sic*]" (Sept. 1931). Boyle struck the right literary chords with the suggestion of Colette, just as she did in 1961 when she urged Caresse to read Howard Nemerov's *Mirrors and Windows,* and poetry by Carolyn Kizer and May Swenson. Boyle delivered sound translator's advice about the title *Le Diable au Corps*—"thorn in the side," or "limb of Satan" just would not be suitable! Gently revising Crosby's literary tastes in an undated letter, she recommended for publication a volume of Russian short stories and the poems of Dylan Thomas, then added: "If you're in Brentano's sometime and in the mood for some 'fornicating stuff,' get a copy of *Sailors Don't Care*—worse than *The Well of Loneliness,* the proprietor insists."

Choice and candor inform Boyle's literary advice to Crosby. Never bombastically prescriptive like Ezra Pound, nor petulantly formulaic like Jacques Porel, Boyle wrote directly, here about André Breton:

> the matter of *selling* the Breton is another thing entirely. It couldn't possibly be a popular book. But as a deluxe thing, it would be important. He had an extraordinary pride—amazing. Nothing to do with American good humor or with French complacency. . . . it could never be a book for your proposed scheme. It would have to be purely of your own choice and let that suffice. (Sept. 1931)

It was Boyle who informed Crosby of the Hemingway hoax, just as she praised her friend for the "pricelessness" of her anger. After a long ordeal with Robert McAlmon's short stories, Boyle could not recommend them for publication on June 11, 1933—at least not the first sixty pages—nor could she send them on with her approval. Her advice to Caresse about Archibald MacLeish? That he was "not a realist—mumbling, bungling, and in a vague state somewhere. To a person of action, this is most unsatisfactory," Kay wrote on January 10, 1942. Such candor extended to Crosby's own poems in an October 3, 1961, letter: "I feel about them as I did on first reading—that they are too intellectual to be successful poems. The music, the abandon of your earlier work is lacking, lacking in these poems, *although not in your nature."* And on July 29, 1961, Boyle urged: "Please do not be through with the past. What would happen to our friendship if you were?" Yet when she heard six years later that Crosby, after heart surgery, was considering a literary advisorship, she wrote: "I don't think it a good idea, your considering being a literary advisor, or anything like that. You are a great individual and must remain so. What compromises one has to make in the usual publishing venture—and what else is there in these tragic times?—*You know as well as I"* (July 21, 1967).

These several decades of literary marginalia—"creative opinion" elicited and given copiously by a bevy of advisers—greatly matured Caresse Crosby's technical "know-how" in her art and literary enterprises of the forties. A decade later Caresse introduced to wartime Washington the work of fledgling contemporary artists (Romare Bearden, Lily Saarinen, Pietro Lazzari, Sam

Rosenberg): "With the Second World War my life took on a clearer pattern. The things that I loved gave colour to that pattern, those I had learnt gave form. My contribution to the 'war effort' was to open the Crosby Gallery of Modern Art, and as a projection of a world ideal I plotted the publication of *Portfolio*. . . . I was not without a plan" (*Passionate Years* 351).

A new openness, a regeneration, *a confidence,* characterized her art and literary ventures. If the old romantic illusionism held that the highest art *concealed* art in hopes of being mistaken for reality, Crosby's *Portfolio* (1945–48) surely undermined this belief.[11] Six issues, published in Paris, Italy, and Greece, as well in as the United States, deconstructed the canon of the "little" magazine with its demure size (Pound's tiny, red, hieroglyphic *Exile,* for example), its thumping manifestos (in the words of *Direction,* Montparnassians were to rid themselves of the past decade's "pretenders, and corpse-raisers, and cheap miracle-men"), and its raids on the cult of intelligibility. Unbound and unbounded, gathered up in stiff twin boards with ends tied in ribbons, *Portfolio* was printed on every colored stock imaginable that could be seized from printers' floors. Paper was scarce. Pages were scraps of papers blazoned in colored inks—blue on orange, scarlet on grey. Motley-sized paper—large and small sizes mixed, speckled and plain, deckled edges—made up a virtual harlequinade of shapes and textures of the thousand copies of each issue that were printed. The diversity was immediately apparent: no two folders were alike. Such a format was surely a wry comment on its editor, who had unbound the constraints of bustles and bones, that "boxlike armor of whalebone and pink cordage with white muslin cover" as early as 1913 by inventing the brassiere.

Caresse's startling new magazine was culturally positioned between Charles Henri Ford's *View* (1940–47)[12] and the appearance of the more decorous *Folio* published by Daisy Aldan (Winter 1953 through Winter 1956). *View* channeled European ideas to New York, adding a "political and social theory to the original explorations of the unconscious made by Freud" (Hoffman 356), while *Folio,* featuring the work of Pier Pasolini, paraded New York poets and painters (James Merrill, Kenneth Koch, Jean Garrigue, Frank O'Hara, Grace "George" Hartigan, Larry Rivers, Jackson Pollock, and John Ashbery) in an attempt to integrate the arts. Out of print since 1938, the Jolases' *transition* had billed itself as "an international laboratory for the study of the magical state of mind," trying to capture the prelogical experience of the creative unconscious. *This Quarter,* particularly under Samuel Putnam, attempted to shape Montparnasse into a cosmopolitan cultural center with contributions from every country in Europe.

Almost titled "Future" or "Generation," the outsized *Portfolio* (11 by 17 inches) was born out of acts of resistance and transgression. First, until the early fifties, there were forty-two little magazines in the United States, most of which were controlled by academic poets (Anderson and Kinzie 264).

Caresse's *Portfolio,* with its masthead of editors (Sam Rosenberg on photography; Selden Rodman on poetry) and its postwar dedication to a new world unity through the arts, violated tight little academic boundaries. The first issue appeared a matter of weeks after V-J Day that summer of 1945: "ideas could prove more valuable than guns," she wrote. "In every age, there have been men [sic] to lead peoples into treacherous conflict, but human achievement lives on through the medium of the artist, be he historian, poet, or painter" (*Portfolio* I, introduction, n.p.).

The "courageous vision of the artist" was no less the vision of Caresse, the editor, who imagined—and then shaped—an international community out of nationalisms, no matter what the odds. Sheer physical energy, not to mention repeated violation of national rules and borders, informed her physical act of scouting material for each of the magazines. Her first act was to lobby Ruth Shipley at the State Department for a passport to London and France at a time when no civilian travel was permitted. Then, in the months following, through an odyssey of "flying boats" and converted bombers, middle-of-the-night military transports and sudden calls from cultural attachés, Caresse was able to transgress enormous political barriers in the wake of French Resistance, the Fascist regime, and then the chaos of the military government in Greece. Not only did she scout newcomers (Robert Lowell, García Lorca, Carlo Levi, Anaïs Nin, Man Ray, Modigliani, Charles Olson, to name a few) long before they were nationally, and internationally, visible, she carried with her for distribution the new work of various U.S. artists, such as Romare Bearden and Pietro Lazzari, usually tucked surreptitiously into her Schiaparelli hatbox!

Her editorial work, her risk taking with unfamiliar artists and writers, did not fail to elicit a certain combativeness from such contributors as Kenneth Rexroth. Without finalizing his fee, she printed his innovative play, "Iphegenia at Aulis," only to receive his tirade about the economic politics and practices of the well-heeled:

> the last thing in the world I wish is to be beholden to you in anyway—I am well aware that the literary bon ton is made up of English assistants, Stalinist gunmen, fairies, professional cunnilinguists [sic] and other swine, who simply love to be kicked around by millionairesses. I am emphatically not such a person. I publish only on invitation. . . . I loathe and despise the world of cocktail literature and art. . . . Of course, I know, when one has so much, one is careless about other people's property, isn't one? Poor dear. (*Portfolio* III)

Facing both political and personal resistances, Crosby reinscribed "world space" not only with a parade of national nomenclatures, but with both well-known and sometimes virtually unknown writers, journalists and artists such as Rexroth, Olson, or the prisoner Edwin Becker. *Portfolio,* her "Guide Bleu of the Avant-Garde," offered a defiant political statement of resistance to the "monoliths" that cultures and types can become. *Portfolio* I, for example, offered a diverse social criticism of American life, amidst editorial laments for the "low grade marketplace of national letters" in the postwar United States. A civil disobedience appeal by English anarchist Alex Comfort; Kay Boyle's translation of part of René Crevel's *Babylon;* poems by Louis Aragon and Rimbaud; attacks on the state of scholarship by David Daiches, who argued for a science of "agniology," the study of ignorance, to complement epistemology; even a story by the young Gwendolyn Brooks, "We're the Only Colored People Here" (four years before she won the Pulitzer for "Annie Allen") marked real, material conditions under all the hoopla about the culturally diverse and the "experimental." A powerful addition to the magazine's debut was Henry Miller's savaging of America in "Staff of Life," from *Air-Conditioned Nightmare* ("If bread is bad, the whole life is bad"),[13] run together with Pietro Lazarri's horses, and the art of Romare Bearden and Henry Moore.

The brilliance, if not the mythology, illuminating Caresse's journal was that it exposed its own contradictions. Like the *Guide Bleu, Michelin,* or *Baedeker* guides, *Portfolio* offered its own geology of bathroom symbols, forks for good restaurants, stars and sundry museum symbols. From the labor-saving device of the editorial masthead (Rodman for poetry, Rosenberg on photos, Harry Moore for reviews, Henry Miller on prose), to each issue's reprints of Harry Crosby's poems that undercut their very nostalgia ("The whole past theory of your life and all conformity / to the lives of those around you would have to be abandoned" [*Portfolio* I]), *Portfolio* challenged its own ideological project with the surprising contradictions of each issue's literary form. If improbable national typologies were set forth, and they often were—"what the young Greek mind, and new Greece, is feeling and hoping" (*Portfolio* VI), or the portrait of "young France" in *Portfolio* II—such monoliths were immediately challenged by the unsuppressible realities of human life and material conditions within the country.

What Roland Barthes calls "the disease of essences" masquerading as the avant-garde, "the new," was brought to that "full armour of light" by the challenging social-historical questions asked within *Portfolio*'s pages. Editors of various resistance journals—Louis Martin-Chauffier of *Liberation,* Valdi-Leduc of *Action,* Albert Camus of *Combat,* even Jean-Paul Sartre, who had just begun writing for *Les Temps Modernes*—discussed the tragedy of postwar French cultural activity, existentialism, and the bomb, from conflicting points of view. Any hint of a homogeneous "monument" to postwar France is surely contradicted and undercut by the various representations that follow—Paul Eluard poems illustrated by Dora Marr; "Blues for Bessie," a poem on the singer's death; animated cartoons and then a musical score from the film "Le Retour"; Henry Cartier-Bresson's photos of refugees freed by Allied armies accompanying a paean to the ordinary "river of human beings" celebrated in the Claude

Roy text "The Return." Picasso, too, added a powerful political commentary on the artist: "What do you believe an artist to be? An imbecile who has only eyes if he is a painter, ears if he is a musician, or a lyre on every rung of his heart if he is a poet . . . a boxer, only muscles? He is at the same time a political being . . . a painting is not made to decorate apartments. It is an instrument of offensive and defensive warfare against the enemy" (*Portfolio* II).

The range of classes, high and low cultural forms of production, and varying material circumstances challenged the homogeneity of a given culture—France, Russia, Italy—demythologizing that gallery of national essences with the generic variety. *Portfolio* IV seemed to set forth in its foreword Italy's new postwar Renaissance, its "devotion of the artist to the 'artisana' of the country and renewed life of culture in great castles and estates" far from cities, in the renovated great halls of Torre Sommi-Peccinardi: "Here the bucolic thespians romp through a Saroyan play, with the gusto of olden times, and the ambitious villagers present latest French and Italian chamber music to willing listeners both country and urban . . . the proprietor [has returned to his lands] with enthusiasm and through harvesting is adding the richness of modern art and its activities to his refurbished estates." Undercutting this *Guide Bleu* picturesque flowering of Italian culture in its various forms of accumulation is another, more irregular terrain of Italian culture. Within the pages of the same issue we find a contradictory portrait in the work of the vigorous, young antifascist radicals who configured themselves around the journal *Il Politichnico:* Carlo Levi, Eugenio Montale, and Ungaretti.

I do not wish to suggest that to read *Portfolio* through its enabling mythology of the *Guide Bleu* or the *Baedeker* is to dismiss the journal as a kind of cultural alibi, a vade mecum that carelessly dispersed art and literature for the many but was unaware of its own ideological project. Not at all. Nor did the seeming conflicts between the ideology proposed by *Portfolio* and the cultural format practiced quite literally loose those binding ties of this brilliant transnational journal. Rather I believe that its sophistication and complexity—so far merely a footnote in little magazine history—were testament to the clever technologies and "creative opinions" learned by its editor, Caresse Crosby, a decade earlier when she transformed a limited-edition press into the Crosby Continental Editions, an egalitarian paperback series ("remakes of really good books"). The intellectual and technical expertise that tutored her through so many epistolary exchanges matured in the bold venture of *Portfolio,* challenging the little magazine industry and influencing the direction of transnational letters. From Paris in the twenties to Cyprus in the sixties, from the pink bathtub on the rue de Lille to plans to mobilize women against war to hang their laundry across the Suez Canal, Caresse Crosby brought new vigor, daring, and accomplishment to the direction of modern arts and letters.

Notes

This essay is dedicated to the memory of Al Cohn, professor, rare book connoisseur and bibliophile, whose spirited knowledge of the era encouraged me during my visits to SIU–C, 1979–82. "Animus incorruptus, aeternus habet cuncta"—Sallust.

An earlier version of this paper was delivered for a Special Session of the Modern Language Association, "Biographical Backgrounds of the Lost Generation," in December 1979. I am particularly grateful to Gianna and the late Roberto Celli, and to the Fondazione Rockefeller: a 1982 residency at the Villa Serbelloni enabled me to continue work on Caresse Crosby. A longer version of the *Portfolio* section, "Caresse Crosby and Literary Iconoclasm: *Portfolio,* 1945–48," was read at the 1984 MLA for the Special Session "American Muses in Paris." Both papers were widely circulated among scholars and friends.

1. In addition to this memoir, the Caresse Crosby papers at Southern Illinois University–Carbondale also contain "Who in the World," an unpublished sequel to *Passionate Years,* as well as several versions of *One Spring: Notes from the Diary of C.C.,* dated "Paris, 1929." The largest collection of Caresse Crosby papers (1912–72)—72 library boxes and 172 free-standing volumes—is in the Morris Library, Special Collections, at Southern Illinois University at Carbondale (SIU 140). The Crosby Collection is abbreviated in this essay as (CColl 140), followed by the series citation, and is quoted by permission of the Morris Library and the Caresse Crosby Estate. The Crosby Collection includes the Black Sun Press rare book catalog and volumes; personal correspondence of the Crosbys; unpublished manuscripts of both Caresse and Harry (poems, short stories, plays, diaries, and a volume of "Letters to the Editor"); and prints, photographs, scrapbooks, drawings, and various memorabilia. Of interest, too, are related materials, including the galley proofs for Hart Crane's *The Bridge* (36/7), bound volumes of letters to Harry and Caresse from D. H. Lawrence (55/7), the artwork of Henry Miller (58/3), and Robert Snyder's 16-mm film of Caresse at Roccasinibalda. The reader should note that often individual letters are collected in two or three archival locations, such as Lawrence correspondence in 5/4 (twelve unpublished letters intended for "Letters to the Editor"), 55/7 (a bound but not commercially published archival volume of Crosby/Lawrence letters), and 55/8 and 55/9, the serial individual letters. This is true for Kay Boyle's and Ezra Pound's correspondence, too. The reader should note that in most cases I cite the original serial correspondence from CColl 140's fifth series, designated "Correspondence." Previously unpublished letters by Ezra Pound, Copyright © 1995 by the Trustees of the Ezra Pound Literary Property Trust; used by permission of New Directions Publishing Corporation, agents for the Trustees. Letters by D. H. Lawrence and Frieda Lawrence are used by permission of Laurence Pollinger Ltd. and the Estate of Frieda Lawrence Ravagli. My thanks to David Koch, curator of special collections, and to Shelley Cox

for their invaluable guidance through the archive. I am also deeply grateful to Harry T. Moore, now deceased, for generously sharing such lively information about Caresse, and to Beatrice Moore for her gracious hospitality.

2. Of the six issues published during these years, issues 1, 3, and 5 were printed in the United States. Issue 2 was published in Paris, featuring primarily French artists and writers; issue 4 was released in Rome and focused on Italian writers and artists, while issue 6 was a Greek issue. As Richard Peabody confirms, "Caresse planned to do Issue 7 on Black American writers and artists, and Issue 8 on the Irish, with material collected towards that end. Issue 9 was to include an anthology of poems by Seferis and Elytis with prose by Kazantzakis and Vanezias. Issue 10 was to be a Near East issue" (11).

3. Between the years of 1979 until his death several years later, Harry T. Moore generously shared with me lively anecdotes and information about Caresse Crosby whenever I came to Carbondale, and later to Carterville, Illinois. Harry and Caresse were particularly close during the war years in Washington when Caresse had the G-Place Gallery with David Porter, and then the Crosby Gallery of Modern Art. When industrialist Henry J. Kaiser first met Vice President Henry Wallace at the gallery, they immediately staged a mock wrestling match. Moore: "That's the way it was at Caresse's." It is largely due to Harry and Beatrice Moore's friendship with Caresse, and their efforts on behalf of the university, that her papers made their way to the Morris Library Special Collections at SIU–Carbondale.

4. "Ezra Pound to Harry Moore: Four Letters from Ezra Pound." This is an unpublished manuscript in CColl. Moore is repeating a quotation from a Feb. 16, 1959, letter from Richard Aldington about a conversation Aldington had with Pound before Pound settled in Venice with Olga Rudge. At the time of Pound's conversation with Aldington, Pound was casting about for an Italian residence, and Moore recommended Roccasinibalda, Caresse's castello in the Abruzzi hills outside Rome.

5. Hugh Ford's *Published in Paris,* as well as more detailed books on the "little magazine" enterprise—Frederick Hoffman, *The Little Magazine,* and the more anecdotal and eclectic *The Little Magazine in America,* ed. Anderson and Kinzie—provide a rich lode of information about the book industry and about individual magazines and publishers. See also Benstock, and Fitch, who detail the lives and work of various bookwomen. Useful, too, are individual chapters from various expatriate essays and memoirs by Margaret Anderson, Kay Boyle and Robert McAlmon, Sisley Huddleston, Edward Dahlberg, Sam Putnam and Malcolm Cowley, and others.

6. Kay Boyle made Crosby aware of this in an October 2, 1931, letter (CColl 140: 33/6).

7. Remarkably, Caresse took some considerable risks. Had money not run out, she was planning to publish Vita Sackville-West, Franz Kafka, John Dos Passos, Richard Aldington, and Somerset Maugham, in addition to Faulkner, Huxley, McAlmon, and Katherine Mansfield.

8. Caresse Crosby, page 1 of "Miller," introductory notes to the unpublished sequel to *The Passionate Years,* "Who in the World." See also Crosby's plans for "Letters to the Editor."

9. Not above mistakes, and misled by the term *southern,* in later years Caresse attempted to withdraw the agreement to deposit her papers at Southern Illinois University when she thought that the demographics of southern Illinois meant that black students could not use the library! In the sixties, she incorrectly formulated an appeal for artists-in-residence at Roccasinibalda, eliciting responses from "hat-hangers," cocktail-bar organists from South Carolina, AND even interior decorators who offered to create "free-standing bamboo mobile room dividers" at the elegant 382-room Italian castle.

10. The Kay Boyle letters are arranged serially by date in CColl 140: 33/6–14. All letters cited below can be found in this section of the archive or in 5/4, which contains ten letters planned for "Letters to the Editor."

11. Two sources have provided useful commentary on the entire run of the journal: Peabody's excellent *D. C. Magazines: A Literary Retrospective* and Conover's *Caresse Crosby,* particularly chapters 9 and 10. Nothing, however, substitutes for the singular experience of reading *Portfolio* in toto in the Morris Library Crosby Collection.

12. *View* published thirty-six issues between 1940 and 1947, channeling European ideas to New York, the postwar center of modern art, through abstract expressionism, surrealism, and existentialism. Breton was a regular contributor, along with Kenneth Burke, Wallace Stevens, Harold Rosenberg, Meyer Schapiro, Albert Camus, Jorge Luis Borges, and Henry Miller, as well as artists Magritte, Man Ray, Noguchi, Leger, and O'Keeffe. Entire numbers were devoted to Max Ernst and Marcel Duchamp; one issue even championed the aesthetic value of "vertigo." In the engagement of politics and aesthetics lacing through *View,* truth was left to the artist who cultivated the irrational and the eccentric, and compromised neither with reality, nor with the professional marketplace. In 1992 Ford edited *View: Parade of the Avant-Garde,* a lavish anthology of selected work from *View* complete with plates of paintings, drawings, and photographs.

13. Miller, in the early days of *Portfolio,* was something of a monument. He had already debuted in the *New Review* as a film critic, was part of Villa Seurat's zany *Booster* (1937–39), and by 1946 was nostalgic for all those French provinces, good breads, faded facades, and mixtures of "bistre and pigeon dung" that were glorified in the long walks around the fourteenth arondissement. We recall, too, that in 1931, when Sam Putnam was out of town, he and Alfred Perles had edited the bawdiest of all literary magazine manifestos on "the new instinctualism."

Works Cited

Anderson, Benedict. *Imagined Communities: Reflections on the Origin and Spread of Nationalism.* London: Verso, 1983.

Anderson, Elliott, and Mary Kinzie, eds. *The Little Magazine in America: A Modern Documentary History.* Yonkers, NY: Pushcart P, 1978.

Anderson, Margaret, ed. *The Little Review Anthology.* New York: Hermitage House, 1953.

Bell, Millicent, ed. *Black Sun Press, 1927–Present*. Providence, RI: Brown UP, 1961.

Benstock, Shari. *Women of the Left Bank: Paris, 1900–1940*. Austin: U of Texas P, 1986.

Boyle, Kay. "The Crosbys: An Afterword." *ICarbS* 3:2 (Spring/Summer 1977): 117–25.

———. Letters to Caresse Crosby. Jan. 14, 1930; Sept. 26, 1930; Oct. 1930; Sept. 1931; Sept. 3, 1931; June 11, 1933; Jan. 10, 1942; Jan. 27, 1956; Oct. 3, 1961; July 29, 1961; July 21, 1967; and undated. CColl 140: 33/6–14. By permission of the Kay Boyle Estate.

Broe, Mary Lynn, and Angela Ingram, eds. *Women's Writing in Exile*. Chapel Hill: U of North Carolina P, 1989.

Cocteau, Jean. Advertising copy for Crosby Continental Editions. CColl 140: 57/12.

Conover, Anne. *Caresse Crosby: From Black Sun to Roccasinibalda*. Santa Barbara, CA: Capra P, 1989.

Cowley, Malcolm. *Exile's Return*. New York: Viking, 1956.

———. Letter to Caresse Crosby. Dec. 14, 1949. CColl 140: 36/4. By permission of the Malcolm Cowley Estate.

———. *A Second Flowering: Works and Days of the Lost Generation*. New York: Viking, 1956.

Crosby, Caresse. *Crosses of Gold*. Paris: Albert Messein, 1925.

———. *Impossible Melodies*. Paris: Editions Narcisse, 1928.

———. Letter to Kay Boyle. Undated. CColl 140: 33/6.

———. "Letters to the Editor." Unpublished manuscript. CColl 140: 5/4–5/6.

———. "Open Letter to Ernest Hemingway." *The Torrents of Spring*. By Ernest Hemingway. Paris: Crosby Continental Editions, 1932.

———. *Painted Shores*. Paris: Black Sun P, 1927.

———. *The Passionate Years*. New York: Ecco, 1979.

———. *Poems for Harry Crosby*. Paris: Black Sun P, 1931.

———. "Who in the World." CColl 140: 1.

Crosby, Harry. *Shadows of the Sun*. Paris: Black Sun P, 1928.

———. *Sonnets for Caresse*. Paris: Editions Narcisse Paris, 1927.

Dahlberg, Edward. *Alms for Oblivion*. Minneapolis: U of Minnesota P, 1964.

Fitch, Noel Riley. *Sylvia Beach and the Lost Generation: A History of Literary Paris in the Twenties and Thirties*. New York: Norton, 1983.

Ford, Charles Henri, ed. *View: Parade of the Avant-Garde, 1940–47*. New York: Thunder's Mouth P, 1992.

Ford, Hugh Douglas. *Published in Paris: American and British Writers, Printers, and Publishers in Paris, 1920–1939*. New York: Macmillan, 1975.

Germain, Edward. "Harry Crosby, His Death, His Diaries." *ICarbS* 3:2 (Spring/Summer 1977): 102–10.

Hoffman, Frederick J., Charles Allen, and Carolyn F. Ulrich. *The Little Magazine: A History and a Bibliography*. Princeton, NJ: Princeton UP, 1946.

Huddleston, Sisley. *Back to Montparnasse: Glimpses of Broadway in Bohemia*. Philadelphia: Lippincott, 1931.

Kahn, Sy M. *Devour the Fire: Selected Poems of Harry Crosby*. Berkeley, CA: Two Windows P, 1983.

Lawrence, D. H. Letters to Caresse Crosby. Aug. 12, 1929; Feb. 14, 1930. CColl 140: 5/4 and 55/7, 55/8 and 55/9.

———. Letters to Harry Crosby. April 1, 1928; May 26, 1928; Aug. 28, 1928; Oct. 20, 1928; Jan. 1929. CColl 140: 5/4, 55/8.

Lawrence, Frieda. Letter to Caresse Crosby. June 6, 1930. CColl 140: 55/8.

Maurois, André. Advertising copy for Crosby Continental Editions. CColl 140: 57/12.

McAlmon, Robert. *Being Geniuses Together, 1920–1930*. Rev. ed., with Kay Boyle. New York: Doubleday, 1968.

Miller, Henry. "Staff of Life." *Remember to Remember*. Vol 2 of *The Air-Conditioned Nightmare*. New York: New Directions, 1947.

Minkoff, George Robert. *A Bibliography of the Black Sun Press*. Great Neck, NY: Minkoff, 1970.

Moore, Harry T. "The Later Caresse Crosby: Her Answer Remained 'Yes!'" *D.C. Magazines: A Literary Retrospective*. Ed. Richard Peabody. Washington, DC: Paycock P, 1981.

Parker, Andrew, Mary Russo, Doris Sommer, and Patricia Yaeger, eds. *Nationalisms and Sexualities*. New York: Routledge, 1992.

Peabody, Richard, ed. *D.C. Magazines: A Literary Retrospective*. Washington, DC: Paycock P, 1981.

Porel, Jacques. Letters to Caresse Crosby. Jan. 1932; Jan. 13, 1932; Mar. 5, 1932. CColl 140: 64/3–4.

Portfolio I. Washington, DC: Black Sun P, Aug. 1945.

Portfolio II. Paris: Black Sun P, Dec. 1945.

Portfolio III. Washington, DC: Black Sun P, Spring 1946.

Portfolio IV. Rome: Black Sun P, 1946.

Portfolio V. Paris: Black Sun P, Spring 1947.

Portfolio VI. Washington, DC: Black Sun P, Spring 1948.

Pound, Ezra. "Ezra Pound to Harry Moore: Four Letters from Ezra Pound." CColl 140: 64/10.

———. Introduction to *Torchbearer*. By Harry Crosby. Paris: Crosby Continental Editions, 1931.

———. Letters to Caresse Crosby. Aug. 2 (from Rapallo, no year); Aug. 25 (no year); Sept. 7 (from Venice, no year); Nov. 10 (no year); May 1930; Aug. 25, 1930; Nov. 15, 1930; Feb. 5, 1931. CColl 140: 5/5 (twelve unpub. letters collected for "Letters to the Editor") and 64/10.

Putnam, Samuel. *Paris Was Our Mistress: Memoirs of a Lost and Found Generation*. Carbondale: Southern Illinois UP, 1970.

Symons, Julian. *Makers of the New: The Revolution in Literature, 1912–1939*. New York: Random House, 1987.

Wickes, George. *Americans in Paris*. New York: Doubleday, 1969.

Wolff, Geoffrey. *Black Sun: The Brief Transit and Violent Eclipse of Harry Crosby*. New York: Random House, 1976.

Selected Bibliography

Anderson, Elliott, and Mary Kinzie, eds. *The Little Magazine in America: A Modern Documentary History.* Yonkers, NY: Pushcart P, 1978.

Anderson, Margaret. *My Thirty Years' War.* New York: Covici, Friede, 1930.

Antler, Joyce. "After College What? New Graduates and the Family Claim." *American Quarterly* 32 (1980): 409–33.

Auerbach, Nina. "Engorging the Patriarchy." *Feminist Issues in Literary Scholarship.* Ed. Shari Benstock. Bloomington: Indiana UP, 1987. 150–60.

Baggett, Holly. "Aloof from Natural Laws: Margaret C. Anderson and the *Little Review*, 1914–1929." Diss. U of Delaware, 1992.

Bald, Wambly. *On the Left Bank, 1929–1933.* Ed. Benjamin Franklin V. Athens: Ohio UP, 1987.

Banta, Martha. *Imaging American Women: Idea and Ideals in Cultural History.* New York: Columbia UP, 1987.

Bardes, Barbara, and Suzanne Gossett. *Declarations of Independence: Women and Political Power in Nineteenth-Century American Fiction.* New Brunswick, NJ: Rutgers UP, 1990.

Baym, Nina. "Between Enlightenment and Victorian: Toward a Narrative of American Women Writers Writing History." *Critical Inquiry* 18 (1991): 22–41.

———. "Melodramas of Beset Manhood: How Theories of American Fiction Exclude Women Authors." *The New Feminist Criticism: Essays on Women, Literature, and Theory.* Ed. Elaine Showalter. New York: Pantheon, 1985. 63–80.

———. *Woman's Fiction: A Guide to Novels by and about Women in America, 1820–1870.* Ithaca, NY: Cornell UP, 1978.

Beatty, Barbara. "'A Vocation from on High': Kindergartning as an Occupation for American Women." *Changing Education: Women as Radicals and Conservators.* Ed. Joyce Antler and Sari Knopp Biklin. Albany: State U of New York P, 1990. 35–50.

Bell, Millicent, ed. *Black Sun Press, 1927–Present.* Providence, RI: Brown UP, 1961.

Bennion, Sherilyn Cox. *Equal to the Occasion: Women Editors of the Nineteenth-Century West.* Reno and Las Vegas: U of Nevada P, 1990.

Benstock, Shari. *Women of the Left Bank: Paris, 1900–1940.* Austin: U of Texas P, 1986.

Berry, Faith. "A Question of Publishers and a Question of Audience." *Black Scholar* 17 (1986): 41–49.

Brigham, Clarence S. "James Franklin and the Beginnings of Printing in Rhode Island." *Massachusetts Historical Society Proceedings* 65 (1936): 536–44.

Broe, Mary Lynn. "My Art Belongs to Daddy." *Women's Writing in Exile.* Ed. Mary Lynn Broe and Angela Ingram. Chapel Hill: U of North Carolina P, 1989. 41–86.

———, and Angela Ingram, eds. *Women's Writing in Exile.* Chapel Hill: U of North Carolina P, 1989.

Brown, Hallie Q. *Homespun Heroines and Other Women of Distinction.* 1926. Freeport, NY: Books for Libraries P, 1971.

Brumberg, Joan Jacobs, and Nancy Tomes. "Women in the Professions: A Research Agenda for American Historians." *Reviews in American History* 10 (1982): 275–96.

Bryer, Jackson R. "Joyce, *Ulysses,* and the *Little Review.*" *South Atlantic Quarterly* 66 (Spring 1967): 148–64.

———. "'A Trial Track for Racers': Margaret C. Anderson and the *Little Review.*" Diss. U of Wisconsin–Milwaukee, 1965.

Buell, Lawrence. *New England Literary Culture from Revolution through Renaissance.* New York: Cambridge UP, 1986.

Bullock, Penelope L. *The Afro-American Periodical Press, 1838–1909.* Baton Rouge: Louisiana State UP, 1981.

Burke, Carolyn. "Getting Spliced: Modernism and Sexual Difference." *American Quarterly* 39 (1987): 98–121.

Chapin, Howard M. "Ann Franklin of Newport, Printer, 1736 –1763." *Bibliographical Essays: A Tribute to Wilberforce Eames.* Cambridge: Harvard UP, 1924. 337–46.

———. "Ann Franklin, Printer." *Americana Collector* 2 (1926): 461–65.

Charvat, William. *Literary Publishing in America, 1790–1850.* Philadelphia: U of Pennsylvania P, 1959.

Chisholm, Anne. *Nancy Cunard: A Biography.* New York: Knopf, 1979.

Clark, Suzanne. *Sentimental Modernism: Women Writers and the Revolution of the Word.* Bloomington: Indiana UP, 1991.

Cody, Morrill, with Hugh Ford. *Women of Montparnasse.* New York: Cornwall Books, 1984.

Conrad, Susan Phinney. *Perish the Thought: Intellectual Women in Romantic America, 1830–1860.* New York: Oxford UP, 1976.

Coultrap-McQuin, Susan. *Doing Literary Business: American Women Writers in the Nineteenth Century.* Chapel Hill: U of North Carolina P, 1990.

Crosby, Caresse. *The Passionate Years.* New York: Ecco, 1979.

Dann, Martin E., ed. *The Black Press, 1827–1890.* New York: Capricorn Books, 1971.

Dannett, Sylvia G. L. *Profiles of Negro Womanhood.* New York: M. W. Lads, 1964.

Darnton, Robert. "What Is the History of Books?" *Reading in America: Literature and Social History.* Ed. Cathy N. Davidson. Baltimore, MD: Johns Hopkins UP, 1989. 27–52.

Davis, Elizabeth Lindsay. *Lifting As They Climb.* Washington, DC: National Association of Colored Women, 1933.

DeKoven, Marianne. *Rich and Strange: Gender, History, Modernism*. Princeton, NJ: Princeton UP, 1991.

Demeter, Richard L. *Primer, Presses, and Composing Sticks: Women Printers of the Colonial Period*. Hicksville, NY: Exposition P, 1979.

Dennison, Sally. *(Alternative) Literary Publishing: 5 Modern Histories*. Iowa City: U of Iowa P, 1984.

Dexter, Elisabeth Anthony. *Career Women of America, 1776–1840*. Francestown, NH: Marshall Jones, 1950.

———. *Colonial Women of Affairs: A Study of Women in Business and the Professions in America before 1776*. Boston: Houghton Mifflin, 1924.

Douglas, Ann. *The Feminization of American Culture*. New York: Avon, 1978.

Emery, Michael, and Edwin Emery. *The Press and America: An Interpretive History of the Mass Media*. 7th ed. Englewood Cliffs, NJ: Prentice-Hall, 1992.

Exman, Eugene. *The Brothers Harper*. New York: Harper and Row, 1965.

Faderman, Lillian. *Odd Girls and Twilight Lovers: A History of Lesbian Life in Twentieth-Century America*. New York: Columbia UP, 1991.

Fetterley, Judith. *Provisions: A Reader from 19th-Century American Women*. Bloomington: Indiana UP, 1985.

Fitch, Noel Riley. *Sylvia Beach and the Lost Generation: A History of Literary Paris in the Twenties and Thirties*. New York: Norton, 1983.

Folkerts, Jean, and Dwight Teeter. *Voices of a Nation: A History of Media in the United States*. New York: Macmillan, 1989.

Ford, Hugh Douglas. "Publishing in Paris." *Women, the Arts, and the 1920s in Paris and New York*. Ed. Kenneth W. Wheeler and Virginia Lee Lussier. New Brunswick, NJ: Transaction Books, 1982. 65–73.

———. *Published in Paris: American and British Writers, Printers, and Publishers in Paris, 1920–1939*. New York: Macmillan, 1975.

Ford, Margaret Lane. "The Types of the Franklin Press of Rhode Island, 1727–1763, with Addenda to Alden's *Rhode Island Imprints*." *Papers of the Bibliographical Society of America* 82 (1988): 83–95.

Gatewood, Willard B. *Aristocrats of Color: The Black Elite, 1880–1920*. Bloomington: Indiana UP, 1990.

Giddings, Paula. *When and Where I Enter: The Impact of Black Women on Race and Sex in America*. New York: William Morrow, 1984.

Gollin, Rita K. "Subordinated Power: Mrs. and Mr. James T. Fields." *Patrons and Protégées: Gender, Friendship, and Writing in Nineteenth-Century America*. Ed. Shirley Marchalonis. New Brunswick, NJ: Rutgers UP, 1988. 141–60.

Hahn, Emily. "Salonists and Chroniclers." *Women, the Arts, and the 1920s in Paris and New York*. Ed. Kenneth W. Wheeler and Virginia Lee Lussier. New Brunswick, NJ: Transaction Books, 1982. 56–64.

Hanscombe, Gillian, and Virginia L. Smyers. *Writing for Their Lives: The Modernist Women, 1910–1940*. Boston: Northeastern UP, 1987.

Harper, J. Henry. *The House of Harper*. New York: Harper and Brothers, 1912.

Harris, William E. "Women in Publishing: The Story of How Carro Morrell Clark Made a Dramatic Success of Publishing Nearly Thirty Years Ago." *Publishers Weekly* 113 (March 24, 1928): 1353–55.

Hart, James D. *The Popular Book: A History of America's Literary Taste.* New York: Oxford UP, 1950.

Henry, Susan. "Ann Franklin of Newport, Rhode Island's Woman Printer." *Newsletters to Newspapers: Eighteenth-Century Journalism.* Ed. Donovan H. Bond and W. Reynolds McLeod. Morgantown: West Virginia U, 1977.

Hersh, Blanche Glassman. *The Slavery of Sex: Feminist-Abolitionists in America.* Urbana: U of Illinois P, 1978.

Hoffman, Frederick J., Charles Allen, and Carolyn F. Ulrich. *The Little Magazine: A History and a Bibliography.* Princeton, NJ: Princeton UP, 1946.

Hudak, Leona M. *Early American Women Printers and Publishers, 1639–1820.* Metuchen, NJ: Scarecrow P, 1978.

Huddleston, Sisley. *Back to Montparnasse: Glimpses of Broadway in Bohemia.* Philadelphia: Lippincott, 1931.

———. *Paris Salons, Cafés, Studios: Being Social, Artistic and Literary Memories.* Philadelphia: Lippincott, 1928.

James, Edward T., Janet Wilson James, and Paul S. Boyer, eds. *Notable American Women, 1607–1950: A Biographical Dictionary.* 3 vols. Cambridge, MA: Belknap P of Harvard UP, 1971.

Jordan, Ellen. "The Christening of the New Woman: May 1894." *Victorian Newsletter* 63 (1983): 19–21.

Joseph, Michael. *The Adventure of Publishing.* London: Allan Wingate, 1949.

Kelley, Mary. *Private Woman, Public Stage: Literary Domesticity in Nineteenth-Century America.* New York: Oxford UP, 1984.

Keyssar, Alexander. "Widowhood in Eighteenth-Century Massachusetts: A Problem in the History of the Family." *Perspectives in American History* 8 (1974): 83–119.

Kolmer, Elizabeth. "Nineteenth Century Woman's Rights Movement: Black and White." *Negro History Bulletin* 35 (1972): 178–80.

Kramer, Dale. *Chicago Renaissance: The Literary Life of the Midwest, 1900–1930.* New York: Appleton-Century, 1966.

Langlois, Karen S. "Mary Austin and Houghton Mifflin Company: A Case Study in the Marketing of a Western Writer." *Western American Literature* 23.1 (1988): 31–42.

Lerner, Gerda, ed., *Black Women in White America: A Documentary History.* New York: Random House, 1971.

Ling, Amy. "Edith Eaton: Pioneer Chinamerican Writer and Feminist." *American Literary Realism* 16.2 (1983): 287–98.

Litwack, Leon, and August Meier. *Black Leaders of the Nineteenth Century.* Urbana: U of Illinois P, 1988.

Logan, Rayford W. *The Negro in American Life and Thought.* New York: Dial, 1954.

———, and Michael R. Winston, eds. *Dictionary of American Negro Biography.* New York: Norton, 1982.

Lottman, Herbert R. *The Left Bank: Writers, Artists, and Politics from the Popular Front to the Cold War*. Boston: Houghton Mifflin, 1982.

Low, W. A., and Virgil Clift, eds. *Encyclopedia of Black America*. New York: McGraw Hill, 1981.

Marchalonis, Shirley, ed. *Patrons and Protégées: Gender, Friendship, and Writing in Nineteenth-Century America*. New Brunswick, NJ: Rutgers UP, 1988.

Mark, Joan. *A Stranger in Her Native Land: Alice Fletcher and the American Indians*. Lincoln: U of Nebraska P, 1988.

Marzolf, Marion. *Up from the Footnote: A History of Women Journalists*. New York: Hastings House, 1977.

Massa, Ann. "Black Women in the 'White City.'" *Journal of American Studies* 8 (1974): 319–37.

McGann, Jerome J. *The Textual Condition*. Princeton, NJ: Princeton UP, 1991.

Mills, Kay. *A Place in the News: From the Women's Pages to the Front Page*. New York: Dodd, Mead, 1988.

Monroe, Harriet. *A Poet's Life: Seventy Years in a Changing World*. New York: Macmillan, 1938.

Morrison, Daryl. *"Twin Territories: The Indian Magazine* and Its Editor, Ora Eddleman Reed." *Chronicles of Oklahoma* 60 (1982): 136–66.

Mott, Frank Luther. *A History of American Magazines, 1741–1850*. New York: D. Appleton, 1930.

Nestor, Pauline A. "A New Departure in Women's Publishing: *The English Woman's Journal* and *The Victoria Magazine*." *Victorian Periodicals Review* 15.3 (1982): 93–106.

Noble, Jeanne L. *Beautiful, Also, Are the Souls of My Black Sisters: A History of the Black Woman in America*. Englewood Cliffs, NJ: Prentice-Hall, 1978.

Norton, Mary Beth. *Liberty's Daughters: The Revolutionary Experience of American Women, 1750–1800*. Boston: Little, Brown, 1980.

Palmieri, Patricia A. "Patterns of Achievement of Single Academic Women at Wellesley College, 1880–1920." *Frontiers* 5 (1980): 63–67.

Penn, I. Garland. *The Afro-American Press and Its Editors*. Springfield, MA: Willey & Co., 1891.

Platt, Susan Noyes. "Mysticism and the Machine Age: Jane Heap and the *Little Review*." *Twenty/One* Fall 1989: 19–44.

Pride, Armistead Scott. "Negro Newspapers: Yesterday, Today and Tomorrow." *Journalism Quarterly* 28 (1951): 179–82.

Putnam, Samuel. *Paris Was Our Mistress: Memoirs of a Lost and Found Generation*. Carbondale: Southern Illinois UP, 1970.

Radway, Janice A. *Reading the Romance: Women, Patriarchy, and Popular Literature*. Chapel Hill: U of North Carolina P, 1984.

Ronda, Bruce A., ed. *Letters of Elizabeth Palmer Peabody, American Renaissance Woman*. Middletown, CT: Wesleyan UP, 1984.

Ross, Ishbel. *Ladies of the Press*. New York: Harper and Brothers, 1936.

Rubin, Joan Shelley. *The Making of Middlebrow Culture*. Chapel Hill: U of North Carolina P, 1992.

Rudnick, Lois Palken. *Mabel Dodge Luhan: New Woman, New Worlds*. Albuquerque: U of
    New Mexico P, 1984.

Russo, Ann, and Cheris Kramarae, eds. *The Radical Women's Press of the 1850s*. New
    York: Routledge, 1991.

Scott, Anne Firor. *Making the Invisible Woman Visible*. Urbana: U of Illinois P, 1984.

Scott, Bonnie Kime, ed. *The Gender of Modernism: A Critical Anthology*. Bloomington:
    Indiana UP, 1990.

Smith-Rosenberg, Carroll. *Disorderly Conduct: Visions of Gender in Victorian America*.
    New York: Knopf, 1985.

Sterling, Dorothy, ed. *We Are Your Sisters: Black Women in the Nineteenth Century*. New
    York: Norton, 1984.

Stern, Madeleine B. *We the Women: Career Firsts of Nineteenth-Century America*. New
    York: Schulte, 1962.

Symons, Julian. *Makers of the New: The Revolution in Literature, 1912–1939*. New York:
    Random House, 1987.

Thomas, Isaiah. *The History of Printing in America*. New York: Weathervane Books, 1970.

Tompkins, Jane. *Sensational Designs: The Cultural Work of American Fiction, 1790–1860*.
    New York: Oxford UP, 1985.

Tuchman, Gaye, with Nina E. Fortin. *Edging Women Out: Victorian Novelists, Publishers,
    and Social Change*. New Haven, CT: Yale UP, 1989.

Ulrich, Laurel. *Good Wives: Image and Reality in the Lives of Women in Northern New
    England, 1650–1750*. New York: Oxford UP, 1983.

Walker, Cheryl. *The Nightingale's Burden: Women Poets and American Culture before
    1900*. Bloomington: Indiana UP, 1982.

Walker, Gay. "Women Printers in Early American Printing History." *Yale University Library
    Gazette* 61 (April 1987): 116–24.

Welch, Deborah Sue. "Zitkala-Sa: An American Indian Leader, 1876–1938." Diss. U of
    Wyoming, 1985.

Welter, Barbara. "The Cult of True Womanhood, 1820–1860." *American Quarterly* 18
    (1966): 151–74.

Wesley, Charles H. *The History of the National Association of Colored Women's Clubs: A
    Legacy of Service*. Washington, DC: National Association of Colored Women's Clubs,
    1984.

Wickes, George. *The Amazon of Letters: The Life and Loves of Natalie Barney*. New York:
    Putnam, 1976.

————. *Americans in Paris*. New York: Doubleday, 1969.

Williams, Ellen. *Harriet Monroe and the* Poetry *Renaissance: The First Ten Years of* Poetry,
    1912–22. Urbana: U of Illinois P, 1977.

Wolseley, Roland E. *The Black Press, U.S.A.* 2d ed. Ames: Iowa State UP, 1990.

Wood, James Playsted. *Magazines in the United States*. 3d ed. New York: Roland, 1971.

Wroth, Lawrence C. *The Colonial Printer*. 2d ed. Charlottesville, VA: Dominion Books,
    1964.

Contributors

Susan Albertine is an associate professor of English and Women's Studies at Susquehanna University, specializing in nineteenth-century American literature. Her work on American career women has appeared in *American Literary Realism, American Literature, Review,* and *biography: an interdisciplinary quarterly.* She learned editing at *Modern Philology* (University of Chicago Press). Currently she is writing a book on women's writing and the language of industrialism in the United States.

Holly Baggett is an assistant professor of history at the University of Oregon. She is working on a biography of Margaret Anderson and editing the letters of Jane Heap.

Barbara Bardes is dean of Raymond Walters College at the University of Cincinnati. A political scientist, she writes on American politics and American literature. Her work includes essays on public opinion and foreign policy, and women and foreign policy attitudes. She is coauthor of *American Government and Politics Today, 1993–94 Edition* (West Publishing), with Mack Shelley and Steffen Schmidt. With Suzanne Gossett she is coauthor of *Declarations of Independence: Women and Political Power in Nineteenth-Century American Fiction* (Rutgers UP, 1990), as well as essays on several American authors.

Mary Lynn Broe is Louise R. Noun Professor of Women's Studies and English at Grinnell College. She has published three books: *Protean Poetic* (U of Missouri P, 1980), *Women's Writing in Exile* (with Angela Ingram; U of North Carolina P, 1989), and *Silence and Power: A Reevaluation of Djuna Barnes* (Southern Illinois UP, 1991). *Cold Comfort,* a biographical portrait of Djuna Barnes through letters, is forthcoming from Random House. She is editing two volumes of Charles Henri Ford's journals for Southern Illinois UP. Her new book in progress is *Reworlding: Life Writings across Cultures,* a critique of western autobiographical genre in the context of postcolonial discourses.

BARBARA DIGGS-BROWN is an assistant professor of public communication at the American University School of Communication. She is currently a scholar of journalism and public relations history with particular emphasis on multicultural issues and the modern civil rights movement and the media. Professor Diggs-Brown is the author of a book chapter and an article on Philippa Duke Schuyler, African-American woman foreign correspondent. She is also coauthor of an article on Marvel Cooke, the first African-American woman to report full-time for an American mainstream newspaper. She is currently researching the lives and work of Simeon Booker, Washington bureau chief for Johnson Publishing Company, and labor activist Lucy E. Parsons.

NOEL RILEY FITCH is the author of the critically acclaimed *Sylvia Beach and the Lost Generation: A History of Literary Paris in the Twenties and Thirties* (Norton, 1983 [11th printing]), *Anaïs: The Erotic Life of Anaïs Nin* (Little, Brown, 1993), *Hemingway in Paris* (St. Martin's Press, 1989), *Literary Cafés of Paris* (Starrhill Press, 1989), and numerous scholarly articles. Her latest published essay is "The Literate Passion of Anaïs Nin and Henry Miller," in *Significant Others: Creativity and Intimate Partnership,* edited by Whitney Chadwick and Isabelle de Courtivron (Thames and Hudson, 1993). Most of her books have been translated into German, Japanese, Dutch, and Spanish. Fitch earned a Ph.D. in literature and was named an NEH Fellow (1980). Currently she teaches nonfiction writing in the graduate program of professional writing at the University of Southern California, and expatriate literature at the American University of Paris. She is presently writing a biography of Julia Child.

MARGARET LANE FORD has worked in the antiquarian trade in New York and London, specializing first in early American printing before turning to earlier centuries, particularly the fifteenth. She was awarded fellowships from the American Antiquarian Society and the Bibliographical Society of America to pursue work on Ann Franklin. Her articles have appeared in the *Papers of the Bibliographical Society of America, The Library,* and *Printing History,* and her two-volume catalogue of incunabula in the Bibliotheca Philosophica Hermetica, Amsterdam, has recently been published. Ford is currently research fellow at the Warburg Institute (University of London) for the collaborative *History of the Book in Britain,* vol. 3, 1400–1557.

SUZANNE GOSSETT is a professor of English at Loyola University Chicago. She writes on Renaissance drama and on American literature. With Barbara Bardes she is coauthor of *Declarations of Independence: Women and Political Power in Nineteenth-Century American Fiction* (Rutgers UP, 1990), as well as essays on Catherine Sedgwick and Sarah Josepha Hale. Her current work includes an edition of *A Fair Quarrel* for the *Collected Works of Thomas Middleton* (Oxford 1994) and *Recent Studies in Masques* for *English Literary Renaissance.*

ELIZABETH HORAN is an assistant professor of English and women's studies and director of studies in comparative literature at Arizona State University. Her first book, *Gabriela Mistral: The Poet and Her People* (Organization of American States, 1994), was awarded first prize by the Organization of American States in a special contest to celebrate the poet's centenary; it will also be appearing in Spanish. In addition to poetry, translations, and book reviews, she has published articles on Mistral and on Dickinson in *Sulfur, Academia,* and *Revista Canadiense de Estudios Hispánicos.* She has held Fulbright and NEH grants and is currently writing a biography of Gabriela Mistral for the University of Texas Press, and a book-length study of the marketing of Emily Dickinson.

KAREN S. LANGLOIS received her doctorate in American history from the Claremont Graduate School in 1987. She is currently affiliated with the California State Polytechnic University, Pomona. In 1989–90 she taught American women's history at San Diego State University. She has also taught American literature, American studies, and women's studies. Langlois has been the recipient of a Haynes Foundation Fellowship and a Herbert Hoover Presidential Library Fellowship for her work on the western American writer Mary Hunter Austin (1867–1934). Her article "A Fresh Voice from the West: Mary Austin and the American Literary Magazines, 1892–1910" appeared in the spring 1990 issue of *California History.* Langlois has also published in the *Huntington Library Quarterly, Western American Literature, Theatre History Studies,* and *Resources in American Literary History.* She is presently completing a full-scale scholarly biography of Mary Austin and an edition of her selected letters.

ANN MASSA studied and has taught American studies and American literature at various universities in the United States and England; she currently teaches in the School of English at the University of Leeds. Her main publications include *Vachel Lindsay, Fieldworker for the American Dream* (1970); *The American Novel since 1945* (1975); and *American Literature in Context, 1900–30* (1982), a collection of fourteen essays. Her articles include a body of work on Harriet Monroe and the Chicago Renaissance. She is currently researching the changing image of England and the English in the work of Henry James.

BRUCE A. RONDA has an A.B. in English from Hope College and M.Phil. and Ph.D. degrees in American studies from Yale University. He taught American studies at Skidmore College, was a Fulbright professor of American studies at Shanghai Foreign Language Institute (1984–85), and is currently teaching in the department of English, Colorado State University, Fort Collins. His research and writing interests include the New England Renaissance, literature and religion, and children and childhood in American culture. He is the editor of *American Renaissance Woman: Letters of Elizabeth Palmer Peabody* (1984) and the author of *Intellect and Spirit: The Life and Work of Robert Coles* (1989). He has also published essays and book reviews on American literature and culture in the mid-nineteenth century. Ronda received an NEH Fellowship for 1993–94 to write a biography of Elizabeth Peabody.

RODGER STREITMATTER is a professor in the School of Communication at the American University in Washington, D.C. His publication credits include *Journalism Quarterly, Journalism History,* and *American Journalism.* His book *Raising Her Voice: African-American Women Journalists Who Changed History* was published by the University Press of Kentucky in 1994.

Index